Modern Trial Advocacy

Law School Edition

Second Edition

Modern Trial Advocacy

Law School Edition

Second Edition

Steven Lubet
Professor of Law
Northwestern University School of Law
Chicago, Illinois

Including Electronic Visuals
by Edward R. Stein

National Institute for Trial Advocacy

Anthony J. Bocchino, NITA Editor in Chief
Temple University Beasley School of Law

Zelda Harris, NITA Associate Editor
University of Arizona College of Law

ISBN: 978-1-55681-924-7

05/07

Lubet, Steven, *Modern Trial Advocacy: Law School Edition*, 2d ed., (NITA 2004)

Library of Congress Cataloging-in-Publication Data Pending

To Bob Burns and Tom Geraghty

— Summary of Contents —

— Table of Contents —

CHAPTER TWELVE—Final Argument

Acknowledgments

I am grateful for the insights and suggestions of Joseph Ben-Or, Donald Beskind, Sheila Block, Anthony Bocchino, Robert Burns, James Duane, James Epstein, Thomas Geraghty, Jonathan Misheiker, Linda Lipton, Fred Lubet, Alex Rose, James Seckinger, Ashley Smith, Paulette Van Zant, and David Zlotnick. Thanks also to Northwestern law students Jennie Levin, Anand Singh, Miriam Szatrowski, and Anne Zellner for research assistance.

Special appreciation to Jill Trumbull-Harris for her exceptional input on "The Basics," and to Edward Stein for "Visual Evidence."

— CHAPTER ONE —
Trial Basics

I. TRIALS AND JUSTICE

The objective of a trial is to do justice. Although that goal may sometimes be obscured in the heat and frustration of combat, it is well worth remembering that the ultimate purpose of the adversary system is to seek the truth, and thereby to distinguish right from wrong. A lawsuit is typically initiated because someone believes that a wrong has been done. Perhaps a crime has been committed or a contract has been broken. Perhaps a large corporation believes that its copyright has been infringed by an equally large competitor, or parents believe that their child has been mistreated in school. Whatever the nature of the dispute, our judicial system provides a forum for resolution. Any person, any business, any club or organization may come to court and ask to be heard. Every defendant may likewise retain counsel to dispute the allegations of the complaint. Some cases are dismissed for legal insufficiency, of course, and many more are compromised or settled. But cases that cannot be resolved—where the parties resolutely disagree about the blame or the consequences—will eventually be set for trial.

Popular imagination notwithstanding, a trial is truly something more than a soap opera or a sporting match. Most of all, a trial is a contest of ideas, a process in which the law is applied to the facts. To tell her client's story, an attorney takes the raw and splintered observations of witnesses and attempts to organize them into a coherent and powerful narrative. To do this, the lawyer must sift through all potential claims and defenses in order to determine the requirements of the applicable law. The lawyer must next consider the vast and indeterminate array of facts and details attendant to every case, separating relevant from irrelevant, admissible from inadmissible, persuasive from unconvincing, truth from deceit.

Eventually, the client's case will take shape. Through the use of logical theories and artful techniques, the advocate will present the most compelling arguments for her client. The opposing parties will do the same. To be sure, one side's gospel is bound to be the other side's subterfuge, but that is inherent in the human condition—a phenomenon long predating the practice of law. In response, we have devised an adversary system designed to sort out competing claims to accuracy and justice.

The system, as we all know, is hardly free of errors. Mistakes happen, injustices are done. The goal of the process, however, is to engage vigorous advocacy on both sides, relying upon the self-interest of the parties (and their counsel) to ensure that no stone is left unturned.

II. GETTING STARTED

Trial preparation begins with a thorough understanding of the substantive law, rules of evidence, rules of procedure, and legal ethics.

Every cause of action and defense may be divided into legal elements, and every item of evidence must be relevant to one or more of the legal issues in the case. In other words, each fact offered at trial must either add some quantum of support to an aspect of your case, or it must detract in some way from the opposition's case. Moreover, there must be some discernable relationship between the item of evidence and a recognized claim or defense.

In an automobile accident case, for example, imagine that the plaintiff wants to introduce evidence that the defendant is nasty and irascible, and often inclined to lose his temper. That testimony would not be allowed simply to show that the defendant is a bad person, since no legal consequences follow from the defendant's disagreeable disposition. On the other hand, it might be possible to connect the evidence to the plaintiff's cause of action for negligence, one element of which is "due care." Was the hotheaded defendant inclined to lose his temper while driving? Did something happen on the day of the accident that might have provoked him? If so, it could be said that the defendant's temperament is relevant to the question of due care, since a splenetic outburst would tend to distract him from his driving. It is the lawyer's knowledge of the substantive law (here quite obvious, but in other situations far more subtle) that allows a trial strategy to emerge.

A process of cross-evaluation continues throughout trial preparation. In light of the applicable law, counsel assesses the usefulness of the available information, considers possible interpretations of the known facts, and determines where and how to search for new evidence. At the same time, the attorney constantly reevaluates her legal theories in light of the evidence at hand. In our hypothetical automobile collision, new information about the defendant's explosive outbursts of temper might prompt the plaintiff's lawyer to amend her complaint, perhaps adding a cause of action for recklessness or wilful and wanton conduct.

The rules of evidence are therefore inseparable from the substantive law. A cause of action must be supported by admissible evidence, but admissibility itself is a function of the particular legal theory.

The law of trial procedure provides a third consideration in trial planning. Evidence must be introduced in an orderly fashion, according to the rules of the court in which the trial is being held. For example, some courts require elaborate pretrial orders, specifying every potential exhibit and document, along with anticipated objections and responses. Some courts even require a list of the facts that each attorney expects to prove at trial. And even in courts where such complex orders are not in use, there will nearly always be pretrial discovery procedures, calling upon the parties to provide extensive disclosures to their adversaries. Failure to comply with such procedural rules may result in the exclusion of otherwise valid evidence; in extreme cases it may lead to a dismissal or default judgment.

Finally, the rules of ethics establish an important constraint on the conduct of trial lawyers, as will be discussed in nearly all of the following chapters.

III. TRIAL PROCEDURES

A trial typically begins when the clerk of the court calls the parties before the bench. One by one, the lawyers will be asked if they are ready to proceed. If the case has been set for trial by court order, this initial question is usually a formality. In the event that a party is not ready to proceed, the court will listen to the reason, determine the position of the other parties, and decide whether the trial will go forward as scheduled. Assuming that the lawyers all answer "Ready," or that the court denies any requests for a continuance or adjournment, the trial will probably track the following broad outline.

The first step will be to resolve any outstanding pretrial motions. Even if there has already been a pretrial conference in the case, there might still be procedural or other matters that need to be decided by the judge. There may be objections to certain evidence or exhibits (motions in limine), questions about witness scheduling or the order of proof, or other issues that need to be addressed before the trial begins.

Following disposition of the pretrial motions, the next step is jury selection, or voir dire.[1] Every jurisdiction approaches jury selection differently. Some allow lengthy, "wide-open" lawyer participation, and in others the entire process is handled much more expeditiously by the trial judge. Whatever the approach, it ordinarily begins by bringing a group of prospective jurors—called the venire or venire panel—into the courtroom. The judge will often address the entire venire, giving them an overview of the case and perhaps asking a series of general questions. Thereafter, individual jurors may be questioned by either the attorneys or the judge. Jury voir dire follows innumerable variations—from jurisdiction to jurisdiction, and even from courtroom to courtroom—regarding number of jurors, form and scope of questioning, and the format for exercising challenges (also called strikes). At some point in the process, however, the attorneys will be allowed to object to certain prospective jurors on either of two bases. Parties are allowed an unlimited number of "challenges for cause," which must be justified to the court. In addition, each party is allowed a set number of "peremptory challenges," which require no explanation.

Once the requisite number of jurors and alternates have been seated, many judges address the panel directly, presenting a more detailed description of the issues in the trial and often providing preliminary instructions regarding the applicable law.

Next come the opening statements of counsel, intended to provide the jury with an overview of each side of the case.[2] This is the attorneys' first opportunity to speak directly to the jury, although the law of opening statements requires that counsel refrain from argument. Nonetheless, lawyers may use their opening statements to begin the process of persuasion by explaining exactly how the expected evidence will lead to the desired verdict.

Following opening statements, the testimonial phase of the trial begins. The plaintiff proceeds first, calling witnesses for direct examination.[3] At the completion of each direct examination the witness is tendered for cross examination by the opposing party or parties.[4] Under the prevailing American rule, cross examinations are limited to the scope of the direct, meaning that new issues may not be raised for the first time on cross examination. It is within the court's discretion, however, to relax that restriction.

---

1. See Chapter 13.
2. See Chapter 11.
3. See Chapter 3.
4. See Chapter 4.

THE BASICS

Outline of a Trial

- Pretrial Motions
    - Objections to evidence
    - Procedural matters
- Jury Selection
    - Voir dire
    - Challenges for cause
    - Peremptory challenges
- Opening Statements
    - Plaintiff (or prosecution)
    - Defendant
- Plaintiff's case in chief
    - For each witness:
    - Direct examination
    - Cross examination
    - Redirect
    - Recross
    - Introduction of exhibits
- Plaintiff rests
- Motions

- Defendant's case in chief
    - For each witness:
    - Direct examination
    - Cross examination
    - Redirect
    - Recross
    - Introduction of exhibits
- Plaintiff's case in rebuttal
- Defendant's surrebuttal
- Final Argument
    - Plaintiff's argument in chief
    - Defendant's argument in chief
    - Plaintiff's rebuttal
- Judge's charge to the jury
    (jury instructions)
- Deliberation
- Verdict (or mistrial)

Once the cross examination is finished, the plaintiff may conduct a redirect examination of the witness, which will similarly be restricted to subjects that were raised or covered on cross.[5] In the same manner, recross examination is confined to the scope of the redirect. The attorneys may continue to alternate redirect and recross examinations so long as the judge is willing to allow it (although they will likely be cut off as soon as the questioning becomes repetitive). Eventually, all of the examinations will be completed and the witness will be excused.

The plaintiff will then call the next witness and the process will be repeated: direct, cross, redirect, recross, and so on. In addition to the testimony of witnesses, the counsel may present evidence in the form of exhibits, primarily either tangible objects or documents.[6] Most exhibits will be offered in the course of a witness's testimony, but they may also be received by agreement of the attorneys, usually called a stipulation. Of course, not all of the proffered testimony and other evidence will be clearly admissible. In that case, opposing counsel may make an objection which will be decided (sustained or overruled) by the court.

---

5.   See Chapter 6.
6.   See Chapter 9.

Once she has presented all of her evidence, plaintiff's counsel will inform the court that she "rests." At that point the defense may present a motion aimed at testing the legal sufficiency of the plaintiff's case. In federal court it is called a "motion for a judgment as a matter of law." Most states continue to use the older term, "motion for a directed verdict." The point of the motion, whatever the terminology, is that the plaintiff has failed to present sufficient evidence, and that some or all of the plaintiff's case should therefore be dismissed. The plaintiff in a civil case has the burden of producing "some evidence" in support of each element of every cause of action (sometimes referred to as claims or counts). In criminal cases the prosecution must meet a higher standard by presenting sufficient evidence upon which a reasonable jury could find the defendant guilty of the crime charged. In either case, a failure of proof regarding one or more elements will result in the midtrial dismissal of the particular charge or cause of action.

The defense case then proceeds in the same manner as the plaintiff's case. Witnesses are called to the stand for direct, cross, redirect, and recross, each of which is limited to the scope of the preceding examination.

After the defense has rested, the plaintiff may call witnesses, or offer other evidence in rebuttal. Rebuttal witnesses may only be called to controvert matters raised during the defense case; rebuttal may not be used merely to accumulate additional evidence in support of plaintiff's claims. The same is true of the defendant's sur-rebuttal, which is only available to refute or deny points raised by plaintiff's rebuttal case.

Following the close of the evidence, the attorneys have another opportunity to speak directly to the jury, this time for final (or closing) argument.[7] In sharp contrast to the opening statements, there is nothing subtle about the level of advocacy in final arguments. The lawyers may—and should—draw inferences, urge conclusions, comment on witness credibility, and otherwise use all of their adversarial and forensic skills to persuade the jury to render a favorable verdict. In most jurisdictions, the plaintiff goes first (argument in chief) and last (rebuttal), while the defendant argues only once.

At the conclusion of the final arguments, the court will instruct the jury on the law and often on the range of verdicts that may be entered. The jury then retires to the jury room for deliberations, which will continue until they reach a verdict or an impasse.

---

7. See Chapter 12.

IV. DEMEANOR

In a very real sense, a lawyer is "on trial" from the first moment he or she steps in front of the fact-finder. Judge and jury will constantly evaluate (and reevaluate) your credibility as they assess your behavior, appearance, bearing, and conduct. They will observe your interactions with your client, with opposing counsel, with witnesses, and with the court. They will be alert to signs of confidence, authority, and professionalism, as well as subtle displays of doubt, misgiving, weakness, or betrayal. All lawyers want to make the right impression, yet there is no formula that tells you how to act, much less how to react. There is a place in the courtroom for lawyers of every background, origin, appearance, temperament, and personality type. Perhaps the only universal indicator of success is sincerity. Insincere lawyers may yet win cases, but they do it in spite of themselves.

This section is not intended as a one-size-fits-all guide to lawyers' preferred appearance. Rather, the following sections will point out three important components of demeanor that can be helpful to all lawyers.

A. Integrity

Throughout every trial you will be asking the fact-finder to trust you, to believe you, to credit your witnesses, to accept your arguments, and, ultimately, to bring back the verdict you request. Why should a judge or jury do that? Certainly, the compelling nature of your evidence should provide one reason, but most trials feature cogent evidence on both sides. And when the evidence is most nearly equal, the credibility of the lawyers can play a large part in shaping the trial's outcome. Integrity inspires trust, and, in trial work, trust leads to success.

What does integrity have to do with demeanor? Isn't integrity something that you have rather than something that you do or show in front of a jury? In the deepest sense, of course, integrity is part of your character, your fiber. You live your life according to principles because they are right, not because their display will help you win a trial. But judges and juries are not blind, and they are not easily fooled. Lawyers who lack integrity almost inevitably reveal themselves in court.

The word integrity comes from the Latin integritas, meaning wholeness or soundness, complete in itself. Thus, our concept of integrity has come to mean unsullied, unbroken, undivided moral principle. In other words, it is a quality of the "whole lawyer." It refers to you and everything you do. When you are seen to depart from a principle, you diminish your standing as an honorable advocate. Thus, there are numerous courtroom behaviors that can add to or detract from your realization as a "whole lawyer."

If nothing else, integrity means honesty. An honest lawyer does not overstate her case, does not promise evidence that she cannot deliver, and does not make arguments that she cannot support. Most important, an honest lawyer does not try to sneak excluded evidence into the trial and does not misuse objections or argument as a means of presenting inadmissible material.

Courtesy is also an aspect of integrity. It means that you do not use bullying tactics to intimidate your opponent or to put a timid witness in a bad light. It means that you do not attempt to distract the fact-finder during your opponent's case, and you do not try to disrupt opposing counsel's legitimate presentation. You do not use facial expressions, grimaces, or gestures to "argue" your case while other arguments or examinations are proceeding.

Much more can be said of integrity as demeanor. For now, suffice it to say that integrity cannot be "faked." It is not a face or costume that you put on and take off. If you are truly committed to trying a case with integrity, it will show. If you are not, it will also show.

B. Confidence

A lawyer demonstrates confidence by knowing and operating within the rules of the court, by understanding how the judge wants the trial to proceed, and by demonstrating her awareness of proper procedure. A confident lawyer has prepared her examinations, is ready to call and cross examine witnesses, and can argue evidentiary objections on the basis of advance preparation. A confident lawyer enters the courtroom knowing what she wants to accomplish, why she wants to accomplish it, and how she intends to do it.

A competent lawyer is well organized and well prepared. He knows where his exhibits can be found, how they are supposed to be numbered, and which witnesses are necessary to introduce them. He understands which documents can be used to impeach which witnesses, as well as the difference between impeachment and refreshing recollection. He realizes that not every valid objection must be made, and he knows how to explain to the court why his objections have merit.

In short, competence leads to confidence, and confidence is apparent to the fact-finder. Disorganization and incompetence lead to insecurity, which is also obvious and can be damning.

C. Consideration

Consideration is a third component of winning demeanor. In a sense, consideration is an aspect of confidence since insecurity and thoughtlessness are surely companion traits. In another sense, consideration is a facet of integrity since the "whole lawyer" will be concerned about the impact of her work upon the court, jury, witnesses, and others in the courtroom. Consideration is discussed as a separate category because it sums up the need to recognize the limits of what a lawyer may do in the name of advocacy.

A considerate lawyer is a forceful advocate who nonetheless understands the impact that his advocacy may have on others. That depth of understanding can be made evident in many ways. He will not interrupt the court, the witnesses, or opposing counsel (other than for an extremely good reason). He will make certain that he can be heard throughout the courtroom. He will listen to the judge's rulings and instructions, and he will try in good faith to comply. (And if his duty to his client ever compels him to talk back to the court or to resist a ruling, he will respectfully explain why.)

A respectful lawyer will not wage a war of attrition against witnesses or other lawyers, and certainly not against the court or the jury. She will know when to request breaks in the proceeding and when to proceed for the benefit of others despite her own preferences. She may attack witnesses, but only when they have shown themselves to deserve it. She may joust with opposing counsel over professional issues, but not over personalities. She will not back down from a fight, but she will not start one as a tactic.

Most important, a respectful lawyer will realize that the trial is being conducted for the benefit of the fact-finder. She will not conduct a seemingly private dialogue between herself and the witnesses. Rather, she will be sure to structure her examinations (both rhetorically and physically) so that they include the fact-finder. Her exhibits will be large enough to be seen. Her language will be straightforward and uncomplicated. Her pace will be intelligible. She will make certain (within her power) that the fact-finder has plenty of time to hear, digest, understand, and appreciate her evidence.

Need it be said? Judges and juries appreciate considerate lawyers.

V. TRIAL ETHICS

There is nothing in the practice of law that is more important than professional responsibility. The entire adversary system is premised on the assumption that attorneys will make the strongest possible arguments for their clients, while remaining scrupulously within the bounds of the law. This means that trial lawyers must be vigorous advocates, but they must also be honest and trustworthy. Therefore, specific ethics issues, as they may arise in a precise context during trial, are discussed in nearly every chapter of this book. What follows here is a broader outline of lawyers' general ethical obligations.

A.   Duties to Clients

An attorney owes her clients three basic duties: competence, confidentiality, and loyalty.

For trial lawyers, the obligation of competence includes the obvious duty of zealous representation. A trial attorney must be her client's champion, taking the case to heart and making every sincere effort to "see it" the way the client sees it. In addition, a competent lawyer must know and understand the law and, perhaps most importantly, must engage in thorough investigation of the facts. No lawyer, of course, would ever care to admit incompetence. But some cases may be too big or too complex for certain individuals, in which case the lawyer must bring in capable cocounsel, or perhaps refer the representation to another office.

Lawyers must also be secret keepers. Confidences entrusted by a client to an attorney must never be misused and may not be revealed without consent except in a few narrowly defined circumstances.[8]

Thus, certain information may remain undisclosed to adversaries and to the courts. The attorney-client privilege, however, protects only the specific communications between attorney and client and does not apply to discovery of the underlying facts. In civil cases, for example, parties are subject to depositions and other discovery requests, and the information sought may not be withheld simply because it has also been communicated to a lawyer. In criminal cases, a defendant may be required to produce physical evidence. The Fifth Amendment, however, prevents compelled testimonial disclosures even in the absence of attorney-client privilege.

The third duty is loyalty, which means that a lawyer's representation of a client must not be diluted by competing interests. Thus, a trial lawyer's advocacy must not be constrained by an obsequious desire to please the court or to remain in the good graces of a powerful

---

8. Lawyers have an ethical obligation to maintain the confidences of their clients. Rule 1.6, Model Rules of Professional Conduct; DR 4-101, Model Code of Professional Responsibility. In addition, the attorney-client privilege, a closely related concept in the law of evidence, permits lawyers to resist disclosure of client confidences unless there is an applicable exception.

adversary. Equally important, an attorney must be extremely cautious about agreeing to represent multiple clients in the same litigation. The possibility of a conflict of interest is ever-present, even if it is not immediately apparent. Even in those situations where multiple representation is permissible, counsel must take care to obtain the knowing consent of everyone involved.

B. Duties to the Court

A lawyer's primary obligation to the court is one of candor and honesty. The adversary system cannot function unless judges can rely upon lawyers to tell them the truth. In certain circumstances, as when protecting client confidences, attorneys are allowed to withhold information, but they may not lie or dissemble.

This duty is never greater than when lawyers make representations about the law. Judges do not have time to check every citation and read every case, especially in the midst of trial, so they often depend upon the lawyers to apprise them of the law. In doing so, counsel must be scrupulously accurate and may even have to provide the court with citations adverse to his or her position.[9]

While there is no corresponding obligation to volunteer "bad facts," attorneys must not make deliberately false statements of fact or otherwise participate in the creation or preservation of false evidence. But what if a lawyer presents testimony in good faith, only to learn later that the witness was lying? Under the Model Rules of Professional Conduct, adopted in most states, the attorney is then required to "take reasonable remedial measures," up to and including disclosure to the court.[10] Moreover, this obligation applies even to testimony by the attorney's client and even if compliance requires disclosure of an otherwise privileged communication.

Fortunately, perjury and false testimony are infrequent occurrences, especially since good lawyers do everything they can to discourage witnesses from lying. A more common problem is the misuse of evidence or the use of unsupportable innuendo, either in argument or during cross examination. In that regard, the rules provide that a lawyer shall not "allude to any matter that the lawyer does not reasonably believe is relevant or that will not be supported

---

9. A lawyer may not knowingly fail to disclose to the tribunal "legal authority in the controlling jurisdiction known to the lawyer to be directly adverse to the position of the client and not disclosed by opposing counsel." Rule 3.3(a)(2), American Bar Association Model Rules of Professional Conduct; DR 7-106(B)(1), American Bar Association Model Code of Professional Responsibility.

10. Rule 3.3(a)(3), Model Rules of Professional Conduct.

by admissible evidence."[11] This is the source of the well-known statement that counsel must have a "good faith basis" for every question on cross examination. The "relevance" requirement also means that a lawyer may not simply throw mud at witnesses or attempt to inject bigotry or intolerance into a trial.

On a more mundane level, attorneys in trial must also refrain from asserting personal knowledge of facts in issue, and must not state their personal opinions as to the justness of the client's case or the credibility of a witness.[12] And of course, lawyers must adhere to the rules of the court and obey the directions of the judge, although a lawyer may test the legal validity of a rule or order by openly refusing to comply.[13]

THE BASICS

Trial Ethics

- Duties to clients
  - Competence
  - Confidentiality
  - Loyalty

- Duties to the court
  - Candor
  - No use of false evidence
  - Good faith basis for examinations
  - No assertions of personal knowledge

- Duties to adversaries and third parties
  - Courtesy and respect
  - No obstruction of access to evidence
  - Good faith fulfillment of agreements
  - No false statements
  - No ex parte communications

C. Duties to Adversaries and Third Parties

There is considerable overlap between a lawyer's obligations to the court and counsel's duties to adversaries and third parties. For example, the citation of adverse legal authority, not to mention the disclosure of a witness's false testimony, will obviously benefit the

---

11. Rule 3.4(e), Model Rules of Professional Conduct; accord DR 7-106(C)(1), Model Code of Professional Responsibility.

12. Rule 3.4(e), Model Rules of Professional Conduct; accord DR 7-106(C)(4), Model Code of Professional Responsibility.

13. Rule 3.4(c), Model Rules of Professional Condcut, accord DR 7-106(A), Model Code of Professional Responsibility.

opposing party. In addition, there are other rules of ethics that apply directly to a lawyer's treatment of adversaries.

First and foremost, a lawyer may not make a "false statement of material fact or law" to a third party.[14] The adversary system gives lawyers tremendous leeway to represent their clients, and a certain amount of "puffing" is expected in litigation, but lies and deceptions can quickly undermine the integrity of the entire process. Closely related is the lawyer's obligation to keep his or her word. Lawyers regularly make commitments to their adversaries in the course of litigation, often orally rather than in writing. Principled advocates will complete their undertakings in good faith, even those that may not be easily enforceable by opposing counsel. If it turns out that a commitment cannot be fulfilled, the reasons should be explained to opposing counsel.

All parties must have fair access to evidence. Consequently, counsel must not "unlawfully obstruct another party's access to evidence or unlawfully alter, destroy, or conceal a document or other material having potential evidentiary value."[15] Nor may an attorney request a person other than a client (or a client's relative or employee) to "refrain from voluntarily giving relevant information to another party."[16]

Similarly, all parties must have equal access to the court— hence the rule against ex parte communications, meaning that a lawyer may not attempt to communicate privately or secretly with the judge outside the presence of the other lawyers (other than in certain narrow circumstances authorized by law). Needless to say, a lawyer may never communicate with jurors or prospective jurors other than in open court.

Every person involved in the legal process is entitled to be treated with dignity and respect. This includes opposing counsel, adverse parties, and all witnesses, even in the most furiously contested trial. Lawyers should not stoop to tactics that are meant only to embarrass, burden, or harass a witness or opponent, no matter how strategically effective that might seem.

---

14. Rule 4.1(a), Model Rules of Professional Conduct; accord DR 7-102(A)(5), Model Code of Professional Responsibility.

15. Rule 3.4(a), Model Rules of Professional Conduct; accord DR 7-109(A), Model Code of Professional Responsibility.

16. Rule 3.4(f), Model Rules of Professional Condcut; accord DR 7-109(A), Model Code of Professional Responsibility.

— CHAPTER TWO —
Case Analysis and Storytelling

I.   THE IDEA OF A PERSUASIVE STORY

A.   Trials as Stories

The function of a trial is to resolve factual disputes. Trials are only held when the parties are in disagreement concerning historical facts. These disagreements commonly involve the existence or occurrence of events or actions, but they may also turn upon questions of sequence, interpretation, characterization, or intent. Thus, trials may be held to answer questions such as these: What happened? What happened first? Why did it happen? Who made it happen? Did it happen on purpose? Was it justified or fair? All of these questions are resolved by accumulating information about past events; if there is no dispute about past events, the case should be resolved on summary judgment.[1]

Trials, then, are held in order to allow the parties to persuade the judge or jury by recounting their versions of the historical facts. Another name for this process is storytelling. Each party to a trial has the opportunity to tell a story, albeit through the fairly stilted devices of jury address, direct and cross examination, and introduction of evidence. The framework for the stories—or their grammar—is set by the rules of procedure and evidence. The conclusion of the stories—the end to which they are directed—is controlled by the elements of the applicable substantive law. The content of the stories is governed, of course, by the truth, or at least by so much of the truth as is available to the advocate. Thereafter, the party who succeeds in telling the most persuasive story should win.

But what is persuasive storytelling in the context of a trial? A persuasive story can establish an affirmative case if it has all, or most, of these characteristics: (1) it is told about people who have reasons for the way they act; (2) it accounts for or explains all of

---

1.   See Rule 56, Federal Rules of Civil Procedure.

the known or undeniable facts; (3) it is told by credible witnesses; (4) it is supported by details; (5) it accords with common sense and contains no implausible elements; and (6) it is organized in a way that makes each succeeding fact increasingly more likely. On the other hand, defense lawyers must often tell "counterstories" that negate the above aspects of the other side's case.

In addition to persuasiveness, a story presented at trial must consist of admissible evidence, and it must contain all of the elements of a legally cognizable claim or defense.

An advocate's task when preparing for trial is to conceive of and structure a true story—comprising only admissible evidence and containing all of the elements of a claim or defense—that is most likely to be believed or adopted by the trier of fact. This is a creative process, since seldom will the facts be undisputed or capable of but a single interpretation. To carry through this process the lawyer must "imagine" a series of alternative scenarios, assessing each for its clarity, simplicity, and believability, as well as for its legal consequences.

B. Planning a Sample Story

Assume, for example, that you represent a plaintiff who was injured in an automobile accident. You know from your law school torts class that in order to recover damages you will have to tell a story proving, at a minimum, that the defendant was negligent. You also know from your evidence class that the story will have to be built on admissible evidence, and you know from your ethics class that the story cannot be based on false or perjured testimony.[2] Your client knows only that when traffic slowed down to allow a fire truck to pass, she was hit from behind by the driver of the other automobile.

How can these basic facts be assembled into a persuasive trial story? First, we know that the story must be about people who act for reasons. Your client slowed down for a fire truck, which explains her actions. But why didn't the defendant slow down as well? Your story will be more persuasive if you can establish his reason.

True, a reason is not absolutely essential. Perhaps the defendant was such a poor driver that he simply drove about banging into other automobiles. On the other hand, consider what the absence of a reason implies. The plaintiff claims that traffic slowed for a fire truck, but the defendant—also part of traffic—did not slow down.

---

2. See Rule 3.3, American Bar Association Model Rules of Professional Conduct (Model Rules); Disciplinary Rules 7-102 and 7-106, American Bar Association Model Code of Professional Responsibility (Model Code).

Could it be that there was no fire truck? Perhaps there was a fire truck, but it was not sounding its siren or alerting traffic to stop. Is it possible that the plaintiff didn't slow down, but rather slammed on her brakes? In other words, the very absence of a reason for the defendant's actions may make the plaintiff's own testimony less believable.

The skilled advocate will therefore look for a reason or cause for the defendant's actions. Was the defendant drunk? In a hurry? Homicidal? Distracted? You can begin to choose from among these potential reasons by "imagining" each one in the context of your story. Imagine how the story will be told if you claim that the defendant was drunk. Could such a story account for all of the known facts? If the police came to the scene, was the defendant arrested? Did any credible, disinterested witnesses see the defendant drinking or smell liquor on his breath? If not, drunkenness does not provide a persuasive reason for the defendant's actions.

Next, imagine telling your story about a homicidal defendant. Perhaps this wasn't an accident, but a murder attempt. Envision your impassioned plea for punitive damages. But wait, this story is too implausible. How would a murderer know that the plaintiff would be driving on that particular road? How would he know that a fire truck would be attempting to bypass traffic? How could he predict that the plaintiff would slow down enough, or that there would be no other cars in the way? Barring the discovery of additional facts that support such a theory, this story is unpersuasive.

Finally, imagine the story as told about a defendant who was in a hurry. This story accounts for the known facts, since it explains why traffic might slow while the defendant did not. Perhaps the defendant saw the fire truck but was driving just a little too fast to stop in time; or he might have been so preoccupied with the importance of getting somewhere on time that he simply failed to notice the fire truck until it was too late. Moreover, there is nothing implausible or unbelievable about this theory. It is in complete harmony with everyone's everyday observations. Furthermore, details that support the story should not be hard to come by. Was the defendant going to work in the morning? Did he have an important meeting to attend? Was he headed home after a long day? The trial lawyer can find details in virtually any destination that will support the theory of the hurried defendant. Note, however, that while such additional evidence of the defendant's haste will be helpful, the story does not rest upon any external witness's credibility. All of the major elements of the story may be inferred from the defendant's own actions.

How can this last story best be organized? Let us assume that the occurrence of the collision itself is not in issue, and recall that it is important that each fact make every succeeding element increasingly more likely. Which aspect should come first: the presence of the fire truck or the fact that the defendant was in a hurry? Since the presence of the fire truck does not make it more likely that the defendant was in a hurry, that probably is not the most effective starting point. On the other hand, the defendant's haste does make it more likely that he would fail to notice the fire truck.

A skeletal version of our story, with some easily obtained details supplied, might go like this: we know there was a collision, but why did it happen? The defendant was driving south on Sheridan Road at 8:20 in the morning. It was the end of rush hour, and he had to be at work downtown. In fact, he had an important meeting that was to begin at 8:30 a.m. sharp. The defendant's parking lot is two blocks from his office. As traffic slowed for a passing fire truck, the defendant didn't notice it. Failing to stop in time, the defendant ran into the plaintiff's car.

Other details might also be available to support this story. Perhaps, immediately following the collision, the defendant took out a cell phone to call his office. Similarly, there might be "counter-details" for the plaintiff to rebut. The point, however, is to organize your story on the principle of successive supporting details.

THE BASICS

A Persuasive Story

- Explains all of the known facts
- Is told about people who have reasons for their actions
- Is told by credible witnesses
- Is supported by details
- Accords with common sense

II. THE ETHICS OF PERSUASIVE STORYTELLING

In the preceding section we discussed the way in which an advocate imagines a persuasive theory or story. We also noted that lawyers are bound to the truth—we are not free to pick stories simply on the basis of their persuasive value. Within this parameter, exactly how much room is there for creative theory choice?

A. Assuming That You "Know" the Truth

Let us begin with the proposition that in most cases neither the lawyer nor the client will know with certainty what we might call all of the "relevant truth." As in the scenario above, for example, the plaintiff knows her own actions but has no special knowledge about the defendant. The lawyer, of course, is not free to persuade or coach the plaintiff to alter her own story simply to make it more effective.[3]

This is not to say, however, that legal ethics permit us to do nothing more than put the plaintiff on the witness stand. The lawyer's duty of zealous representation requires further inquiry into the existence of additional details, not to mention the artful use of sequencing and emphasis. For instance, let us assume that the plaintiff has informed her lawyer with certainty that the fire truck was flashing its lights but not sounding its siren or bell. There is no doubt that an attorney absolutely may not coach the plaintiff to testify that the siren and bell were sounding. Such testimony would be false, perjurious, and unethical.

On the other hand, there is no requirement that the absence of bell and siren be made the centerpiece of the plaintiff's direct examination. Sequencing and emphasis may be used to minimize the adverse impact of this information. Therefore, the direct examination could be developed as follows: "The fire truck was the largest vehicle on the road. It was the standard fire-engine red. All of its lights were flashing brightly—headlights, taillights, and red dome lights. It could be seen easily from all directions. All of the traffic, save the defendant, slowed down for the fire truck. It was not necessary to hear a siren in order to notice the fire truck." Thus, the lawyer has held closely to the truth, while establishing the irrelevance of the damaging information.

B. Assuming That You Do Not Know the Truth

A different situation arises when the advocate is not able to identify truth so closely, as in the example above concerning the defendant's reasons for failing to notice the fire truck in time. Recall that we considered a variety of possible reasons, including inattention, drunkenness, and aggression. Some reasons have clear forensic advantages over others. What are the ethical limitations on the attorney's ability to choose the best one?

First, it should be clear that we are not bound to accept the defendant's story in the same way that we must give credence to our own client. The duty of zealous representation requires that we resolve doubts in our client's favor.[4] Moreover, we speak to our client within a relationship of confidentiality, which not only protects

---

3. Rules 3.1, 3.4, and 4.1, Model Rules of Professional Conduct; Disciplinary Rule 7-102(A)(6), Model Code of Professional Responsibility.

4. See Rule 1.2, Model Rules of Professional Conduct; Disciplinary Rule 7-101, Model Code of Professional Responsibility.

her communication, but also gives her additional credibility. Without her consent, what our client tells us will go no further, and this knowledge gives her every reason to make a full disclosure.[5] When our client gives us damaging facts (such as the absence of the fire truck's siren), it is even more likely to be true, since she obviously has no reason to inject such information falsely. Conversely, statements that we obtain from the defendant are not necessarily accompanied by comparable indicia of reliability, and we are entitled to mistrust them.

This is not to say that we must always accept information from our clients as revealed wisdom. Clients may mislead us as the result of misperception, forgetfulness, mistake, wishful thinking, reticence, or ignorance, and, unfortunately, they occasionally lie. Moreover, opposing parties in litigation usually tell what they perceive as the truth. As a tactical matter, trial lawyers must always examine every statement of every witness for potential error or falsehood. As an ethical matter, however, we should be more ready to assume that our client's words—both helpful and damaging—are likely to be true. It is, after all, the client's case.[6]

Recognizing, then, that we must go beyond the opposite party's version of the facts, we next evaluate the entire universe of possible stories. In our example we determined that the "in a hurry" story would be the most persuasive. Simultaneously, we must also determine whether it is an ethical story to tell.

The key to determining the ethical value of any trial theory is whether it is supported by facts that we know, believe, or have a good faith basis to believe, are true. In other words, the story has to be based on facts that are "not false."[7]

Returning to our fire truck case, assume that the defendant has denied that he was in a hurry. He has the right to make this denial, but as plaintiff's lawyers we have no duty to accept it. Assume also that we have not been able to locate a witness who can give direct evidence that the defendant was in a hurry. We do know where and when the collision occurred, and assume that we have also been able to learn numerous facts about the defendant's home, automobile,

---

5. See Rule 1.6, Model Rules of Professional Conduct; Disciplinary Rule 4-101, Model Code of Professional Responsibility.

6. Note that a lawyer is generally required to accept the client's goals and objectives with regard to litigation. Rule 1.2(a), Model Rules of Professional Conduct. (A lawyer shall abide by a client's decisions concerning the objectives of representation...and shall consult with the client as to the means by which they are to be pursued.

7. See Rules 3.1, 3.4(e), and 4.1, Model Rules of Professional Conduct, Disciplinary Rules 7-102(A)(2) and 7-106(C), Model Code of Professional Responsibility.

occupation, and place of employment. The following story emerges, based strictly on facts that we would have no reason to doubt.

> The defendant lives sixteen miles from his office. He usually takes a commuter train to work, but on the day of the accident he drove. The accident occurred on a major thoroughfare approximately eleven miles from the defendant's office. The time of the accident was 8:20 a.m., and the defendant had scheduled an important, and potentially lucrative, meeting with a new client for 8:30 a.m. that day. The parking lot nearest to the defendant's office is over two blocks away. The first thing that the defendant did following the accident was telephone his office to say that he would be late.

Our conclusion is that the defendant was in a hurry. Driving on a familiar stretch of road, he was thinking about his appointment, maybe even starting to count the money, and he failed to pay sufficient attention to the traffic. We are entitled to ask the trier of fact to draw this inference because we reasonably believe its entire basis to be true. The known facts can also support numerous other stories, or no story at all, but that is not an ethical concern. Perhaps the defendant was being particularly careful that morning, knowing how important it was that he arrive on time for his appointment. Perhaps the appointment had nothing to do with the accident. Those arguments can be made, and they may turn out to be more persuasive stories than our own. Our ultimate stories might be ineffective, or even foolish, but they are ethical so long as they are not built on a false foundation.

C.   The Special Case of the Criminal Law

The analysis above, regarding both persuasion and ethics, applies to civil and criminal cases alike. In the criminal law, however, the prosecutor has additional ethical obligations and the defense lawyer has somewhat greater latitude.

A criminal prosecutor is not only an advocate, but also a public official. It is the prosecutor's duty to punish the guilty, not merely to win on behalf of a client. Therefore, a public prosecutor may not rely upon the "not false" standard for determining the ethical value of a particular theory. Rather, the prosecutor must personally believe in the legal validity of each case and must refrain from bringing any prosecution that is not supported by probable cause.[8]

---

8.   See Rule 3.8, Model Rules of Profession Conduct; Disciplinary Rule 7-103(A), Model Code of Professional Responsibility.

Conversely, a criminal defendant is always entitled to plead not guilty, thereby putting the government to its burden of establishing guilt beyond a reasonable doubt.[9] A plea of not guilty need not in any sense be "true," since its function is only to insist upon the constitutional right to trial. Of course, a criminal defendant has no right to introduce perjury or false evidence. However, a criminal defendant need not present any factual defense, and in most jurisdictions a conviction requires that the prosecution "exclude every reasonable hypothesis that is inconsistent with guilt." Thus, so long as she does not rely upon falsity or perjury, a criminal defense lawyer may argue for acquittal—that is, tell a story—based only upon "a reasonable hypothesis" of innocence.

III. PREPARING A PERSUASIVE TRIAL STORY

Assume that you have decided upon the story that you want to tell. It is persuasive. It is about people who have reasons for the way they act. It accounts for all of the known facts. It is told by credible witnesses. It is supported by details. It accords with common sense. It can be organized in a way that makes each succeeding fact more likely.

How do you put your story in the form of a trial?

A.   Developing Your Theory and Your Theme

Your case must have both a theory and a theme.

1. Theory

Your theory is the adaptation of your story to the legal issues in the case. A theory of the case should be expressed in a single paragraph that combines an account of the facts and the law in such a way as to lead to the conclusion that your client must win. A successful theory contains these elements:

It is logical. A winning theory has internal logical force. It is based upon a foundation of undisputed or otherwise provable facts, all of which lead in a single direction. The facts upon which your theory is based should reinforce (and never contradict) each other. Indeed, they should lead to each other, each fact or premise implying the next, in an orderly and inevitable fashion.

---

9.   Rule 3.1, Model Rules of Professional Conduct. (A lawyer for the defendant in a criminal proceeding...[may] defend the proceeding as to require that every element of the case be established.)

It speaks to the legal elements of your case. All of your trial persuasion must be in aid of a "legal" conclusion. Your theory must not only establish that your client is good or worthy (or that the other side is bad and unworthy), but also that the law entitles you to relief. Your theory therefore must be directed to prove every legal element that is necessary both to justify a verdict on your behalf and to preserve it on appeal.

It is simple. A good theory makes maximum use of undisputed facts. It relies as little as possible on evidence that may be hotly controverted, implausible, inadmissible, or otherwise difficult to prove.

It is easy to believe. Even "true" theories may be difficult to believe because they contradict everyday experience, or because they require harsh judgments. You must strive to eliminate all implausible elements from your theory. Similarly, you should attempt to avoid arguments that depend upon proof of deception, falsification, ill motive, or personal attack. An airtight theory is able to encompass the entirety of the other side's case and still result in your victory by sheer logical force.

To develop and express your theory, ask these three questions: What happened? Why did it happen? Why does that mean that my client should win? If your answer is longer than one paragraph, your theory may be logical and true, but it is probably too complicated.

2. Theme

Just as your theory must appeal to logic, your theme must appeal to moral force. A logical theory tells the trier of fact the reason that your verdict must be entered. A moral theme shows why it should be entered. In other words, your theme—best presented in a single sentence—justifies the morality of your theory and appeals to the justice of the case.

A theme is a rhetorical or forensic device. It has no independent legal weight, but rather it gives persuasive force to your legal arguments. The most compelling themes appeal to shared values, civic virtues, or common motivations. They can be succinctly expressed and repeated at virtually every phase of the trial.

In a contracts case, for example, your theory will account for all of the facts surrounding the formation and breach of the contract, as well as the relevant law, say, of specific performance. Your theory will explain why a particular verdict is compelled by the law. Your theme will strengthen your theory by underscoring why entering that verdict is the right thing to do. Perhaps your theme will be, "The defendant would rather try to make money than live up to a promise." Or you might try, "This defendant tried to sell some property and keep it too." Whatever the theme, you will want to introduce it during your opening statement, reinforce it during direct and cross examinations, and drive it home during your final argument.

THE BASICS	
Theory and Theme	
Trial Theory	• Logical—facts reinforce each other, leading to a single conclusion • Legal—proves every element of a valid claim or defense • Simple—makes maximum use of undisputed evidence • Easy to believe—meets the test of "plausibility"
Trial Theme	• Moral—appeals to shared values, civic virtues, common understandings • Succinct—may be summarized in a single phrase or sentence • Instrumental—may be invoked and repeated at all stages of the trial

B. Planning Your Final Argument

Good trial preparation begins at the end. It makes great sense to plan your final argument first, because that aspect of the trial is the most similar to storytelling; it is the single element of the trial where it is permissible for you to suggest conclusions, articulate inferences, and otherwise present your theory to the trier of fact as an uninterrupted whole.

In other words, during final argument you are most allowed to say exactly what you want to say, limited only by the requirement that all arguments be supported by evidence contained in the trial record. Thus, by planning your final argument at the beginning of your preparation, you will then be able to plan the balance of your case so as to ensure that the record contains every fact that you will need for summation.

Ask yourself these two questions: What do I want to say at the end of the case? What evidence must I introduce or elicit in order to be able to say it? The answers will give you the broad outline of your entire case.

C. Planning Your Case in Chief

Your goal during your case in chief is to persuade the trier of fact as to the correctness of your theory, constantly invoking the moral leverage of your theme. To accomplish this, you have four basic tools: (1) jury address, which consists of opening statement and final argument; (2) testimony on direct examination, and to a lesser extent on cross examination; (3) introduction of exhibits, including real and documentary evidence; and (4) absolutely everything else that you do in the courtroom, including the way you look, act, react, speak, move, stand, and sit. The skills involved in each of these aspects of a trial will be discussed at length in later chapters. What follows here is an outline of the general steps to take in planning for trial.

1. Consider Your Potential Witnesses and Exhibits

Your first step is to list the legal elements of every claim or defense that you hope to establish. If you represent the plaintiff in a personal injury case, then you must offer evidence on all of the elements of negligence: duty, foreseeability, cause in fact, proximate cause, and damages. Next, list the evidence that you have available to support each such element. Most likely the bulk of your evidence will be in the form of witness testimony, but some of it will consist of documents, tangible objects, and other real evidence. For each such exhibit, note the witness through whom you will seek its introduction.

You are now ready to make decisions concerning your potential witnesses by inverting the informational list that you just created.

2. Evaluate Each Witness Individually

Imagine what you would like to say in final argument about each witness you might call to the stand: What does this witness contribute to my theory? What positive facts may I introduce through this witness? Are other witnesses available for the same facts? Is this witness an effective vehicle for my theme? What can I say about this witness that will be logically and morally persuasive?

Once you have assembled all of the "positive" information about each witness, you must go on to consider all possible problems and weaknesses.

a. Factual weaknesses

Are there likely to be inconsistencies or gaps in the witness's testimony? Does the witness have damaging information that is likely to be elicited on cross examination? If the answer to either question is affirmative, how can you minimize these problems? Can you resolve the inconsistencies by reevaluating your theory? Can another witness fill the gaps? Can you defuse the potentially damaging facts by bringing them out on direct examination?

b. Evidentiary problems

Each witness's testimony must be evaluated for possible evidentiary problems. Do not assume that any item of evidence or testimony is automatically admissible. Instead, you must be able to state a positive theory of admissibility for everything that you intend to offer during your case in chief. To prepare for objections ask yourself, "How would I try to keep this information out of evidence?" Then plan your response. If you are not absolutely confident in your ability to counter any objections, you have to go back to the law library.

c. Credibility problems

How is the witness likely to be attacked? Is the witness subject to challenge for bias or interest? Will perception be in issue? Is there potential for impeachment by prior inconsistent statements? Can you structure your direct examination so as to avoid or minimize these problems?

3. Decide Which Witness to Call

Having evaluated the contributions, strengths, and weaknesses of all of your potential witnesses, you are now in a position to decide which ones you will call to the stand. Your central concern will be to make sure that all of your necessary evidence is admitted. You must call any witness who is the sole source of a crucial piece of information. Except in rare or compelling circumstances, you will also want to call any witness whose credibility or appearance is central to the internal logic or moral weight of your case.

All nonessential witnesses must be evaluated according to their strengths and weaknesses. You will want to consider eliminating witnesses whose testimony will be cumulative or repetitive of each other, since this will increase the likelihood of eliciting a damaging contradiction. You must also be willing to dispense with calling witnesses whose credibility is seriously suspect, or whose testimony has the potential to do you more harm than good.

Once you have arrived at your final list of witnesses, arrange them in the order that will be most helpful to your case. While there are no hard and fast rules for determining witness order, the following three principles should help you decide:

Retention. You want your evidence not only to be heard, but also to be retained. Studies have consistently suggested that judges and juries tend to best remember the evidence that they hear at the beginning and at the end of the trial. Following this principle, you will want to call your most important witness first and your next most important witness last. Start fast and end strong.

Progression. The "first and last" principle must occasionally give way to the need for logical progression. Some witnesses provide the foundation for the testimony of others. Thus, it may be necessary to call "predicate" witnesses early in the trial as a matter of both logical development and legal admissibility. To the extent possible, you may also wish to arrange your witnesses so that accounts of key events are given in chronological order.

Impact. You may also order your witnesses to maximize their dramatic impact. For example, you might wish to begin a wrongful death case by calling one of the grieving parents of the deceased child. Conversely, a necessary witness who is also somewhat unsavory or impeachable should probably be buried in the middle of your case in chief. A variant on the impact principle is the near universal practice of calling a criminal defendant as the last witness for the defense. This practice has arisen for two reasons. First, it postpones until the last possible moment the time when the lawyer must decide whether to call the defendant to the stand for exposure to cross examination. Second, and far more cynically, calling defendants last allows them to hear all of the other testimony before testifying. (While all occurrence witnesses are routinely excluded from the courtroom, the defendant has a constitutional right to be present throughout the trial.)

D.   Planning Your Cross Examinations

It is inherently more difficult to plan a cross examination than it is to prepare for direct. It is impossible to safeguard yourself against all surprises, but the following four steps will help keep them to a minimum.

First, compile a list of every potential adverse witness. Imagine why the witness is likely to be called. Ask yourself, "How can this witness most hurt my case?" Always prepare for the worst possible alternative.

Second, consider whether there is a basis for keeping the witness off the stand. Is the witness competent to testify? Is it possible to invoke a privilege? Then consider whether any part of the expected testimony might be excludable. For every statement that the witness might make, imagine all reasonable evidentiary objections. Do the same thing concerning all exhibits that might be offered through the witness. For each objection plan your argument and prepare for the likely counterargument. You won't want to make every possible objection, but you will want to be prepared.

Third, consider the factual weaknesses of each opposing witness. Are there inconsistencies that can be exploited or enhanced? Is the witness's character subject to attack? Can the witness be impeached from prior statements? How can the witness be used to amplify your own theme?

Finally, catalog all of the favorable information that you will be able to obtain from each opposing witness.

E. Reevaluating Everything That You Have Done

Now that you have planned your case in chief and cross examinations, it is imperative that you go back and reevaluate every aspect of your case. Do your direct examinations fully support and establish your theory? Do they leave any logical gaps? Are you satisfied that all of your necessary evidence will be admissible? Will it be credible? Do the potential cross examinations raise issues with which you cannot cope? Will you be able to articulate your moral theme during most or all of the direct and cross examinations? If you are unable to answer these questions satisfactorily, you may need to readjust your theory or theme.

Assuming that you are satisfied with your theory, you should now have an excellent idea of what the evidence at trial will be. With this in mind, go back again and rework your final argument. Make sure that it is completely consistent with the expected evidence and that it makes maximum use of the uncontroverted facts. Consider eliminating any parts of the argument that rest too heavily on evidence that you anticipate will be severely contested. Be sure that you structure your argument so that you can begin and end with your theme, and invoke it throughout. Finally, outline your opening statement, again beginning and ending with your theme, and raising each of the points to which you will return on final argument.

IV. CONCLUSION

The following chapters discuss all aspects of persuasion at trial, from the opening statement to the final argument. Trial lawyers must master numerous forensic skills, procedural rules, and examination techniques, but your starting point must always be your theory of the case—the story that you want to tell.

— CHAPTER THREE —
Direct Examination

I. THE ROLE OF DIRECT EXAMINATION

Cases are won as a consequence of direct examination.

Direct examination is your opportunity to present the substance of your case. It is the time to offer the evidence available to establish the facts that you need to prevail. Having planned your persuasive story, you must now prove the facts upon which it rests by eliciting the testimony of witnesses.

Direct examination, then, is the heart of your case. It is the fulcrum of the trial—the aspect upon which all else turns. Every other aspect of the trial is derivative of direct examination. Opening statements and final arguments are simply the lawyer's opportunity to comment upon what the witnesses have to say; cross examination exists solely to allow the direct to be challenged or controverted. While we could easily imagine a reasonably fair trial system consisting solely of direct examinations, it is impossible to conceive of anything resembling accurate fact finding in their absence.

Direct examinations should be designed to accomplish one or more of the following basic goals.

A. Introduce Undisputed Facts

In most trials there will be many important facts that are not in dispute. Nonetheless, such facts cannot be considered by the judge or jury, and will not be part of the record on appeal, until and unless they have been placed in evidence through a witness's testimony. Undisputed facts will often be necessary to establish an element of your case. Thus, failing to include them in direct examination could lead to an unfavorable verdict or reversal on appeal.

Assume, for example, that you represent the plaintiff in a case involving damage to the exterior of a building, and that the defense in the case is consent. Even if the question of ownership of the premises is not in dispute, it is still an element of your cause of action.

Thus, you must present proof that your client had a possessory or ownership interest in the building, or run the risk of a directed verdict in favor of the defendant.

B. Enhance the Likelihood of Disputed Facts

The most important facts in a trial will normally be those in dispute. Direct examination is your opportunity to put forward your client's version of the disputed facts. Furthermore, you must not only introduce evidence on disputed points, you must do so persuasively. The true art of direct examination consists in large part of establishing the certainty of facts that the other side claims are uncertain or untrue.

C. Lay Foundations for the Introduction of Exhibits

Documents, photographs, writings, tangible objects, and other forms of real evidence will often be central to your case. With some exceptions, it is necessary to lay the foundation for the admission of such an exhibit through the direct testimony of a witness. This is the case whether or not the reliability of the exhibit is in dispute.

It is not unusual for a witness to be called only for the purpose of introducing an exhibit. The "records custodian" at a hospital or bank may know absolutely nothing about the contents of a particular report, but nonetheless may be examined solely in order to qualify the document as a business record.

D. Reflect Upon the Credibility of Witnesses

The credibility of a witness is always in issue. Thus, every direct examination, whatever its ultimate purpose, must also attend to the credibility of the witness's own testimony. For this reason, most direct examinations begin with some background information about the witness. What does she do for a living? Where did she go to school? How long has she lived in the community? Even if the witness's credibility will not be challenged, this sort of information helps to humanize her and therefore adds weight to what she has to say.

You can expect the credibility of some witnesses to be attacked on cross examination. In these situations you can blunt the assault by bolstering the witness's believability during direct examination. You can strengthen a witness by eliciting the basis of her knowledge, her ability to observe, or her lack of bias or interest in the outcome of the case.

You may also call a witness to reflect adversely on the credibility of the testimony of another. Direct examination may be used, for example, to introduce negative character or reputation evidence concerning another witness. Alternatively, you may call a witness to provide direct evidence of bias or motive, to lay the foundation for an impeaching document, or simply to contradict other testimony.

E.   Hold the Attention of the Trier of Fact

No matter which of the above purposes predominates in any particular direct examination, it must be conducted in a manner that holds the attention of the judge or jury. In addition to being the heart of your case, direct examination also has the highest potential for dissolving into boredom, inattention, and routine. Since it has none of the inherent drama or tension of cross examination, you must take extreme care to prepare your direct examination so as to maximize its impact.

II.   THE LAW OF DIRECT EXAMINATION

The rules of evidence govern the content of all direct examinations. Evidence offered on direct must be relevant, authentic, not hearsay, and otherwise admissible. In addition, there is a fairly specific "law of direct examination" that governs the manner and means in which testimony may be presented.

A.   Competence of Witnesses

Every witness called to testify on direct examination must be legally "competent" to do so. This is generally taken to mean that the witness possesses personal knowledge of some matter at issue in the case,[1] is able to perceive and relate information, is capable of recognizing the difference between truth and falsity, and understands the seriousness of testifying under oath or on affirmation.[2]

In the absence of evidence or other indications to the contrary, all individuals called to the stand are presumed competent to testify.[3] If the competence of a witness is reasonably disputed, it may be necessary to conduct a preliminary examination in order to "qualify" the witness.[4] Such inquiries are usually conducted by the direct examiner but may also be conducted by the trial judge. In either case, the examination must be directed toward that aspect of competence that has been called into question.

---

1.   Rule 602, Federal Rules of Evidence.
2.   Rule 603, Federal Rules of Evidence.
3.   Rule 601, Federal Rules of Evidence.
4.   Rule 104(a), Federal Rules of Evidence.

In the case of a very young child, for example, the qualifying examination must establish that the witness is capable of distinguishing reality from fantasy, is able to perceive such relationships as time and distance, and appreciates that it is "wrong to tell a lie." Following the preliminary examination, the adverse party should be allowed an opportunity to conduct a "voir dire," which is a preliminary cross examination limited to a threshold issue such as competence.[5]

Note that there are several exceptions to the general rules of competence. Expert witnesses, for example, are excused from the requirement of testifying exclusively from personal knowledge.[6] Judges and jurors are generally disqualified from giving evidence in cases in which they are involved.[7]

B. Nonleading Questions

The principal rule of direct examination is that the attorney may not "lead" the witness. A leading question is one that contains or suggests its own answer. Since the party calling a witness to the stand is presumed to have conducted an interview and to know what the testimony will be, leading questions are disallowed in order to ensure that the testimony will come in the witness's own words.

Whether a certain question is leading is frequently an issue of tone or delivery, as much as one of form. The distinction, moreover, is often finely drawn. For example, there is no doubt that this question is leading:

QUESTION: Of course you crossed the street, didn't you?

Not only does the question contain its own answer, its format also virtually requires that it be answered in the affirmative.

On the other hand, this question is not leading:

QUESTION: Did you cross the street?

Although the question is highly specific and calls for a "yes" or "no" answer, it does not control the witness's response.

Finally, this question falls in the middle:

QUESTION: Didn't you cross the street?

If the examiner's tone of voice and inflection indicate that this is meant as a true query, the question probably will not be considered leading. If the question is stated more as an assertion, however, it will violate the leading question rule.

---

5. See Chapter 8, Section IIC(1)(e), *infra* at p. 213.
6. Rule 703, Federal Rules of Evidence.
7. Rules 605 and 606, Federal Rules of Evidence.

There are, in any event, numerous exceptions to the rule against leading questions on direct examination. A lawyer is generally permitted to lead a witness on preliminary matters, on issues that are not in dispute, in order to direct the witness's attention to a specific topic, in order to expedite the testimony on nonessential points, and, in some jurisdictions, to refresh a witness's recollection. In addition, it is usually permissible to lead witnesses who are very young, extremely old, infirm, confused, or frightened. Finally, it is always within the trial judge's discretion to permit leading questions in order to make the examination effective for the ascertainment of the truth, avoid needless consumption of time, protect the witness from undue embarrassment, or as is otherwise necessary to develop the testimony.

In the absence of extreme provocation or abuse, most lawyers will not object to the occasional use of leading questions on direct. It is most common to object to leading questions that are directed to the central issues of the case or that are being used to substitute the testimony of counsel for that of the witness.

C. Narratives

Another general rule is that witnesses on direct examination may not testify in "narrative" form. The term narrative has no precise definition, but it is usually taken to mean an answer that goes beyond responding to a single specific question. Questions that invite a lengthy or run-on reply are said to "call for a narrative answer."

An example of a non-narrative question is, "What did you do next?" The objectionable, narrative version would be, "Tell us everything that you did that day."

As with leading questions, the trial judge has wide discretion to permit narrative testimony. Narratives are often allowed, indeed encouraged, when the witness has been qualified as an expert.

D. The Nonopinion Rule

Witnesses are expected to testify as to their sensory observations. What did the witness see, hear, smell, touch, taste, or do? Witnesses other than experts generally are not allowed to offer opinions or to characterize events or testimony. A lay witness, however, is allowed to give opinions that are "rationally based upon the perception of the witness." Thus, witnesses will usually be permitted to draw conclusions on issues such as speed, distance, volume, time, weight, temperature, and weather conditions. Similarly, lay witnesses may characterize the behavior of others as angry, drunken, affectionate, busy, or even insane.

E. Refreshing Recollection

Although witnesses are expected to testify in their own words, they are not expected to have perfect recall. The courtroom can be an unfamiliar and intimidating place for all but the most "professional" witnesses, and witnesses can suffer memory lapses due to stress, fatigue, discomfort, or simple forgetfulness. Under these circumstances it is permissible for the direct examiner to "refresh" the witness's recollection. It is most common to rekindle a witness's memory through the use of a document such as her prior deposition or report. It may also be permissible to use a photograph, an object, or even a leading question.

In order to refresh recollection with a document, you must first establish that the witness's memory is exhausted concerning a specific issue or event. You must then determine that her memory might be refreshed by reference to a certain writing. Next, show the writing to the witness, allow her time to examine it, and inquire as to whether her memory has returned. If the answer is yes, remove the document and request the witness to continue her testimony. Note that in this situation the testimony must ultimately come from the witness's own restored memory; the document may not be offered as a substitute.

THE BASICS

Direct Examination Checklist ☑	
❏ Are all of your questions nonleading?	Do any of the questions you plan to ask suggest the answer desired? *If so, they are leading and you should rephrase them.*
❏ Did you avoid asking questions that call for narrative answers?	Do any of your questions call for answers that will be longer than a few sentences? *If so, you should break up the testimony by asking more specific questions.*
❏ Did you avoid speculative testimony and refrain from asking the witness to offer an opinion she is not qualified to give?	Do any of your questions call for answers outside of the witness's personal knowledge or sensory perception? *If so, it is likely that the witness will be speculating. Rephrase your questions so that they call for facts instead of conclusions.*
❏ Are you prepared to refresh the witness's recollection if necessary?	Have you practiced refreshing recollection, and are you able to do it on a moment's notice? *If not, keep practicing until you are comfortable refreshing recollection.*

III. PLANNING DIRECT EXAMINATIONS

There are three fundamental aspects to every direct examination plan: content, organization, and technique.

Your principal tool in presenting a persuasive direct examination is, of course, the knowledge of the witness. If the underlying content of the examination is not accurate and believable, the lawyer's technique is unlikely to make any noticeable difference. Your primary concern, then, must be content—the existence of the facts that you intend to prove.

The content of a direct examination can be enhanced through the use of organization, language, focus, pacing, and rapport. Effective organization requires sequencing an examination in a manner that provides for logical development, while emphasizing important points and minimizing damaging ones. Questions should be asked in language that directs the progress of the examination without putting words in the witness's mouth. A direct examination uses focus to underscore and expand upon the most crucial issues, rather than allow them to be lost in a welter of meaningless details. Pacing varies the tone, speed, and intensity of the testimony to ensure that it does not become boring. Finally, the positive rapport of the direct examiner with the witness is essential to establish the witness's overall trustworthiness and believability.

A. Content

Content—what the witness has to say—must be the driving force of every direct examination. Recall that direct examination provides your best opportunity to prove your case. It is not meant merely as a showcase for the witness's attractiveness or for your own forensic skills. The examination must have a central purpose. It must either establish some aspect of your theory, or it must contribute to the persuasiveness of your theme. Preferably, it will do both.

Begin by asking yourself, "Why am I calling this witness?" Which elements of your claims or defenses will the witness address? How can the witness be used to controvert an element of the other side's case? What exhibits can be introduced through the witness? How can the witness bolster or detract from the credibility of others who will testify? How can the witness add moral strength to the presentation of the case, or appeal to the jury's sense of justice?

Since a witness might be called for any or all of the above reasons, you must exhaustively determine all of the possible useful information. List every conceivable thing that the witness might say to explain or help your case.

Now you must begin to prioritize and discard. This is a ruthless process. In direct examination, length is your enemy. You must work to eliminate all nonessential facts that are questionable, subject to impeachment, cumulative, distasteful, implausible, distracting, or just plain boring.

1. What to Include

First, go through a process of inclusion. List the witness's facts that are necessary to the establishment of your theory. What is the single most important thing that the witness has to say? What are the witness's collateral facts that will make the central information more plausible? What is the next most important part of the potential testimony? What secondary facts make that testimony more believable? Continue this process for every element of your case.

For example, assume that in our fire engine case you have located a witness who saw the defendant driver at an automobile repair shop just a few days before the accident. The witness told you that the defendant was advised that his brakes were in poor repair, but that he left without having them fixed. This is a fact of central importance, and you will no doubt present it in the direct examination. Collateral or supportive facts will include corroborative details such as the time of day, the witness's reason for being in the auto shop, the witness's location during the crucial conversation about the brakes, the reason that the witness can remember the exact language used, and why the witness can identify the defendant. These details, while not strictly relevant to your theory, give weight and believability to the crucial testimony.

You must also be sure to include those "thematic" facts that give your case moral appeal. Returning to the intersection case, perhaps you have an additional witness who will testify that at the time of the collision the defendant was already late for an important meeting. Your theme, then, might be that the defendant was "too busy to be careful." How can this theme be developed in the testimony of the "auto shop" witness? The answer is to look for supportive details. Was the defendant curt or abrupt with the repairperson? Was he constantly looking at his watch? Was he trying to read "important-looking papers" while discussing the brakes? Did the defendant rush out of the shop? In other words, search for details that support your image of the defendant as busy, preoccupied, and unconcerned with safety.

In addition to central facts and supporting details, your "content checklist" should include consideration of the following sorts of information:

Reasons. Recall that stories are more persuasive when they include reasons for the way people act. A direct examination usually should include the reasons for the witness's own actions. Some witnesses can also provide reasons for the actions of another.

Explanations. When a witness's testimony is not self-explanatory, or where it raises obvious questions, simply ask the witness to explain. In the above "repair shop" scenario it may not be immediately apparent that a casual observer would recall the defendant's actions in such detail. Ask for an explanation:

QUESTION: How is it that you can remember seeing and hearing what the defendant did that morning?

ANSWER: I was at the shop to have my brakes fixed, and it really made an impression on me that he was leaving without taking care of his.

Credibility. The credibility of a witness is always in issue. Some part of every direct examination should be devoted to establishing the credibility of the witness. You can enhance credibility in numerous ways. Show that the witness is neutral and disinterested. Demonstrate that the witness had an adequate opportunity to observe. Allow the witness to deny any expected charges of bias or misconduct. Elicit the witness's personal background of probity and honesty.

2. What to Exclude

Having identified the facts that most support your theory and most strengthen your theme, you may now begin the process of elimination. It should go without saying that you must omit those facts that are "untrue." While you are not required to assure yourself beyond reasonable doubt of the probity of each witness, neither may you knowingly elicit testimony that you believe to be false. By the time you are preparing your direct examinations you certainly will have abandoned any legal or factual theory that rests upon evidence of this sort.

More realistically, unless you have an extraordinarily compelling reason to include them, you will need to consider discarding facts that fall into the following categories:

Clutter. This may be the single greatest vice in direct examination. Details are essential to the corroboration of important evidence, and they are worse than useless virtually everywhere else. Aimless detail will detract from your true corroboration. In the "auto shop" example, for instance, the witness's proximity to the service counter is an essential detail. The color of the paint in the waiting room is not.

How do you determine whether a certain fact is clutter? Ask what it contributes to the persuasiveness of your story. Does it supply a reason for the way that someone acted? Does it make an important fact more or less likely? Does it affect the credibility or authority of a witness? Does it enhance the moral value of your story? If all of the answers are negative, you're looking at clutter.

Unprovables. These are facts that can successfully be disputed. While not "false," they may be subjected to such vigorous and effective dispute as to make them unusable. Is the witness the only person who claims to have observed a certain event, while many other credible witnesses swear to the precise contrary? Is the witness herself less than certain? Is the testimony contradicted by credible documentary evidence? It is usually better to pass up a line of inquiry than to pursue it and ultimately have it rejected. This is not, however, a hard and fast rule. Many true facts will be disputed by the other side, and your case will virtually always turn upon your ability to persuade the trier of fact that your version is correct. Sometimes your case will depend entirely upon the testimony of a single witness who, though certain and truthful, will come under massive attack. Still, you must be willing to evaluate all of the potential testimony against the standards of provability and need. If you can't prove it, don't use it. Especially if you don't need it.

Implausibles. Some facts need not be disputed in order to collapse under their own weight. They might be true, they might be useful, they might be free from possible contradiction, but they still just won't fly. Return to the "auto shop" witness and assume that she informed you that she recognized the defendant because they had once ridden in the same elevator fifteen years previously. You may have no reason to disbelieve the witness, and it is certainly unlikely that anyone could contradict or disprove her testimony. The testimony might even add some support to your theme, say, if the defendant rushed out of the elevator in an obvious hurry to get to work. Nonetheless, the testimony is simply too far-fetched. If offered, it will give the trier of fact something unnecessary to worry about; it will inject a reason to doubt the other testimony of the witness.

Note, however, that implausibility must be weighed against importance. If the case involved a disputed identification of the defendant, then proof of an earlier encounter might be of sufficient value to risk its introduction.

Impeachables. These are statements open to contradiction by the witness's own prior statements. By the time of trial, many witnesses will have given oral or written statements in the form of interviews, reports, and depositions. Many also will have signed or authored documents, correspondence, and other writings. With some limitations, the witnesses' previous words may be used to cast doubt upon their credibility; this is called impeachment by a prior inconsistent statement.[9] The demonstration that a witness has previously made statements that contradict her trial testimony is often one of the most dramatic, and damning, aspects of cross examination. Unless you can provide an extremely good explanation of why the witness has changed—or seems to have changed—her story, it is usually best to omit "impeachables" from direct testimony.

Door openers. Some direct testimony is said to "open the door" for inquiries on cross examination that otherwise would not be allowed. The theory here is that fairness requires that the cross examiner be allowed to explore any topic that was deliberately introduced on direct. For example, in the intersection case the defendant almost certainly would not be allowed to introduce the fact that the plaintiff had been under the care of a psychiatrist. On the other hand, assume that the plaintiff testified on direct that the accident had forced her to miss an important appointment with her doctor, and that the appointment could not be rescheduled for a week due to the nature of the doctor's schedule. In these circumstances the door would be opened, at a minimum, to a cross examination that covered the nature of the appointment and the reason that it could not be rescheduled; in other words, that the plaintiff was on her way to see her psychiatrist.

Another common door opener is the misconceived "defensive" direct examination. It is considered a truism in many quarters that the direct examiner should defuse the cross by preemptively bringing out all of the bad facts. The danger, however, is that you will "defensively" bring out facts that would have been inadmissible on cross examination. Assume, for example, that your client has a prior juvenile conviction for theft. While you might ordinarily want to raise a prior crime yourself in order to explain it or otherwise soften the impact of the evidence, juvenile convictions are almost never admissible. Thus, a defensive direct examination would not only introduce otherwise excludable information, it could very well open the door to further exploitation of those facts on cross. You cannot always avoid door openers, but you must learn to recognize them.

B.   Organization and Structure

Organization is the tool through which you translate the witness's memory of events into a coherent and persuasive story. This requires idiom, art, poetry. An artist does not paint everything that

---

9.   See Chapter 5, Section II, *infra* at p. 124.

she sees. Rather, she organizes shapes, colors, and light to present her own image of a landscape. In the same manner, a trial lawyer does not simply ask a witness to "tell everything you know," but instead uses the placement and sequence of the information to heighten and clarify its value.

The keys to this process are primacy and recency, apposition, duration, and repetition.

Primacy and recency refer to the widely accepted phenomenon that people tend best to remember those things that they hear first and last. Following this principle, the important parts of a direct examination should be brought out at its beginning and again at its end. Less important information should be "sandwiched" in the middle. In our intersection case the presence of the fire truck may well be the most important part of the plaintiff's testimony. It should therefore be introduced early in her direct examination and perhaps alluded to again at the end.

Apposition is the placement or juxtaposition of important facts in a manner that emphasizes their relationship. Again looking at the intersection case, a strictly chronological direct examination might have the plaintiff begin by explaining where she was headed on the morning of the accident. Assume now that she was going to an art exhibit that would not open for another hour. The importance and value of this seemingly innocuous fact can be heightened tremendously by "apposing" it to the conduct of the defendant immediately following the accident. Imagine the impact of contrasting the plaintiff's unhurried trip with the following information about the defendant:

> QUESTION: Where were you going on the morning of the accident?
>
> ANSWER: I was going to the Art Institute.
>
> QUESTION: Were you in any hurry to get there?
>
> ANSWER: It wasn't going to open for an hour, so I was in no hurry at all.
>
> QUESTION: What did you do immediately after the accident?
>
> ANSWER: I asked the defendant if he was all right.
>
> QUESTION: What did the defendant do immediately following the accident?

ANSWER: He jumped out of his car and took out his cell phone. He shouted that he would talk to me later, but first he had to cancel an important appointment.

Duration refers to the relative amount of time that you spend on the various aspects of the direct examination. As a general rule you should dwell on the more important points, using the very length of coverage to emphasize the significance of the topic. Less important matters should consume less of the direct examination. In the fire truck example it should be obvious that the presence and noticeability of the fire engine is central to the plaintiff's case. Although the plaintiff's initial observation of the truck could be established in a single question and answer, the importance of the subject dictates greater duration for this part of the direct examination:

QUESTION: What did you see as you drove south on Sheridan Road?

ANSWER: I saw a fire truck.

QUESTION: Describe it, please.

ANSWER: It was your basic fire truck. It was red, and it had firefighters riding on it. It had lights and a bell.

QUESTION: Were the lights flashing?

ANSWER: Yes, and it was sounding its siren.

QUESTION: How far away were you when you first noticed the fire truck?

ANSWER: I would say almost a block away.

Repetition is a corollary of duration. Important points should be repeated, preferably throughout the direct examination, to increase the likelihood that they will be retained and relied upon by the trier of fact.

Even applying these principles, there is no set pattern for the structure of a direct examination, just as there is no correct way to paint a landscape. The following guidelines, however, will always be useful.

1. Start Strong and End Strong: The Overall Examination

Every direct examination, no matter how else it is organized, should strive to begin and end on strong points. The definition of a strong point will differ from trial to trial. It may be the most gripping and dramatic aspect of the entire examination; it may be the single matter on which the witness expresses the greatest certainty; it may be the case's most hotly disputed issue; or it may be a crucial predicate for other testimony. Whatever the specifics, the strong points of your overall examination should have some or all of these features:

Admissibility. There is little worse than having an objection sustained right at the beginning, or end, of a direct examination. You must be absolutely certain of the admissibility of your opening and closing points.

Theory value. The very definition of a strong point is that it makes a significant contribution to your theory. What does the witness have to say that is most central to the proof of your case?

Thematic value. Ideally, your strongest points will reinforce the moral weight of your case. Try to phrase them in the same language you use to invoke your theme.

Dramatic impact. Dramatic impact at the beginning of an examination will keep the judge or jury listening. Dramatic impact at the end of the examination will help fix the testimony in their memories.

Undeniability. Choose strong points in the hope that they will be vividly remembered. It will do you little good if they are remembered as being questionable or controverted.

In most cases, of course, it will be necessary to use the opening part of the direct examination to introduce the witness and establish some of her background. Thus, the actual "beginning" of the examination should be understood as the beginning of the substantive testimony.

2. Start Strong and End Strong: The Sub-examinations

Each full direct examination is actually a combination of many smaller sub-examinations. As you move from topic to topic you are constantly concluding and reinitiating the sub-parts of the direct testimony. The "start strong/end strong" rule should not be applied only to the organization of the full direct; it should also be used to structure its individual components.

In our intersection case you might wish to begin and end the substantive part of the plaintiff's examination with evidence about the fire truck. In between, however, you will cover many other issues, including the plaintiff's background, the scene of the collision, and the plaintiff's damages. Each of these component parts of the direct should, if possible, begin and end on a strong point.

In something as simple as setting the scene, consider what elements of the description are most important to your case. Then begin with one and end with another. In the intersection case you might want to lead off with the clarity of the weather conditions in order to establish visibility. Perhaps you would then conclude the scene-setting portion of the examination with this description of the traffic:

QUESTION: Of all of the cars that were present, how many stopped for the fire truck?

ANSWER: All of them, except the defendant.

3. Use Topical Organization

Chronology is almost always the easiest form of organization. What could be more obvious than beginning at the beginning and ending at the end? In trial advocacy, however, easiest is not always best. In many cases it will be preferable to utilize a topical or thematic form of organization. In this way, you can arrange various components of the witness's testimony to reinforce each other, you can isolate weak points, and you can develop your theory in the most persuasive manner. The order in which events occurred is usually fortuitous. Your duty as an advocate is to rearrange the telling so that the story has maximum logical force.

Assume that you are the prosecutor in a burglary case. Your first witness is the police officer who conducted a stakeout and arrested the defendant on the basis of a description that she received from a superior officer. A strict chronology in such a case could be confusing and counterproductive. The witness would have to begin with the morning of the arrest, perhaps explaining the time that she came on duty, the other matters that she worked on that day, and her instructions in conducting the stakeout. She no doubt would have received the description somewhere in the middle of all this activity. Even if relevant, the importance of the surrounding details is not likely to be well understood at the outset of the examination. The officer, sticking to chronological order, would then describe the people she saw at the stakeout location whom she did not arrest. Finally, the witness would come to the defendant's arrival on the scene. Assume, however, that she did not immediately arrest him. Rather, she observed him for some time; perhaps he even left the scene (and returned) once or twice before the eventual arrest.

In plain chronological order, all of this can add up to a rather diffuse story. The officer's reasons for conducting the stakeout are separated from the activity itself; the receipt of the description has no immediate relationship to the apprehension of the suspect. The trier of fact is required to reflect both forward and back on the significance of the data.

A topical organization, however, could provide a framework that adds clarity and direction to the story. A structure based upon the description of the defendant, rather than chronology, would begin with a description of the arrest itself; then:

QUESTION: Officer, why did you arrest the defendant?

ANSWER: Because he fit a description that I had been given earlier of a wanted burglar.

QUESTION: Did you arrest him as soon as you saw him?

ANSWER: No. I wanted to make sure that he fit the description completely, so I waited until he was standing directly below a street light.

QUESTION: Was there anyone else in the vicinity at that time?

ANSWER: There had been a few people, but nobody who matched the description.

QUESTION: Officer, please go back and tell us how you received the description that led to the arrest of the defendant.

Even in a matter as simple as our automobile collision case, a strictly chronological direct examination of the plaintiff could fail to be either dramatic or persuasive. Imagine beginning the examination with the time that the plaintiff left home that morning. State her destination and her estimated travel time. Describe the weather and traffic conditions. Trace her route from street to street until she arrives at the fateful intersection. Describe the appearance of the fire truck, the plaintiff's reaction, and finally the collision. After slogging through a series of details, some important and some not, the direct examination finally arrives at the most important event—the accident itself.

It would be more dramatic to (1) begin with the collision, (2) explain why the plaintiff had stopped her car, (3) describe the fire truck, (4) describe the response of the surrounding traffic, and (5) contrast that with the actions of the defendant.

4. Do Not Interrupt the Action

Every direct examination is likely to involve one, two, or more key events or occurrences. The witness may describe physical activity such as an automobile accident, an arrest, the failure of a piece of equipment, or a surgical procedure. Alternatively, the witness may testify about something less tangible, such as the formation of a contract, the effect of an insult, the making of a threat, the breach of a promise, or the existence of pain following an injury. Whatever the precise subject, it will always be possible to divide the testimony into "action" on the one hand and supporting details and descriptions on the other.

A cardinal rule for the organization of direct examination is never to interrupt the action. Do not disrupt the dramatic flow of your story, the description of the crucial events, in order to fill in minor details. There can be no more jarring or dissatisfying an experience during trial than when the witness, who has just testified to the sound of a gunshot or the screech of automobile tires, is then calmly asked the location of the nearest street light. The lighting conditions may be important, but they cannot possibly be important enough to justify the discontinuity created by fracturing the natural flow of occurrence testimony.

Many lawyers subscribe to the theory that you should "set the scene" before proceeding to the activity. Following this approach in our automobile case, you would first have the witness describe the intersection, the surrounding traffic, the condition of the streets, and the location of her car, all before proceeding to the events of the collision. This approach is based on the concept that the trier of fact can then place the activities within the framework that you have created.

An alternative approach is first to describe the events themselves and then to go back and redescribe them while filling in the details of the scene. Assume that the plaintiff in the automobile case has already testified about the events of the accident. You can now go back to set the scene, effectively telling the story a second time: What were the weather conditions when you entered the block where the collision occurred? How much traffic was there when you first saw the fire truck? What direction were you traveling when the defendant's car struck yours?

5. Give Separate Attention to the Details

We have seen that details add strength and veracity to a witness's testimony. Unfortunately, they can also detract from the flow of events. It is therefore often best to give separate attention to the details, an approach that also allows you to explain their importance.

Assume, for example, that you are presenting the testimony of a robbery victim and that the central issue in the case is the identification of the defendant. You know that you don't want to detract from the action, so you will present the events of the robbery without interruption. Then you will go back to supply the details that support the witness's ability to identify the defendant:

QUESTION:	How far was the defendant from you when you first noticed him?
ANSWER:	About twelve or fifteen feet.
QUESTION:	How much closer did he come?
ANSWER:	He came right up to me. His face wasn't more than a foot from mine.
QUESTION:	Did you look at his face?
ANSWER:	Yes, absolutely. He stared right at me.
QUESTION:	For how long?
ANSWER:	It was at least a minute.
QUESTION:	Was it still light out?
ANSWER:	Yes, it was.
QUESTION:	Could you see the color of his clothing?

There will be dozens of details available to support the witness's identification. Dispersing them throughout the description of events would both disrupt the testimony and diminish their cumulative importance. The remedy for this problem is to give the details separate attention.

6. Try Not to Scatter Circumstantial Evidence

Circumstantial evidence is usually defined as indirect proof of a proposition, event, or occurrence. The identity of a burglar, for example, could be proven directly through eyewitness testimony. It could also be proven indirectly through the accumulation of circumstantial evidence such as the following: The defendant was seen near the scene of the burglary on the evening of the crime; her scarf was found in the doorway of the burglarized house; she had been heard complaining about her need for a new radio; two days after the crime she was found in possession of a radio that had been taken in the burglary.

None of the above facts taken individually amount to direct proof that the defendant committed the crime. There could be a perfectly innocent explanation for each one. In combination, however, they raise an extremely compelling inference of guilt. In other words, the indirect circumstances accumulate to establish the likelihood of the prosecution's case.

Inferential evidence is at its strongest when a series of circumstances can be combined to lead to the desired conclusion. It is therefore effective to present all of the related circumstantial evidence at a single point in the direct examination, rather than scatter it throughout. This will not always be possible. The logic of a witness's testimony may require that items of circumstantial evidence be elicited at different points in the testimony. Chronological organization will dictate introducing the circumstances in the order that they occurred or were discovered. Even topical organization may require assigning individual circumstances to separate topics. In the burglary case, for example, a topical approach might divide the testimony into areas such as "condition of the premises" and "apprehension of the defendant." The discovery of the scarf and the recovery of the radio would consequently be separated in the testimony.

Nonetheless, it is a good idea to attempt to cluster your circumstantial evidence. Abandon this technique only when you have settled upon another that you believe will be more effective.

7. Defensive Direct Examination

From time to time it may be advisable to bring out potentially harmful or embarrassing facts on direct in order to blunt their impact on cross examination. The theory of such "defensive" direct examination is that the bad information will have less sting if the witness offers it herself and, conversely, that it will be all the more damning if the witness is seen as having tried to hide the bad facts. As we noted above, you should conduct a defensive direct examination only when you are sure that the information is known to the other side and will be admissible on cross examination.

Assuming that you have determined to bring out certain damaging information, be sure not to do it at either the beginning or the end of the direct examination. Remember the principles of primacy and recency. By definition, bad facts cannot possibly be the strong points of your case, so you will always want to bury them in the middle of the direct examination.

An extremely useful technique is to allow the trier of fact to "make friends" with your witness before you introduce harmful information. It is a normal human tendency to want to believe the best of people whom you like. Thus, you should give the judge or jury every possible reason to like your witness before offering anything that might have a contrary effect. Recall the last time that you saw a television interview of the neighbors of an arrested crime suspect. They almost inevitably say something like, "He was such a nice man. I can't believe that he would do a thing like that."

If, for example, you have a witness who was previously convicted of a felony, you can reasonably assume that to be fair game for cross examination. You will therefore want to bring out the conviction, in sympathetic terms, during your direct examination. Do not elicit such a fact until you have spent some time "personalizing" the witness. Give the trier of fact a reason to discount the conviction before you ever mention it.

8. Affirmation Before Refutation

Witnesses are often called both to offer affirmative evidence of their own and to refute the testimony of others. In such cases it is usually best to offer the affirmative evidence before proceeding to refutation. In this manner you will accentuate the positive aspects of your case and avoid making the witness appear to be a scold.

As with all principles, this one should not be followed slavishly. Some witnesses are called solely for refutation. Others are far more important for what they negate than for their affirmative information. As a general organizing principle it is useful to think about building your own case before destroying the opposition's.

9. Get to the Point

A direct examination is not a treasure hunt or murder mystery; there is seldom a reason to keep the trier of fact in suspense. The best form of organization is often to explain exactly where the testimony is headed and then to go directly there.

10. End with a Clincher

Every examination should end with a clincher, a single fact that capsulizes your trial theory or theme. To qualify as a clincher a fact must be (1) absolutely admissible, (2) reasonably dramatic, (3) simple and memorable, and (4) stated with certainty. Depending upon the nature of the evidence and the theory on which you are proceeding, the final question to the plaintiff in our automobile case might be any of the following:

> QUESTION: How long was the fire engine visible before the defendant's car struck yours?
>
> ANSWER: It was visible for at least ten seconds because I had already seen it and stopped for a while when the defendant ran into me.

Or,

> QUESTION: Did the defendant make his telephone call before or after he checked on your injuries?
>
> ANSWER: He took out his cell phone without even looking at me.

Or,

> QUESTION: Do you know whether you will ever be able to walk again without pain?
>
> ANSWER: The doctors say that they can't do anything more for me, but I am still praying.

11. Ignore Any Rule When Necessary

By now you will no doubt have noticed that the above principles are not completely consistent with one another. In any given case you will probably be unable to start strong, organize topically, and separate the details, while still getting to the point without interrupting the action. Which rules should you follow? The answer lies in your own good judgment and can only be arrived at in the context of a specific case. If you need another principle to help interpret the others, it is this: Apply the rules that best advance your theory and theme.

THE BASICS

Direct Examination Organization
• Start strong and end strong in the overall and subexaminations
• Use topical organization
• Get to the point
• Tell the story
• Do not interrupt the action
• Affirm before refuting
• Draw the sting
• End with a clincher
• Ignore any rule when necessary

IV. QUESTIONING TECHNIQUE

Since content is the motive force behind every direct examination, you must use questioning technique to focus attention on the witness and the testimony. It is the witness's story that is central to the direct examination; the style and manner of your questioning should underscore and support the credibility and veracity of that story. The following questioning techniques can help you to achieve that goal.

A. Use Short, Open Questions

You want the witness to tell the story. You want the witness to be the center of attention. You want the witness to be appreciated and believed. None of these things can happen if you do all of the talking. Therefore, ask short questions.

Using short questions will help you to refrain from talking, but not every short question will get the witness talking. To do that, you will need open questions.

Don't ask a witness, "Did you go to the bank?" The answer to that short question will probably be an even shorter "Yes." Instead, as much of your direct examination as possible should consist of questions that invite the witness to describe, explain, and illuminate the events of her testimony. Ask questions such as these:

QUESTION: Where did you go that day?

QUESTION: What happened after that?

QUESTION: Tell us who was there.

QUESTION: What else happened?

QUESTION: Describe where you were.

Your witness will almost always be more memorable and believable if you can obtain most of her information in her own words. Short, open questions will advance that goal.

B.   Use Directive and Transitional Questions

You cannot use open questions to begin an examination or to move from one area of the examination to another. To do so you would have to start with "When were you born?" and proceed to ask "What happened next?" in almost endless repetition.

A better approach is to use directive and transitional questions. Directive questions, quite simply, direct the witness's attention to the topic that you want to cover. Suppose that you want the witness to address the issue of damages. Ask,

QUESTION: Were you in any pain after the accident?

Having directed the witness's attention, you can now revert to your short, open questions:

QUESTION: Please describe how you felt.

QUESTION: Where else did you hurt?

QUESTION: How has this affected your life?

You may need to use more than one directive question during any particular line of testimony. To fill out the subject of damages, for example, you may need to ask additional questions such as,

QUESTION: Do you currently suffer any physical disabilities?

Or,

QUESTION: Did you ever have such pains before the accident?

Remember that the purpose of a directive question is to direct the witness's attention, not to divert the jury's.

Another problem with short, open questions is that they are not very good at underscoring the relationship between one fact and another. The best way to do this is through "transitional" questions that utilize one fact as the predicate, or introduction, to another. Here are some examples of transitional questions:

QUESTION: After you saw the fire truck, what did you do?

QUESTION: Do you know what the defendant did as the other traffic slowed to a stop?

QUESTION: Once the defendant's car hit yours, did you see him do anything?

Note that directive and transitional questions will tend to be leading. As a technical matter, however, these questions are permissible so long as they are used to orient the witness, expedite the testimony, or introduce a new area of the examination. As a practical matter, objections to directive and transitional questions are not likely to be sustained so long as they are used relatively sparingly and are not asked in a tone that seems to insist upon a certain answer. It is unethical to abuse transitional or directive questions in a way that substitutes your testimony for that of the witness.

C. Reinitiate Primacy

The doctrine of primacy tells us that the trier of fact will pay maximum attention to the witness at the very beginning of the testimony. You can make further use of this principle by continuously "re-beginning" the examination. That is, every time you seem to start anew, you will refocus the attention of the judge or jury. This technique can be called reinitiating primacy, and there are several ways to achieve it:

1. Use General Headline Questions

Most direct examinations, including even those that are organized chronologically, will consist of a number of individual areas of inquiry. If you treat each such area as a separate examination you can reinitiate primacy every time you move to a new topic. You can divide the direct into a series of smaller examinations through the use of verbal headlines. Rather than simply move from area to area, insert a headline to alert the judge or jury to the fact that you are shifting gears or changing subjects.

The introduction should be overt. Don't ask,

QUESTION: What happened as you were driving south on Sheridan Road?

Instead, announce the new subject by asking,

QUESTION: Were you involved in an accident at the corner of Sheridan and Chase?

Similar headlines might include:

QUESTION: Had you kept your own car in good repair?

Or,

QUESTION: Were you hospitalized?

Or,

QUESTION: Are you still disabled today?

None of these introductory questions would really be necessary to begin the particular segment of testimony. You could simply proceed to the detailed questioning, relying upon the witness to provide the necessary information. You could also write an entire novel without using chapter titles, paragraphs, or even punctuation. The headline question, however, serves the same function as a chapter heading in a book. It divides the "text" and reinitiates primacy.

2. Explain Where You Are Going

You can reinitiate primacy even more directly through the use of a few, well-chosen, declaratory statements. Everything that you say during a direct examination does not have to be in the form of a question. You may say to the witness, "Let's talk about the aftermath of the accident," or, "We need to move on to the subject of your injuries." Such statements are permissible so long as they are truly used to make the transition from one part of the testimony to another or to orient the witness in some other manner. You cannot, of course, use declaratory statements to instruct the witness how to testify.

3. Use Body Movement

Another way to segment your examination, and thereby reinitiate primacy, is through the use of body movement. Most jurisdictions, although not all, allow lawyers to move rather freely about the courtroom as they conduct their examinations. Unless you are in a court that requires you to remain seated at counsel table or standing at a lectern, you can effectively announce the beginning of a new topic by pausing for a moment and then moving purposefully to a different part of the room. You needn't stride dramatically—a few short steps will usually suffice.

The key to this technique is to stop talking as you move. The silence and movement will reinforce each other, making it clear that one topic has ended and another is about to begin.

D. Use Incremental Questions

Information usually can be obtained in either large or small pieces. Incremental questions break the "whole" into its component pieces so that the testimony can be delivered in greater, and therefore more persuasive, detail.

A large, nonincremental question might be,

QUESTION: What did the robber look like?

Even a well-prepared witness will probably answer this question with a fairly general description. A common response might be,

ANSWER: He was a white male, about twenty or twenty-five years old, maybe six feet tall.

You might be able to go back to supply any omitted information, but in doing so you will risk giving the unfortunate impression of doing just that—filling in gaps in the witness's testimony. Furthermore, at some point in the backtracking a judge might sustain an objection on the ground that the question—"Describe the robber"—had been asked and answered.

An incremental approach to the issue of identification, on the other hand, would be built upon a set of questions such as these:

QUESTION: Were you able to get a good look at the robber?

ANSWER: Yes, I was able to see him clearly.

QUESTION: How tall was he?

ANSWER: About six feet tall.

QUESTION: How heavy was he?

ANSWER: He was heavy, almost fat, over 200 pounds.

QUESTION: What race was he?

ANSWER: He was white.

QUESTION: And his complexion?

ANSWER: He was very fair, with freckles.

QUESTION: What color was his hair?

ANSWER: He was blond.

QUESTION: How was his hair cut?

ANSWER:	It wasn't really cut at all—just sort of long and stringy.
QUESTION:	Did he have any facial hair?
ANSWER:	A small mustache.
QUESTION:	Could you see his eyes?
ANSWER:	Yes, he came right up to me.
QUESTION:	What color were they?
ANSWER:	Blue.
QUESTION:	Was he wearing glasses?
ANSWER:	Yes, he was.
QUESTION:	What sort of frames?
ANSWER:	Round wire rims.
QUESTION:	Did he have any scars or marks?
ANSWER:	Yes, he had a birthmark on his forehead.
QUESTION:	Was he wearing a jacket?
ANSWER:	He had on a Philadelphia Flyers jacket.

Depending upon the witness's knowledge, further questions could inquire into other facts. Could the witness see the robber's shirt? What color was it? His trousers? His shoes? Any jewelry? Tattoos?

As you can plainly see, the use of incremental questions, each seeking a single small bit of information, can drive home the accuracy of the identification without seeming to put words in the witness's mouth.

The incremental technique should be used sparingly. It will not work as an overall principle since the unrestrained use of details will quickly overwhelm the trier of fact. Use it only where the details are available, significant, and convincing.

First and foremost, the details must be available. It will only damage your case for you to ask a series of incremental questions that elicit negative or blank responses.

Second, the details must be significant. You will produce only boredom by providing every conceivable detail regarding every conceivable fact. No one will be interested in the location of the bell on the fire truck or the number of spots on the fire house dalmatian. Rather, you want the fine emphasis on small facts to come as a clear departure from the balance of the examination. What you are implying by the shift should be obvious: "Details weren't crucial before, but they are now. So pay close attention."

Finally, the incremental details have to be convincing; they have to lend verity to the larger point that you are trying to establish. Some details will be meaningless. It is unlikely to help an identification, for example, for the witness to testify that the robber was chewing gum. Other details may not be credible. Even if the witness claims absolute certainty, you probably won't want to offer testimony about the number of fillings in the assailant's teeth.

E.   Reflect Time, Distance, Intensity

The very best direct examinations virtually re-create the incidents they describe, drawing verbal images that all but place the trier of fact at the scene of the events. Your pace and manner of questioning are essential to this process.

The timing or duration of an event, for example, is often crucial in a trial; one side claims that things happened quickly and the other asserts that they were drawn out. It is possible to use the pace of questioning to support your particular theory. Assume that you represent the defendant in our fire truck case. His defense is that the fire engine appeared only a moment before the collision and that he just didn't have enough time to stop his car. The goal of the defendant's direct examination must be to re-create that scene by collapsing the time available to react to the fire truck. Hence, you will ask only a few, fast-paced questions:

QUESTION: When did the fire truck first become visible?

ANSWER: It approached the intersection just as I did.

QUESTION: What was the very first action that you took?

ANSWER: I slammed on my brakes.

QUESTION: How much time did that take?

ANSWER: Less than a second.

Note that this direct examination proceeds quickly, emphasizing both shortness of time and immediacy of response. This result will be enhanced if you fire off the questions, and if the witness doesn't pause before answering. Strive for the appearance of all but panting for breath.

In contrast, the plaintiff will claim that there was ample time for the defendant to stop. Her direct examination should therefore be drawn out in order to demonstrate exactly how much time there was:

QUESTION: Where was the fire truck when you first saw it?

ANSWER: It was about a quarter of a block away from the intersection.

QUESTION: How far away from you was it?

ANSWER: About one hundred yards.

QUESTION: How many other cars were between you and the fire truck?

ANSWER: Three or four.

QUESTION: What did they do in response?

ANSWER: They all stopped.

QUESTION: How long did it take those other cars to stop?

ANSWER: Normal stopping time—a few seconds.

QUESTION: What was the first thing that you did?

ANSWER: I started to pull over to the side.

QUESTION: How long did that take?

ANSWER: Five seconds or so.

QUESTION: What did you do after that?

ANSWER: I brought my car to a stop.

QUESTION: How long did that take?

ANSWER: Well, I applied my brakes right away, and it took a few seconds for the car to stop.

QUESTION: Then what happened?

ANSWER: That's when the other car rear-ended me.

QUESTION: How much time elapsed between the moment when you first saw the fire truck and the time that the defendant's car hit yours?

ANSWER: At least ten or fifteen seconds.

There is every reason not to hurry through this part of the examination. The length, detail, and pace of your questions should be used to demonstrate the validity of your theory: The defendant had plenty of time to stop.

Similar techniques can be used to establish distance and intensity. Draw out your questions to maximize distance; move through them quickly to minimize it. Ask questions at a rapid pace to enhance the intensity of an encounter; slow down to make the situation more relaxed.

A word about ethics is important at this point. Lawyers are often accused of using verbal tricks to turn night into day. That is not what we are discussing here. Rather, the purpose of using "reflective" questioning is just the opposite—to ensure that the witness conveys her intended meaning. The techniques and examination styles discussed above are not deceptive, but are useful to illuminate or underscore the content of a witness's testimony. If a witness says that an event took only moments, you can assist in the accurate presentation of that testimony by using a questioning style reflective of suddenness and speed. Use of the wrong style can actually inhibit the witness's communication and positively mislead the trier of fact.

F.   Repeat Important Points

In every direct examination there will be several essential ideas that stand out as far more important than the rest. Do not be satisfied to elicit those points only once. Repeat them. Restate them. Then repeat them again. Then think of ways to restate them again. Since you are not allowed to ask the same question twice (Objection: asked and answered), you will need to employ your lawyer's creativity to fashion numerous slightly different questions, each stressing the same point. Repetition is the parent of retention, and your most important points should arise again and again throughout the testimony to ensure that they are retained by the trier of fact.

The corollary to this principle is that less important points should not be repeated in like manner. Increased attention should be used to make key subjects stand out. If too many points are given this treatment, they will all be made to seem equally unimportant. How do you decide which facts are sufficiently important to bear repetition? The answer is to consider your theory and theme. You will want to repeat those facts that are basic to your logical theory and those that best evoke your moral theme.

In our automobile accident case the gist of the plaintiff's theory is that she stopped for a passing fire truck while the defendant did not. Her single most important fact is definitely the observable presence of the fire truck. Thus, the words "fire truck" should be inserted at every reasonable point during the examination. At the close of her testimony you want to have created the image that the fire truck dominated the scenery. How many different ways can the witness describe the fire truck? In how many locations can she place it? How many ways can she use it as a reference point for other testimony?

Thematic repetition may be more elusive or subtle. If the plaintiff's theme is that the defendant was "too busy to be careful," you will want to use repetition to emphasize how unbusy the plaintiff was.

Bench and jury trials differ significantly regarding the use of repetition. Juries consist of six or twelve individuals whose attention may sometimes drift. You can never be certain that every juror will have heard and retained every point, so repetition is particularly important. You not only need to drive your key points home, you need to drive them home to everyone. Judges are usually aware of this problem, and they typically will allow a fair amount of latitude for repetition during jury trials.

Bench trials are a different matter. Judges usually expect bench trials to move along swiftly. They don't like to be battered with constant reiteration of the same points. Of course, judges may also be inattentive, but they don't like to be reminded of it. In short, many judges do not like to be treated like jurors, and they will cut off attempts at repetition. Use this technique sparingly in bench trials.

G. Use Visual Aids

Seeing is believing. In daily life we are accustomed to receiving as much as seventy percent of our information through the sense of sight. Ordinary witness testimony is received primarily through the sense of hearing. This makes it harder to follow and harder to retain. You can enhance the effectiveness of almost any witness by illustrating the testimony through the use of charts, photographs, maps, models, drawings, and other visual aids.

Always consider whether the witness's testimony can be illustrated. If the witness is going to testify about a pivotal document, determine whether it can be enlarged or projected on a screen in the courtroom. If the witness is going to testify about an event, create a map or produce an oversize photograph. If the witness will testify about a series of numbers or transactions, use a visual "time line" as your visual aid.

Demonstrations can also serve as visual aids. Ask the witness to reenact crucial events or to re-create important sounds. "Please show the jury exactly how the defendant raised his hand before he struck you." "Please clap your hands together to show us how loud the sound was." "Please repeat the plaintiff's words in exactly her tone of voice."

Demonstrations must be carefully planned. They have an inevitable tendency to backfire when ill-prepared. Be certain that your expectations are realistic. A witness will not be able to illustrate the loudness of a rifle shot by clapping her hands. Nor will a witness be able to demonstrate the movement of a vehicle by walking about the courtroom. Finally, make sure that your demonstration doesn't look silly. Many lawyers have lost more ground than they gained by asking witnesses to roll around on the floor, climb up on chairs, or dash from one end of the courtroom to the other.

H. Avoid Negative, Lawyerly, and Complex Questions

For reasons unknown and unknowable, many lawyers think that it makes them sound more professional when they phrase questions in the negative:

QUESTION: Did you not then go to the telephone?

No advocate, judge, juror, witness, English teacher, or speaker of our common language can possibly understand the meaning of that question. Even harder to understand are the two potential answers. What would "yes" mean? "Yes, I did not then go to the telephone?" Or, "Yes, I did." What would "no" mean? "No, I did then go to the telephone?" Or, "No, I didn't."

Furthermore, on direct examination your goal typically is to establish an affirmative case. It is therefore beneficial to phrase your questions so that your witnesses can answer them affirmatively. Do not use negative questions.

You must also avoid "lawyer talk." Many jurors and witnesses will not understand lawyerese and virtually all will resent it. On the other hand, everyone, including judges, will appreciate plain language. Do not ask,

QUESTION: At what point in time did you alight from your vehicle?

Ask instead,

QUESTION: When did you get out of your car?

Do not ask,

> QUESTION: What was your subsequent activity, conduct, or response with regard to the negotiation of an offer and acceptance?

Opt for,

> QUESTION: What did you agree to next?

Finally, do not pose questions that call for more than a single item or category of information. Although a witness may be able to sort through a fairly simple compound question—such as, "Where did you go and what did you do?"—many will become confused, and more will simply fail to answer the second part. Truly complex questions will almost certainly fail to elicit the answer that you seek.

THE BASICS

Direct Examination Techniques

- Maximize use of descriptive language and minimize "legalese"
- Make use of primacy and recency
- Use repetition and duration to emphasize important points
- Use reflective questioning to illustrate time, distance, and intensity
- Use apposition to compare related facts
- Use headlines for emphasis and transitions
- Use enumeration when addressing related points

V. ADVERSE AND HOSTILE WITNESSES

From time to time it may be necessary to call a witness, such as the opposing party, who will be hostile to your case. Because unfriendly witnesses cannot be expected to cooperate in preparation, most jurisdictions allow the use of leading questions for the direct examination of such witnesses.[10] They fall into two broad categories: adverse and hostile witnesses.

A. Adverse Witnesses

Adverse witnesses include the opposing party and those identified with the opposing party. Examples of witnesses identified with the opposing party include employees, close relatives, business partners, and others who share a community of interest. It is within the court's discretion to determine whether any particular witness

---

10. Rule 611(c), Federal Rules of Evidence.

is sufficiently identified with the opposition as to allow leading questions on direct examination.

It is important to alert the court to the fact that you are calling an adverse witness, lest the judge sustain objections to leading questions. In the case of the opposing party, counsel's right to ask leading questions on direct will be obvious. Nonetheless, there is no harm in stating that the witness is being called "as an adverse witness pursuant to Rule 611(c)" or its local analog.

In the case of a nonparty adverse witness, it will usually be necessary at the outset to lay a foundation that establishes the witness's identification with the opposition. It may be as simple as in this example:

QUESTION: Please state your name.

ANSWER: My name is Merkys Gomez.

QUESTION: Mr. Gomez, are you employed by the defendant, South Suburban Country Club?

ANSWER: Yes, I am.

Note that more foundation may be needed, depending upon the nature of the witness's relationship to the adverse party.

In some jurisdictions it may be necessary to request that the court specifically find that the witness is adverse. In others one may lay the foundation and proceed to conduct the examination with leading questions.

B.   Hostile Witnesses

A hostile witness is one who, while not technically adverse, displays actual hostility to the direct examiner or her client. The necessary characteristic may be manifested either through expressed antagonism or evident reluctance to testify. Additionally, a witness may be treated as hostile if his testimony legitimately surprises the lawyer who called him to the stand. Whatever the circumstances, it is generally necessary to have the court declare a witness to be hostile before proceeding with leading questions.

C.   Strategy

There are limited situations in which it may be profitable to call an adverse witness. The first is where the adverse witness is the only person who can supply an essential element of your case. Thus the witness will have to be called in order to prevent a directed verdict. For the same reason, an adverse witness might also be called to authenticate a necessary document or to lay the foundation for some other exhibit. Finally, and most perilously, an adverse or hostile witness might be called solely for the purpose of making a bad impression on the trier of fact. Needless to say, this tactic has a strong potential to backfire.

In general, adverse (and potentially hostile) witnesses should not be called unless it is clearly necessary. As noted in the introduction to this section, direct examination provides counsel with an opportunity to build a case. There is therefore great risk involved in calling a witness who will be troublesome, uncooperative, or worse. Moreover, calling an adverse witness allows opposing counsel to conduct, in the midst of your case, a "cross examination" that is very likely to resemble a final argument for the other side. The scope of adverse testimony should therefore be made as narrow as possible.

VI. ETHICS OF DIRECT EXAMINATION

Most of the ethical issues in direct examination involve the extent to which it is permissible to "assist" a witness to prepare or enhance her testimony.

Some issues are relatively easy to resolve. As was discussed earlier in this chapter, for example, it is not unethical to employ "reflective" questioning on direct examination in order to make events seem as though they occurred quickly or slowly.[11] At most, reflective questions will assist a witness to communicate accurately; they cannot alter the truth. A witness who testifies that an incident happened quickly can be helped, through reflective questioning, to make that point clear. If, on the other hand, the witness states that the events were slow-paced, no amount of reflective direct will effectively change that conclusion.[12]

At the other end of the spectrum, it is absolutely unethical to participate in the creation of false testimony. Lawyers must not ever collude with witnesses in the invention of untrue facts. It is an underpinning of adversary justice that lawyers will act as guardians of the system to prevent the offer of perjured evidence. Without this safeguard the very justification of adversary litigation is weakened if not destroyed.

The following subsections will discuss variations on this theme.

---

11. See Section IV E, *supra* at p. 56.

12. This is true of direct examination. On cross examination, of course, the pacing of questions can be used to undermine a witness's conclusory testimony. Regarding the ethics of this sort of examination, see Chapter 4, Section VI D, *infra* at p. 113.

A. Preparation of Witnesses

A recurring question is the extent to which lawyers may "coach" witnesses in preparation for their testimony. In many countries it is considered unethical for a lawyer even to meet alone with a witness prior to the trial, such is the aversion to the possibility for contamination of the testimony. In the United States, however, we take a far different view. Here it is generally considered incompetent for a lawyer to fail to meet with and prepare a witness in advance of offering her testimony.

The practice of witness preparation is so widespread and entrenched as to be unassailable. It is justified on the theory that witnesses, especially clients, are entitled to the lawyer's help in ensuring that their testimony is presented accurately and persuasively. The justification is compelling. A witness, left to her own devices, might be forgetful, inarticulate, or unaware of the significance of the facts that she relates or omits. People come to lawyers precisely because they want, and are entitled to, assistance in presenting their claims and defenses. It smacks of abandonment to submit a client to examination without first reviewing the potential testimony.

Few would doubt that a lawyer's pretrial counsel should extend to advising a witness to be polite and well-dressed, to answer all of the questions, and to avoid losing her temper. In a sense this advice might be seen as disguising an otherwise ill-mannered, boorish, and evasive client. The more realistic view, however, is that the lawyer is assisting the client to ensure that externalities do not obstruct effective communication. To be sure, there is a point where even recommendations on appearance can verge on fraud. It would, for example, be improper to urge an Muslim or Jewish client to wear a visible cross in order to testify before an all-Christian jury.

More difficult issues arise when counsel attempts to refresh a witness's recollection, to fill in gaps in her story, or to suggest alternative possibilities. Again, this practice is usually justified on the ground that it is necessary to ensure that the truth emerges fully. Witnesses can be forgetful, especially when they are unaware of the legal importance of certain facts.

Thus, a client complaining of a defective product would probably place greatest emphasis on the way that it malfunctioned; he might not think it important that the salesperson helped him select it. A lawyer, however, should know that the seller's participation in selection can result in an implied warranty of fitness for a particular use. It would be wrong to withhold this information from the client and equally wrong to avoid probing the client's memory for the nature and extent of the seller's representations. Most would agree that the following inquiries are proper:

"Did you speak to a salesperson when selecting the product?"

"What did the salesperson say?"

"Did you tell the seller why you needed the product?"

"Did you tell her the use to which you would put it?"

"Did she recommend a particular product to you?"

"Did the salesperson make any promises to you?"

While this line of questioning runs some slight risk of inducing memories, rather than simply recalling them, it is essential to adequate representation.

Now consider this scenario. The client was asked whether he spoke to the salesperson, and he replied, "Well, I pretty much picked the item out for myself. I really didn't want or need any help." The lawyer continued:

"I've shopped in those appliance stores and my experience is that the salespeople just won't leave you alone. They're all on commission, and they pretty much stay with you until you buy something. You might not want their help, but sometimes you can't really avoid it. Did anything like that happen to you?"

Is this an aid to the witness's memory or a not-so-subtle suggestion as to how to improve the story?

There is no good answer to the conundrum, as it essentially rests on the lawyer's intent.[13] It is permissible to invoke common experience in order to help a witness remember details that might have seemed unimportant when they occurred. It is flatly impermissible, even when utilizing an ostensible question, to prompt a witness to add facts that did not really take place.

The key is that counsel must, explicitly and implicitly, prepare the witness to give his or her own testimony and not the testimony that the lawyer would favor or prefer. Most efforts to assist or empower the witness are ethical. Efforts at substitution or fabrication, no matter how well-cloaked, are not.

---

13. Needless to say, blatant efforts to influence the witness's testimony are unethical. The lawyer could not, for example, importune the witness this way: "You cannot win this case unless you testify that the salesperson assured you a specific level of performance. You need to tell me exactly how the seller induced you to buy and how you were promised that the product would meet your needs."

B. Offering Inadmissible Evidence

When evidence is admissible only for a limited purpose it is unethical to attempt to put it to further use.[14] The obligation of zealous advocacy does not require counsel to ignore or evade the court's rulings with regard to the restricted admissibility of evidence.

By the same token, it is impermissible to prepare a witness to interject clearly inadmissible evidence. Where a motion in limine[15] has been granted, for example, counsel cannot suggest or encourage a witness to use a narrative answer to volunteer the excluded information.

Of course, counsel is not obligated to resolve all evidentiary doubts in favor of the opposition. It is ethical to offer any evidence with regard to which there is a reasonable theory of admissibility. In other words, it is proper to offer evidence so long as counsel can articulate at least one specific and recognizable argument in favor of its admission.[16]

C. Disclosing Perjury

The appropriate response to witness and client perjury has perplexed our profession endlessly. While no ethical lawyer would willingly be a party to perjury, questions arise as how best to prevent it without damaging the principles of confidentiality and zealous advocacy.

There is no doubt that a lawyer may not call a non-client witness who is going to testify falsely,[17] and must "take reasonable remedial measures should non-client perjury occur despite counsel's efforts to avoid it."[18]

---

14. Regarding the misuse of evidence during final argument, see Chapter 11, Section VI A(3), *infra* at p. 382.

15. See Chapter 8, Section II A(2), *infra* at p. 205.

16. This issue is discussed further in Chapter 8, Section III A, *infra* at p. 226.

17. Rules 3.3(a) and 3.4(b), Model Rules of Professional Conduct.

18. A lawyer shall not "falsify evidence [or] counsel or assist a witness to testify falsely." Rule 3.4(b), Model Rules of Professional Conduct.

Moreover, "[i]f a lawyer ... has been offered material evidence and the lawyer comes to know of its falsity, the lawyer shall take reasonable remedial measures." Rule 3.3, Model Rules of Professional Conduct.

The Commentary to Rule 3.3 provides a three-step approach to "reasonable remedial measures." The lawyer must first remonstrate with the witness to correct the false testimony. If that fails, the lawyer should seek to withdraw "if that will remedy the situation." Since withdrawal will usually be inappropriate in the case of perjury by a non-client, the final step is to make disclosure to the court.

The thorny problem is the client. An attorney must certainly take all reasonable steps to dissuade a client from presenting untrue testimony. But what if the client insists on presenting a story that the lawyer firmly believes is false? Or what if the client's perjury on the stand takes the lawyer by surprise and becomes *a fait* accompli before the lawyer can stop it?

The dilemma is especially acute in criminal cases. Many believe that a criminal defendant has a constitutional right to take the stand and "tell his story," whether the lawyer believes it or not. One commentator has gone so far as to urge that a lawyer's duties of loyalty and confidentiality require actively presenting a criminal defendant's perjured testimony.[19] The great majority of lawyers, judges, and scholars, however, reject this extreme position. The United States Supreme Court has held that there is no constitutional right to testify falsely.[20] The Model Rules of Professional Conduct provide that counsel, in both civil and criminal cases, must take reasonable steps to remedy client perjury, even at the cost of revealing a confidential communication.[21]

The full dimension of the debate over responses to client perjury is beyond the scope of this text. Numerous approaches have been suggested over the years, each supported by its own policies and justifications. It is fair to say, however, that the trend, as outlined in the preceding paragraph, is toward diminished latitude for the client and increased disclosure by counsel.

---

19. Monroe Freedman, *Understanding Lawyer's Ethics*, (2d Ed. 2000).
20. *Nix v. Whiteside*, 474 U.S. 157, 106 S.Ct. 988, 89 L.Ed.2d 123 (1966).
21. Rule 3.3(b), Model Rules of Professional Conduct.

— CHAPTER FOUR —
Cross Examination

I. THE ROLE OF CROSS EXAMINATION

Cross examination is hard. It is frequently dramatic, often exciting, and in many ways it defines our adversarial system of justice. Cross examination is the ultimate challenge for the trial lawyer. Can you add to your case or detract from the opposition's case by extracting information from the other side's witnesses?

If direct examination is your best opportunity to win your case, cross examination may provide you with a chance to lose it. A poor direct can be aimless and boring, but the witnesses are generally helpful. Your worst fear on direct examination is usually that you have left something out. A poor cross examination, on the other hand, can be truly disastrous. The witnesses can range from uncooperative to hostile, and you constantly run the risk of actually adding weight or sympathy to the other side's case. Moreover, most cross examinations will inevitably be perceived by the trier of fact as a contest between the lawyer and witness. You can seldom afford to appear to lose.

In other words, cross examination is inherently risky. The witness may argue with you. The witness may fill in gaps that were left in the direct testimony. The witness may make you look bad. You may make yourself look bad. And whatever good you accomplish may be subject to immediate cure on redirect examination.

None of these problems can be avoided entirely, but they can be minimized. Although some cross examination is usually expected of every witness, and the temptation is difficult to resist, as a general rule you should cross examine carefully. You must always set realistic goals.

Brevity is an excellent discipline. Many trial lawyers suggest that cross examinations be limited to a maximum of three points. While there may often be reasons to depart from such a hard and fast rule, there is no doubt that short cross examinations have much to commend themselves. In terms of your own preparation, setting a mental limit for the length of the cross will help you to concentrate and to organize your thinking. Actually conducting a short examination will minimize risk, add panache, and usually make the result more memorable.

This chapter discusses the general law, content, organization, and basic technique of cross examination. Several more advanced aspects of cross examination—such as impeachment and the use of character evidence—are treated separately in later chapters.

II. THE LAW OF CROSS EXAMINATION

Cross examination is the hallmark of the Anglo-American system of adversary justice. Protected as a constitutional right in criminal cases, it is also understood as an aspect of due process in civil cases. The law of cross examination varies somewhat from jurisdiction to jurisdiction, but the following rules are nearly universal.

A. Leading Questions Permitted

The most obvious distinction between direct and cross examination is the permissible use of leading questions. It is assumed that your adversary's witnesses will have little incentive to cooperate with you, and that you may not have been able to interview them in advance. Consequently, virtually all courts allow the cross examiner to ask questions that contain their own answers. Moreover, the right to ask leading questions is usually understood to include the right to insist on a responsive answer.

As we will see below, the ability to use leading questions has enormous implications for the conduct of cross examination.

B. Limitations on Scope

The general rule in the United States is that cross examination is limited to the scope of the direct. Since the purpose of cross examination is to allow you to inquire of your adversary's witnesses, the scope of the inquiry is restricted to those subjects that were raised during the direct examination.

Note that the definition of scope will vary from jurisdiction to jurisdiction, and even from courtroom to courtroom. A narrow application of this rule can limit the cross examiner to the precise events and occurrences that the witness discussed on direct. A broader approach would allow questioning on related and similar events. For example, assume that the defendant in our collision case testified that his brakes had been inspected just a week before the accident. A strict approach to the "scope of direct" rule might limit the cross examination to questioning on that particular inspection. A broader interpretation would allow inquiries into earlier brake inspections and other aspects of automobile maintenance.

A more generous approach to the scope of cross examination is definitely the modern trend. Undue restriction of cross examination can result in reversal on appeal. Nonetheless, there is no way to predict how an individual judge will apply the scope limitation in any given case; much will depend on the nature of the evidence and the manner in which the lawyers have been conducting themselves.

A few American jurisdictions have adopted the "English rule," · which allows wide-open cross examination concerning any issue relevant to the case. In the federal jurisdiction, and some others, the trial judge has discretion to allow inquiry beyond the scope of the direct examination, but the cross examiner is then limited to nonleading questions. Also, in most states a criminal defendant who takes the stand and waives the Fifth Amendment is thereafter subject to cross examination regarding all aspects of the alleged crime.

There are two general exceptions to the "scope of direct" rule. First, the credibility of the witness is always in issue. You may therefore always attempt to establish the bias, motive, interest, untruthfulness, or material prior inconsistency of a witness without regard to the matters that were covered on direct examination. Second, you may cross examine beyond the scope of the direct once the witness herself has "opened the door" to additional matters. In other words, a witness who voluntarily injects a subject into an answer on cross examination may thereafter be questioned as though the subject had been included in the direct.

C. Other Restrictions

Cross examination is also limited by a variety of other rules, most of which involve the manner or nature of questioning.

Argumentative questions. You may ask a witness questions. You may suggest answers. You may assert propositions. But you may not argue with the witness. As you may have guessed, the definition of an argumentative question is elusive. Much will depend on your demeanor; perhaps an argumentative question is one that is asked in an argumentative tone. The following is a reasonable working definition: An argumentative question insists that the witness agree with an opinion or characterization, as opposed to a statement of fact.

Intimidating behavior. You are entitled to elicit information on cross examination by asking questions of the witness and insisting upon answers. You are not allowed to loom over the witness, to shout, to make threatening gestures, or otherwise to intimidate, bully, or (yes, here it comes) badger the witness.

Unfair characterizations. Your right to lead the witness does not include a right to mislead the witness. It is objectionable to attempt to mischaracterize a witness's testimony or to ask "trick" questions. If a witness has testified that it was dark outside, it would mischaracterize the testimony to begin a question, "So you admit that it was too dark to see anything..." Trick questions cannot be answered accurately. The most famous trick question is known as the "negative pregnant," as in Senator McCarthy's inquisitional, "Have you resigned from the Communist Party?"

Assuming facts. A frequently heard objection is that "Counsel has assumed facts not in evidence." Of course, a cross examiner is frequently allowed to inquire as to facts that are not yet in evidence. This objection should only be sustained when the question uses the non-record fact as a premise rather than as a separate subject of inquiry, thus denying the witness the opportunity to deny its validity. Imagine a witness in the fire truck case who was standing on the sidewalk at the time of the accident. Assume that the witness testified on direct that the defendant never even slowed down before the impact, and that the witness said absolutely nothing about having been drinking that morning. At the outset of the cross examination, then, there would be no "facts in evidence" concerning use of alcohol. The cross examiner is certainly entitled to ask questions such as, "Hadn't you been drinking that morning?" The cross examiner should not be allowed, however, to use an assumption about drinking to serve as the predicate for a different question: "Since you had been drinking, you were on foot instead of in your car that morning?" The problem with this sort of bootstrapping is that it doesn't allow the witness a fair opportunity to deny having been drinking in the first place.

Compound and other defective questions. Compound questions contain more than a single inquiry: "Are you related to the plaintiff, and were you wearing your glasses at the time of the accident?" The question is objectionable since any answer will necessarily be ambiguous. Cumulative or "asked and answered" questions are objectionable because they cover the same ground twice (or more). Vague questions are objectionable because they tend to elicit vague answers.

THE BASICS
Limitations on Cross Examination
• Must be within "scope of direct" • No argumentative questions • No unfair characterizations • No compound, vague, or cumulative questions • Do not intimidate, insult, demean, or harass the witness • Every question must have a "good faith basis"

III. THE CONTENT OF CROSS EXAMINATION

The first question concerning any cross examination is whether it should be brief or extensive. Although it is standard advice in many quarters that you should refrain from cross examining a witness who hasn't hurt you, in practice almost every witness is subjected to at least a short cross examination. You will seldom wish to leave the testimony of an adverse witness appear to go entirely unchallenged. Moreover, as we will see below, there will often be opportunities to use cross examination to establish positive, constructive evidence. The most realistic decision, then, is not whether to cross examine, but how much. This evaluation must be made at least twice: once in your pretrial preparation and again at the end of the direct examination.

In preparation, you must consider the potential direct examination. What do you expect the witness to say, and how, if at all, will you need to challenge or add to the direct? At trial you must make a further determination. Did the actual direct examination proceed as you expected? Was it more or less damaging than you anticipated? You must always reevaluate your cross examination strategy in light of the direct testimony that was eventually produced. This process will often lead you to omit portions of your prepared cross because they have become unnecessary. It is considerably more dangerous to elaborate on or add to your plan, although this is occasionally unavoidable. In either situation always remember the risk inherent in cross examination and ask yourself, "Is this cross examination necessary?"

A. Consider the Purposes of Cross Examination

Though often an invigorating exercise, cross examination should be undertaken only to serve some greater purpose within your theory of the case. A useful cross examination should promise to fulfill at least one of the following objectives:

Repair or minimize damage. Did the direct examination hurt your case? If so, can the harm be rectified or minimized? Can the witness be made to retract or back away from certain testimony? Can additional facts be elicited that will minimize the witness's impact?

Enhance your case. Can the cross examination be used to further one of your claims or defenses? Are there positive facts that can be brought out that will support or contribute to your version of events?

Detract from their case. Conversely, can the cross examination be used to establish facts that are detrimental to your opponent's case? Can it be used to create inconsistencies among the other side's witnesses?

Establish foundation. Is the witness necessary to the proper foundation for the introduction of a document or other exhibit, or for the offer of evidence by another witness?

Discredit direct testimony. Is it possible to discredit the witness's direct testimony through means such as highlighting internal inconsistencies, demonstrating the witness's own lack of certainty or confidence, underscoring lack of opportunity to observe, illustrating the inherent implausibility of the testimony, or showing that it conflicts with the testimony of other, more credible witnesses?

Discredit the witness. Can the witness be shown to be biased or interested in the outcome of the case? Does the witness have a reason to stretch, misrepresent, or fabricate the testimony? Has the witness been untruthful in the past? Can it be shown that the witness is otherwise unworthy of belief?

Reflect on the credibility of another. Can the cross examination be used to reflect, favorably or unfavorably, on the credibility of a different witness?

The length of your cross examination will generally depend upon how many of the above goals you expect to be able to fulfill. It is not necessary, and it may not be possible, to attempt to achieve them all. You will often stand to lose more by over-reaching than you can possibly gain by seeking to cover all of the bases in cross examination. Be selective.

B. Risk Averse Preparation

There are many ways to prepare for cross examination. The following is a "risk averse" method designed to result in a solid, if generally unflashy, cross that minimizes the potential for damage to your case.

Risk averse preparation for cross examination begins with consideration of your anticipated final argument. What do you want to be able to say about this particular witness when you address the jury at the end of the case? How much of that information do you expect to be included in the direct examination? The balance is what you will need to cover on cross.

Next, write out the portion of a final argument that you would devote to discussing the facts presented by this particular witness. This will at most serve as a draft for your actual closing,[1] and you should limit this text to the facts contained in the witness's testimony. You need not include the characterizations, inferences, arguments, comments, and thematic references that will also be part of your real final argument. Depending upon the importance of the witness, the length of this argument segment can range from a short paragraph to a full page or more.

It is important that you write your text using short, single-thought, strictly factual sentences. You are not attempting to create literature. Do not worry about continuity, style, or transition. Simply arrange the declarative sentences one after another in the order that you believe will be the most persuasive, referring to the witness in the third person. For example, your argument concerning the defendant in the fire truck case might, assuming that all of these facts were readily available, include the following:

> The defendant awoke on the morning of the accident at 7:00 a.m. He had to be downtown later that morning. He was meeting an important new client. He wanted to get that client's business. He stood to make a lot of money. The meeting was scheduled for 8:30 a.m. The defendant lived 16 miles from his office. He rented a monthly parking spot. That spot was in a garage located two blocks from his office. He left his home at 7:55 a.m. There was a lot of traffic that morning. The accident occurred at an intersection seven miles from downtown. It happened at 8:20 a.m.

An effective paragraph will include the facts that underlie your theory of the case. It should now be a simple matter to convert the text into a cross examination plan. You merely need to take each

---

1. Final argument is treated in Chapter 12. At this point it is sufficient to note that, while it may be a useful exercise to write out a draft, it is a mistake to read your closing argument from a prepared text.

sentence and rephrase it into a second-person question. In fact, it is often best to leave the sentence in the form of a declaration, technically making it a question through voice inflection or by adding an interrogative phrase at the end. The above paragraph then becomes the following cross examination of the defendant:

QUESTION: You awoke at 7:00 a.m. on the morning of the accident, isn't that right?

QUESTION: You had to be downtown later that morning, correct?

QUESTION: You were meeting an important new client?

QUESTION: You wanted to get that client's business?

QUESTION: You stood to make a lot of money?

QUESTION: The meeting was scheduled for 8:30 a.m., correct?

QUESTION: You lived 16 miles from your office?

QUESTION: You rented a monthly parking spot?

QUESTION: That spot was in a garage located two blocks from your office?

QUESTION: You left your home at 7:55 a.m., right?

QUESTION: There was a lot of traffic that morning?

QUESTION: The accident occurred at an intersection seven miles from downtown?

QUESTION: It happened at 8:20 a.m., isn't that right?

This technique is useful for developing the content of your cross examination. The organization of the examination and the structure of your individual questions will depend upon additional analysis.

IV. THE ORGANIZATION OF CROSS EXAMINATION

A. Organizing Principles

As with direct examination, the organization of a cross examination can be based on the four principles of primacy and recency, apposition, repetition, and duration. Unlike direct examination, however, on cross examination you will often have to deal with a recalcitrant witness. You may therefore have to temper your plan in recognition of this reality, occasionally sacrificing maximum clarity and persuasion in order to avoid "telegraphing" your strategy to the uncooperative witness. Thus, we must include the additional organizing principles of indirection and misdirection when planning cross examinations.

Three further concepts are basic to the organization, presentation, and technique of virtually every cross examination.

First, cross examination is your opportunity to tell part of your client's story in the middle of the other side's case. Your object is to focus attention away from the witness's direct testimony and onto matters that you believe are helpful. On cross examination, you want to tell the story. To do so, you must always be in control of the testimony and the witness.

Second, cross examination is never the time to attempt to gather new information. Never ask a witness a question simply because you want to find out the answer. Rather, cross examination must be used to establish or enhance the facts that you have already discovered.

Finally, an effective cross examination often succeeds through the use of implication and innuendo. It is not necessary, and it is often harmful, to ask a witness the "ultimate question." Final argument is your opportunity to point out the relationship between facts, make characterizations, and draw conclusions based upon the accumulation of details. Do not expect an opposing witness to do this for you.

Lay the groundwork for your eventual argument, then stop. This technique is premised on the assumption that many witnesses will be reluctant to concede facts that will later prove to be damaging or embarrassing. Thus, it may be necessary to avoid informing the witness of the ultimate import of the particular inquiry. This can be accomplished through indirect questioning, which seeks first to establish small and uncontrovertible factual components of a theory and only later addresses the theory itself.

For example, a witness may be loath to admit having read a certain document before signing it; perhaps the written statement contains damaging admissions that the witness would prefer to disclaim. Direct questioning, therefore, would be unlikely to produce the desired result. The witness, if asked, will deny having read the item in question. Indirect questioning, however, may be able to establish the point:

QUESTION: You are a businessman?

QUESTION: Many documents cross your desk each day?

QUESTION: It is your job to read and respond to them?

QUESTION: Your company relies upon you to be accurate?

QUESTION: You often must send written replies?

QUESTION: Large amounts of money can change hands on the basis of the replies that you send?

QUESTION: You have an obligation to your company to be careful about its money?

QUESTION: So you must be careful about what you write?

QUESTION: Of course, that includes your signature?

By this point you should have obtained through indirection that which the witness would not have conceded directly. The final question should be superfluous.

Misdirection is an arch-relative of indirection, used when the witness is thought to be particularly deceptive or untruthful. Here the cross examiner not only conceals the object of the examination, but actually attempts to take advantage of the witness's own inclination to be uncooperative. Knowing that the witness will tend to fight the examination, the lawyer creates, and then exploits, a "misdirected" image. In our fire truck case, for example, the defendant is extremely unlikely to admit that he should have seen the fire engine; perhaps he would go so far as to deny the obvious. The lawyer may therefore misdirect the defendant's attention, as follows:

QUESTION: Isn't it true that you expected to see a fire truck at that corner?

ANSWER: Certainly not, I never expected a fire truck.

QUESTION: You weren't looking for a fire truck?

ANSWER: No.

QUESTION: You didn't keep your eye out for one?

ANSWER: No.

QUESTION: And you never saw one?

ANSWER: No.

QUESTION: Until, of course, after it was too late?

To be effective in the use of this technique, the cross examination must be organized first to obtain the "misdirected" denial. Note that the above example would not work at all if the questions were asked in the opposite order. In other words, the principle of misdirection works best with an intentionally elusive witness who needs only to be given sufficient initial rope with which to hoist himself.

B. Guidelines for Organization

There are many ways in which you can employ the principles discussed above.

1. Do Not Worry About Starting Strong

It would be desirable to be able to begin every cross examination with a strong, memorable point that absolutely drives home your theory and theme. Unfortunately, this will not always be possible. Many cross examinations will have to begin with a shakedown period during which you acclimate yourself to the tenor of the witness's responses, and when you also attempt to put the witness in a cooperative frame of mind. Unless you are able to start off with a true bombshell, it will usually be preferable to take the time necessary to establish predicate facts through indirection.

2. Use Topical Organization

Topical organization is essential in cross examination. Your goal on cross examination is not to retell the witness's story, but rather to establish a small number of additional or discrediting points. A topical format will be the most effective in allowing you to move from area to area. Moreover, topical organization also allows you to take maximum advantage of apposition, indirection, and misdirection. You can use it to cluster facts in the same manner that you would on direct examination or to separate facts in order to avoid showing your hand to the witness.

Assume that you want to use the cross examination of the defendant in the automobile accident to show how busy he was on the day of the collision. You know that he had an important meeting to attend that morning, but he will be unlikely to admit that he might lose the client (and a lot of money) if he arrived late. You can solve this problem by using topical organization to separate your cross examination into two distinct segments: one dealing with the nature of the defendant's business and the other covering his appointment on the fateful morning.

In the first topical segment you will show that the defendant is an independent management consultant. It is a very competitive business in which client relations are extremely important. Part of his work involves seeking out potential new clients, whom he is always anxious to please. Since he is a sole proprietor, every client means more money. As a consultant, he must pride himself on professionalism, timeliness, and efficiency. He bills his clients by the hour. Time is money. In short, examine the witness on his business background without ever bringing up the subject of the accident. (The defendant's own lawyer almost certainly will have introduced his stable, business-like background; your examination on the same issue would then be within the scope of the direct.)

Later in the examination, after covering several other areas, you will shift topics to the defendant's agenda on the day of the accident. Now it is time to establish the details of his planned meeting and the fact that he was still miles from downtown shortly before it was scheduled to begin. You do not need to obtain an admission that he was running late or that he was preoccupied. Topical organization has allowed you to develop the predicate facts for that argument before the witness was aware of their implications.

There is another advantage to topical organization on cross examination. Assume, in the example above, that the witness was well-prepared and that he immediately recognized your reasons for inquiring into his business practices. Because your examination was segmented, however, he could scarcely deny the facts that you suggested. In a portion of the examination limited to the operation of his business it would be implausible for him to deny that his clients value "professionalism, efficiency, and timeliness." Denying your perfectly reasonable propositions would make him look either untrustworthy or defensive. Note that you would not obtain the same result without topical organization. In the middle of the discussion of the morning of the accident it would be quite plausible for the defendant to testify that this particular new client was not dominating his thoughts.

3. Give the Details First

Details are, if anything, more important on cross examination than they are on direct. On direct examination a witness will always be able to tell the gist of the story; details are used in a secondary manner to add strength and veracity to the basic testimony. On cross examination, however, the witness will frequently disagree with the gist of the story that you want to tell, and use of details therefore becomes the primary method of making your points. You may elicit details to lay the groundwork for future argument, to draw out internal inconsistencies in the witness's testimony, to point out inconsistencies between witnesses, to lead the witness into implausible assertions, or to create implications that the witness will be unable to deny later.

Within each segment of your cross examination it will usually be preferable to give the details first. No matter what your goal, the witness will be far more likely to agree with a series of small, incremental facts before the thrust of the examination has been made apparent. Once you have challenged, confronted, or closely questioned a witness, it will be extremely difficult to go back and fill in the details necessary to make the challenge stick.

Assume that the weather conditions turn out to be of some value to you in the automobile accident case. If you begin your examination of the defendant with questions about the weather, you will be likely to obtain cooperative answers. As a preliminary matter you may have no difficulty establishing that it was clear and sunny that day. Perhaps you will have additional details available—the defendant left home without an umbrella, he wasn't wearing overshoes, he didn't turn on his headlights. Conversely, imagine a first question such as, "Isn't it true that you never even tried to stop before the collision?" Now what is the witness likely to say when you ask whether the pavement was dry? Suddenly, the witness may remember all manner of fog and puddles; of course he tried to stop, but the street was just too wet.

There is an additional advantage to beginning a cross examination with details. It allows you to learn about the witness with a minimum of risk. We know that cross examination is not the time to try to gather new information about the case. You should only ask questions to which you know the answer, or where you at least have a good reason to expect a favorable answer. On the other hand, you frequently will not know how a particular witness will react to your questions. Will the witness be cooperative or compliant, or can you expect a struggle every inch of the way? Worse, is the witness slippery and evasive? Even worse, is the witness inclined to mislead and prevaricate? Worst of all, have you misinterpreted the information or made some other blunder in your own preparation? You must learn the answers to these questions before you proceed to the heart of your cross examination. While it may be mildly uncomfortable to receive an unexpectedly evasive answer to a question about a preliminary detail, it can be positively devastating to discover that you are unable to pin down a witness on a central issue. Beginning with details will allow you to take the witness's measure (and to evaluate your own preparation) at a time of minimum impact and risk.

4. Scatter the Circumstantial Evidence

Inferential or circumstantial evidence[2] is most persuasive when a series of facts or events can be combined in such a way as to create a logical path to the desired conclusion. Unfortunately, facts arranged in this manner on cross examination will also be highly transparent to the witness. As you stack inference upon inference, your direction will become increasingly clear. A hostile or unfriendly witness will then become increasingly uncooperative, perhaps to the point of thwarting your examination. A far safer approach is to scatter the circumstantial evidence throughout the examination, drawing it together only during final argument.

THE BASICS

Cross Examination Organization

- Do not worry about starting strong
- Use topical organization
- Give the details first
- Scatter the circumstantial evidence
- Follow the classic format to maximize witness cooperation
- Save a zinger for the end

---

5. Save a Zinger for the End

The final moment of cross examination may well be the most important. No matter how low-key or friendly your style, almost every cross examination will in some sense be viewed as a contest between you and the witness. Were you able to shake the adverse testimony? Were you able to help your client? In short, did you do what you set out to do? In this regard the final impression that you leave is likely to be the most lasting. Were you able to finish on a high note, or did you simply give up?

It is therefore imperative that you plan carefully the very last point that you intend to make on cross examination. It must be a guaranteed winner, the point on which you are willing to make your exit. Indeed, you should write this point down at the very bottom of your note pad, underlined and in bold letters. It should stand alone with nothing to obscure it or distract you from it. Then if your entire examination seems to fail, if the witness denies every proposition, if the judge sustains every objection, if the heavens fall and doom impends, you can always skip to the bottom of the page and finish with

---

2. Circumstantial evidence is defined and described in Chapter 3, Section III B(6), *supra* at p. 46.

a flourish. Satisfied that you have made this single, telling, case-sealing point, you may proudly announce, "No further questions of this witness," and sit down.

How do you identify your fail-safe zinger? The following guidelines should help:

a. It must be absolutely admissible

There can be no doubt about the admissibility of your intended final point. Nothing smacks more of defeat than ending a cross examination on a sustained objection. If you suspect even for a moment that your zinger might not be allowed, abandon it and choose another. In fact, you should make an entry in the margin of your notes that reminds you of your theory of admissibility. Why is the point relevant? Why isn't it hearsay? How has the foundation been established? Why isn't it speculation?

b. It should be central to your theory

Since your closing point is likely to be the most memorable, you would be best served to make it one of the cornerstones of your theory. If there are eight facts that you must establish in order to prevail, you would like to end each cross examination on one of them. This may not always be possible. Not every opposing witness will testify about an essential matter, and it is important to ensure admissibility by keeping your zinger well within the scope of the direct. Or it may be possible to undermine the witness's credibility by ending on a point that is collateral to your basic theory.

c. It should evoke your theme

The very purpose of a trial theme is to create a memorable phrase or invocation that captures the moral basis of your case. The closing moments of cross examination, therefore, constitute the perfect time to evoke your theme. Attention will never be more focused and memorability will never be higher. Imagine that the plaintiff in the fire truck case was taken directly to a hospital but that the unhurt defendant went on to his office after filling out a police report. If your theme is "Too busy to be careful," you can close your cross examination with these two questions: "You made it to your office later that morning, didn't you? Taking care of business, I suppose?" You know that the answer to the first question will be "Yes." You don't care about the answer to the second one.

d. It must be undeniable

It should be obvious by now that your final question must be undeniable. The end of your cross is not the time to argue or quibble with the witness. There are two good ways to ensure undeniability.[3]

First, choose a fact that you can document. Look for something that can be proven from a prior statement of the witness or some other tangible exhibit or writing. If evidence of that sort is unavailable, select a point that has already been made in the testimony of other opposition witnesses, thereby making a denial either implausible or inconsistent with the balance of the other side's case.

Second, phrase your question in terms of bedrock fact, making sure that it contains nothing that approaches a characterization. The more "factual" your question, the less possible it is for the witness to deny you a simple answer. In the automobile accident case, for example, a purely factual closing question would be, "You arrived at your office later that morning?" The same point, but made with a characterization, would be, "You were so busy that you went straight to your office?" The witness can argue with you about the interpretation of the word "busy," but arrival at his office is a fact.

Remember that cross examination may be followed immediately by redirect examination. Your closing question on cross may provide the opening subject for redirect. Thus, another aspect of undeniability is that the point must not be capable of immediate explanation. For example, the fire truck defendant may have gone straight to his office, but only to retrieve medicine for his heart condition. After that he might not have worked for the next three days. You can omit those facts on cross examination, but you can be sure that they will be developed on redirect. Since that point can be explained, it is not sufficiently "undeniable" for use as a closing question.

e. It must be stated with conviction

No matter what your closing question, you must be able to deliver it with an attitude of satisfied completion. If the subject makes you nervous, worried, or embarrassed, then you must choose another. It is neither necessary nor desirable to smirk, but you must exhibit confidence that your parting inquiry has done its work.

C. A Classic Format for Cross Examination

Because almost all cross examinations will be topical, there can be no standard or prescribed form of organization. The following

---

3. The subject of controlling the witness and insuring favorable answers is discussed at greater length in Section V, *infra* at p. 86.

"classic format" is designed to maximize witness cooperation. Of course, you may have a goal in mind for your cross examination other than witness cooperation; in that case, feel free to ignore or alter this approach. As a rule of thumb, however, you can best employ principles such as indirection and "detail scattering" by seeking information in this order.

1. Friendly Information

Be friendly first. Begin by asking all questions that the witness will regard as nonthreatening. These will often be background questions. For example, medical malpractice cases are often based upon errors of omission, and you may intend to argue in closing that the defendant physician, by virtue of her extraordinary training, should have known about certain available tests. You can start your cross examination, then, by asking friendly questions about the defendant's medical education, residency, fellowships, and awards. Most people, even defendants on trial, like to talk about their achievements. There is little doubt that a witness will be the most forthcoming when asked about aggrandizing information at the very outset of the cross examination.

2. Affirmative Information

After exhausting the friendly information, ask questions that build up the value of your case rather than tear down the opposition's. Much of this information will fill in gaps in the direct testimony. In fact, a good way to plan this portion of the cross is to list the information that you reasonably hope will be included in the direct. Whatever is omitted from the witness's actual testimony will form the core of your affirmative information section. Although adverse witnesses may not be enthusiastic about supplying you with helpful information, they will be unlikely to fight you over answers that might logically have been included in their own direct.

3. Uncontrovertible Information

You can now proceed to inquire about facts that damage the opposition's case or detract from the witness's testimony, so long as they are well-settled or documentable. On these questions a witness may be inclined to hedge or quibble, but you can minimize this possibility by sticking to the sort of information that ultimately must be conceded.

4. Challenging Information

It is unlikely that a witness will cooperate with you once you begin challenging her memory, perception, accuracy, conduct, or other aspects of her testimony. Therefore, it is usually desirable to proceed through friendly, affirmative, and uncontroverted information before you begin to take sharper issue with the witness. At some point, of course, you will have to ask most witnesses questions that they will recognize as challenges: "Mr. Defendant, the fact is that the first thing you did after the collision was to telephone your office?" Such questions are necessary. When used in their proper place they will not prevent you from first exploiting the other, more cooperative testimony from the witness.

5. Hostile Information

Hostile information involves confronting the witness directly. You may be able to extract the necessary answers to hostile questions, but certainly you can eliminate all hope of cooperation both then and thereafter. Hostile questions involve assaults on the witness's honesty, probity, peacefulness, character, or background. "Didn't you spend time in prison?" "You never intended to live up to the contract?" "That was a lie, wasn't it?"

6. Zinger

Always end with a zinger. You know why.

V. QUESTIONING TECHNIQUE

You know what you want to cover on cross examination and you know the order in which you want to cover it. How do you ask questions that will ensure your success?

The essential goal of cross examination technique is witness control. As we noted above, your object on cross examination is to tell your client's story. This requires that you set the agenda for the examination, that you determine the flow of information, and that you require answers to your questions. In short, you must always be in control of the witness and the testimony. This does not, by the way, mean that you must appear to be in control, and it certainly does not mean that you must be domineering, rude, or overbearing toward the witness. In this context, control means only that the examination follow the course that you have selected and that the information produced be only that which you have determined helpful.

Control, therefore, can be either nonassertive or assertive. With a cooperative or tractable witness, control may mean nothing more than asking the right questions and getting the right answers. A hostile, evasive, or argumentative witness may require that you employ more assertive means.

There are numerous questioning techniques, to be discussed below, that you can employ to ensure witness control. At a minimum, however, every question on cross examination should have all of the following bedrock characteristics:

Short. Questions on cross examination must be short in both execution and concept. If a question is more than ten words long, it is not short in execution. Try to shorten it. If a question contains more than a single fact or implication, it is not short in concept. Divide it.

Leading. Every question on cross examination should be leading. Include the answers in the questions. Tell the witness exactly what to say. Cross examination is no time to seek the witness's interpretation of the facts. It is the time for you to tell a story by obtaining the witness's assent. A nonleading question invites the witness to wander away from your story.[4]

Propositional. The best questions on cross examination are not questions at all. Rather, they are propositions of fact that you put to the witness in interrogative form. You already know the answer— you simply need to produce it from the witness's mouth. Every question on cross examination should contain a proposition that falls into one of these three categories: (1) you already know the answer; (2) you can otherwise document or prove the answer; or (3) any answer will be helpful. An example of the last sort of question would be the classic inquiry to a witness who must admit having previously given a false statement: "Were you lying then, or are you lying now?"

---

4.   There are a few situations in which you may want to ask a nonleading question on cross examination. This chiefly occurs when you are absolutely certain that the witness must answer in a certain way and you believe that the dramatic value of the answer will be enhanced by having it produced in the witness's own words. If, for example, you are cross examining a witness with a prior felony conviction, you might ask the nonleading question, "How many years did you spend in prison after you were convicted of perjury?" Even in low-risk situations such as this, however, the technique has been known to backfire. Use it sparingly, if at all.

THE BASICS

Cross Examination Checklist ☑	
❑ Are all of your questions leading?	Does each question you plan to ask suggest the answer desired? *If not, rephrase your questions so that they do.*
❑ Did you get in and get out?	Are you covering more than three or four topics? *If so, consider cutting down your cross to make it as short as possible.*
❑ Are you asking only questions to which you already know the answers?	Is there any answer that the witness might give that will surprise you? *If so, rephrase the question to eliminate this possibility or strike the question altogether.*
❑ Are your questions short, fair, and propositional?	Can opposing counsel object that any of your questions are compound, cumulative, vague, argumentative, or other otherwise improper? *If so, rephrase those questions now to avoid unnecessary interruptions at trial.*
❑ Did you avoid asking that ultimate question?	Did you ask any questions that summarize an argument you will make during your closing? *If so, skip the question and save the point for closing argument.*

A. Planning for Control

Control of a witness on cross examination begins with your plan and is achieved, in large measure, on your note pad or laptop.[5] In other words, a cross examination is only as good as your outline.

1. Avoid Written Questions

Many beginning lawyers like to write out all of the questions that they intend to ask on cross examination. This can be an excellent drill since it will concentrate your thinking and sharpen your specific questions. As we will see below, much of the art of cross examination involves asking short, incremental, closely sequenced questions. Since this is an unnatural style for many lawyers, it can

---

5. No matter how tech savvy you may be, it usually makes sense to keep your cross examination notes on paper, rather than your laptop. A note pad gives you maximum physical flexibility, preserves eye contact, and allows you to take notes without turning away from the witness. Even if your cross examination uses computer-generated displays, it is a good idea to have a colleague handle the technical aspects while you concentrate on asking questions.

be useful indeed to write out the questions first in order to make sure that they conform to this ideal.

When it comes to the actual examination, however, it is usually a mistake to read from a prepared list of questions. The great majority of lawyers use notes, of course, but not in the form of written questions. Reading your questions will deprive your examination of the appearance of spontaneity. For all but the most accomplished thespians, reading from a script will sound just like reading from a script, or worse, a laundry list. It will be almost impossible to develop any rhythm with the witness.

Reading from a set of questions will also deprive you of the control that comes from eye contact with the witness. The witness will be less likely to follow your lead, and you will be less able to observe the witness's demeanor for telltale signs of nervousness or retraction. Witnesses often betray themselves or open doors during cross examination, and you must constantly be ready to exploit such an unplanned opportunity. Needless to say, that will not happen if you are tied to a set of written questions.

There are even drawbacks simply to keeping your notes in the form of a set of written questions. First, this format encourages bobbing your head up and down from pad to witness. Even if you do not read the questions, you will spend an inordinate amount of time looking away from the witness. A more serious difficulty is the increased likelihood of losing your place. This is not a small problem. Notes based on written questions will be much longer than an outline, and the questions will all tend to look alike. The possibility of losing your place on a page, or being unable to find the page that you need, is extreme. Almost nothing is more embarrassing or damaging than being unable to continue a cross examination because your notes have become disorganized.

Written questions are best used as a pre-examination device. Write them out, study them, hone them, rearrange them, and then discard them in favor of a topical outline.

2. Using an Outline

The purpose of your outline should be to remind yourself of the points that you intend to make on cross examination and to ensure that you do not inadvertently omit anything. Do not regard your notes as a script, but rather as a set of cues or prompts, each of which introduces an area of questioning. Beneath each of the main prompts you will list the key details that you intend to elicit from the witness.

Your outline can follow the same format that you have used since high school. Principal topics are represented by Roman numerals, subtopics are denoted by capital letters, and smaller points or component details are represented by Arabic numerals. Although the form for academic outlines goes on to involve lower case letters, small Roman numerals, and other levels ad infinitum, the outline for a cross examination will become too complex if it extends beyond the third level.

The main topics for the cross examination of the defendant in the fire truck case would probably include the defendant's background, the events of the accident, and his post-accident conduct. In abbreviated form, an outline for that cross examination might look like this:

Cross Examination of Defendant	
I. Background	B. Weather
A. Business Consultant	C. Fire Truck
1. Sole Proprietor	1. Didn't see
2. Clients are important	2. Didn't hear
3. Timeliness and efficiency	3. Didn't stop
B. Locations and distances	III. Post-accident
1. His home	A. Immediately phoned office/client
2. His office	B. Didn't call ambulance for plaintiff
3. Parking lot	
II. Accident	
A. Plans for day	
1. Left home at 7:55 A.M.	
2. Meeting at 8:30 A.M.	

Note that the use of sub-parts will vary according to the importance of, and your need to remember, discrete details. Depending upon your level of confidence, for example, you might want to fill in additional details for the weather conditions. On the other hand, you can usually expect to remember what was important to your case about the weather.

More importantly, note that the indented headings make it very easy to follow an outline in this form. It is not organized merely to tell the story, it also has a visual pattern that allows you to keep your place. Even when you lose your place, the sparsity of words makes recovery that much simpler. Moreover, the use of single-word or short-phrase headings should allow you to keep your outline short. It may be possible to limit your notes to a single sheet of paper, and it should almost never be necessary to use more than a few pages.

Finally, your zinger has to be the very last Roman numeral at the bottom of the final page of your outline. Even if you do not fill the last page, put the zinger at the bottom so that it will have maximum visual impact. You will want it to stand out when you need it.

3. "Referencing" Your Outline

Once you have drafted the outline for your cross examination you should proceed to "reference" it. Referencing allows you to refresh the recollection of forgetful witnesses and to impeach or contradict witnesses who give you evasive, unexpected, or false answers.

Across from every important subtopic and crucial detail, make a note that records the source for the point that you intend to make. You need not reference the major topic headings, but other than that it will often prove useful to reference your notes line by line. At a minimum, you must reference every point that you consider essential to your case, as well as those that you expect to be controverted or challenging to the witness. For example, assume that you know about the defendant's meeting plans because he testified to them at his deposition. At the point in your outline where you reach the defendant's intended destination on the morning of the accident, make a note of the page and line in his deposition where he testified that he had an 8:30 a.m. meeting with an important client.

In addition to deposition transcripts, reference sources can come from letters, reports, memoranda, notes, and even photographs. The best sources, of course, are the witness's own prior words. Adequate secondary sources may include documents that the witness reviewed, acted upon, or affirmed by silence. In most circumstances, the testimony of a different person, though perhaps useful, will not be a reliable source for referencing a cross examination.

Many lawyers prepare their outlines by first drawing a vertical line slightly to the right of the center of the page. They then write the outline for the examination on the left side of the line, while references are noted on the right side. The right column may also be used for note-taking during the witness's direct examination.

The first part of such a note pad would look like this:

Cross Examination of Defendant	
I. Background	
A. Business Consultant	Dep., p. 6, line 11
1. Sole proprietor	Dep., p. 7, line 2
2. Clients important	Dep., p. 26, line 23
3. Timeliness	Dep., p. 19, line 4
B. Locations and distance	
1. His home	Dep., p. 2, line 6
2. His office	Lease
3. Parking lot	Rental contract

It is also useful to devote the top of your first page to a sort of mini-reference chart where you list all of the important times, dates, and addresses in the case. Although by the time of trial you may think that you know these details as well as your own name, no lawyer is forever safe from "drawing a blank" on crucial details at crucial moments. The last thing you want to do is cross examine a witness as to her whereabouts for the wrong date. Cautious lawyers have even been known to write the names of the key witnesses—including their own clients—at the top of the first page.

B. Questions That Achieve Control

Having organized and outlined the cross examination, we are now ready to consider the precise techniques that provide maximum control over a witness's testimony. Many of the following rules will seem familiar since most are based upon the principles of apposition, duration, indirection, and misdirection. As with all of trial advocacy, it will seldom be possible to apply every rule in any given examination (although some lawyers have managed somehow to break every rule during a single examination). Rather, you must use your own good judgment to determine which principles will be most effective in your particular situation.

1. Use Incremental Questions

Cross examination should proceed in a series of small, steady steps. No matter how certain you are that a witness must grant you an answer, there is always a risk that she will disagree. Disagreement can hurt. While it is true that you may often bring a witness back under control, at a minimum that effort will generally waste time and distract attention from your more important goals.

The larger the scope of your question, the more likely you are to give the witness room to disagree. It is therefore preferable to divide areas of questioning into their smallest component parts. For example, assume that you are about to cross examine the defendant in the fire truck case. You want to establish the distance from his parking garage to his office in order to show that he was in a hurry to get to his meeting that morning. You could ask one question: "Your parking garage is located three blocks from your office, isn't it?" If the witness says "yes," you will have achieved your purpose, but what will you do if the witness says "no"? Make no mistake about it: no matter how carefully you have planned your cross examination, some witnesses will find a way to say "no." In the above scenario, for example, the defendant may decide that the distance is somewhere between two and three blocks, since his office building is not exactly on the corner. Or he may quibble with you over whether you can call the parking lot "his" garage. You may even have made a mistake about the facts. In any event, you can head off such potential problems by asking incremental questions, such as these:

QUESTION: You have a monthly parking contract at the Garrick garage?

QUESTION: The Garrick is located at the northwest corner of Randolph and Dearborn?

QUESTION: Your office is located at 48 South Dearborn?

QUESTION: The shortest distance from the Garrick to your office is to go south on Dearborn?

QUESTION: First you must cross Randolph? Then you must cross Washington? Then you must cross Madison?

QUESTION: And your office is further south on that block, isn't it?

This technique allows you to do two things. First, it cuts off the escape route for a witness who is inclined to argue or prevaricate. The incremental questions provide small targets for a witness's inventiveness. More importantly, it lets you know early in the sequence whether the witness is likely to disagree with you. The use of incremental questions allows you to test the witness for cooperation, and to determine whether your own factual assumptions are correct, before you reach an embarrassing point of no return.

2. Use Sequenced Questions for Impact

Sequencing may be used on cross examination for a variety of purposes. First, as on direct, you may use sequencing (or apposition) to clarify your story or enhance its impact upon the trier of fact. Eliciting two facts in close proximity can underscore relationships, contrasts, inconsistencies, connections, or motives. In the fire truck case you may sequence your cross examination so that the defendant testifies within a very short time about the important meeting that he had to attend on the morning of the accident and his earlier decision to leave the auto repair shop without servicing his brakes. The apposition of these otherwise disparate facts can help develop your theme, "Too busy to be careful."

The defendant, of course, will not want to draw the connection for you that his busy professional life leads him to neglect safety. You may be able to control the witness, however, by sequencing your examination in a way that multiplies the impact of two otherwise unconnected facts.

3. Use Sequenced Questions for Indirection

Unfortunately, what is clear to the jury will also be clear to the witness. Alerted that you have decided to exploit his busy schedule, the defendant may decide not to concede so readily the key details of his visit to the mechanic. In such situations you may use sequencing not for clarity and impact, but for indirection. You may therefore decide simply to abandon apposition and instead to "scatter" the information about the defendant's busy schedule.

Alternatively, however, you may still use sequencing to make your point. The key lies in the order of the examination. Assume that you still want to elicit in close proximity the information about the repair shop and the client meeting. Neither event is a necessary predicate to the other; which one should you establish first?

Although it may seem counterintuitive, the answer is to save the "surest" topic for last. In the above example you can probably be the most "sure" that the defendant will admit going directly to his office following the accident. The issue is purely factual, and there are, no doubt, other witnesses who will place him at the office that morning. You can also be fairly sure that the witness will admit having been at the repair shop, since again there will be witnesses to place him there. On the other hand, you must be decidedly less sure that he will concede that he opted not to have his brakes fixed because he was busy that day. The defendant's motivations are his own, and they can seldom be established from a collateral source.[6]

---

6. This discussion assumes that you do not have available a prior statement from the defendant that admits the facts that you are seeking to establish.

Thus, motivation is your touchiest subject. It should therefore come at the beginning of your sequence, for two reasons. First, recall that the witness will be most cooperative before he understands where the examination is headed. Since proof of motivation depends most on the witness's own cooperation, you will want to address that issue at the beginning of that part of the examination. Second, you know that you want to conclude every area of the examination successfully. You will therefore save your more "provable" points for last.

How will this particular exercise in sequencing work? Assume that the brake shop incident occurred on Monday and that the accident was on Friday. Begin by asking the witness about his business schedule on that Monday. Do not bring up automobile repairs until you have completely established all of his appointments and time commitments for that day. Then ask him about his visit to the mechanic, concluding with the fact that he did not leave his car there. You may now go on to the day of the accident, establishing that the defendant went on to his office following the collision. Through careful sequencing you should be able to maintain sufficient control of the witness and keep both events in close apposition.

4. Use Sequenced Questions for Commitment

Using sequenced questions in combination with incremental questions may occasionally allow you to compel an unwilling witness to make important concessions. Facts can often be arranged in a manner that gives their progression a logic of its own. When the initial facts in a sequence are sufficiently small and innocuous, a witness may be led to embark upon a course of concessions that will be impossible to stop.

Suppose that you represent the defendant in the fire truck case, and you want to prove that the plaintiff was not as seriously injured as she claims. There is, of course, absolutely no possibility that the witness will admit flatly to having exaggerated her injuries. On the other hand, she may initially admit the accuracy of a series of smaller, more innocuous assertions. Note that the sequencing of the following questions commits the witness to a premise that will later be expanded in a way that she will not be able to deny:

QUESTION: You have testified that the accident has interfered with your enjoyment of life?

QUESTION: For example, you have given up playing tennis?

QUESTION: Tennis, of course, requires considerable physical exertion?

QUESTION: Because of that, you have dropped your membership in the North Shore Tennis Club?

QUESTION: One of your other interests is the fine arts, isn't that right?

QUESTION: In particular, you admire the French impressionists, correct?

QUESTION: Of course, the accident has not diminished your appreciation for the French impressionists?

QUESTION: In fact, you are a fairly serious student of nineteenth century art?

QUESTION: You share that interest with your friends and children, don't you?

QUESTION: You have maintained your membership in the Art Institute, haven't you?

QUESTION: You attended the special Monet exhibition, didn't you? And your membership allowed you to bring along some friends as guests, correct?

QUESTION: And in fact, you have continued to serve as a guide for schoolchildren?

QUESTION: Being a guide, of course, involves accompanying the children throughout the museum?

Sequencing was used in this example to commit the witness to several premises that were later expanded in a way that she would be unable to deny. Tennis is strenuous. She continues to enjoy the French impressionists. She was able to keep up with her friends at a crowded museum exhibit. And eventually, she is still capable of chasing children around the Art Institute.

5. Create a "Conceptual Corral"

As we have seen, the purpose of cross examination is often to "box in" a witness so that crucial facts cannot be averted or denied. It is often useful to think of this process as building a "conceptual corral" around the witness. After building the first three sides of the corral, you may then close the gate with your final proposition.

Each side of the conceptual corral is formed by a different sort of question. One side consists of the witness's own previous admissions or actions, another is formed by undeniable facts, and the third is based upon everyday plausibility. The length of any particular side, or the extent to which you will rely on any of the three sorts of information, will differ from case to case. With almost every witness, however, the three sides of the corral can be constructed to form an enclosure from which the witness cannot escape.

Suppose that you want to prove that the defendant in the accident case ignored the fire truck. That proposition will be the gate of your corral; you won't make it obvious until all three sides have been put into place.

The first side is formed by the witness's own admissions, gathered from his deposition, documents in the case, or his earlier testimony on direct: He was driving south on Sheridan Road, he was late for an appointment, he had over ten miles yet to go, he had to park a few blocks from his office, and he didn't hit his brakes before the collision.

Side two consists of undeniable facts that have already been established or that can readily be proved by other witnesses: The fire truck was the largest vehicle on the road. It was red. The other traffic stopped. The weather was clear.

The last side is based upon plausibility: A fire truck can be seen at a distance of over one hundred yards. Fire trucks have red lights to increase their visibility. Traveling at thirty miles per hour it only takes about ninety feet to stop an automobile.

The three sides having been constructed, the gate will simply fall into place: The defendant could only have missed the fire truck by ignoring the roadway.

Note that the fourth side of the corral often will not require any questions at all. Admissions, facts, and plausibility will frequently be all that you need to establish your ultimate point. And, as we will discuss below, it is usually preferable not to confront the witness with your ultimate proposition.

6. Avoid Ultimate Questions

It will often be tempting to confront an adverse witness with one last conclusory question: "So you just ignored the fire truck, didn't you?" Resist this temptation. If you have already established all of the incremental facts that lead to your conclusion, then you will have little to gain by making the question explicit. At best you will repeat what has become obvious, and at worst you will give the witness an opportunity to recant or amend the foundational testimony.

Even worse, you may not have established the incremental facts as fully as you thought. Under these circumstances you can expect the witness not only to disagree with your ultimate proposition but to be prepared to explain exactly why you are wrong.

The classic approach to cross examination calls for the lawyer to elicit all of the facts that lead to the ultimate conclusion, and to then stop. The final proposition is saved for final argument. By saving the ultimate point for final argument, you ensure that the witness will not be able to change or add to the testimony. To a certain extent you also avoid informing opposing counsel of your argument, and you diminish the likelihood of having your position refuted either on redirect or through another witness.

While some writers state flatly that you should always save your ultimate point for argument, a more flexible rule is also more realistic. Perhaps it could best be stated as "Save the ultimate point for argument unless you are certain that it will be inescapable." For example, the witness may already have admitted your ultimate point during her deposition. Or your proposition might have been so firmly established by the evidence as to be undeniable. Occasionally, you might even want the witness to disagree with your conclusion so that you may exploit the sheer implausibility of the denial. Short of these circumstances, however, the safest route is generally to be satisfied with establishing a chain of incremental facts and to reserve the capstone for argument.

THE BASICS

Cross Examination Techniques	
Leading questions	• Tells witness what to say, rather than open-ended inquiry
Incremental questions	• Short, single-fact, small steps
Propositional questions	• Assertion of fact, requesting affirmation from witness
Sequenced questions	• Arranged either to underscore related facts or to avoid "telegraphing" your point to the witness
No "ultimate" questions	• Save conclusions, characterizations, and other ultimate points for final argument

7. Listen to the Witness and Insist on an Answer

There is more to controlling a witness on cross examination than asking the right questions. You must also make sure that you have gotten the correct answers. This requires that you listen to the witness. Even the most painstakingly prepared question can elicit the wrong answer. The witness may not have understood you, or she may have detected an ambiguity in your inquiry. Some witnesses will argue with you for the sake of argument, some will try to deflect your examination, and some will simply answer a question different from the one that you asked. In any event, you must always recall that it is the witness's answer that constitutes evidence, and you must listen carefully to ensure that the evidence is what you expected.

You can often correct an answer by restating your question. Consider the following scenario from the fire truck case:

QUESTION: Isn't it true that all of the other traffic stopped for the fire truck?

ANSWER: How would they know to stop? There was no siren.

QUESTION: You didn't answer my question. All of the other cars did stop?

ANSWER: Yes.

In the above example, the defendant apparently decided that he did not want to respond to the cross examiner's question, so he deflected it by answering a different question. An inattentive lawyer might have interpreted that answer as a denial or otherwise let it go by. The advocate listened more carefully, however, and was able to obtain the precise information sought.

Note as well that the cross examiner in this situation would be equally satisfied with either an affirmative or a negative answer. If the defendant admitted that all of the other traffic stopped, then the point is made. If the defendant insisted that the traffic hadn't stopped, he would be subject to contradiction by numerous other witnesses. Either way, the cross examination would be successful. The greater problem, then, is the non-answer. There are many techniques for requiring difficult or evasive witnesses to answer your questions, but the first step is always to listen to the witness and to insist upon an answer.

C. Questions That Lose Control

The pitfalls of cross examination are well known: refusals to answer, unexpected answers, argumentative witnesses, evasive and slippery witnesses. Significantly, virtually all of these problems derive from the same basic error on the part of the cross examiner—failure to control the testimony.

Control of testimony on cross examination means ensuring (1) that all of your questions are answered with the information that you want, and (2) that no information is produced other than what you have requested. In other words, the witness must answer your questions and only your questions. An examination goes slightly out of control when a witness hedges or withholds answers. It goes seriously out of control when a witness begins to spout entirely new information.

While some witnesses are intractable by nature, it is more usual that lawyers bring these problems upon themselves. Certain questions and styles of questioning constitute virtual invitations to a witness to set up an independent shop. The most common of these are detailed below. From time to time there may be a reason to use one of the following sorts of questions, but as a general proposition they are all to be avoided.

1. Nonleading Questions

The cardinal rule on cross examination is to use leading questions. The cardinal sin is to abandon that tool. We have discussed at length the advantages of stating your questions in the form of leading propositions. For some reason, however, many lawyers seem impelled to drift into nonleading questions once an examination has begun. You can control a witness this way:

> QUESTION: You were thirty feet away from plaintiff's car when you first applied your brakes, correct?

But you lose control when you ask,

> QUESTION: How far from the plaintiff's car were you when you applied your brakes?

Why would a lawyer make such an elementary mistake? The principal reason no doubt lies in lack of confidence. It is awkward to put words in another person's mouth. We do not generally conduct conversations by telling others exactly what to say. It is even more uncomfortable when you are uncertain about the content yourself. How odd it feels to tell the driver of an automobile exactly where and when he applied his brakes. An easy response mechanism to this unease is to revert to a more natural style of discourse: Just ask what happened. We all occasionally fall into the trap of turning control of the examination over to the witness.

The solution to this problem is preparation. If you are unsure of where the witness applied his brakes, of course you will not tell him that it was thirty feet. So be sure. Read his deposition, scour the police report, measure the skid marks, talk to other witnesses, calculate his speed and stopping distance. Then, once you are certain that there is no plausible denial, tell him exactly what he did. Because your leading question is based upon verifiable facts, the great likelihood is that the witness will agree with you. If the witness disagrees, all is still well and good. After all, you have the facts to use in further cross examination or to introduce through another witness.

There are two legitimate reasons to suspend temporarily the use of leading questions. Neither is without its risks, and both should be used with care. First, you will occasionally need to learn a bit of information from a witness in order to continue a cross examination. For example, there might have been two routes available for the fire truck defendant to reach his office from the scene of the accident. Having prepared thoroughly, you know that you will be able to show that he was already so late that neither route would have gotten him to his appointment on time. Thus, even if you don't know the answer to the question, you can safely ask a nonleading question: "What road did you intend to take downtown?" You need that information to structure the balance of your examination, and you can handle whichever answer you are given. Never employ this approach because you are curious or because you hope that the answer will be helpful. The potential for backfiring is great. You must truly be certain that you need to ask an informational question and that you have prepared alternate examinations depending on which answer you are given.

Second, and even less frequently, you may believe that an answer will have more impact if it comes in the witness's words instead of yours. Sometimes this works, but often it does not. Suppose that you are cross examining the fire truck plaintiff on the extent of her injuries. You know that she is still able to work at her job and that she recently went on a three-day camping trip. It would indeed heighten the drama of the moment if you could obtain the damning testimony in her own words:

QUESTION: Ma'am, please tell us all of the things that you were able to do on your recent camping trip.

ANSWER: Oh, I was able to hike, fish, swim, pitch the tent, carry my backpack, and sleep on the ground.

Perhaps the witness testified to all of that during her deposition. By the time of trial, however, the more likely scenario will be:

QUESTION: Ma'am, please tell us all of the things that you were able to do on your recent camping trip.

ANSWER: I was hardly able to do anything. Everything I tried caused me pain, even sleeping.

Nonleading questions might have a terrific potential impact, but leading questions have the incalculable advantage of greater safety. Consider:

QUESTION: Ma'am, you went on a three-day camping trip?

ANSWER: Yes.

QUESTION: You went hiking?

ANSWER: Yes, but it caused me pain.

QUESTION: You went fishing and swimming?

ANSWER: Yes.

QUESTION: You pitched the tent?

ANSWER: Yes, but that hurt too.

QUESTION: You stayed out in the woods for three days?

ANSWER: Yes.

Note that the witness may be able to argue with you notwithstanding your use of leading questions. The difference, however, is that short, leading questions limit her ability to do so, while increasing your ability to bring her back under control. Furthermore, the "yes, but" nature of her embellishments necessarily makes them less convincing.

Still, there may be times when it is truly advantageous to extract cross examination testimony in a witness's own words. This technique is most likely to work when the information you are after is well-documented, factual, and short. In the above example, assuming that you have adequate deposition testimony, you might be able to use nonleading questions to the following extent:

QUESTION: Where did you spend last Labor Day week-
            end?

ANSWER: At Eagle River Falls.

QUESTION: What is Eagle River Falls?

ANSWER: It is a campground.

That is enough; do not push your luck. Since the last thing you want to do is lose control of the testimony, now is the time to go back to leading questions.

2. "Why" or Explanation Questions

It is almost impossible to imagine a need to ask a witness to explain something on cross examination. If you already know the explanation, then use leading questions to tell it to the witness. If you do not already know the explanation, then cross examination surely is not the time to learn it. No matter how assiduously you have prepared, no matter how well you think you understand the witness's motives and reasons, a witness can always surprise you by explaining the unexplainable.

The greatest temptation to ask for an explanation arises when a witness offers a completely unexpected answer. The dissonance between the expectation and the actual response cries out for reso- lution. The natural reaction is to resolve the inconsistency by asking the witness, "Please explain what you mean by that." Unfortunately, the witness will be more than happy to explain, almost always to the detriment of the cross examiner. The following scenario is not unrealistic:

QUESTION: Your parking garage was located three blocks
            from your office, correct?

ANSWER: Yes.

QUESTION: And the sidewalks are always very crowded
            between 8:00 and 8:30 in the morning?

ANSWER: That's right.

QUESTION: You usually have to wait for one or more traf-
            fic lights between the garage and your office,
            don't you?

ANSWER: I do.

QUESTION:	So you have to plan on at least ten minutes to get from your garage to your office, right?
ANSWER:	No, that is not right. I usually make it in three to five minutes.
QUESTION:	Please explain how you can travel that distance, under those circumstances, in only three to five minutes.
ANSWER:	It's simple. There is an express bus that travels that route in a bus lane. I get on in front of the garage and its next stop is right in front of the office. Even in heavy traffic it never takes more than five minutes since the bus lane is always clear and the traffic lights are coordinated.

There are numerous common questions that invite such long, unwelcome answers. They should all be excised from your cross examination vocabulary. Do not ask a witness to explain. Do not ask a "why" question. Do not ask a question that begins with "How do you know" or "Tell us the reason." If you receive an unexpected answer, the fault probably lies with the original question. The best solution is usually to move on or rephrase your inquiry. It cannot help you to allow the witness to dig the hole a little deeper.

Asking a witness to explain is the equivalent of saying, "I've grown tired of controlling this cross examination. Why don't you take over for a while?"

3. "Fishing" Questions

Fishing questions are the ones that you ask in the hope that you might catch something. It has been said before and it is worth repeating here: Do not ask questions to which you do not know the answers. For every reason that you have to think that the answer will be favorable, there are a dozen reasons you haven't thought of, all of which suggest disaster.

Very few lawyers actually intend to go fishing during cross examination; most lawyers plan only to elicit information that they have developed during preparation for trial. Nonetheless, temptation has been known to strike. A witness, during either direct or cross, may expose an enticing, but incomplete, morsel of information. It is difficult to resist exploring such an opening, just to see if anything is really there. That is how the fishing starts.

In our intersection case, for example, suppose that during discovery the plaintiff produced medical reports indicating that she would need to participate in extensive physical therapy for the next several years. During her direct testimony at trial, however, she has unexpectedly stated, "My doctor said that I did not need to go to physical therapy any longer, and I ended it several months ago." The suggestion seems obvious; her injuries are not as severe as was previously thought, and she is now well on the way to resuming her normal life. Defense counsel immediately sees a vision of reduced damages. The temptation to go fishing on cross is now nearly irresistible; the defendant's lawyer wants to make sure that the record is clear as to the plaintiff's recovery.

Unfortunately, defendant's counsel is likely to "catch" information sharply different from that which was sought:

QUESTION: You have told us that your doctor terminated your physical therapy.

ANSWER: That is correct.

QUESTION: Isn't that because your recovery has been quicker than was expected, and you don't need the therapy any longer?

ANSWER: No. It is because the therapy was too painful and I wasn't making any progress.

The defendant's lawyer in the above scenario had a good reason to hope that the "therapy" questions would produce helpful information. The most important part of the answer, however, was unknown. Counsel simply had no way of predicting what the witness would say as to why the physical therapy ended. Reasonably hoping to turn up a good answer, counsel instead made the plaintiff's case stronger. That is what can happen when you go fishing.

4. Long Questions

Long questions have an almost limitless capacity to deprive a cross examiner of witness control. Recall that short, single-fact, propositional questions give a witness the least room to take issue with your point. By contrast, long questions, by their very nature, multiply a witness's opportunity to find something with which to disagree. The more words you use, the more chance there is that a witness will refuse to adopt them all.

A second problem with long questions is that they are easily forgotten or misunderstood. Even a witness with every reasonable intention can be misled or baffled by a lengthy question. Thereafter, the witness may insist on answering the question that she thought you asked rather than the one that you meant to ask.

Finally, long questions diminish your ability to enlist the judge in your efforts to control a witness. It is a little-known, and even less acknowledged, characteristic of trial judges that they do not all tend to pay close attention to attorneys' questions, particularly in jury trials. It is, after all, the answer that constitutes evidence. Given the principle of primacy, long questions have the greatest potential to lose a judge's attention. In ordinary circumstances this is not of great moment, since the judge's impression, or even understanding, of the question may not be essential. Once a witness has avoided answering, however, the judge's perception of the question can become crucial.

Counsel will often want to request the judge to direct a witness to answer a question "yes" or "no." Understandably, a judge will only be inclined to do this if she has heard and comprehended the entire question. Even if your question is completely susceptible of a "yes or no" answer, a judge who has tuned out the last two-thirds of your inquiry is extremely unlikely to restrict the witness's answer.

There is no fixed point at which a question becomes "long." Some inquiries, depending upon the nature of the concept and the cooperativeness of the witness, may call for more words than others. A useful rule of thumb is that any question of ten words or fewer may be considered "short." You may wish to exceed this length, but only for a reason.

5. "Gap" Questions

"Gap" questions constitute an especially enticing subset of explanation questions. Interestingly, they are often most irresistible to lawyers who are particularly well-prepared or attentive.

Imagine that you are the prosecutor in a hit-and-run case. You know the date on which the crime occurred, but because there were no eyewitnesses, you have been able to narrow the time of the crime only to a six-hour window. The defendant has raised the defense of alibi. You have thoroughly researched the law and meticulously prepared the facts of your case, which is based entirely on circumstantial evidence. The defendant has taken the stand and testified in his own defense. Listening carefully, you were surprised to notice that he left several half-hour gaps in his alibi.

The defendant is now available for cross examination. The temptation may be overwhelming to alert the jury to the gaps in the defendant's alibi: "Mr. Defendant, you told us where you were at 2:00 p.m., but you didn't say anything about 2:30 p.m., did you?" Do not ask that question; you will lose control. It is an unspoken invitation to the witness to fill in the gap. Even if the witness does not take the opportunity to complete his alibi, you can be certain that opposing counsel will do it for him on redirect. The far better tactic is to allow the omission to remain unexplained and then to point it out during final argument.

Gaps are found in direct testimony more often than one might expect. A witness may neglect to testify about one of a series of important events or may omit testimony concerning a crucial document. Alternatively, a witness might leave out important evidence on damages or may fail entirely to testify as to an element, such as proximate cause, of the opposition's case.

How can you avoid the temptation to ask "gap" questions? The key is to remember that it is the opposition's burden to prove their case. Everything that they leave out of their case works in your favor. In most circumstances the absence of proof can be interpreted as negative proof.[7]

Of course, your opposition may also create gaps in their testimony by design, purposely leaving out facts that damage their case but are helpful to yours. Needless to say, you will want to address these omissions during your cross examination. The fatal "gap" questions are the ones that are directed at omissions in the other side's case. A useful way to keep this distinction in mind is the following: Do not cross examine on omissions in testimony. Do cross examine on the absence of facts.

Thus, when your opposition has failed to prove something, simply allow the gap to remain. Comment on it during final argument, not cross examination.

6. "You testified" Questions

Another common method of surrendering control to a witness is through the use of questions that seem to challenge the witness to recall the content of her earlier direct testimony. These can be referred to as "you testified" questions because they inevitably contain some variant on those words. Each of the following is a "you testified" question:

> QUESTION: You testified that the assailant had brown
> hair?

---

7.   The most obvious exception to this rule is a criminal defendant's decision not to testify at all, from which no negative inference may be drawn.

QUESTION: Wasn't it your testimony that you left your house at 8:00 a.m.?

QUESTION: On direct examination you testified that the last possible delivery date was May 17, didn't you?

What is wrong with these questions? In each case they seem to call for relevant information. They are all leading. They are all short. They are all propositional.

The problem with "you testified" questions is that they invite the witness to quibble over the precise wording used on direct examination. The exact language of the witness's earlier answer is seldom essential,[8] but the "you testified" format inflates its apparent importance, often almost to the point of seeming to pick a fight. Imagine these answers to the above questions, with the witness's unspoken thoughts given in parentheses:

QUESTION: You testified that the assailant had brown hair?

ANSWER: No. (I testified that he had sort of sandy brown hair.)

QUESTION: Wasn't it your testimony that you left your house at 8:00 a.m.?

ANSWER: That was not my testimony. (I said that I believed that I left my house at approximately 8:00 a.m.)

QUESTION: On direct examination you testified that the last possible delivery date was May 17, didn't you?

ANSWER: I do not believe that is correct. (I think I said that we could not accept delivery any later than May 17.)

---

8.   The precise wording of a witness's previous answer can be essential when you intend to impeach the witness through the use of a prior inconsistent statement. In that situation it is usually necessary, and indeed some courts require, that you "recommit" the witness to the testimony that you intend to impeach. Thus, the classic foundation for impeachment by a prior inconsistent statement includes a preliminary "you testified" question. Note, however, that the subject of the impeachment is the witness's earlier testimony and not the actual underlying events. For further information on the specifics of impeachment, see Chapter 5, Section II *infra* at p. 124.

Even if you have correctly remembered the witness's precise testimony down to the last word, there is no guarantee that the witness will remember it equally well. At best, you may end up with a response on the order of, "I cannot remember whether those were my exact words." At that point you have lost control, since the examination has now shifted away from your agenda and onto the issue of the superiority of your memory. The court reporter can be called upon to resolve the dispute, but that exercise, at a minimum, will be disruptive to your pace. Besides, you might turn out to be embarrassingly wrong.

It is far less risky, and generally much more effective, to cross examine witnesses on facts and events, rather than on prior testimony: "You left your home at 8:00 a.m.?" "You expected delivery no later than May 17?" In situations where you want to make it clear that you challenge the witness's version of events, use a formulation such as this one: "You now claim that the assailant had brown hair?"

It may be helpful to think of possible cross examination questions using the following hierarchy. As a general rule, you should prefer questions that are higher on the list: Best, direct your questions to what happened. Next, direct your questions to what the witness claims happened. Last, direct your questions to what the witness said happened.

The closer you can stay to "real life," the less likely you are to lose witness control.

7. Characterizations and Conclusions

Another way to risk losing control on cross examination is to request that a witness agree with a characterization or conclusion. Assume that you are cross examining the complaining witness in a robbery case. The witness testified on direct that the crime occurred at midnight on a seldom-traveled country road. Your defense is misidentification. Wishing to take advantage of the time and place of the events, you ask this question:

"It was too dark to see very well, wasn't it?"

You have just asked the witness to agree with your characterization of the lighting conditions. The witness, being nobody's fool, answers:

"I could see just fine."

Instead, you should have asked the witness about the facts that led you to the characterization: the sun had gone down, there was no moon that night, there were no street lamps, there were no house lights, and there were no illuminated signs. The characterization could then be saved for final argument.

Some outstanding trial lawyers, through force of personality, splendid preparation, or stunningly good luck, have been quite successful in obtaining a witness's agreement to their characterizations. In the above example it would be of inestimable value to have the witness concede that it was too dark to see very well. For most lawyers, however, the risk to these questions usually outweighs the gain.

Bear in mind that it may be difficult to draw the line between characterization and fact. It will depend on the specifics of the case, the inclinations of the witness, the context of the question, and numerous other factors. On the one hand, a question such as, "It was midnight?" is clearly one of fact. On the other hand, a question such as, "Your identification was mistaken?" is no doubt a characterization. There are numerous possibilities in between. Even the question, "It was too dark to see?" might be regarded as either characterization or fact, depending upon the witness's background. While most people would regard that statement as conclusory—who is to say when it becomes too dark to see?—a photo-physicist, or perhaps a forensic ophthalmologist, might regard the inquiry as calling for an absolute fact.

Recognizing the impossibility of stating an absolute rule, the wisest course is to examine your questions for their potential to be taken as characterizations. Then make sure that you phrase them as facts.

VI. ETHICS OF CROSS EXAMINATION

While lawyers generally consider cross examination to be an "engine" of truth-seeking, we are often criticized for using cross as a device for distortion and obfuscation. And in truth, as with all powerful rhetorical tools, cross examination can be used to mislead and deceive. Accordingly, certain ethical principles have developed that circumscribe a lawyer's use of cross examination.

A. Basis for Questioning

1. Factual Basis

Many cross examinations contain inherent assertions of fact. Indeed, many of the best cross examination questions are strictly "propositional." Consider these examples from the fire engine case:

QUESTION: You did not have your brakes fixed, did you?

QUESTION: You slept on the ground while on your camping trip, correct?

QUESTION: You were on your way to an important business meeting, right?

QUESTION: You have continued to work as a guide at the Art Institute, haven't you?

Each question contains a single fact that counsel is urging to be true. The danger arises that counsel might also propose baseless or knowingly false points. The witness, of course, can deny any untrue assertions, but the denials are likely to ring hollow in the face of an attorney's presumably superior persuasive skills. Enormous damage can be done by false or groundless accusations. Imagine the impact of this examination:

QUESTION: Isn't it true that you had been drinking on the morning of the accident?

ANSWER: No, not at all.

QUESTION: Didn't you arrive at Mayer's Bar at 7:00 a.m.?

ANSWER: Certainly not.

QUESTION: Well, the truth is that you ran up a $12.00 tab that morning, didn't you?

ANSWER: No.

QUESTION: $12.00 would cover at least four drinks, right?

ANSWER: I'm telling you that I wasn't drinking.

The precision of the details in the questions appears to add verity to the cross examination, while the denials can be made to appear superficial. The cross examiner's ability to control the interchange puts the witness at an extreme disadvantage. This cross examination raises no problems if the witness was indeed drinking at Mayer's Bar, but it is intolerable if the charge is untrue.

To protect against the unscrupulous use of cross examination, it is required that every question have a "good faith basis" in fact.[9] Counsel is not free to make up assertions or even to fish for possibly incriminating material. Rather, as a predicate to any "propositional"

---

9.   A laywer shall not "in trial, allude to any matter that the lawyer does not reasonably believe is relevant or that will not be supported by admissible evidence." Rule 3.4(e), Model Rules of Professional Conduct.

question, counsel must be aware of specific facts that support the allegation.

2. Legal Basis

The "good faith basis" for a cross examination question cannot be comprised solely of inadmissible evidence. Counsel cannot allude to any matter "that will not be supported by admissible evidence."[10] Thus, a good faith basis cannot be provided by rumors, uncorroborated hearsay, or pure speculation.

Allegations lacking a basis in admissible evidence may lead to a sustained objection, an admonition by the court, or even a mistrial. Moreover, many jurisdictions require counsel to offer admissible extrinsic evidence to "prove up" certain assertions made on cross examination, such as past conviction of a felony.

B. Assertions of Personal Knowledge

It is unethical to "assert personal knowledge of facts in issue… or state a personal opinion as to the justness of a cause, the credibility of a witness, the culpability of a civil litigant or the guilt or innocence of an accused."[11] While this problem most frequently occurs during final argument,[12] it also arises during cross examination.

Cross examination questions sometimes take a "Do you know?" or "Didn't you tell me?" format. Both types of question are improper because they put the lawyer's own credibility in issue. "Do you know?" questions suggest that the lawyer is aware of true facts which, while not appearing on the record, contradict the witness's testimony. "Didn't you tell me?" questions argue that the witness and the lawyer had a conversation, and that the lawyer's version is more believable. In either case, the questions amount to an assertion of personal knowledge.[13]

C. Derogatory Questions

It is unethical to ask questions that are intended solely to harass, degrade, or humiliate a witness, or to discourage him from testifying.

---

10. *Id.*

11. Rule 3.4(e), Model Rules of Professional Conduct.

12. See Chapter 11, Section VI A(1), *infra* at p. 380.

13. "Do you know?" questions may be permissible in limited circumstances. A witness claiming compendious knowledge, for example, could legitimately be questioned as to her lack of certain information. Similarly, a character witness could be questioned concerning unknown facts about a witness's reputation. In each situation, however, the question must have a good faith basis.

D. Discrediting a Truthful Witness

To what extent may cross examination be used to discredit the testimony of a witness whom counsel knows to be telling the truth?

The answer to this question is reasonably straightforward in criminal cases. Defense counsel is entitled to insist that the government prove its case through evidence that is persuasive beyond a reasonable doubt. Thus, witnesses must not only be truthful, they must also be convincing to the required degree of certainty. A discrediting cross is simply an additional safeguard.

Conversely, a criminal prosecutor has a public duty to avoid conviction of the innocent. A truthful witness, therefore, should not be discredited simply for the sake of the exercise.

The rule is less certain in civil cases. It is clear, however, that a witness cannot be degraded or debased simply to cast doubt on otherwise unchallenged testimony. On the other hand, true factual information may be used to undermine the credibility of a witness whose testimony is legitimately controverted.

E. Misusing Evidence

The same rules apply on cross as on direct with regard to misusing evidence that has been admitted for a limited purpose.[14]

14. See Chapter 3, Section VI B, *supra* at p. 66.

— CHAPTER FIVE —
Impeachment

I.   INTRODUCTION

A.   Categories of Impeachment

While much cross examination consists of demonstrating inaccuracies or rebutting a witness's testimony, impeachment is intended actually to discredit the witness as a reliable source of information.[1] Successful impeachment renders the witness less worthy of belief, as opposed to merely unobservant, mistaken, or otherwise subject to contradiction. There are three basic categories of witness impeachment, each of which provides a reason to place less credence in a witness's testimony.

Perhaps the most common method of impeachment is the use of a prior inconsistent statement, action, or omission. The elicitation of a prior inconsistency demonstrates that the witness's current testimony is at odds with her own previous statements or actions. In essence, this examination says, "Do not believe this witness because her story has changed."

A second method of impeachment is the use of character, or "characteristic" evidence. This form of impeachment is aimed at demonstrating that the witness possesses some inherent trait or characteristic, unrelated to the case at hand, that renders the testimony less credible. Perhaps the witness is a convicted felon or suffers a memory defect. This examination says, "This witness is not trustworthy on any matter, because of who he is."

---

1.   It was once considered improper for a lawyer to "impeach one's own witness" on the theory that a lawyer who called a witness to the stand for direct examination had "vouched" for the witness's credibility. The techniques of impeachment, therefore, arose in the context of cross examination. The rule against impeaching your own witness has been abolished. See Rule 607, Federal Rules of Evidence. As a technical matter, impeachment may now occur during either direct or cross examination. As a practical matter, however, impeachment during direct examination is unusual. This chapter, therefore, will treat impeachment as a device to be used on cross examination.

Finally, "case data" impeachment involves the establishment of facts that make the witness less reliable, although only within the context of the case at trial. The witness might have a financial interest in the outcome of the case or might be prejudiced against one of the parties. In other words, "Give less weight to the witness because of her relationship to the case."

THE BASICS	
The Forms of Impeachment	
Type:	**Used When:**
• Prior Inconsistent Statement	A witness's trial testimony conflicts with a prior statement.
• Omission	A witness adds facts to trial testimony that were not included in the prior statement.
• Character and Bias	An aspect of the witness's character, or the witness's relationship to a party, renders trial testimony less credible.

B. Tactical Considerations

Impeachment is a powerful tool. Unlike "standard" cross examination, which may rely on unspoken premises and subtle misdirection, there should be no mistaking or hiding the intended impact of impeachment. All three kinds of impeachment are inherently confrontational. They challenge the witness's believability, perhaps even her veracity. For this reason it is best to use the techniques of impeachment sparingly, both to preserve the potency of the method and to avoid crying wolf over unimportant details.

1. Impeach the Witness Only on Significant Matters

It is important to avoid impeaching witnesses on irrelevant, trivial, or petty inconsistencies. The process of impeachment, particularly through the use of prior inconsistency, can become so confrontational that there is a great risk of creating an annoying dissonance between expectation and reward. If the "punch line" fails to justify the buildup, the result can be embarrassing or damaging to your case. Imagine this scenario, for example, in the trial of the fire truck case that we have been using throughout; the plaintiff is being cross examined:

QUESTION: You testified on direct examination that you heard the siren, saw the flashing lights, and then slowed down, correct?

ANSWER: Correct.

QUESTION: You have given an earlier statement?

ANSWER: Why, yes I did.

QUESTION: You spoke to the investigating police officer?

ANSWER: That is right.

QUESTION: You knew that you had to be truthful with the police officer?

ANSWER: Of course.

QUESTION: Didn't your earlier statement say, "I saw the flashing lights, then I heard the siren, which caused me to slow down at once"?

ANSWER: Yes, I believe that is what I said.

Although the plaintiff has, in some technical sense, been impeached, the inconsistency involved is so slight as to be inconsequential. What difference does it make whether the witness first heard the siren or saw the lights? The essential point—that the fire truck was using its warning signals and that traffic slowed down—remains completely intact. The cross examiner, however, has squandered valuable capital by confronting the witness, wasting time, and emerging with nothing to show for those efforts. A jury's near certain response would be, "Is that all you can do?" A judge's response would be even less charitable.

This principle of "significance" does not apply only to prior inconsistencies. Other forms of impeachment also should only be used on important matters. Charges of prejudice or bias, for instance, should only be made when they are truly likely to make a difference to the way in which the witness will be perceived.

2. Impeach the Witness Only on True Inconsistencies

The purpose of impeachment through the use of a prior inconsistency is to show that the witness has made contradictory statements. The technique works only when the two statements cannot both be true. If the two statements can be harmonized, explained, or rationalized, the impeachment will fail. For example:

QUESTION: You testified on direct that the bank robbers drove away in a blue car, correct?

ANSWER: Yes.

QUESTION: You gave a statement to the police right after the robbery, didn't you?

ANSWER: Yes, I did.

QUESTION: You told the police that the robbers drove off in a turquoise car, didn't you?

Although different words were used, the two statements are not inconsistent. It does not detract from the witness's credibility that she once referred to the car as turquoise and that she later called it blue.

3. Impeach a Witness Only When Success Is Likely

Failed impeachment can be disastrous. A lawyer who begins an assault that cannot be completed will look ineffective at best and foolishly overbearing at worst.

Impeachment can succeed only when the source of the impeachment is readily available. For that reason the outline of your cross examination must be indexed to the sources of your information, including all of the witness's prior statements. Do not begin your impeachment until you have the prior statement firmly in hand and have located the precise page and line that you intend to use to contradict the current testimony.

Do not rely on your memory. Even your clear recollection that the witness's deposition was diametrically contrary to her new testimony will have a way of betraying you when you turn to the transcript and read her exact words. It makes much more sense to pause and review your notes before attempting to impeach a witness than it does to have to stop in the middle when you cannot find the right material.

4. Do Not Impeach Favorable Information

Impeachment is not like mountain climbing. It should not be undertaken simply because it is there. The purpose of impeachment is to cast doubt on the credibility of some or all of a witness's testimony. There is nothing to be gained by casting doubt on testimony that was helpful to your own case. Thus, even if an opposing witness has given a prior inconsistent statement, it should not be used to impeach favorable trial testimony.

Assume that the defendant in the fire engine case testified at trial that immediately after the accident he took out a cell phone to call his office. In contrast, at deposition he testified that his first action was to check the damage to his BMW and that he used his cell phone only after making sure that the plaintiff was not seriously injured.

The two statements are clearly inconsistent, and the witness is technically open to impeachment. The trial testimony, however, is actually more helpful to the cross examiner's case. Recall the possible plaintiff's theme that the defendant was "too busy to be careful." The defendant's admission that his first thought was to telephone his office fits beautifully into that theme. While his hard-heartedness in checking on his BMW before looking into the plaintiff's injuries might also be useful to the cross examiner's case, this information does not go directly to any theory of liability or damages. The cross examiner therefore will not want to undercut the trial testimony (about the immediate phone call) by impeaching it with the deposition transcript (about checking on his BMW).

5. Consider the Impact of Multiple Impeachment

In some cases, a witness may have made a number of potentially impeaching statements. Though no single statement may be of great significance, it is possible that the sheer volume of self-contradiction may be sufficient to take on a life of its own. Thus, it may be worthwhile to impeach a witness on a series of relatively minor facts. Consider this, somewhat truncated, impeachment of a bystander witness in the fire engine case:

QUESTION: You testified today that you were standing on the northeast corner, correct?

QUESTION: But you told the police officer that you were standing on the southeast corner, didn't you?

QUESTION: You told the jury that you saw the accident while you were waiting for a bus?

QUESTION: But your pretrial statement said that you were out for a walk.

QUESTION: Today you said that you were on your way to work that day.

QUESTION: In your deposition, though, you said you were going to the beach.

QUESTION: Today's testimony was that you were the only person on the corner.

QUESTION: You told the police, however, that there was a jogger standing right next to you.

In isolation, none of the above details would make much difference to the witness's credibility. In aggregation, however, they paint a picture of a confused person who is very likely confused about precisely what he saw.

Multiple impeachment is a refined tool. It can be overdone, and the point may be easily lost. On the other hand, when deftly executed and well-conceived, the whole impeachment can actually turn out to be much greater than the sum of its parts.

6. Consider the "Rule of Completeness"

The "Rule of Completeness" provides that once a witness has been impeached from a prior inconsistent statement, opposing counsel may request the immediate reading of additional, explanatory portions of the same statement. Under the Federal Rules of Evidence, for example, the adverse party may introduce any other part of the statement "which ought in fairness to be considered contemporaneously with it."[2]

Thus, even a true gem of an impeaching statement may be immediately undercut if some other part of the impeaching document explains or negates the apparent contradiction. Assume that the following impeachment of the plaintiff has taken place in our fire truck case:[3]

QUESTION: You testified on direct examination that as a result of the accident you are no longer able to ride your bicycle, correct?

ANSWER: Correct.

QUESTION: On deposition, however, didn't you testify as follows: "Just last week I rode my bicycle over four miles to the Botanic Garden"?

ANSWER: Yes, I did say that.

The above impeachment obviously hurts the plaintiff's claim for damages.

---

2. See Rule 106, Federal Rules of Evidence.

3. The form of the impeachment has been truncated so as to emphasize the point about the Rule of Completeness.

The effectiveness of the impeachment is undercut, if not entirely destroyed, however, if the following statement from the same deposition is immediately admitted into evidence: "I try to do everything I can to minimize the limitations of my injury. Sometimes I try too hard. That bike trip to the Botanic Garden put me back in the hospital for two days; I'll never try that again."

There is little to gain and much to lose by impeaching a witness only to see the impeachment come completely undone within a matter of minutes. Always scour the impeaching document for other information "which ought in fairness to be considered contemporaneously" with the impeachment.

THE BASICS

Impeachment Checklist ☑	
❑ Is this worth impeaching?	Does this testimony actually tend to hurt your case? *If not, skip the impeachment.*
❑ Is this an actual inconsistency?	Does this testimony truly conflict with the witness's prior testimony? *If not, there is no point in impeaching.*
❑ Are you sure to succeed?	Is the inconsistency found in the witness's own statement or in some other usable document? *If not, consider skipping the impeachment to save yourself from the possibility of a failed attempt.*
❑ Is this information actually favorable to your case?	Do the additional or changed facts actually support your theory of the case? *If so, there is no need to point out an earlier inconsistency.*
❑ Can you perform a multiple impeachment?	Are the points you plan to impeach so small such that they will be stronger if grouped together? *If so, impeach the witness in a series of questions.*
❑ Is this the right time to impeach on this fact?	Are you impeaching based on the witness's direct examination testimony? *If so, add the impeachment into the confrontational section of your cross.* Are you impeaching based on the witness's response to a question during cross examination? *If so, launch into the impeachment right away.*

7. Consider Refreshing the Witness's Recollection

Not every gap or variation in a witness's testimony is the result of an intentional change. Witnesses often become confused or forgetful. A witness may have testified inconsistently with her prior statements quite innocently or inadvertently. In these circumstances it will often be possible to use the prior statement to refresh the witness's recollection, rather than to impeach her credibility. The technique for refreshing recollection is the same on cross examination as it is on direct.[4] In many courts, however, a cross examiner will be allowed to refresh a witness's recollection without first being required to establish that the witness's memory has been exhausted. For example:

QUESTION: You testified on direct examination that you went directly from the scene of the accident to the hospital?

ANSWER: That is right.

QUESTION: You also testified to these matters when your deposition was taken, didn't you?

ANSWER: I am sure that I did.

QUESTION: Please look at page 725 of your deposition, which I am now handing to you, and tell me when you have finished reading it.

ANSWER: I am done.

QUESTION: Does that refresh your recollection as to whether you did anything before going to the hospital?

ANSWER: Yes, it does.

QUESTION: In fact, you took your cell phone and called your office first, didn't you?

ANSWER: Yes, I did.

The strict requirements for refreshing recollection are usually somewhat relaxed on cross examination because the cross examiner cannot expect much cooperation from the witness. It is one thing on direct examination to refresh the recollection of a witness who admits to a memory lapse, but it is quite another on cross examination

---

4. See Chapter 3, Section II E, *supra* at p. 34.

to refresh the memory of a witness who has omitted some fact without realizing it. Judges therefore tend toward leniency, and opposing counsel often abstain from objecting, if only to avoid the unpleasant necessity of impeachment.

C. Evidentiary Considerations

Prior inconsistent statements that were given under oath are admissible as substantive evidence; they can be used to prove the truth of the original statement.[5] Prior inconsistent statements that were not given under oath are generally admissible for the limited purpose of impeachment; they can be used only to reflect on the credibility of the witness.[6]

Under traditional theories of evidence, prior out-of-court statements of witnesses are hearsay and therefore not admissible as substantive evidence. They are admissible, however, as impeachment under the theory that the offer is intended only to reflect on the witness's credibility and not actually as proof of the facts contained in the statement. Consider the following example:

QUESTION: You testified on direct examination that the southbound traffic had the green light?

ANSWER: Yes.

QUESTION: In your statement to the police officer, didn't you say that the southbound traffic had a red light?

ANSWER: I did.

The witness's earlier statement to the police officer was obviously made out of court. It therefore would be hearsay if offered to prove that the light actually was red, since that would go to the "truth of the matter asserted."[7] The statement is not hearsay, however, if it is only offered to show that the witness has changed her testimony. Under those circumstances, the statement is not offered to prove that the light was red, but only that the witness is an unreliable source for the color of the light.

---

5. Rule 801(d)(1)(A), Federal Rules of Evidence.

6. Prior inconsistent statements that were not given under oath may occasionally be used as substantive evidence if they qualify for some exception to the hearsay rule. For example, the prior statement of a party is admissible as a party admission whether or not it was made under oath. See Rule 801(d)(2), Federal Rules of Evidence. The same would be true of declarations against interest, excited utterances, or present sense impressions. Rule 803, Federal Rules of Evidence.

7. See Rule 801(c), Federal Rules of Evidence.

The traditional rule has been altered somewhat by modern practice. Under the Federal Rules of Evidence a prior inconsistent statement is not considered hearsay if it was originally made under oath at a trial, hearing, other proceeding, or in a deposition.[8] Thus, if the witness in the example above had made the earlier statement at her deposition, rather than to a police officer, it would then be admissible as substantive proof that the light was indeed red.

What is the importance of this distinction? Isn't the difference between substantive evidence and impeaching evidence simply too fine for most juries to comprehend? It is true that judges' limiting instructions are frequently ignored or misunderstood. In some situations, however, it may make a difference if the judge instructs the jury to "consider the witness's prior statement only as impeachment, and not as substantive evidence."

More frequently, the difference between impeaching and substantive evidence will be relevant to the determination of issues of law. For example, only substantive evidence should be considered in deciding whether the plaintiff has made out a prima facie case. Similarly, a reviewing court should not consider strictly impeaching evidence in deciding whether a verdict was supported by sufficient evidence. Finally, a court may restrict a lawyer's final argument if evidence that was admitted for a limited purpose is sought to be used as substantive proof.

In consequence, it is usually preferable to impeach a witness through the use of a sworn statement if one is available, since that approach allows the greatest latitude for later use of the evidence.

II. PRIOR INCONSISTENT STATEMENTS

One of the most dramatic aspects of any trial is the confrontation of a witness with his own prior inconsistent statement. This is the moment that cross examiners live for—the opportunity to show that the witness's current testimony is contradicted by his own earlier words. Properly conducted, this form of impeachment is not only effective on cross examination; it also can provide extremely fruitful final argument:

"Ladies and Gentlemen, Mr. Kaye is simply unworthy of belief. He couldn't even keep his story straight himself. Right after the accident he told Officer Berkeley that the light was red. By the time of trial it had mysteriously changed to green. The best you can say about Mr. Kaye is that he doesn't know what color the light was."

---

8. Rule 801(d)(1)(A), Federal Rules of Evidence.

Prior inconsistent statements damage a witness's credibility because they demonstrate that the witness has changed his story. Depending upon the nature and seriousness of the change, the witness may be shown to be evasive, opportunistic, error-prone, or even lying. To accomplish any of these goals, of course, it is necessary that the prior statement be clearly inconsistent with the current testimony, and that it be directed to a subject of true significance to the case. Semi-inconsistencies concerning tangential matters will have little or no impact.[9]

There are three steps necessary to impeach a witness with a prior inconsistent statement: (1) recommit; (2) validate; and (3) confront. Each of the three steps will be treated in detail below. Before proceeding to consider the separate elements of impeachment, the following illustration, though somewhat truncated, will place the entire process in perspective.

Recommit:

QUESTION: Mr. Kaye, you testified during your direct examination that the traffic light was green for the southbound traffic?

ANSWER: That is right.

Validate:

QUESTION: Immediately after the accident you spoke to Officer Berkeley?

ANSWER: I did.

QUESTION: You understood that it was important to tell Officer Berkeley exactly what you saw?

ANSWER: Yes.

QUESTION: You spoke to the police officer on the very day of the accident?

ANSWER: Correct.

QUESTION: So obviously the events were fresh in your mind?

ANSWER: Yes.

QUESTION: Since then over a year has gone by?

ANSWER: Yes.

---

9.   For discussion of tactical considerations in impeachment, see Section I B, *supra* at p. 125.

QUESTION: After you spoke to Officer Berkeley, she asked you to sign a statement, didn't she?

ANSWER: Yes, she did.

QUESTION: You read and signed the statement, didn't you?

ANSWER: Yes.

Confront:

QUESTION: Please look at Exhibit Number 39 for identification and tell me if you recognize your signature at the bottom of the page.

ANSWER: I do.

QUESTION: Isn't this the statement that you signed for Officer Berkeley?

ANSWER: It is.

QUESTION: Please read it through and tell me when you have finished.

ANSWER: I am finished.

QUESTION: Doesn't your statement say the following: "At the time of the accident, the traffic light was red for the southbound traffic."

ANSWER: Yes, that is what the statement says.

QUESTION: That is the statement that you signed for Officer Berkeley?

ANSWER: Yes.

This illustration contains all of the elements of impeachment with a prior inconsistent statement. We will discuss each of those elements in considerably more detail below.

A. The Process of Impeachment

1. Recommit the Witness

The first step in impeaching a witness with a prior inconsistent statement is to recommit the witness to his current testimony:

QUESTION: Mr. Kaye, you testified on direct examination that the light was green for the southbound traffic, correct?

The purpose of recommitting the witness is to underscore the gulf between the current testimony and the prior statement. There is no evidentiary requirement that the witness be allowed to repeat the direct testimony. On the other hand, it is difficult to imagine how the two statements could be effectively contrasted without restating the testimony that is about to be impeached.

The traditional method of recommittal is to restate the witness's direct testimony and to ask the witness to reaffirm it. Thus, the witness's current statement is made absolutely clear so that there can be no doubt about its content when it is eventually impeached. You must restate the direct testimony as accurately as possible. Paraphrases or summaries may result in a series of arguments or quibbles with the witness that can detract from the impeachment.

It is equally important, however, for the cross examiner to avoid giving the witness an unbridled opportunity simply to repeat the direct testimony. It is therefore crucial to use short, leading questions during this phase of recommittal. Do not, as in the example that follows, ask a witness to repeat his direct testimony:

QUESTION: Mr. Kaye, what color did you say that the light was for the southbound traffic?

Instead, tell the witness what his previous testimony was:

QUESTION: Mr. Kaye, you testified on direct examination that the light was green for the southbound traffic?

The difference between these two approaches is that the leading question retains control over the witness and prevents the witness from embellishing upon or improving his answer. Moreover, the second approach allows you to use vocal inflection and facial expression to inject a note of doubt as to the accuracy of the testimony that you are repeating. When you ask a witness to repeat his testimony, there is an inevitable suggestion that the testimony is important. On the other hand, when the cross examiner repeats the testimony, it is possible to inject a note of skepticism that will convey just the right measure of doubt.

Depending upon the severity of the impending impeachment, it may be possible to ask the question in a form that is doubtful indeed:

QUESTION: Mr. Kaye, on direct examination you told defendant's counsel that the light was green for the southbound traffic?

Or in extreme cases,

> QUESTION: Mr. Kaye, the story that you told on direct examination was, and I quote, that "the light was green for the southbound traffic"?

2. Validate the Prior Statement

Once the witness has been recommitted, the next step in the impeachment is to validate the prior statement. The initial purpose of validation is to establish that the witness actually made the impeaching statement. Depending upon the circumstances of the case, further validation may be employed to accredit or demonstrate the accuracy of the earlier statement, as opposed to the witness's direct testimony.

a. Basic validation of written statements

The basic format for validating a witness's prior written statement is simply to establish when and how the earlier statement was made:

> QUESTION: Did you give a statement to Officer Berkeley immediately after the accident?

Or,

> QUESTION: Your deposition was taken at my office in March of last year, correct?

Although the basic process of validation is straightforward, care must still be taken to avoid ambiguity. For example, while lawyers understand what is meant by "giving" a statement, to some witnesses that may suggest a level of formality that was not actually present. Remedy this problem by eliciting constituent facts:

> QUESTION: You spoke to Officer Berkeley immediately after the accident?

> QUESTION: Officer Berkeley was taking notes during your conversation?

> QUESTION: At the end of the conversation Officer Berkeley gave you a handwritten statement to read?

> QUESTION: That statement contained a description of what you had seen that day?

> QUESTION: You read the statement?

> QUESTION: After reading it, you signed it?

In the same fashion, the witness's deposition can be validated without the use of compound questions and also in a manner that explains the deposition process to a jury:

QUESTION: You came to my office in March of last year?

QUESTION: There was a court reporter present?

QUESTION: Your attorney was also there?

QUESTION: You were placed under oath?

QUESTION: I asked questions and you gave answers, correct?

QUESTION: While you were being questioned, the court reporter was taking down your testimony?

QUESTION: Several weeks later you were given a copy of the transcript?

QUESTION: You read and signed the transcript?

The final step in basic validation is to show the written statement to the witness in order to have her confirm that it is indeed her own. As with all exhibits, the statement must be marked and shown to opposing counsel.[10] The validation may then proceed as follows:

QUESTION: Let me show you Exhibit 9; please tell me when you are done examining it.

QUESTION: Isn't this the statement that you signed after speaking to Officer Berkeley?

This method can be used to validate business documents, memoranda, signed depositions and interrogatories, letters, and other writings that carry the witness's signature. In the case of an unsigned deposition transcript,[11] other means of final validation will have to be used, such as:

QUESTION: At the end of the deposition you were asked if you wanted to read and sign it, correct?

---

10. Regarding the handling of exhibits, see Chapter 9.

11. Depositions may be recorded by audio or videotape, in which case, even if later transcribed, they may not result in a signed transcript. Rule 30(b)(4), Federal Rules of Civil of Procedure. In any event, the signing of a transcript can be, and frequently is, waived by the witness and the parties. Rule 30(e), Federal Rules of Civil Procedure. Finally, a witness may have failed, neglected, or refused to sign the transcript. In these circumstances the transcript generally can still be used as though it had been signed. *Id.*

QUESTION: And you stated that you would waive your right
to read and sign the deposition transcript?

As we will see below, the witness will later be given an opportunity to admit or deny having given the specific deposition testimony being used for impeachment.

b. Accreditation of prior statements

The fact that a witness has made a prior inconsistent statement is impeaching, but it does not necessarily demonstrate that the witness's current testimony is false or inaccurate. After all, the earlier statement may have been erroneous and the direct testimony correct. It is therefore frequently advantageous to show that the first statement was made under circumstances that make it the more accurate of the two. Since the two statements are by definition mutually exclusive (otherwise there would be no impeachment), there is a natural syllogism: If the earlier statement is true, then the current testimony must be wrong. Thus, the "accreditation" of the prior inconsistent statement can further detract from the witness's credibility.

Of course, no witness is likely to admit that her out-of-court statement was more accurate than her sworn testimony. It is therefore usually necessary to accredit the prior statement through the use of circumstantial evidence. Many indicia of accuracy can be attributed to the witness's earlier statement, including importance, duty, and proximity in time.

i. Accreditation through importance

A witness's earlier statement can be accredited by showing that the witness had an important reason to be accurate when giving it. Assume that the victim of a robbery testified on direct examination that the robber was wearing a Chicago Bulls sweatshirt:

QUESTION: Immediately after the robbery you called the police?

QUESTION: Officer Epstein came to your home?

QUESTION: At that time, the robber was still at large?

QUESTION: Of course, you wanted to help Officer Epstein catch the criminal?

QUESTION: So it was very important that you give Officer Epstein a full and complete description?

QUESTION: A careless or incomplete description would make Officer Epstein's job harder, wouldn't it?

QUESTION: You certainly didn't want anyone else to be robbed?

QUESTION: So you gave Officer Epstein the best information that you could?

QUESTION: Didn't you tell Officer Epstein that the robber was wearing a Philadelphia Flyers shirt?

This form of validation establishes the witness's reason to be as accurate and truthful as possible at the time that the original description was given. The inconsistent later description will therefore be less credible.

ii. Accreditation through duty

A prior statement can also be accredited by showing that the witness was under either a legal or a business duty to be accurate. The most common example of a statement given under a legal duty is prior testimony, either at trial or at deposition. Here is an example of accrediting deposition testimony:

QUESTION: You came to my office in March of last year?

QUESTION: There was a court reporter present?

QUESTION: Your attorney was also there?

QUESTION: You were sworn to tell the truth?

QUESTION: That was the same oath that you took here today?

QUESTION: You did tell the truth at your deposition?

QUESTION: You promised to give accurate answers?

QUESTION: You promised to tell me if there were any questions that you did not understand?

QUESTION: I asked questions and you gave answers, correct?

QUESTION: All of your answers at the deposition were under oath?

An even greater duty can often be shown if the prior testimony occurred in court:

QUESTION: You testified in an earlier hearing in this case?

QUESTION: That testimony took place right here in this courtroom?

QUESTION: Judge Castillo was presiding, just as he is here today?

QUESTION: You were sworn to tell the truth?

QUESTION: You knew that Judge Castillo wanted you to tell the truth?

Business duties may also be used to accredit a prior statement. Assume that a high school student has been charged with a crime and that one of her teachers has testified that the student was present in his class at the time of the offense. The attendance report, however, has the student marked absent.

QUESTION: One of your jobs as a high school teacher is to take attendance?

QUESTION: You fill out an attendance form and send it down to the school office?

QUESTION: Your attendance figures are entered onto a master roll?

QUESTION: And that roll is eventually sent on to the superintendent's office?

QUESTION: Attendance figures are used to determine state funding for your school?

QUESTION: They are also used to determine allocation of resources?

QUESTION: The filing of attendance reports is considered in your own annual review?

QUESTION: The filing of attendance reports is part of your job description?

QUESTION: The filing of attendance reports is included in your union contract?

QUESTION: A teacher could be suspended for serious errors in his attendance reports, isn't that right?

This accreditation creates a circumstantial basis for preferring the information in the attendance report to the witness's later inconsistent testimony.

iii. Accreditation through proximity in time

Because human memory inevitably fades, an earlier statement can be accredited because it was given closer in time to the events being described. This source of accreditation can be employed whether the impeaching material is a written statement, a deposition transcript, or a business document.

The value of proximity in time can be emphasized by pointing out intervening events that may have caused the witness's memory to dim. In the robbery case, assume that Officer Epstein testified on direct testimony that she arrested the defendant, who was wearing a Chicago Bulls sweatshirt. Her police report, however, states that the defendant was wearing a Philadelphia Flyers shirt:

QUESTION: Officer Epstein, immediately after you arrested the defendant you filled out a police report, correct?

QUESTION: You completed your report within an hour of making the arrest?

QUESTION: At the time that you wrote your report, the defendant was still in a holding cell?

QUESTION: The defendant was still available to you, if you had wanted to confirm any of the details of your report?

QUESTION: In any event, when you wrote the report, the events of the arrest were still fresh in your mind?

QUESTION: And now over a year has gone by, correct?

QUESTION: During the intervening year you have made at least fifty additional arrests?

QUESTION: You have had to write reports concerning each of those fifty arrests?

QUESTION: And you always try to write arrest reports as soon as you can, while the events are fresh in your mind, correct?

Proximity in time will only accredit a statement that was given significantly earlier than the trial testimony. You can scarcely use this method to accredit a deposition that was taken two weeks before trial.

3. Confront the Witness with the Prior Statement

The final stage of impeachment is to confront the witness with the prior statement. The purpose of this confrontation is to extract from the witness an admission that the earlier statement was indeed made; recall that it is the fact of the prior inconsistency that is admissible as impeachment. This confrontation need not always be "confrontational." It can be sufficient merely to require the witness to admit making the impeaching statement, particularly when the impeachment is based upon the witness's forgetfulness, confusion, or embellishment. Hostility or accusation should be reserved for those situations when the witness can be shown to be lying or acting out of some other ill motive.

To be effective, the confrontation must be accomplished in a clear and concise manner that leaves the witness no room for evasion or argument. The classic approach is simply to read the witness's own words. In confronting the gas station owner from the fire truck case, the cross examiner will end the impeachment by reading from the witness's statement:

QUESTION: Now just after the accident, didn't you tell the investigator, "I saw the fire truck's lights, and I was surprised that there was no siren"?

ANSWER: Yes, I did.

The confrontation can be enhanced, and counsel can be more assured of agreement from the witness, by directing the witness to read along from the impeaching statement. Give a copy to the witness and proceed:

QUESTION: Please take a look at Exhibit 14; isn't that the statement that you signed?

ANSWER: Yes, it is.

QUESTION: Now please look at the first sentence of the last paragraph and read along with me. Doesn't your statement say, "I saw the fire truck's lights, and I was surprised that there was no siren"?

There are two rules to be followed in confronting a witness with a prior inconsistent statement: (1) Do not ask the witness to read the statement aloud, and (2) do not ask the witness to explain the inconsistency. Both of these rules are applications of basic principles of cross examination.

Asking a witness to read aloud from an impeaching document is the same as asking a wide-open, nonleading question; it surrenders control of the examination to the witness. The cross examiner has no way of knowing how clearly, loudly, or accurately the witness will read the statement. It is not unknown for a witness, either mistakenly or intentionally, to read from an entirely different portion of the document. It is nearly certain that the witness will not read with inflection that emphasizes the inconsistency.

Impeachment will be more effective when the cross examiner reads the impeaching matter in a loud, clear, contrasting tone of voice. While some attorneys believe that they can make a dramatic point by eliciting the words from the witness's own mouth, for most lawyers the risk of this approach will far outweigh the possible gain.

An even riskier way to lose control of the examination is to ask the witness to explain the inconsistency between a prior statement and the trial testimony. There is almost never a reason to ask a witness to explain something on cross examination, and the middle of impeachment is no time to experiment with exceptions to this rule. At best, the witness will take the opportunity to muddle the clarity of the impeachment; at worst, the witness will launch into a facile explanation that undercuts the entire line of examination. A variety of questions might function as invitations to explain. Do not ask a witness to agree that the two statements are inconsistent or different. Except in unusual circumstances, do not ask a witness to concede that she has "changed her story." Questions of this sort are likely only to produce argument, and argument is likely to engender explanation.

Properly conducted, each line of impeachment will conclude on a lawyer's highlight. You will read the impeaching statement in a manner that underscores the inconsistency between the witness's own previous words and the testimony just given in court. There will be no mistaking the implication, and the witness will necessarily concede that the prior statement was indeed given.

THE BASICS		
Impeachment by Prior Inconsistent Statement		

- Recommit the witness
- Validate the prior statement
- Confront the witness with his prior statement

4. Special Cases

a. The denying witness

Some witnesses may deny some or all of the predicates to impeachment. They may refuse to reconfirm their own direct testimony, they may resist validating the circumstances of the impeaching statement, or they may deny ever having made the prior statement. Most of these difficulties can be dealt with through the use of basic cross examination principles.

The simplest problem is the witness who refuses to reaffirm the direct testimony. The easy remedy is to have the court reporter read back the original testimony and then to re-put the question to the witness. In any but the shortest trial, however, it may take the court reporter some time to find the precise place in the transcript where the testimony can be found. Indeed, if the testimony to be impeached occurred on an earlier day of the trial, the court reporter may have changed. Unfortunately, not every trial judge will have the patience to wait while the exact testimony is located.[12]

There are a number of solutions to this problem. The first solution is to avoid the problem entirely by making sure that your notes contain a word-for-word rendition of the testimony that you intend to impeach. That will make it more difficult for the witness to deny your accuracy, and it will also make the judge and jury more inclined to view a denying witness as a quibbler. Second, you can break the question into its constituent parts.

QUESTION:　You testified on direct testimony that you clearly heard the siren of the fire engine, correct?

ANSWER:　I do not believe that I said that.

---

12. This problem is obviated if counsel has been able to afford the purchase of "daily copy" of the transcript. Testimony likely to be impeached can be marked by the court reporter. In that case, you need only turn to the appropriate page and read the testimony to the witness. The court reporter's certification at the end of the transcript is sufficient proof of authenticity.

QUESTION: You did testify about the fire engine?

ANSWER: Yes, I did.

QUESTION: Are you telling me that you did not hear the siren?

ANSWER: No.

QUESTION: All right, so your current testimony is that you did hear the siren?

ANSWER: That is right.

A witness who will not validate the circumstances of a prior statement can be handled in the same manner. Break the cross examination into small, constituent facts that the witness cannot deny. It is also effective to confront the witness with the negative implications of the denial. In the robbery scenario, for example, imagine that the witness will not agree to the importance of the description given to Officer Epstein:

QUESTION: Immediately after the robbery Officer Epstein came to your home?

ANSWER: Yes.

QUESTION: At that time the robber was still at large?

ANSWER: I guess so.

QUESTION: Of course, you wanted to help Officer Epstein catch the criminal?

ANSWER: I just wanted to get my things back.

QUESTION: Well, the robber had your things, didn't he?

ANSWER: Yes.

QUESTION: So it was very important that you give Officer Epstein a full and complete description?

ANSWER: I did the best I could under the circumstances.

QUESTION: You did the best you could to give a good description, right?

ANSWER: Yes.

QUESTION:	You certainly wouldn't have intentionally misled Officer Epstein?
ANSWER:	No, of course not.
QUESTION:	And you wouldn't have left anything out?
ANSWER:	Not on purpose.
QUESTION:	You certainly didn't want anyone else to be robbed?
ANSWER:	Of course not.
QUESTION:	And you were the only one that Officer Epstein could talk to about a description?
ANSWER:	Yes.
QUESTION:	So you gave Officer Epstein the best information that you could, didn't you?
ANSWER:	I did.

Since the true circumstances of the statement contribute to its validity, the witness cannot avoid supplying the cross examiner with the accrediting information.

Finally, some witnesses will disclaim ever having made the impeaching statement:

QUESTION:	Didn't you tell Officer Epstein that the robber was wearing a Philadelphia Flyers shirt?
ANSWER:	No, I never said that.

If the prior statement was in writing, the witness can then be confronted with the impeaching document. Further denial may lead to the admission of the impeaching document into evidence.

A stickier problem arises when the prior statement was oral rather than written. Assume that the robbery victim spoke to Officer Epstein but did not sign a written statement. Even if Officer Epstein included verbatim notes in the police report, that document cannot be used to complete the impeachment because it is not a prior statement of the witness. Thus the officer would have to be called to the stand and examined about the description that the witness gave orally during the investigation:

QUESTION:	Didn't you interview the victim immediately after the robbery?

ANSWER: Yes.

QUESTION: And he told you that the robber was wearing a
             Philadelphia Flyers shirt?

ANSWER: Yes, he did.

Should Officer Epstein also deny the cross examiner's assertion, then the police report can be utilized either for impeachment
or to refresh recollection.

b. The lying witness

Prior inconsistent statements are generally used to cast doubt
on witnesses' credibility but not to accuse them of outright falsehood. It is usually enough to argue that a witness has forgotten the
facts or has exaggerated her testimony, without attempting to paint
her as a liar. Viewed purely as a matter of persuasion, it is easier to
get a jury to accept that a witness is in error than it is to establish
that the witness is guilty of lying. The witness may have a tolerable
explanation for the inconsistency, or she may have other redeeming
personal qualities that can create juror sympathy if he is attacked
too harshly.

Nonetheless, some witnesses are liars. Some of the liars can be
exposed through the use of their own prior inconsistent statements.
Some witnesses even admit having contradicted their testimony by
lying in the past.

Lying witnesses can be confronted directly, since almost nothing will be more damaging to a witness's credibility than proof of
past deceit. Perhaps the most frequently encountered admitted liar
is the criminal defendant who has become the government's witness
against a codefendant:

QUESTION: You testified on direct that you participated in
             the crime with Mr. Camozzi?

ANSWER: I did.

QUESTION: You were arrested for that crime on December
             19?

ANSWER: Yes, I was.

QUESTION: Right after your arrest you were questioned by
             Officer Benno?

ANSWER: That is right.

QUESTION: You told Officer Benno that you didn't know anything about the crime?

ANSWER: Yes, but that was not true.

QUESTION: You claim now that you were lying to Officer Benno?

ANSWER: That is right.

QUESTION: You claim that you lied to Officer Benno in order to keep yourself out of trouble?

ANSWER: Yes.

QUESTION: So you admit to being a liar?

ANSWER: I guess so.

Note that the cross examiner has taken care not to validate the witness's claim that the original denial was a lie. Defense counsel wants the original denial of involvement to be true and the current testimony, which implicates the defendant, to be false. Thus, the cross examiner uses the prior inconsistent statement only to establish the witness's willingness to lie.

5. The Timing of Impeachment

To be used effectively, impeachment should fit into the overall strategy of your cross examination. If you intend to impeach a statement that was made during the witness's direct examination, you can decide where to place it in your own cross examination. Assuming that you have multiple points to make, at what stage of the cross examination should you make use of the prior inconsistent statement?

The basic principles for the organization of cross examination also apply to impeachment. It is usually advisable to maximize cooperation by beginning with inquiries that do not challenge or threaten the witness. For the same reason, initial questions are usually employed to build up your own case, as opposed to controverting the opposition's. These are not hard and fast rules, but they do form a sound framework within which to begin thinking about organization.

Since impeachment can easily become threatening or confrontational it is usually advisable to save it until you have exhausted the favorable information that you intend to obtain from the witness. Only once the witness's cooperation is no longer important to your success should you move on to the past inconsistency.

B. Ethical Concerns

Two primary ethical issues arise in the context of impeaching a witness through the use of a prior inconsistent statement. The first issue, attempting to use the statement for a purpose other than that for which it was admitted, was discussed at some length earlier. It bears repeating.

It is unethical for a lawyer to "allude to any matter which the lawyer does not reasonably believe is...supported by admissible evidence."[13] Once a judge has ruled that certain evidence is admissible only for a limited purpose, it is inadmissible on those issues for which it has been excluded. In light of a limiting instruction, no lawyer can reasonably believe otherwise. Thus, it is unethical to "allude" to a purely impeaching statement as though it had been admitted as substantive evidence.[14]

The second ethical issue in impeachment involves the admonition not to allow a witness to explain the inconsistency. Assuming that there may be a perfectly reasonable explanation for the discrepancy between two statements, is it ethical to prevent the witness from explaining?

The answer lies in the fact that it is not truly possible for a cross examiner to prevent a witness from providing an explanation. It will always be possible for opposing counsel to ask the witness to elaborate during redirect examination. No admissible evidence can ultimately be excluded as the result of cross examination tactics. Thus, the most that the cross examiner can accomplish will be to prevent the witness from explaining an inconsistency during cross examination. As an advocate it is the cross examiner's task to present the evidence that is favorable to her client; the very purpose of redirect is to allow the other side to fill in gaps, remedy errors, and correct misperceptions. Leaving potential explanations to redirect is perfectly permissible under the adversary system.

An explanation would carry more weight if it could be given in the midst of cross examination. It will necessarily seem somewhat hollow and apologetic occurring after the fact during redirect. That again is a consequence of advocacy. Recall that the witness had an opportunity during direct examination to offer the earlier statement and explain its seeming inconsistency with current testimony. Having passed up the chance to offer that testimony during direct examination, a witness can hardly complain that it is unethical for the cross examiner not to allow it during cross.

---

13. Rule 3.4(e), Model Rules of Professional Conduct.

14. As has been noted previously, many prior statements may be admitted both for impeachment and as substantive evidence.

III. OTHER PRIOR INCONSISTENCIES

In addition to prior inconsistent statements, witnesses may also be impeached through the use of prior omissions or silence, as well as on the basis of prior inconsistent actions.

A. Impeachment by Omission or Silence

Impeachment by omission generally follows the same theory as impeachment with a prior inconsistent statement. The witness's current testimony is rendered less credible because when she told the same story earlier it did not contain facts that she now claims are true. In essence, the impeachment is saying, "Do not believe this witness because she is adding facts to her story." Or, in other words, "If those things are true, why didn't you say them before?"

To be impeaching, the witness's prior omission must be inconsistent with the current testimony. A prior omission is not impeaching, or even admissible, if it occurred in circumstances that do not render it incompatible with the witness's testimony from the stand. The following example, as should be obvious, does not constitute impeachment by omission:

QUESTION: You have testified today that the fire engine was sounding its siren, correct?

ANSWER: Yes.

QUESTION: You took a final examination in your Property class last week, didn't you?

ANSWER: Yes, I did.

QUESTION: Nowhere on your final exam did you write that you heard a fire engine's siren, did you?

The cross examination misses the mark because the omission is entirely consistent with the witness's testimony about the siren. There was no reason for the witness to include the facts of the accident on a final examination.

Impeachment by omission, then, rests upon the establishment of circumstances that create a dissonance between the witness's previous silence and the story that is now being told. The stronger the dissonance, the more effective the impeachment.

What circumstances create the necessary discontinuity between omission and testimony? We can begin by looking at opportunity, duty, and natural inclination.

1. Opportunity

The first requirement is opportunity. A witness cannot be impeached by virtue of previous silence if she was not given the opportunity to speak. Moreover, this must include the opportunity to provide the information that is now being challenged at trial. Thus, a witness cannot be impeached on the basis of omission at a deposition unless a question was asked that reasonably called for that information. The following example illustrates the minimum necessary for impeachment:[15]

QUESTION: You have testified that you heard the fire truck siren?

ANSWER: Yes.

QUESTION: During your deposition I asked you this question: "After you first saw the fire truck, what else did you see or hear?"

ANSWER: That is right.

QUESTION: And you answered, "I heard the screech of brakes and I saw the BMW slam into the back of the other car."

ANSWER: I believe that was my testimony.

The witness was impeached, if not devastated, by the omission of the sound of the siren in response to a question that reasonably called for it. In contrast, the following example is not impeaching:

QUESTION: During your entire deposition you never once mentioned hearing the fire truck's siren, did you?

ANSWER: I do not believe that anyone asked me about what I heard.

Proof of opportunity, however, is not always sufficient to allow impeachment by omission. A witness who neglects the opportunity to provide information may have misunderstood the question or may have been temporarily forgetful or confused. The cross examiner must usually go further to show that the absent statement would

---

15. For the sake of brevity, most of the buildup for the use of the deposition has been omitted.

have been made if it had been true. This can be shown by virtue of either duty or natural inclination.

2. Duty

A witness who was under a duty to provide or record information cannot easily be forgiven its absence. Under these circumstances the natural conclusion to be drawn from the omission of a fact is that the fact did not occur.

Duty is easily established when the witness previously testified under oath. Duty can also be shown in a wide variety of other circumstances. A prime example is the police report. Assume that the officer in the scenario below arrested the defendant on a charge of narcotics possession; on direct examination the officer testified that the defendant also vigorously resisted arrest:

QUESTION:	Officer, immediately after the arrest you filled out a police report, correct?
QUESTION:	It is one of your official duties to fill out such a report?
QUESTION:	In fact, police reports are required by both municipal statute and state law, isn't that right?
QUESTION:	There are also departmental regulations on the manner in which the reports are to be filled out?
QUESTION:	Doesn't one of those regulations state, quote, "Every felony arrest report must contain all information relevant to the apprehension and prosecution of the offender"?
QUESTION:	So it is your duty to include in your report "all information relevant to the apprehension and prosecution of the offender," right?
QUESTION:	On the day that you arrested the defendant, you certainly wanted to do your duty?
QUESTION:	Now, you testified here today that the defendant resisted your arrest, and even took a swing at you?
ANSWER:	Yes, that is right.
QUESTION:	Resisting a police officer is a crime, isn't it?

ANSWER: Yes, it is.

QUESTION: And trying to hit a police officer can surely lead to "prosecution of the offender," can't it?

ANSWER: It can.

QUESTION: Please look at your police report, which has been marked as Exhibit 6. Read it through carefully, and tell me when you are finished.

ANSWER: I am done reading.

QUESTION: Isn't this the report that you were under a duty to complete?

ANSWER: Yes.

QUESTION: A duty imposed both by law and by departmental regulations?

ANSWER: Yes.

QUESTION: There is not a single word in your report about the defendant resisting arrest?

ANSWER: No.

QUESTION: And there is not a single word in your official report about the defendant taking a swing at you, is there?

ANSWER: No, there is not.

Business duty can also be used as a predicate to impeachment by omission. It can be shown that a witness did not include facts in a docket entry, a sales record, a service report, a transmittal letter, a bill of lading, an invoice, or any of numerous other documents that are expected to contain complete records of transactions.

3. Natural Inclination

Even if no duty can be established, impeachment by omission can still be accomplished. Previous silence can be inconsistent with a current statement if the earlier omission occurred in circumstances where the witness should have been naturally inclined to speak. Imagine that a witness testified at trial that he had seen several children break into a neighbor's garage and steal a bicycle. It would impeach the witness to point out that he had never mentioned this occurrence to either the neighbor or to the children's parents, since a natural inclination is to report such matters to the persons affected. In other words, "If you really saw the kids steal a bicycle, why didn't you say anything at the time?" While it is true that the witness was under no legal or business duty to alert his neighbor to the theft, it is nonetheless a reasonable inference that he would have told his neighbor if the theft had really happened. It is a natural inclination to help your friends and neighbors.

Natural inclination can be found in a wide variety of circumstances and relationships. A crime victim should be naturally inclined to give the police a complete description of the criminal. Parents should be naturally inclined to give safety warnings to their children. Employees should be naturally inclined to complain about adverse working conditions to their employers. The key to this form of impeachment by omission is accreditation of the circumstances that give rise to the inclination to speak.

An example can be found in "missing complaint" situations. Assume that the tenant in a commercial lease case seeks to break a tenancy on the ground that the building did not provide adequate security. The plaintiff's testimony concerning poor security could be impeached if there had been no previous complaints about conditions:

QUESTION: You testified on direct that the security situation in the building makes it impossible for you to do business there?

ANSWER: That is absolutely correct.

QUESTION: That is because security is very important to you and your customers, right?

ANSWER: Yes, it obviously is.

QUESTION: You have never written a letter to building management complaining about security, have you?

ANSWER: No.

QUESTION: You never requested a meeting to discuss secu-
               rity, did you?

ANSWER: Well, no.

QUESTION: You paid your rent by check each month?

ANSWER: Yes.

QUESTION: But you never sent a note complaining about
               security along with the rent check, did you?

ANSWER: No, we didn't.

The absence of complaints is impeaching because a business
owner would naturally be inclined to complain about something so
important to business. Since there were no complaints, the logic of
the impeachment is that conditions could not have been so bad as
the plaintiff is now claiming.

B.   Prior Inconsistent Actions

Finally, a witness may be impeached on the basis of prior inconsistent actions. The witness's current testimony is rendered less
credible by pointing out that she did not act in conformity with her
own story on some previous occasion: "If what you are saying now is
true, why did you act inconsistently in the past?"

Unlike impeachment through prior inconsistent statements
or omissions, no elaborate setup is necessary for the use of prior
inconsistent actions. It is sufficient simply to put the questions to
the witness. Return to the commercial lease case from the preceding section and assume that the business owner testified about the
poor security in the building. With no further elaboration, the cross
examiner may proceed as follows:

QUESTION: Your business hours are 9:00 a.m. to 10:00
               p.m.?

QUESTION: You have not shortened your hours?

QUESTION: You have not installed closed circuit television
               cameras?

QUESTION: You have not put in additional lighting?

QUESTION: You have allowed your own teenage children
               to work the evening shift?

Each of these instances of the witness's own conduct, if admitted or otherwise proven, detracts from the credibility of the plaintiff's testimony that security conditions were intolerable.

The impeachment might be enhanced further still through the use of a setup that takes advantage of the principle of apposition:

QUESTION: You testified on direct examination that security conditions are intolerable?

ANSWER: That is right.

QUESTION: You claim to be in fear for your customers' safety?

ANSWER: Absolutely.

QUESTION: You keep your store open until 10:00 p.m.?

ANSWER: Yes.

QUESTION: And security conditions are so bad that you have had your own teenage children work the evening shift?

The witness's claim of danger is flatly inconsistent with his actions in allowing his children to work in the store at night. Note, however, that the use of sarcasm is often risky. Many lawyers would prefer simply to make this point during final argument.

IV. CHARACTER AND "CHARACTERISTIC" IMPEACHMENT

Character impeachment refers to the use of some inherent trait or particular characteristic of the witness, essentially unrelated to the case at hand, to render the testimony less credible. The thrust of the impeachment is to show that the witness, for some demonstrable reason, is simply not trustworthy.

The most common forms of characteristic impeachment include conviction of a crime, defect in memory or perception, and past untruthfulness.

A. Conviction of a Crime

A witness may be impeached on the basis of his or her past conviction of certain crimes. While the specifics vary from state to state, under the Federal Rules of Evidence a conviction is admissible for impeachment only if the crime

(1) was punishable by death or imprisonment in excess of one year under the law under which the witness was convicted, and ... the court determines that the probative value of admitting this evidence outweighs its prejudicial effect to the accused, or (2) involved dishonesty or false statement, regardless of the punishment.[16]

In addition, the Federal Rules provide that convictions generally may not be used if they are more than ten years old[17] and that juvenile adjudications are inadmissible under most circumstances.[18]

The theory behind impeachment on the basis of conviction of a crime is that criminals are less trustworthy than other witnesses. Thus, the characteristic of having been convicted of a qualifying crime may be admissible to discredit a witness, without regard to the issues in the particular case. This makes great sense with regard to crimes such as perjury, forgery, and theft by deception, but it is somewhat less compelling concerning crimes such as assault or criminal damage to property. Why would a six-year-old conviction for, say, vandalism have any bearing on a witness's credibility in a current contract dispute? It is for this reason that Federal Rule 609(a)(1) provides that before allowing the impeachment to proceed, the court must determine whether the probative value of admitting the evidence outweighs its prejudicial effect. Note, however, that the balancing test is not required if the impeaching crime involved dishonesty or false statement.

Once it has been determined that a conviction can be used for impeachment, relatively little technique is involved in the cross examination:

QUESTION: Isn't it true, Ms. Roth, that you were once convicted of the crime of aggravated battery?

ANSWER: Yes.

QUESTION: You were convicted on October 12, 1992, correct?

ANSWER: Yes.

QUESTION: That was a felony?

---

16. Rule 609(a), Federal Rules of Evidence.

17. Specifically, evidence of a conviction under this rule is not admissible if a period of more than ten years has elapsed since the date of the conviction or of the release of the witness, whichever is the later date, unless the court determines, in the interests of justice, that the probative value of the conviction substantially outweighs its prejudicial effect. Rule 609(b), Federal Rules of Evidence.

18. See Rule 609(d), Federal Rules of Evidence.

ANSWER: It was.

QUESTION: And you were sentenced to two years of proba-
             tion?

ANSWER: I was.

QUESTION: That conviction took place in this very court-
             house?

ANSWER: It did.

As a rule, the impeachment is limited to the details of the conviction; the facts and circumstances of the crime are generally inadmissible.[19] Because of this, the importance of the impeachment can
easily be lost if the cross examiner collapses it all into one or two
questions. It is far more effective to draw out the impeaching information, as in the above example, into a series of short questions,
each of which deals with a single fact. Repetition of terms such as
"crime," "conviction," and even "convicted felon" will add weight to
the impeachment.

If the witness denies having been convicted, the cross examiner must be able to complete the impeachment by introducing a
certified copy of the judgment or order of conviction.

B.   Past Untruthfulness and Other Bad Acts

We have discussed the rules governing impeachment on the
basis of a criminal conviction. What about a witness's bad acts that
were not the subject of a conviction? A witness who has lied in the
past, whether or not prosecuted and whether or not under oath, may
well be likely to lie during current testimony. On the other hand,
past misconduct of some sort is a near universal human condition,
and trials could easily become bogged down if lawyers are allowed
free rein to cross examine witnesses on any and all of their old
misdeeds.

The Federal Rules of Evidence strike a balance by allowing the
impeachment of witnesses on the basis of specific instances of past
misconduct, apart from criminal convictions, only if they are probative of untruthfulness. Thus, a witness can be impeached with evidence that he has lied on a specific previous occasion, but not on the
basis of previous violence. Moreover, the trial judge has discretion
to exclude evidence even of past untruthfulness. Finally, incidents of

---

19. The facts and details of the crime may become admissible, however, if the witness or opposing counsel "opens the door."

prior untruthfulness may not be proven by extrinsic evidence.[20] The cross examiner is stuck with the witness's answer.

Impeachment on the basis of past untruthfulness is therefore a very tricky matter. You must be certain that the witness will "own up" to the charge since you will be unable to prove it otherwise.

THE BASICS

Character Impeachment	
Conviction of a crime	• Must have been punishable by more than one year of imprisonment, <u>or</u> • Must have involved dishonesty or false statement, <u>and</u> • Must usually be within the past ten years, <u>and</u> • Probative value must outweigh prejudicial effect
Past "bad acts"	• Must be probative of untruthfulness, <u>and</u> • Probative value must outweigh prejudicial effect, <u>but</u> • May not be proven by extrinsic evidence

C. Impaired Perception or Recollection

A witness can also be impeached on the basis of inability to perceive or recall events.

Perception can be adversely affected by a wide variety of circumstances. The witness may have been distracted at the time of the events, or his vision may have been obscured. The witness may have been sleepy, frightened, or intoxicated. The witness may have poor eyesight or may suffer from some other sensory deficit. Any of these, or similar, facts can be used to impeach the credibility of a witness's testimony.

As with so much else in cross examination, this form of impeachment is usually most effective when counsel refrains from asking the ultimate question. Assume, for example, that a witness in a burglary case identified the defendant during direct examination. The cross examiner is primed for impeachment, knowing that the witness had just awakened from a nap when he observed the burglar. The focus of the impeachment will be on the witness's diminished ability to perceive:

QUESTION: The burglary occurred in the middle of the afternoon?

ANSWER: Yes.

---

20. Rule 608(b), Federal Rules of Evidence.

QUESTION: You had been taking a nap on the couch?

ANSWER: Yes.

QUESTION: It was light outside?

ANSWER: It was.

QUESTION: But you were still able to sleep, correct?

ANSWER: Yes.

QUESTION: Then you heard a sound?

ANSWER: I did.

QUESTION: It must have taken a moment to awaken you?

ANSWER: I suppose so.

QUESTION: You couldn't have known right away where the sound was coming from?

ANSWER: No, I guess not.

QUESTION: So you had to orient yourself?

ANSWER: Yes.

QUESTION: Then you sat up?

ANSWER: I did.

QUESTION: Then you looked around?

ANSWER: That's right.

QUESTION: You saw someone by the window?

ANSWER: Right.

QUESTION: That must have come as quite a shock?

ANSWER: It certainly did.

QUESTION: The man had his back to the window?

ANSWER: Yes.

QUESTION: And the light was coming through the window?

ANSWER: Yes, it must have been.

At this point the cross examiner will stop. The constituent facts of the impeachment have been established; the witness's perception was obviously impeded. Any further questioning is likely to be taken by the witness as an invitation to explain, thus threatening counsel's control of the examination. The argument is certainly clear: The witness was groggy, surprised, and a little frightened; the burglar's face was in a shadow; the identification is therefore suspect. The point is to save these conclusions for final argument rather than to attempt to extract them directly from the witness.

The concept of impaired perception relates to the witness's ability to perceive at the time of the original events. In contrast, the concept of impaired recollection involves the occurrence of intervening events damaging to the witness's recall. Such events can be as mundane as the mere passage of time or as dramatic as a head injury.

V. "CASE DATA" IMPEACHMENT

Some facts are impeaching only within the circumstances of a particular case. They would be innocuous, or perhaps even helpful, in any other context. The most common forms of case data impeachment are based on the witness's personal interest, motive, and bias or prejudice.

A. Personal Interest

A witness who is personally interested in the outcome of a case may be inclined to testify with less than absolute candor. Whether consciously or subconsciously, it is a well-recognized human tendency to shape one's recollection in the direction of the desired outcome.

Impeachment on the basis of personal interest is therefore geared to take advantage of this phenomenon by pointing out just how the witness stands to gain or lose as a consequence of the resolution of the case. The technique is common in both civil and criminal cases, and it may be applied to both party and nonparty witnesses.

In civil matters the parties often stand to receive (or lose) great amounts of money depending upon the verdict in the case. As with the criminal defendant, the interest of both civil plaintiffs and defendants is generally apparent. Moreover, since there is always a plaintiff and defendant in each case, this form of interest will generally cancel itself out. The financial interest of nonparty witnesses, however, may not be quite so obvious and will therefore frequently be the target of impeachment.

In the following example assume that the witness has been called to the stand on behalf of the plaintiff in a will contest. The witness testified on direct that the testator did not appear to be "of sound mind" at the time that the challenged will was executed:

QUESTION: You are not a party to this case, are you?

ANSWER: I am not.

QUESTION: But you are the plaintiff's business partner?

ANSWER: Yes, I am.

QUESTION: You will receive no funds directly if the will is thrown out?

ANSWER: Right. I am not involved at all.

QUESTION: But your business partner is involved?

ANSWER: Yes, I suppose so.

QUESTION: He will become the sole beneficiary if the will is found invalid?

ANSWER: I believe that is true.

QUESTION: Your business showed a large loss last year, didn't it?

ANSWER: Yes, we did.

QUESTION: You lost over $1,000,000, didn't you?

ANSWER: Something like that.

QUESTION: You have loaned over $400,000 to the business yourself, haven't you?

ANSWER: I have.

QUESTION: You could lose that money if the business enters bankruptcy?

ANSWER: Yes.

QUESTION: Your business needs an infusion of capital?

ANSWER: We do.

QUESTION: And if that doesn't come from someone else, it might have to come from you?

ANSWER: I suppose that is right.

QUESTION: If this will is upheld, your business partner will not receive a penny?

ANSWER: I guess that is right.

QUESTION: And you have testified that the testator was not of sound mind when she left her estate to someone other than your business partner?

Two things about this example are noteworthy. First, the value of the impeaching fact is strictly dependent upon the circumstances of this case. This impeachment would be impossible, even laughable, if it were attempted in a case that did not involve this unique confluence of events: challenged will, business partner, failing company, and personal loan. Unlike "characteristic" impeachment, which can be used in virtually any matter, "case data" impeachment is limited to its particular circumstances.

This observation leads to the second point. Case data impeachment is most valuable when the cross examiner takes full advantage of the technique of apposition. The impeaching facts have the most weight when they are developed in conjunction with the other "case data" that explain their significance. The above witness's status as the plaintiff's business partner might be viewed as mildly impeaching, standing alone. The witness's credibility is eroded far more significantly, however, when the additional facts—failing business, cash shortage, and outstanding personal loan—are elicited in close succession.

B. Motive

A witness's testimony may be affected by a motive other than financial interest. The witness may have a professional stake in the issues being litigated or may have some other reason to prefer one outcome to another. In the will contest from the previous section, imagine that the lawyer who drew the will was called to the stand to testify with regard to its validity:

QUESTION: You are the lawyer who drew the will?

ANSWER: Yes.

QUESTION: You also arranged for it to be executed?

ANSWER: I did.

QUESTION: You were there at the signing?

ANSWER:	I was.
QUESTION:	You called your secretary and receptionist into your office to act as witnesses?
ANSWER:	That is correct.
QUESTION:	You could not have done those things if the testator had been incompetent?
ANSWER:	Of course not.
QUESTION:	You could not arrange for an incompetent person to execute a will?
ANSWER:	No, I couldn't.
QUESTION:	It would be unprofessional for you not to notice a person's obvious lack of mental faculties?
ANSWER:	It would be a mistake.
QUESTION:	So the challenge to this will is also a challenge to your own professional observations?
ANSWER:	I suppose you could put it that way.
QUESTION:	And, of course, your testimony today is that the testator was perfectly lucid at all times?

This witness may be inclined to testify in such a way as to vindicate her earlier judgment. While she has no direct interest in the distribution of the estate, she is still impeachable on the basis of motive. Other commonly encountered motives include emotional attachment, revenge, chauvinism, preexisting belief, or adherence to a school of thought.[21] In all cases, apposition is the key.

C. Bias or Prejudice

Bias and prejudice generally refer to a witness's relationship to one of the parties. A witness may be well-disposed, or ill-inclined, toward either the plaintiff or the defendant. Sadly, some witnesses harbor prejudices against entire groups of people.

Bias in favor of a party is often the consequence of friendship or affinity:

QUESTION: You are the defendant's younger brother?

---

21. This motive is most frequently used to impeach expert witnesses.

QUESTION:	You grew up together?
QUESTION:	You have helped each other out throughout your lives?
QUESTION:	Now your brother is charged with a crime?
QUESTION:	He is in trouble?
QUESTION:	He needs help?
QUESTION:	And you are here to testify?

Nothing is more case-specific than this sort of impeachment. It has forensic value if and only if the witness's brother is the defendant in the case. Nothing can be presumed about case data; research and exploration are always required. When it comes to bias and prejudice, even close familial relationships have the potential to cut both ways:

QUESTION:	You are the defendant's younger brother?
QUESTION:	You grew up together?
QUESTION:	He was always beating you up?
QUESTION:	He seemed to have all of life's advantages?
QUESTION:	It was hard to follow in his successful footsteps?
QUESTION:	Everyone was always comparing you to him?
QUESTION:	He teased you and called you names?
QUESTION:	You were always resentful of him?
QUESTION:	You swore that you would get even?
QUESTION:	Now your older brother is charged with a crime?
QUESTION:	After all these years, his success seems to have run out?
QUESTION:	And you have come to court today to testify against him?

As with all case data impeachment, the establishment of bias or prejudice requires careful development through the use of small, individual facts. This sort of impeachment is made doubly difficult by the fact that it is hard to avoid "telegraphing" your strategy. Once the witness realizes that you intend to impugn his objectivity, he will very naturally attempt to avoid admitting the component facts of your impeachment. In the fraternal scenario above, for example, the typical witness would do everything possible to deny the existence of lifelong resentment of his older brother. Thus, the cross examiner would not risk this line of examination unless the witness's grudge could be sufficiently documented through letters, prior statements, or the testimony of other witnesses.

Witnesses are similarly loath to admit to racial, ethnic, or other group prejudices. Effective impeachment on this basis therefore depends upon the initial elicitation of incontrovertible facts such as prior statements, organizational memberships, or other provable past actions.

— CHAPTER SIX —
Redirect Examination and Rehabilitation

I.   PURPOSE OF REDIRECT

Redirect examination, which allows counsel an opportunity to respond to the cross examination, may be used for a number of purposes. The witness may be asked to explain points that were explored during the cross, to untangle seeming inconsistencies, to correct errors or misstatements, or to rebut new charges or inferences. In other words, the purpose of redirect is to minimize or undo the damage, if any, that was effected during the cross examination.

Cross examiners are universally cautioned not to ask "one question too many." In a nutshell, redirect is the time to ask exactly those additional questions that the cross examiner purposefully left out.

II.   LAW AND PROCEDURE

A.   Scope

Because redirect is allowed for counteracting or responding to the cross examination, the material that can be covered on redirect is technically limited to the scope of the cross. The interpretation of this rule varies from court to court; some are quite strict and others are fairly lenient. Almost all courts, however, insist that counsel is not free to introduce a wholly new matter on redirect. The redirect must always have some reasonable relationship to the cross examination.

The scope rule adds considerable hazard to the tactic of "sandbagging," or withholding crucial evidence from the direct examination in order to raise it following the cross. Counsel who reserves an important item of testimony from direct runs the risk that the issue will not be covered on cross and that it will therefore be excluded from redirect as well. Accordingly, there is little to be gained and much to lose by sandbagging, especially since redirect examination is usually followed by recross. Even when successful in deferring certain testimony to redirect, counsel cannot succeed in insulating the witness from recross examination.

There is, however, one situation in which reserving evidence until redirect may be helpful. A witness may have an effective response to a potential line of cross examination. Counsel, however, may have no way of knowing whether the cross examiner will pursue those particular issues. Thus, it can be prudent to withhold the explanation until redirect rather than to insert it defensively during the main direct.[1]

B. Rules of Evidence

All of the rules of direct examination apply equally to redirect examination. Leading questions are prohibited, witnesses may not testify in narrative form, testimony must come from personal knowledge, lay opinions are limited to sensory perceptions, and the proper foundation must be laid to refresh recollection.

Many courts, however, allow a certain amount of latitude during redirect, especially with regard to leading questions. Even without indulgence, leading questions are always permissible to direct the witness's attention or to introduce an area of questioning. A certain amount of leading may be necessary on redirect in order to focus the examination on the segment of the cross examination that you wish to explain or rebut.

C. Recross Examination and Additional Redirect

Redirect examination may be followed by recross, which may be followed by additional redirect, and so on into the night. Each additional examination is limited to the scope of the one that immediately preceded it. Thus, recross is restricted to the scope of the redirect and a second redirect would be confined to the scope of the recross. There is no right to continue an infinite regression of successive "re-examinations." Rather, it is within the court's discretion to allow or deny a request for, say, re-recross. Most judges routinely allow at least one redirect and one recross.

D. Reopening Direct Examination

Reopening direct examination is an alternative to redirect. It can be employed where counsel needs to pursue a line of questioning that is beyond the scope of the cross examination. It is strictly within the court's discretion to allow counsel to reopen a direct examination.

---

1. Situations that may call for this approach are addressed below in Section III, at p. 161.

III. PLANNED REDIRECT

Most redirect examinations cannot be thoroughly planned, since each must be closely responsive to the preceding cross examination. Nonetheless, it is possible to anticipate that certain areas will have to be covered on redirect and to prepare accordingly.

It is not always possible to know which lines of cross examination will actually be pursued. Counsel would not want to use the direct examination to explain away a cross that might never materialize. Thus, an explanation may be best reserved for redirect in the event that the cross examination ultimately probes that particular area. It is both possible and necessary to plan for such contingencies.

For example, a witness may have given a prior statement that is arguably impeaching. While there may be a perfectly reasonable response to any apparent inconsistency, it would undermine the witness to bring up the earlier statement during the direct. An explanation would only make sense once the cross examiner actually effected the impeachment. Consequently, the best approach in this situation is probably to defer the explanation until the redirect.

A similar situation arises where there is credible objection to the anticipated cross examination. A witness's past criminal act, for example, might be excludable.[2] The direct examiner certainly would not want to bring up a prior crime or other bad act, even to justify the circumstances, without first determining whether an objection to the cross examination will be sustained. Again, the wisest approach may be to hold the explanation for redirect.

In both of these situations, and others like them, it is possible to plan a segment of the redirect—including preparation of the witness—just as one would plan a direct examination. Note, however, that both examples involve only rejoinders to potential cross examination. The technique of withholding testimony until redirect is not recommended for affirmative evidence or elements of your case.

IV. WAIVING REDIRECT

Redirect examination is not always necessary. As with all witness examinations, redirect should only be pursued if it will contribute to your theory of the case.

There is no need to ask additional questions if the witness was not appreciably hurt by the cross examination. Additionally, some damage cannot be repaired; it is a mistake to engage in redirect

2. Rule 404(b), Federal Rules of Evidence.

examination if the situation cannot be improved. The worst miscalculation, however, is to surprise the witness with a redirect question. Do not ask for an explanation unless you are certain that the witness has one.

As a further hazard, redirect exposes the witness to recross. If redirect is waived there can be no additional cross examination. Even a single question on redirect, however, can subject the witness to significant further cross examination, so long as it stays within the applicable scope.

Finally, an unnecessary redirect risks repeating, and therefore reemphasizing, the cross examination. It can also trivialize the effect of the direct by rehashing minor points.

V. CONDUCTING REDIRECT

Content is the most important aspect of redirect examination. The redirect should concentrate on a few significant points that definitely can be developed. As noted above, these can typically include explanations, clarifications, or responses.

A. Explanations

Explanations are best obtained by asking for them. Focus the witness's attention on the pertinent area of the cross examination and then simply ask her to proceed:

QUESTION: Defense counsel pointed out that you did not visit your doctor immediately following your camping trip at Eagle River Falls. Why didn't you go to the doctor right away?

This approach can also be used to bring out clarifying facts, made relevant by the cross examination:

QUESTION: How soon after the camping trip did you visit the doctor?

A witness may have been frustrated by the control exerted by the cross examiner. If the level of control seemed unfair or unjustified, this can be pointed out during the redirect. Consider:

QUESTION: Defense counsel seemed very concerned that you did not go to the doctor immediately after your camping trip, but she didn't ask you for an explanation. Would you like to explain?

Or,

    QUESTION: I noticed that defense counsel cut you off when you tried to continue your answer about the camping trip. What was it that you wanted to say?

Or,

    QUESTION: There was a lot of cross examination about your camping trip, but counsel didn't ask you anything about what your doctor eventually prescribed for you. What treatment did you get?

While the introductions in the above examples are arguably leading, they are probably permissible efforts to direct the witness's attention. Nonetheless, preambles of this sort should not be overused. They are likely to be effective only where the cross examination truly was overbearing or oppressive.

B. Rehabilitation

Redirect can be used specifically for rehabilitation of a witness who has been impeached with a prior inconsistent statement.

1. Technique

The technique for rehabilitation is similar to that used for any other explanation. Direct the witness's attention to the supposed impeachment and request a clarification. It may be that the alleged inconsistency can be easily resolved or that the earlier statement was the product of a misunderstanding or misinterpretation. Whatever the explanation, it is important to conclude the rehabilitation with an affirmative statement of the witness's current testimony.

In the following example the plaintiff in the fire truck case testified on direct examination that the fire engine had been sounding its siren and flashing its lights. On cross examination she was impeached with her deposition in which she stated that the fire truck "had not been using all of its warning devices." She might be rehabilitated on redirect as follows:

    QUESTION: In your deposition you said that the fire truck was not using all of its warning signals. Can you explain how that fits in with your testimony today about the lights and the siren?

    ANSWER: When I answered the deposition question I was thinking about the horn as an additional

> warning signal, and as far as I can recall the fire truck was not sounding its horn.

QUESTION: Which warning devices was the fire truck using?

ANSWER: It was definitely sounding its siren and flashing all of its red lights.

2. Prior Consistent Statements

A witness can also be rehabilitated through the introduction of a prior consistent statement. Although a witness's own previous out-of-court account would ordinarily be hearsay, a prior consistent statement is admissible to "rebut an express or implied charge…of recent fabrication or improper influence or motive."[3]

Accordingly, once the cross examiner suggests that the witness has changed her story, the direct examiner may show that the witness's testimony is consistent with an earlier report or other statement. Note that in some jurisdictions a prior consistent statement is admissible only if it predates the inconsistent statement used for impeachment.

THE BASICS	Redirect Examination	Recross Examination
Purpose:	Offering explanations for, clarifications of, or responses to, evidence brought out on cross examination.	Discrediting the explanation, clarification, or response of a witness offered on redirect examination.
Evidentiary Rules:	Follow the same rules of evidence that apply to direct. All redirect questions must be within the scope of the cross.	Follow the same rules of evidence that apply to cross. All recross questions must be within the scope of the redirect.
Length:	Ideally, five questions or fewer.	The shorter the better, or none at all.

---

3. Rule 801(d)(1)(B), Federal Rules of Evidence.

— CHAPTER SEVEN —
Expert Testimony

I.   INTRODUCTION

Most witnesses are called to the stand because they have seen, heard, or done something relevant to the issues in the case. Such persons are often referred to as ordinary witnesses, lay witnesses, or percipient witnesses. Whatever the term used, the testimony of witnesses is generally limited to those things they have directly observed or experienced, as well as reasonable conclusions that can be drawn on the basis of their sensory perceptions. In short, lay witnesses must testify from personal knowledge,[1] and they may not offer opinions.

Expert witnesses comprise an entirely different category. An expert witness is not limited to personal knowledge and may base her testimony on information that was gathered solely for the purpose of testifying in the litigation. Moreover, under the proper circumstances an expert witness may offer an opinion that goes well beyond her direct sensory impressions. An expert may opine on the cause or consequences of occurrences, interpret the actions of other persons, draw conclusions on the basis of circumstances, comment on the likelihood of events, and even state her beliefs regarding such seemingly nonfactual issues as fault, damage, negligence, avoidability, and the like.

Expert witnesses may be helpful in a wide variety of cases. Experts can be used in commercial cases to interpret complex financial data, in tort cases to explain the nature of injuries, or in criminal cases to translate underworld slang into everyday language. Properly qualified, an expert can be asked to peer into the past, as when an accident reconstructionist re-creates the scene of an automobile collision. Other experts may predict the future, as when an economist projects the expected life earnings of the deceased in a wrongful death case. In some cases expert testimony is required as a matter

---

1.   See Chapter 9, Section II A, *infra* at p. 247 concerning the requirement of personal knowledge.

of law. In legal or medical malpractice cases, for example, it is usually necessary to call an expert witness in order to establish the relevant standard of care; in narcotics cases the prosecution usually must call a chemist or other expert to prove that the substance in question is actually an illegal drug.

Given the extraordinarily broad scope of expert testimony, and its extreme potential for influencing the judgment of the trier of fact, certain rules have developed regarding the permissible use, extent, and nature of expert testimony.

II. STANDARDS FOR EXPERT TESTIMONY

A. Areas of Expertise

Rule 702 of the Federal Rules of Evidence provides that expert opinions may be admissible where the expert's "scientific, technical, or other specialized knowledge will assist the trier of fact to understand the evidence or to determine a fact in issue." Thus, there are two threshold questions: Does the witness possess sufficient scientific, technical, or other specialized knowledge? If so, will that knowledge be helpful to the trier of fact?

In a recent series of cases the United States Supreme Court held that a trial judge must also make a preliminary assessment of the validity of the reasoning and methods that support proffered expert testimony.[2] The Federal Rules of Evidence subsequently codified that requirement, specifying that opinion testimony is admissible only if (1) the testimony is based upon sufficient facts or data, (2) the testimony is the product of reliable principles and methods, and (3) the witness has applied the principles and methods reliably to the facts of the case.

In the federal system, then, the trial judge has become a gatekeeper and must hold a hearing whenever the validity of opinion evidence has been challenged. A number of states have also adopted this approach. In other jurisdictions, however, the soundness of an expert's methodology will still be a question for the jury. Needless to say, it is always essential to determine which test for admissibility will be used for scientific or other expert evidence.

B. Scope of Opinion

The Federal Rules of Evidence provide that expert testimony, if otherwise admissible, "is not objectionable because it embraces an

---

2. *Daubert v. Merrell Dow Pharmaceuticals, Inc.*, 509 U.S. 579 (1993); *Kumho Tire v. Carmichael*, 526 U.S. 137 (1999).

ultimate issue to be decided by the trier of fact."[3] The only exception is that an expert in a criminal case may not state an opinion as to whether the defendant "did or did not have the mental state or condition constituting an element of the crime charged or a defense thereto."[4]

Judges vary on their interpretations of the "ultimate issue" rule. Some courts will allow experts to opine on virtually any issue, including such case-breakers as whether the plaintiff in a personal injury case was contributorily negligent or whether the defendant in a tax evasion case had unreported income. Other judges draw the line at what they consider to be legal conclusions. So, for example, a medical expert in a malpractice case would no doubt be allowed to state that certain tests were indicated and that the defendant had not performed them. Many judges would also allow the expert to testify that the failure to order the tests fell below the standard of care generally exercised by practitioners in the relevant community, although this might be considered an "ultimate issue in the case." Most judges, though not all, would balk at permitting the expert to testify that the defendant's conduct constituted malpractice, on the theory that malpractice is a legal conclusion that is not within the specialized knowledge of a medical expert.

THE BASICS

Standards for Expert Testimony	
Areas of Expertise	An expert's opinion is only admissible if the witness's scientific, technical, or other specialized knowledge will assist the fact-finder in understanding the evidence.
Scope of Opinion	An expert's opinion may embrace an ultimate issue to be decided by the fact-finder (exception in criminal cases where an expert may not opine as to the defendant's state of mind when it is an element of the crime).
Bases for Opinion	An expert's opinion need not be preceded by an explanation of the underlying data. Also, the underlying data need not be admissible so long as it is the type reasonably relied upon by experts in the field.

---

3. Rule 704(a), Federal Rules of Evidence.
4. Rule 704(b), Federal Rules of Evidence.

C. Bases for Opinion

Under the Federal Rules of Evidence an expert can testify to her opinion with or without explaining the facts or data on which the opinion is based.[5] In theory, then, an expert, once qualified, could simply state her opinion on direct examination, leaving the cross examiner to search for its basis.[6] In practice this approach is rarely followed since the expert's opinion could hardly be persuasive until its foundation is explained. The practical effect of the rule is to allow the witness to state her opinion at the beginning of the examination, followed by explication, rather than having to set forth all of the data at the outset.

A related issue is the nature of the information that an expert may rely upon in arriving at an opinion. Under the Federal Rules of Evidence, an expert witness may testify on the basis of "facts made known to him at or before the hearing."[7] Moreover, those facts or data need not be admissible in evidence so long as they are "of a type reasonably relied upon by experts in the particular field."[8]

While it is certain that an expert may rely upn inadmissible data, it is less clear when the expert may recite that data as support for her testimony. For example, forensic pathologists regularly rely upon toxicology reports in determining the cause of death. A pathologist could presumably reach an opinion based upon such a written report even if it would be hearsay when offered at trial. The question, however, is whether the expert, having accepted the report, may also testify as to its contents.

According to Rule 703, othewise inadmissible facts or data may not be disclosed to the jury by the proponent of the opinion "unless the court determines that their probative value in assisting the jury to evaluate the expert's opinion substantially outweighs their prejudicial effect." Thus, the pathologist in the above example could read the language of the toxicology report to the jury only if the cort first determines that it is substantially more helpful than it is prejudicial. Otherwise, the witness would be limited tostatinghow and why she relied on the report, but would not be allowed to testify to its contents. Note, however, that there is no such limitation on the opponent of the proffered opinion, who may always require an expert "to disclose the underlying facts or date on cross examination."[9]

---

5. Rule 705, Federal Rules of Evidence.

6. "The expert may in any event be required to disclose the underlying facts or data on cross examination." Rule 705, Federal Rules of Evidence.

7. Rule 703, Federal Rules of Evidence.

8. *Id.*

9. Rule 705, Federal Rules of Evidence.

III. OFFERING EXPERT TESTIMONY

There is a certain logic to the direct examination of most experts. While the particulars and details will vary, there are a limited number of possible patterns for organizing the testimony. It is absolutely necessary, for example, to qualify the expert before proceeding to her opinion. The following is a broad outline that can accommodate the specifics of most expert testimony.

A. Introduction and Foreshadowing

The first step is to introduce the expert and explain her involvement in the case. Since expert testimony is qualitatively different from lay testimony, it is a good idea to clarify its purposes for the jury so that they will understand what they are about to hear.[10] Ask the witness how she came to be retained and why she is present in court.

Moreover, the technical requirements of presenting expert testimony often result in a considerable time gap between the introduction of the witness and the substantive high points of her testimony. Thus, it is generally desirable to foreshadow the expert's opinion at the very outset of the examination.

A plaintiff's damages expert might be introduced as follows:

QUESTION: Please state your name.

ANSWER: Dr. Andrea Longhini.

QUESTION: Dr. Longhini, have you been retained to reach an expert opinion in this case?

ANSWER: Yes.

QUESTION: Did you reach an opinion concerning the plaintiff's lost profits?

ANSWER: Yes, I have calculated the amount of money that the plaintiff would have earned.

QUESTION: We'll talk about your opinion in detail in a few minutes, but right now we have to talk about your qualifications to testify as an expert in this case.

---

10. It is obviously unnecessary to explain the purpose of expert testimony in bench trials.

B.   Qualification

To testify as an expert, a witness must be qualified by reason of knowledge, skill, experience, training, or education.[11] This is a threshold question for the judge, who must determine whether the witness is qualified before permitting her to give opinion testimony. The qualification of the witness, then, is a necessary predicate for all of the testimony to follow. Care must be taken to qualify the expert in a manner that is both technically adequate and persuasive.

1. Technical Requirements

The technical requirements for qualifying an expert witness are straightforward. It is usually adequate to show that the witness possesses some specialized skill or knowledge, acquired through appropriate experience or education, and that the witness is able to apply that skill or knowledge in a manner relevant to the issues in the case.

Thus, the minimal qualifications for the financial expert could be established as follows:

QUESTION: Dr. Longhini, could you please tell us something about your education?

ANSWER: Certainly. I have an undergraduate degree in business from the University of Michigan and a Ph.D. in economics from the University of California.

QUESTION: What work have you done since receiving your doctorate?

ANSWER: I was a professor in the economics department at Washington University for six years. Then I left to start my own consulting firm, which is called Longhini & Associates.

QUESTION: Do you have a specialty within the field of economics?

ANSWER: Yes, my specialty is business valuation.

QUESTION: Has business valuation been your specialty both at Washington University and at Longhini & Associates?

---

11. Rule 702, Federal Rules of Evidence.

ANSWER: Yes.

QUESTION: What is the field of business valuation?

ANSWER: It is the study of all of the components that contribute to the fair value of a business, including anticipated future profits, assets, receivables, good will, and investment potential.

The above examination confirms the expert's qualifications by reason of both education and experience. Dr. Longhini should now be able to give an opinion as to the value of the business in question.

There are, of course, many other areas of basic qualification beyond education and business experience. Examples include specialized training, continuing education courses, teaching and lecturing positions, licenses and certifications, publications, consulting experience, professional memberships, awards, and other professional honors.

The establishment of basic qualifications, however, should not be counsel's entire objective. It is equally if not more important to go on to qualify the witness as persuasively as possible.

2. Persuasive Qualification

The technical qualification of an expert merely allows the witness to testify in the form of an opinion. Counsel's ultimate goal is to ensure that the opinion is accepted by the trier of fact. Persuasive qualification is particularly important in cases involving competing experts, since their relative qualifications may be one basis on which the judge or jury will decide which expert to believe.

It is a mistake, however, to think that more qualifications are necessarily more persuasive. An endless repetition of degrees, publications, awards, and appointments may easily overload any judge or juror's ability, not to mention desire, to pay careful attention to the witness. It is often better to introduce the witness's detailed résumé or curriculum vitae[12] and to use the qualification portion of the actual examination to focus in on several salient points.[13]

---

12. An expert's résumé might technically be considered hearsay. Expert qualifications, however, are notoriously boring, and most judges will jump at the chance to move things along by allowing the introduction of a résumé. For the same reason, it is common for counsel to stipulate to the introudction of résumés for all expert witnesses. Alternatively, a résumé might be admissible as a business record.

13. The expert's résumé should rarely be used as a complete substitute for examination on qualifications since this would deprive counsel of the opportunity to emphasize the witness's most compelling virtues.

It is usually more persuasive to concentrate on a witness's specific expertise, as opposed to her more generic or remote qualifications. Every economist, for example, is likely to hold a doctorate, so there is comparatively little advantage to be gained by spending valuable time expounding your expert's academic degrees. Similarly, there is usually scant reason to go into matters such as the subject of the witness's doctoral thesis, unless it bears directly on some issue in the case.

On the other hand, an expert's credibility can be greatly enhanced by singling out qualifications that relate specifically to the particular case. Thus, it would be important to point out that the witness has published several articles directly relevant to the issues in the case. It would be less useful to take the witness through a long list of extraneous articles, even if they appeared in prestigious journals. Other case-specific qualifications may include direct experience, consulting work, or teaching that is connected to an issue in the case.

Experience is often more impressive than academic background. So, for example, a medical expert may be more impressive if she has actually practiced in the applicable specialty, as opposed to possessing knowledge that is strictly theoretical. When presenting such a witness, then, counsel should typically dwell on her experience, pointing out details such as the number of procedures she has performed, the hospitals where she is on staff, and the number of other physicians who have consulted her.

Finally, it is frequently effective to emphasize areas of qualification where you know the opposing expert to be lacking. If your expert has a superior academic background, use the direct examination to point out why academic training is important. If your expert holds a certification that the opposing expert lacks, have her explain how difficult it is to become certified.

THE BASICS

An expert's qualifications may include:

• Education	• Consulting Experience
• Professional Experience	• Licenses and Certification
• Specialized Training	• Publications
• Continuing Education Courses	• Teaching and Lecturing Positions
• Professional Memberships	• Professional Awards or Honors

3. Tender of the Witness

In some jurisdictions it is necessary, once qualifications have been concluded, to tender the witness to the court as an expert in a specified field. The purpose of the tender is to inform the court that qualification has been completed and to give opposing counsel an opportunity either to conduct a voir dire examination of the witness or to object to the tender.[14] In the restaurant example above, the financial expert would be tendered as follows:

COUNSEL: Your Honor, we tender Dr. Andrea Longhini as an expert witness in the field of business valuation and the projection of profits.

It may be an effective tactic to tender an expert witness to the court even in jurisdictions where a formal tender is not required. First, tendering the witness signals that the qualification segment has been completed and requires opposing counsel either to object or to accede to the witness's qualifications. By forcing the issue early in the examination, the direct examiner can avoid being interrupted by an objection to the witness's qualifications at some more delicate point in the testimony. Additionally, assuming that the judge rules favorably on the tender, counsel in effect has obtained the court's declaration that the witness is, indeed, an expert. This will give additional weight to the opinions that follow.

C. Opinion and Theory

Following qualification, the next step in the direct examination of an expert witness is to elicit firm statements of opinion and theory.

1. Statement of Opinion

The Federal Rules of Evidence provide that an expert "may testify in terms of opinion or inference and give reasons therefor without first testifying to the underlying facts or data, unless the court requires otherwise."[15] Consequently, once the witness has

---

14. Opposing counsel may utilize voir dire examination to attempt to develop deficiencies in the witness's qualifications. This is done in the midst of the direct examination for two reasons. First, if it can be shown that the witness truly is not qualified, there will be no reason to continue the direct examination. Second, objections raised as a consequence of voir dire can often be cured through additional direct examination. Note that voir dire on qualifications, as with all voir dire examination, should be limited to the eventual admissibility of the expert testimony and should not be used as a substitute for cross examination regarding weight or credibility. See Section V A(1), *infra* at p. 186.
15. Rule 705, Federal Rules of Evidence.

been qualified (and accepted as an expert in jurisdictions requiring a formal tender and ruling), she may proceed to express her opinion without additional foundation. In other words, she may state her conclusions without first detailing the nature or extent of her background work or investigation.

Many attorneys believe strongly in taking advantage of the "opinion first" provision. Expert testimony tends to be long, arcane, and boring. The intricate details of an expert's preparation are unlikely to be interesting or even particularly understandable. They will be even less captivating if they are offered in a void, without any advance notice of where the details are leading or why they are being explained. On the other hand, a clear statement of the expert's conclusion can provide the context for the balance of the explanatory testimony. Compare the two following vignettes.

QUESTION: Dr. Longhini, what did you do to arrive at your opinion in this matter?

ANSWER: My first step was to gather all of the available data regarding vehicle registrations and anticipated population growth in the state.

QUESTION: Then what did you do?

ANSWER: I correlated population growth with expected vehicle miles to arrive at a reasonable estimate of "miles per person" over each of the next five years.

QUESTION: How was that calculation performed?

Even the most diligent and attentive juror would be baffled by this examination. What is the relevance of vehicle miles and population growth to the issues in the case? The nature of the witness's computation is meaningless in the absence of some connection to his opinion in the case. Indeed, the more thoroughly the witness explains her calculations, the more incomprehensible they will become. In contrast, consider the following:

QUESTION: Dr. Longhini, do you have an opinion as to the profits that the plaintiff's restaurant chain would have made, if they hadn't been forced out of business?

ANSWER: Yes, I do.

QUESTION: What is your opinion?

ANSWER: I believe that the restaurant chain would have earned at least $3.2 million over the next five years, if they had been able to stay in business.

QUESTION: How did you reach that opinion?

ANSWER: I based my calculations on the state's projected population growth, combined with the probable demand for fast-food, drive-in restaurants.

This examination is far more understandable. By providing her opinion at the outset, the expert allows the trier of fact to comprehend the significance of the following details. The jury will be much more able to understand the relationship between lost profits and the data on vehicle registration and population growth.

2. Statement of Theory

Once the expert's opinion has been stated, immediately provide the underlying theory. The theory should furnish the nexus between the expert's conclusion and the data used to support the conclusion. In other words, the examination should follow this pattern: (1) here is my opinion; (2) here are the principles that support my opinion; (3) here is what I did to reach my final conclusion.

QUESTION: Dr. Longhini, why did you base your calculations on the state's projected population growth?

ANSWER: The demand for fast food will rise as population grows. This is particularly true because teenagers and parents of young children are the largest purchasers of fast food, and they are also two of the groups that increase most rapidly as population goes up.

QUESTION: Why did you also consider growth in vehicle miles?

ANSWER: Drive-in restaurants are especially sensitive to vehicle miles. As people drive more they are exposed to more drive-in restaurants, and they therefore buy more meals.

QUESTION: What did you conclude from these relationships?

ANSWER: I concluded that the profitability of a drive-in restaurant chain will rise in proportion to a combination of general population growth and increases in miles driven.

QUESTION: Did you consider only population growth and vehicle miles?

ANSWER: Of course not. I began by determining the chain's profits under current conditions, and I used those figures as a base. Then I projected them forward for five years, using the government's statistics for population and driving.

QUESTION: Please tell us now exactly how you did that.

Note how this examination provides the context for the explanation to follow.

D. Explanation and Support

Having stated and supported her theory choice, the expert can now go on to detail the nature of her investigation and calculations. The trier of fact cannot be expected to take the expert at her word, so the validity and accuracy of her data and assumptions must be established.

1. Data

The expert should be asked how she chose and obtained her data. She should also explain why her information is reliable. In the scenario above, for example, the expert could point out that government statistics on population and vehicle miles are used to make many crucial decisions such as the configuration of traffic lights, the expansion of highways, and even the construction of schools. The expert should also be asked to describe any tests or computations that she performed.

The treatment of underlying data is one of the trickiest aspects of expert testimony. Many experts will be in love with their data, and they will be anxious to lay them out in excruciating detail. Unfortunately, most judges and jurors will have little tolerance for lengthy descriptions of enigmatic scientific or technical processes. Counsel must therefore strike a balance, eliciting a sufficiently detailed treatment of the data to persuade the jury of its reliability but stopping well short of the point where their attention span is exhausted.

It is not sufficient for the expert simply to relate the nature of the data. Rather, the expert should go on to explain how and why the data support her conclusions.

2. Assumptions

Most experts rely upon assumptions. The financial expert in the restaurant case, for example, would no doubt assume that the relationship between sales and population growth would continue at historical rates. The expert would also probably assume a certain financial "discount rate" for reducing the dollars in his projection to present value. There is obviously nothing wrong with using appropriate presumptions, but their validity should be explained:

> QUESTION: Dr. Longhini, did you make any assumptions in reaching your opinion that the plaintiff's restaurant chain would have earned $3.2 million in profits?

> ANSWER: Yes, I assumed that fast food sales would continue to increase in proportion to population at the same rate as they had in the past.

> QUESTION: Why did you make that assumption?

> ANSWER: The restaurant chain was put out of business, so there were no actual sales to look at. I therefore had to project their most likely sales, and for that I had to assume a base figure to project forward.

> QUESTION: What did you use as your base figure?

> ANSWER: I used the average growth for the entire industry.

> QUESTION: Why did you use the industry average?

> ANSWER: I used the industry average precisely because it is an average of all of the companies in that particular business. That way I could be sure that I wasn't using a figure that was abnormally high or abnormally low.

It is not necessary to explain or outline every hypothesis used by your expert, but the more important assumptions should be noted and supported.

E.   Theory Differentiation

In cases involving dueling experts there will also be competing theories. Properly prepared and presented, each expert will attempt to explain to the trier of fact why her theory ought to be accepted. It can be particularly effective, therefore, to ask your expert to comment on the opposing expert's work. This technique can be called theory differentiation because it is most convincing when your expert discusses the shortcomings of the opposition theory.

The timing of theory differentiation can be important. Plaintiff's counsel generally will want to establish her own theory first, before proceeding to criticize the defense expert. Depending upon the circumstances of the case, plaintiff's counsel might even want to forego theory differentiation entirely during her case in chief, and recall her expert for that purpose on rebuttal.

The defense, on the other hand, should address the plaintiff's expert's theory at some point during the direct examination of the defendant's own expert. This can be done early in the examination (in order to rebut the plaintiff's expert immediately and forcefully), or it can be done toward the end of the testimony (in order to allow the defense expert to build up the positive aspects of his own theory before turning his attention to the opposition).

F.   Conclusion

An expert's direct examination should conclude with a powerful restatement of his most important conclusions.

THE BASICS

Organization of an Expert's Direct

- Introduce the expert and foreshadow the testimony
- Elicit the expert's qualifications
- Obtain a clear statement of the expert's opinion
- Ask the expert to explain the "theory" for the opinion
- Elicit the expert's factual, experimental, or other support for the opinion
- Utilize theory differentiation in cases with competing experts
- Ask the expert to restate the most important conclusions

IV.   TECHNIQUES FOR DIRECT EXAMINATION

Most of the direct examination methods discussed in Chapter Three can be used effectively with expert witnesses. In addition, the following techniques are specifically applicable to expert testimony.

A. Humanize the Witness

Many experts from scientific, technical, or financial backgrounds may appear aloof, intimidating, or even arrogant to jurors who do not share their special expertise. It is therefore important to humanize these witnesses as much as possible in the course of the direct examination. If permitted in your jurisdiction, this can be done by bringing out personal and family background information and by allowing the witness to talk about more than strictly professional matters.

B. Use Plain Language

Virtually every field of expertise creates its own technical and shorthand terms, and expert witnesses will often be inclined to use arcane and jargon-laden speech without even thinking about it. It is counsel's job to guide the witness away from the use of jargon and into the realm of everyday speech. There are three basic means to accomplish this task.

First, thoroughly prepare the witness to avoid complex, professional terms. Spend sufficient time with the witness before trial so that she will understand the importance of plain, simple language.

Second, ask for an explanation when your witness lapses into her native tongue, whether it is finance-talk, engineeringese, or accounting-speak. This should be done gently and without reprimand or condescension, as in this example:

QUESTION: Dr. Schenkier, do you have an opinion as to why the pressure plate failed?

ANSWER: Yes. My tests indicate that the fastening bolts were over-torqued.

QUESTION: What do you mean when you say over-torqued?

ANSWER: I mean that the bolts were turned too far when they were tightened.

Finally, and possibly most important, counsel must avoid the temptation to adopt the expert's word choices. Too many lawyers, perhaps out of a desire to appear erudite or knowledgeable, tend to examine expert witnesses using the expert's own jargon. Such examinations can take on the characteristics of a private, and completely inaccessible, conversation between the lawyer and the witness. It is bad enough when lawyers use legalese; it is worse when they embrace the private speech of another profession. Consider the following:

QUESTION: Dr. Breskin, what injuries did you observe?

ANSWER: I observed multiple contusions on the anterior upper extremities.

QUESTION: Was there anything remarkable about the contusions?

ANSWER: Yes. They varied in color, which indicated that they had been inflicted at different times.

QUESTION: Did the anterior location of the contusions indicate anything further to you?

ANSWER: Yes. Their anterior location suggested that they had been inflicted from a superior position.

The lawyer and doctor are talking about bruises. The witness chose to use the term "contusions" because it is medically precise, and the lawyer's adoption of the term encouraged the doctor to continue using it. While the lawyer may have succeeded in demonstrating his medical sophistication, he may have done so at the cost of the jury's comprehension.

C.   Avoid Narratives

Most judges will allow expert witnesses considerable freedom to testify in narrative fashion. Many lawyers believe that they should take advantage of this leeway, and they therefore encourage their experts to present their testimony in long, uninterrupted segments. This is a mistake. Long narratives are hard to follow and hard to digest.

Anyone who ever sat through a long lecture or speech should understand how difficult it is to pay attention to a speaker for an extended period of time. This is particularly true of expert testimony, which often concentrates on complex or intricate details. Allowing an expert to testify in a long, unbroken stretch invites juror inattention.

Recall the discussion of the importance of primacy in basic direct examination: the judge and jury remember best what they hear first. This concept applies to individual answers as well as to complete examinations. A new answer begins every time counsel asks a question. In other words, every question to the expert reinitiates primacy and refocuses the listeners' attention. Unless the expert is an extraordinarily skilled speaker, a narrative answer will have no comparable points of reinitiation. The opportunity to continuously highlight the testimony will be lost.

Counsel can avoid narrative answers and reinitiate primacy by punctuating the expert's testimony at logical breaking points:

QUESTION: Dr. Haruo, what is the significance of location in projecting profits for a chain of drive-in restaurants?

ANSWER: Location is probably the single most important factor when it comes to profitability in any retail business. Even if the overall trend in an industry is upward, a poorly located business is unlikely to benefit. This is especially true of the restaurant business.

QUESTION: Please explain.

ANSWER: The restaurant business is intensely local in nature. There are very few restaurants that attract people from great distances. Most people eat near their homes, their places of work, or their shopping destinations. So a restaurant in an undesirable neighborhood or in a declining business district simply will not draw customers.

QUESTION: Why is that?

ANSWER: Many restaurants depend heavily on luncheon trade. People on their lunch break usually do not have more than an hour, so a restaurant will not be able to draw this business unless it is located near a fairly large number of employers. No matter how well the economy is doing, a restaurant will not do well at lunchtime if it is located in an area that happens to have experienced a downturn.

Note that the lawyer in this example did not cut off the witness and did not limit the expert to unnaturally short answers. The lawyer did, however, use strategically interjected questions to break up the narrative, thereby continually reemphasizing the expert's testimony.

D. Use Examples and Analogies

Many complex ideas can be made understandable with examples, analogies, or metaphors. Expert witnesses should be encouraged to clarify their testimony through the use of such imagery. Consider the following use of an example to flesh out a relatively abstract concept:

QUESTION: Dr. Haruo, please give us an example of how a restaurant chain might do poorly, even in a state with an expanding population and increasing vehicle miles.

ANSWER: Certainly. Many urban areas have experienced population growth that is basically limited to the suburbs. A restaurant chain that was concentrated in the central city would show almost no increased profitability as a result of that growth. In fact, its profits might well decline because of the population shift. That is why location is such an important factor.

An analogy could serve the same purpose:

QUESTION: Dr. Haruo, could you please explain the importance of location a little further?

ANSWER: Well, maybe it would help to think about it this way. Imagine a baseball league with eight teams. If the top two or three pennant contenders are all located in big cities, they will obviously draw a lot of fans. On the other hand, a cellar-dwelling team in a small city would probably play to an empty stadium. So even if the league's overall attendance went up, that wouldn't help to fill the seats for the last-place team. A poor location is a lot like being stuck in last place.

Counsel should not take the witness by surprise with a request for an example or metaphor. The time to consider using these explanatory tools is during preparation, not on the spur of the moment in the midst of direct examination.

E. Use Visual Aids

The direct examination of almost every expert can be enhanced through the use of visual displays. Since expert testimony may be hard to follow, it can be particularly effective to portray the expert's concepts with charts, graphs, drawings, or models.

A physician's testimony, for example, can be brought to life with an anatomical model or a series of colored overlays. Financial experts should illustrate their testimony with graphs or tables. An architectural or engineering expert should use diagrams or scale models. The possibilities for visual aids are practically infinite, limited only by counsel's (and the expert's) imagination.[16]

THE BASICS

Expert Testimony Checklist ☑	
☐ Does your expert's testimony have a clear theory?	Does your expert's testimony explain why the findings should be believed by the fact-finder? *If not, rework your direct examination to include an overriding theory of the expert's testimony.*
☐ Are you encouraging your expert to use plain language?	Do you prompt your expert to explain complicated concepts using plain language? Do you refrain from using the expert's jargon yourself? *If not, the content and purpose of your expert's testimony may be not be understood by the fact-finder.*
☐ Are you helping the expert to avoid giving narrative answers?	Do any of your questions call for answers longer than a few sentences? *If so, you should use directive questions to divide the witness's answers, to ensure that the fact-finder will remain interested throughout the testimony.*
☐ Are you encouraging your expert to use imagery in the testimony?	Does your expert give examples and make analogies where appropriate during the direct examination? *If not, consider working them in to help explain difficult concepts.*
☐ Are you prompting your expert to give internal summaries?	Is there an internal summary at the end of each major section of your expert's testimony? *If not, consider adding them to clarify and emphasize the witness's testimony.*
☐ Did you make use of visual aids?	Does your expert use maps, charts, diagrams, or the like to explain the testimony? *If not, consider creating demonstrative exhibits that will enable your expert to better explain the testimony.*

---

16. See Chapter 10.

F.   Use Leading Questions When Called For

Two recurrent problems in expert testimony are boredom and pomposity. Many experts are inclined to drone on at length over unimportant details. Others present themselves with an air of over-weening self-importance, especially in the course of presenting their credentials. Both of these difficulties can be resolved through the judicious use of leading questions.

Counsel can often cut through a welter of details by using a leading question to direct the witness to the heart of the matter. Consider the examination of a chemist, called to testify as to the composition of a substance. The process used by the witness may have been comprised of many steps. A judge or jury, however, would quickly become bored with a blow-by-blow recitation of the entire procedure. Counsel can shorten the questioning by using a few leading questions:

QUESTION: Did you perform a chemical analysis?

ANSWER: Yes.

QUESTION: Did that analysis consist of a six-step process?

ANSWER: Yes, it did.

QUESTION: Did you perform all six steps in accordance with accepted procedures?

ANSWER: Yes.

QUESTION: What were your results?

Leading questions were permissible in the above example because they were preliminary. If the adequacy or scrupulousness of the chemist's tests was in issue, however, leading questions would neither be allowed nor be advisable. While it is a useful technique to use leading questions to skip over minor details, they should not be used as a substitute for the witness's own testimony concerning important issues.

G.   Encourage Powerful Language

There is a tradition in many technical fields of hedging or qualifying the language in which conclusions are expressed. This makes great sense when discussing research since one's results are always subject to further inquiry. Thus, it is not uncommon for professionals to use terms such as "to the best of my knowledge," or "according to current indications," or "as far as we can tell." While this language is meant to convey open-mindedness as opposed to uncertainty, it can be fatal to a witness's testimony in a courtroom.

To prevent inadvertent miscommunication, expert witnesses should be prepared to testify in straightforward, unequivocal terms. Experts should be cautioned to avoid language that unintentionally qualifies or hedges their results, using instead wording that emphasizes accuracy and certainty.

Here is an example of weak language:

ANSWER: My best estimate at this time is that the restaurant chain would have earned approximately $3.2 million.

In fact, the witness has conducted an exhaustive study and is completely certain, within the bounds of professional competence, that $3.2 million is the correct figure. That certainty can be better expressed through more powerful language:

ANSWER: I have calculated lost profits at $3.2 million.

Or,

ANSWER: My projections show that the restaurant chain would have earned $3.2 million.

Or,

ANSWER: The result of my study is a determination of lost profits in the amount of $3.2 million.

The substitution of authoritative terminology for weak language may require a process of education for the witness. Of course, if the expert's conclusions really are tentative or provisional, counsel should not attempt to persuade the witness to testify otherwise.

H. Use Enumeration

Audiences most often pay closer attention to information presented in numbered lists. Expert witnesses should therefore be encouraged to introduce concepts in terms of factors or considerations rather than launching into extended explanations. The following is a good example of enumeration:

QUESTION: Dr. Haruo, what is your opinion of Dr. Longhini's study?

ANSWER: There are three basic problems with Dr. Longhini's study.

QUESTION: What are those problems?

ANSWER: First, she projected profits on the basis of only two factors. Second, she failed to consider location, which should have been the most important element. Third, she doesn't seem to recognize that population growth can be extremely uneven.

Counsel can now ask the witness to explain each of the three points. Note that the introduction of each point will reinitiate primacy and therefore heighten the jury's attention.

I.   Consider Inoculation

Expert witnesses may be open to several distinct lines of cross examination.[17] Counsel should therefore consider conducting a certain amount of explanatory or defensive direct examination to "inoculate" the witness against cross examination on such matters as the payment of fees, the use of presumptions, reliance on secondary sources, and the like.

V.   CROSS EXAMINATION OF EXPERT WITNESSES

Most of the basic approaches to cross examination can also be adapted to expert testimony. In addition, there are certain tools that can be used primarily or most effectively with expert witnesses.

A.   Challenge the Witness's Credentials

An expert witness's credentials are subject to challenge either on voir dire or during cross examination. Voir dire may be used to object to the legal sufficiency of the expert's qualifications, while cross examination is the time to attack their weight.

1. Voir Dire on Credentials

Once the proponent of an expert has concluded the qualification segment of the direct examination, opposing counsel is entitled to conduct a voir dire of the witness. A voir dire examination temporarily suspends the direct so that the opponent of the proffered evidence can inquire as to its evidentiary sufficiency. With regard to the qualification of experts, this means that opposing counsel can interrupt the direct examination in order to conduct a mini-cross limited to the issue of the witness's credentials.

---

17. Cross examination of expert witnesses is discussed in Section V, *infra*, at p. 186.

In jurisdictions that require the tender of expert witnesses, voir dire typically proceeds once the witness is proffered to the court:

> PROPONENT: Your Honor, we tender Dr. Benjamin Haruo as an expert on the subject of lost profits.
>
> COURT: Any objection, counsel?
>
> OPPONENT: Your Honor, we would like the opportunity to conduct a voir dire examination.
>
> COURT: You may examine the witness on the subject of his qualifications to testify.

In jurisdictions where tender is not utilized, it is necessary for opposing counsel to interpose an objection at the point where the witness begins to offer an opinion. Do not wait to be invited by the court:

> PROPONENT: Dr. Haruo, do you have an opinion as to the profits that the plaintiff would have earned if the restaurant chain had not been driven out of business?
>
> OPPONENT: Objection. Your Honor, we would like an opportunity for voir dire of this witness before he is allowed to give opinion testimony.
>
> COURT: You may examine the witness on the subject of his qualifications to testify.

Note that voir dire is limited generally to the question of the admissibility of evidence. Thus, voir dire regarding an expert's credentials is restricted to the foundation for the witness's ability to opine on the issues in the case. In other words, is the witness "qualified as an expert by knowledge, skill, experience, training, or education"?[18] The witness may proceed with his testimony so long as he meets this minimum requirement. Voir dire is not the time to launch into a wide-ranging attack on the expert's integrity, methods, data, or bias.

It is frequently an uphill battle to persuade a judge that a proffered witness should not be allowed to testify as an expert. Judges often respond to such objections by ruling that they go only to the weight and not the admissibility of the expert testimony.

Nonetheless, it is possible to disqualify an expert through the use of voir dire. Purported experts can be disqualified by establishing

---

18. Rule 702, Federal Rules of Evidence.

the remoteness of their credentials, the inapplicability of their specialties, the lack of general acceptance of their purported expertise, or the unreliability of their data.

One caution. Counsel must decide whether to request that voir dire be conducted outside the presence of the jury. On one hand, it never hurts for the jury to hear negative information about a witness. On the other hand, a witness's credibility may be strengthened if an aggressive voir dire is unsuccessful and the court rules that the witness is indeed an expert.

2. Cross Examination on Credentials

The court's ruling that a witness may testify as an expert means only that the witness possesses sufficient credentials to pass the evidentiary threshold. It still may be possible to diminish the weight of the witness's qualifications during cross examination. There are three basic methods for discrediting the value of a witness's credentials.

a. Limit the scope of the witness's expertise

Although a witness may be well-qualified in a certain area or subspecialty, it may be possible to recast the issues of the case in such a way as to place them beyond the witness's competence. Assume, for example, that the plaintiff's expert in the restaurant scenario was tendered and accepted as an expert on lost profits:

QUESTION: Dr. Longhini, your primary consulting work involves business valuation, correct?

ANSWER: That is my profession.

QUESTION: Issues of valuation usually involve an existing business, right?

ANSWER: That is the usual case.

QUESTION: People come to you when they want to buy or sell a business, or when they have to value it for estate tax purposes, or perhaps when there is a divorce?

ANSWER: Yes, those are all typical situations for business valuation.

QUESTION: You wouldn't call yourself a management consultant, would you?

ANSWER:	No, I do not get involved in operations.
QUESTION:	Because your work is basically evaluative?
ANSWER:	Exactly.
QUESTION:	So someone who wanted assistance in expanding a business would need to go to a different consultant, wouldn't they?
ANSWER:	Correct.
QUESTION:	For example, there are consultants who specialize in site evaluation, correct?
ANSWER:	Yes, there are.
QUESTION:	But you do not do that yourself?
ANSWER:	No, I do not.
QUESTION:	So if I wanted to evaluate the best possible locations for my business outlets, you would recommend that I consult someone else, isn't that right?
ANSWER:	Yes, I suppose that I would refer you.

Counsel may now argue that the crucial issue of location is beyond Dr. Longhini's expertise and that her opinion regarding lost profits should therefore be discounted.

b. Stress missing credentials

An expert witness may be minimally qualified to testify but still lack certain important certifications, degrees, or licenses. Assume, for example, that the plaintiff in a personal injury case has called his psychotherapist to testify on the issue of damages. The witness was tendered and accepted as an expert and has completed his direct testimony. This cross examination followed:

QUESTION:	Mr. Meizlish, your degree is in social work, correct?
ANSWER:	Yes, I have a MSW, and I am a licensed psychotherapist.
QUESTION:	You do not have a doctorate in clinical psychology, do you?

ANSWER: No, I do not.

QUESTION: And of course you are not a psychiatrist?

ANSWER: That is correct.

QUESTION: I notice that your stationery lists your name as Alex Meizlish, MSW.

ANSWER: Yes, that is right.

QUESTION: I have seen other social workers with the letters ACSW after their names. What does ACSW stand for?

ANSWER: It stands for Accredited Clinical Social Worker.

QUESTION: That is an additional certification that some social workers earn, correct?

ANSWER: Yes, that is correct.

QUESTION: But you have not achieved that certification, have you?

B. Obtain Favorable Information

It will often be possible to obtain favorable concessions from the opposing party's expert witness. As with all cross examination, it is usually wisest to attempt to extract such information near the beginning of the examination. Needless to say, one must be positive of the answers before launching into this sort of cross examination.

In general, the helpful material available from opposing experts will fall into the following categories.

1. Affirm Your Own Expert

Even experts who ultimately disagree may have many shared understandings. You may therefore contribute to the accreditation of your own expert by asking the opposing expert to acknowledge the reliability of your expert's data, the validity of her assumptions, or the caliber of her credentials.

2. Elicit Areas of Agreement

In addition, it may be possible to elicit concessions from the opposing expert that go to the merits of the case. The adverse expert may, for example, be willing to agree with several of your major premises, even while disagreeing with your ultimate conclusion.

Consider this cross examination of the defense expert in the drive-in restaurant case:

QUESTION: Dr. Haruo, you are dissatisfied with the nature of Dr. Longhini's study of lost profits, correct?

ANSWER: Yes, I have trouble with Dr. Longhini's methodology.

QUESTION: But you do agree, don't you, that the chain had been operating as a going concern?

ANSWER: Yes, I do.

QUESTION: In fact, the restaurant chain had made a profit every year they were in business?

ANSWER: I believe that is correct.

QUESTION: And every one of their outlets was profitable, correct?

ANSWER: I think that is right.

QUESTION: So someone must have been able to select profitable locations, right?

ANSWER: I suppose so.

QUESTION: Dr. Longhini assumed that the chain would continue to choose good locations, isn't that right?

ANSWER: That is implicit in her model.

QUESTION: And you did not conduct an independent study of favorable or unfavorable restaurant locations, did you?

ANSWER: No, I did not.

QUESTION: So you have no data that you can point to that would contradict Dr. Longhini's assumption?

ANSWER: I do not.

3. Criticize the Opposing Party's Conduct

Finally, it may be possible to draw from an opposing expert significant criticism of her own party's conduct. Though the expert reached a final conclusion favorable to the party, she may be unwilling to approve of all of their underlying actions. For example:

QUESTION: Dr. Longhini, in order for you to reach your opinion on damages it was necessary for you to review all of the plaintiff's financial records, correct?

ANSWER: Yes, that is correct.

QUESTION: Isn't it true that the plaintiff company did not keep accurate store-by-store records?

ANSWER: Yes, they aggregated their financial information, rather than breaking it down store-by-store.

QUESTION: The absence of store-by-store information must have made your job more difficult.

ANSWER: I found that I was able to achieve accurate results on the basis of statewide projections.

QUESTION: I understand your position. Still, you could have projected profits for each individual restaurant if the available financial data had been more precise, isn't that true?

ANSWER: Yes, that is true.

QUESTION: But because of the plaintiff's aggregate record keeping, you were not able to do that?

ANSWER: No one could have made such projections on the basis of that data.

C.   Use of Learned Treatises

One form of cross examination unique to expert witnesses is impeachment through the use of a learned treatise. Under the Federal Rules of Evidence an expert witness may be confronted with statements contained in "published treatises, periodicals, or pamphlets on a subject of history, medicine, or other science or art," so long as they are established as reliable authority.[19]

Contrary to the belief of many lawyers and judges, it is not necessary to establish that the witness has relied on the particular treatise, or even that the witness acknowledge it as authoritative.

---

19. Rule 803(18), Federal Rules of Evidence.

Under the Federal Rules the reliability of a learned treatise may be established by admission of the witness, or by other expert testimony, or by judicial notice.[20] Impeachment, then, could conceivably take this form:

QUESTION: Are you familiar with Lubet's *Modern Trial Advocacy*?

ANSWER: Certainly.

QUESTION: Do you regard it as authoritative in the field?

ANSWER: Absolutely not.

QUESTION: I want to read you a passage from Lubet's *Modern Trial Advocacy*.

OPPONENT: Objection, Your Honor. The witness testified that Lubet is not regarded as an authority.

QUESTION: Your Honor, we will produce other expert testimony that Lubet's *Modern Trial Advocacy* is regarded as an authoritative text.

COURT: You may proceed.

Of course, it is far more persuasive when the witness agrees that the treatise is indeed recognized as a leading authority. You can ensure such a favorable response by restricting your impeachment to widely recognized sources. Alternatively, you can utilize the expert's deposition to determine exactly what treatises she will accept as reliable.

In either case, once the reliability of the treatise is confirmed, the impeachment may proceed one of two ways. You may read a passage from the treatise into evidence without asking the expert any questions about it; the Federal Rules require only that the passage be called to the witness's attention. The more traditional approach is to ask the witness whether she agrees with the particular quotation. At that point the witness must either accede or disagree. If she accepts the statement, your job is done. If she disagrees, you may argue later that she is out of step with recognized authority.

Finally, note that this rule allows an excerpt from a learned treatise to be read into evidence but that the treatise itself may not be received as an exhibit.

---

20. Rule 803(18), Federal Rules of Evidence.

D. Challenge the Witness's Impartiality

Expert witnesses are supposed to be independent analysts, not advocates. The worst accusation you can make against an expert witness is that he has altered his opinion to fit a party's needs. Accordingly, it can be very effective to cross examine an expert on the issue of bias if the material is there to be exploited. Cross examination on bias falls into three basic categories.

1. Fees

Most experts in litigation are retained and paid significant fees.[21] While the acceptance of money in exchange for testimony would initially seem to be a fruitful area for cross examination, the reality is somewhat less promising.

First, the trier of fact is likely to understand that no witness could afford to perform extensive tests or analyses without being compensated. Second, all experts in the case are probably being paid, so there is little ground to be gained by making a point of it on cross examination when your own expert is equally vulnerable. Finally, most experienced experts will be adept at turning such challenges aside.

It is generally productive to cross examine an expert concerning her fee only in fairly limited circumstances. For example, it may demonstrate bias if the fee is extraordinarily large. Similarly, it may be evidence of something less than objectivity if the witness has a large unpaid fee outstanding at the time that she testifies.

2. Relationship with Party or Counsel

An expert's relationship with a party or with counsel may also indicate a lack of impartiality. Some witnesses seem to work hand in glove with certain law firms, testifying to similar conclusions in case after case. While such an ongoing relationship is not proof of bias, it does suggest that the association may have been sustained for a reason.

The extent of the repeated retention is important. It will usually be of little significance that an expert worked on two or three cases for one law firm over a fairly lengthy period. After all, the firm might prize the witness precisely for her independence. On the other hand, it can become questionable when a firm has engaged the same expert on a dozen or more occasions. While there may be a perfectly

---

21. It is permissible to compensate experts for their time, but contingency fees are unethical.

innocent explanation for this constancy, it is certainly reasonable to bring it out on cross examination.

The same analysis obtains to witnesses who have testified repeatedly for the same party, although retained by different law firms.

Finally, some cases may involve testimony by in-house experts, perhaps a company's own accountant or engineer. In most cases, such experts are susceptible to no more suggestion of bias than would be any other employee. In some situations, however, the in-house expert's own judgment will be at issue in the case. An accountant, for example, may have failed to see that a debt was under-collateralized; an engineer may not have foreseen the need for more exacting tolerances. In these circumstances the cross examination must bring out the witness's personal stake in the outcome of the litigation.

3. Positional Bias

With or without regard to past retention, some experts seem wedded to certain professional, scientific, or intellectual positions. Experts frequently come to testify only for plaintiffs or only for defendants. Others reach only one of a range of conclusions. For example, it is said that some psychiatrists have been known never to find a single criminal defendant to be sane or competent. Where they exist, these rigidly held positional biases can be exploited effectively on cross examination.

4. Preparation for Cross Examination on Bias

Diligent preparation is required before cross examining an expert witness on bias. Partiality is a serious charge to level against an expert witness, and it should not be advanced without a good faith basis for the claim. Cross examination is not the time to make random inquiries as to lack of objectivity or independence, much less baseless attacks.

It is essential that counsel use discovery and investigation to explore thoroughly all of an expert's potential biases. Cross examination can then be limited to those assertions that can be supported in fact.

E. Point Out Omissions

An expert may be vulnerable on cross examination if she has failed to conduct essential tests or procedures, or if she has neglected to consider all significant factors. The question of neglected tests or experiments will depend upon the unique factors of each case. You must pursue thorough discovery to determine whether processes were shortcut or slighted, preferably after first consulting your own expert.

Other sorts of omissions are more commonplace. Witnesses are frequently asked to give evaluations concerning the validity or accuracy of other experts' work. A consulting pathologist, for example, might be asked to reevaluate the protocol of an autopsy conducted by the local medical examiner. No matter how prominent, a "second-opinion" witness can almost always be undermined by the fact that she did not conduct the primary investigation:

QUESTION: Dr. Elliot, you reach a conclusion quite different from the conclusions reached by Dr. Arlington, correct?

ANSWER: Yes.

QUESTION: Of course, you did not perform an autopsy yourself, did you?

ANSWER: No, I did not.

QUESTION: In fact, your information comes exclusively from Dr. Arlington's autopsy protocol?

ANSWER: That is right.

QUESTION: So you have relied on Dr. Arlington for all of your factual information, isn't that right?

ANSWER: Yes, I have.

QUESTION: Dr. Elliot, you know nothing of the actual circumstances of the autopsy, other than what you have learned from Dr. Arlington's report?

ANSWER: Correct.

QUESTION: So at least with regard to gathering information, you have trusted Dr. Arlington's work?

This technique is not limited to "reevaluating" experts. It can be employed, in different form, with regard to any witness who relies exclusively on information provided by others:

QUESTION: Dr. Elliot, you base your opinion solely on an examination of hospital records, correct?

ANSWER: Correct.

QUESTION: You did not examine the decedent yourself, did you?

ANSWER: No, I did not.

QUESTION: So your opinion can only be as good as the information you received, right?

ANSWER: I suppose so.

QUESTION: If any of that information were faulty, that could affect the basis for your opinion, correct?

ANSWER: Yes, depending upon the circumstances.

QUESTION: The same would be true of missing information, right?

ANSWER: Right.

QUESTION: You'll agree with me, won't you, Dr. Elliot, that firsthand observation is preferred for the purpose of diagnosis?

ANSWER: Yes, it is preferred.

Finally, many experts will testify on the basis of statistics or studies compiled from other sources. Frequently, such experts will not have investigated the reliability of the underlying data, and this can leave them vulnerable to cross examination.

F.   Substitute Information

1. Change Assumptions

As we have seen, almost all experts must use assumptions of one sort or another in the course of formulating their opinions. An expert's assumptions, however, might be unrealistic, unreliable, or unreasonably favorable to the retaining party. It can be extremely effective, therefore, to ask the witness to alter an assumption, substituting one that you believe to be more in keeping with the evidence in the case. Consider this scenario from the drive-in restaurant case:

QUESTION: Dr. Longhini, your lost-profits calculation includes an assumption that vehicle miles will continue to grow at the rate of 4 percent, correct?

ANSWER: Yes, that is the figure I used.

QUESTION: Will you agree that numerous factors can influence the growth of vehicle miles?

ANSWER: Yes, I think that is obvious.

QUESTION: For example, vehicle miles actually fell during the oil embargo?

ANSWER: I believe that is true.

QUESTION: And if vehicle miles were to rise at a rate of less than 4 percent, your estimate of lost profits would have to be reduced, correct?

ANSWER: Yes, that is right.

QUESTION: In fact, if we used an assumption of 2 percent, your estimate of lost profits would have to be reduced by over $600,000?

ANSWER: I haven't done the calculation, but it should be something in that range.

When the substituted assumption calls for recalculation, it is generally most effective to do the math in advance, rather than asking the witness to do it on the spot. A request that the witness perform the computation is an invitation to quibble.

2. Vary the Facts

A related technique is to vary the facts upon which the expert has relied, or to suggest additional facts, as in this example from the restaurant case:

QUESTION: Dr. Longhini, you are aware that the plaintiff's most profitable outlet was in the Lincoln Walk Mall, correct?

ANSWER: Yes.

QUESTION: And the continued existence of that outlet was a fact that you relied on in calculating your result, right?

ANSWER: That is right.

QUESTION: But if the entire Lincoln Walk Mall were to close due to bankruptcy, then you would have to change your conclusion, isn't that right?

ANSWER: I suppose that is correct.

QUESTION: Well, you couldn't have a profitable restaurant in a closed mall, could you?

ANSWER: Of course not.

As with all cross examination questions, counsel must have a good faith basis for asserting new or varied facts to an expert witness.

3. Degree of Certainty

It is also possible to challenge an expert's degree of certainty by suggesting alternative scenarios or explanations:

QUESTION: Dr. Haruo, you believe that the plaintiff's history of profitability is largely attributable to location, correct?

ANSWER: Yes, I think that location is, and has been, the most important factor.

QUESTION: But there are other factors that contribute to profitability, correct?

ANSWER: Certainly.

QUESTION: Some of those factors would be product quality, value, or market demand, correct?

ANSWER: Yes.

QUESTION: You are surely familiar with the term "destination shopping," aren't you?

ANSWER: Of course.

QUESTION: That means that people will travel to seek out value or quality or amenities, regardless of the location, correct?

ANSWER: That does happen.

QUESTION: Well, you didn't interview the plaintiff's customers, did you?

ANSWER: Of course not.

QUESTION: So you cannot be sure that location was of primary importance to them, can you?

ANSWER: I can't look into their minds.

QUESTION: Isn't it possible that the plaintiff's customers sought out their restaurants because of value or quality?

ANSWER: It is possible.

QUESTION: So it is also possible that location was not the primary factor in plaintiff's profitability?

4. Dependence on Other Testimony

The opinion of an expert witness often depends upon facts to be established by other witnesses. Thus, the expert's testimony may be undermined, not by anything you ask the expert directly, but rather by challenging its factual underpinnings during the cross examination of the fact witnesses. It is necessary only to obtain the expert's concession that the other witnesses' facts are essential to her opinion:

QUESTION: Dr. Longhini, part of your opinion is based on Ms. Van Zant's statement that she was certain that the restaurant chain would have been able to obtain funding for continued expansion, correct?

ANSWER: Correct.

Counsel need examine the expert no further, so long as Ms. Van Zant's certainty of funding can later be shaken or refuted. The connection—that the expert's opinion is weakened—may be drawn during final argument. Alternatively, counsel could ask the expert to concede that the opinion would have to be changed if the expansion money were not available.

G. Challenge Technique or Theory

The most difficult, though frequently the most tempting, form of expert cross examination is to challenge the witness's method, theory, or logic. It is possible, but extremely unlikely, that an expert will agree that she made a mistake or that her reasoning is faulty. In most cases you have little to gain by confronting an expert with any but the most glaring flaws, since that will only afford her an op-portunity to explain. It is usually far more effective to use your own expert to point out the opposition's errors and then to draw your own conclusions during final argument.

THE BASICS

Expert Testimony Opposition Checklist ☑	
❑ Can you challenge the witness's credentials?	Are the witness's credentials inadequate for an expert in the field? If so, point out that insufficiency by conducting voir dire during the direct examination. *If possible, object to the tender of the witness as an expert.* Are the expert's credentials weak or flawed in some area? *If so, underscore that weakness during cross examination.*
❑ Can you obtain favorable information from the witness?	Can you get the expert to affirm your expert, agree with her in certain areas, or criticize her own party's conduct? *If so, elicit this helpful information early in your cross examination.*
❑ Can you challenge the witness's impartiality?	Are the expert's fees unusually high? Does the expert have an ongoing relationship with the party or counsel calling her? Does the witness seem wedded to certain positions? *If so, exploit this information during cross examination.*
❑ Can you point out omissions by the witness?	Did someone besides the expert conduct the tests or compile the information upon which the expert relied? *If so, point out the expert's reliance on others during crossexamination.*
❑ Can you substitute information to make the witness's opinion more favorable to your case?	Will the expert's opinion be altered in your favor if you change the assumptions or facts upon which she relied or if you point out her uncertainty? *If so, change any of the assumptions or facts that you have a good faith basis to believe are incorrect or ambiguous.*
❑ Can you challenge the witness's technique or theory?	Are there glaring flaws in the witness's technique or theory that can be exposed? *If so, point them out during your cross examination, but only if you cannot elicit them from another witness.*

— CHAPTER EIGHT —
Objections

I. MAKING THE RECORD

There is a technical, as well as an artistic, side to trial advoca-cy. The laws of evidence and procedure govern the manner in which a trial proceeds. It is not sufficient for information to be persuasive and elegant, or even true; it must also be admissible under the law of evidence and presented properly under the rules of trial proce-dure. The process of bringing and contesting information before the court and jury is called making the record.

Making the record involves a series of steps. Attorneys offer ev-idence in the form of testimony and exhibits. Some of this evidence may become the subject of objections, in which case the trial judge is called upon to make rulings on admissibility. The admissible evi-dence is presented before the fact-finder. If properly preserved, both the evidence and the objections may eventually be reviewed by an appellate court.

In order to make a record, it is necessary to internalize the rules of evidence and procedure. It is not enough to understand the theory of the hearsay rule; one must also be able to recognize hear-say on an almost instinctual level and to articulate a persuasive objection at virtually any given moment. It is not enough to com-prehend the foundation for the admission of a past recollection; it is also necessary to be able to elicit the foundation in a manner that will be persuasive to the trier of fact. In other words, making the record calls for knowledge, judgment, decisiveness, adaptability, and reflexes.

This chapter will discuss the use of objections. The next chap-ter will cover two related aspects of making a trial record: exhibits and foundations.

Objections are the means by which evidentiary disputes are raised and resolved. Objections may be made to an attorney's ques-tions, to a witness's testimony, to the introduction or use of exhibits, to a lawyer's demeanor or behavior, and even to the conduct of the judge.

Most of a trial advocate's energy is understandably devoted to the content of her case. What do the witnesses have to say? What facts are available to prove the case? How can the opposition be undermined? Which events are central to the proof? Is it possible for several different stories to be harmonized? A persuasive story rests upon the manner in which facts can be developed, arranged, and presented to the trier of fact. It is equally and sometimes more important, however, that the advocate also be well-versed in the technical side of trial advocacy. A well-conceived and tightly constructed story cannot persuade a jury if its crucial elements are not admitted into the record, or if the opposition has had the benefit of using substantial amounts of inadmissible evidence.

II. OBJECTIONS

A. Purpose and Function

1. Use of Objections at Trial

An objection is a request that the court rule on the admissibility of certain testimony or evidence. The purpose of objecting is to prevent the introduction or consideration of inadmissible information. Although the process of objecting has become associated with contentiousness and even hostility, that need not be the case. Our adversary system relies upon opposing attorneys to present evidence and the judge to decide upon its admissibility. An objection, then, is nothing more than a signal to the judge that there is a disagreement between counsel concerning the rules of evidence or procedure. When there are no objections—which is the overwhelming majority of the time—the judge can allow evidence to come into the record without the need for a specific ruling. If we had no process of objecting, the trial judge would have to rule upon every separate answer and item of evidence. Unless the process is abused or misused, trials are actually expedited by the judge's ability to rely upon counsel to object to questionable evidence.

Objections can be made to questions, answers, exhibits, and virtually anything else that occurs during a trial.

An attorney's question may be objectionable because of its form or because it calls for inadmissible evidence. A question is objectionable as to form when it seeks to obtain information in an impermissible way. For example, a leading question on direct examination is improper because it tells the witness what answer is expected.[1] Even if the answer itself would be admissible, the question is disallowed because of its suggestiveness. Compound questions, vague questions, and argumentative questions, to name a few, are also objectionable as to form.

Conversely, a question phrased in proper form may nonetheless call for inadmissible evidence. The information sought may be irrelevant, privileged, or hearsay. An objection may be made when it is apparent from the question itself that the answer should not be admitted. The question, "What is your religious belief?" is in proper form. Any answer, however, would be inadmissible under most circumstances by virtue of the Federal Rules of Evidence.[2] The question is therefore objectionable.

Even in the absence of an objectionable question, a witness may respond with an inadmissible answer. The answer might volunteer irrelevant information, it might contain unanticipated hearsay, or it might consist entirely of speculation. For example, a direct examiner could ask the perfectly allowable question, "How do you know that the traffic light was red?" only to receive the hearsay reply, "Because someone told me just last week." Opposing counsel would no doubt object to the answer and move that it be stricken from the record.

Finally, objections may be made to anything else that might have an impermissible impact on the trier of fact. A lawyer can object if opposing counsel raises her voice to a witness or approaches the witness in an intimidating manner. Objections can be made to the manner in which exhibits are displayed or to the position of chairs and tables in the courtroom. Even the judge's words and actions are not immune to objection, although it is admittedly awkward to ask the court to rule on the permissibility of its own conduct.

2. Use of Objections Before Trial

It is not always necessary to wait until trial to move for the exclusion of evidence. Motions in limine are available to obtain pretrial rulings on evidence that is potentially so harmful that even mention of it may prejudice the jury. A motion in limine asks the

---

1. Leading questions are discussed in greater detail in Section IV A(1), *infra* at p. 229.

2. Evidence of the beliefs or opinions of a wintess on matters of religion is not admissible for the purpose of showing that by reason of their nature his credibility is impaired or enhanced. Rule 610, Federal Rules of Evidence.

judge to rule that the offending evidence be found inadmissible and that it not be offered or introduced at trial.[3]

A motion in limine can be based on any of the substantive rules of evidence. Note, however, that the motion generally will not be granted merely because the subject evidence is objectionable. An additional showing is usually required that the evidence is so damaging that once it is mentioned a sustained objection at trial will not be sufficient to undo its prejudicial impact.

3. Preservation of the Record on Appeal

Appellate courts typically will not consider issues that were not originally raised in the trial court. The admission of evidence generally cannot be reviewed unless it was the subject of a motion in limine or a timely objection was made at trial.[4] Thus, objections serve not only to alert the trial judge to the need for a ruling, they also define the scope of the evidentiary issues that can be considered on appeal.

B. The Decision to Object

In the heat of trial the decision on whether to object to some item of evidence must usually be made literally on a split-second basis. A question on either direct or cross examination typically lasts less than ten seconds; a long question will go on for no more than twenty seconds. Yet within that time counsel must recognize, formulate, and evaluate all possible objections. The concentration required is enormous, and there is no opportunity for letup; counsel must pay exquisite attention to every question and every answer, lest some devastating bit of inadmissible evidence sneak its way into the record. There is no room for even the slightest lapse.

The decision-making process consists of three distinct phases. Counsel must first recognize the objectionability of the particular question, answer, or exhibit. This is often the easiest step since many questions simply "sound wrong." In addition, it is often possible to rely upon certain key words and phrases to jog the objection reflex.

---

3. A motion in limine may also be used to obtain an advance ruling that evidence is admissible. With such a ruling in hand counsel can better frame her trial theory, and can also plan witness examinations so as to avoid the possiblity of reversible error. Nonetheless, this "reverse" use of the motion in limine is fairly unusual.

4. See Rule 103(a)(1), Federal Rules of Evidence. The only exception is in the case of "plain error," in which case the appellate court can take notice of egregious errors affecting substantive rights, even if they were not brought to the attention of the trial judge. See Rule 103(d), Federal Rules of Evidence. On the other hand, once the court has made a definitive ruling, either before or at trial, "a party need not renew an objection or offer of proof to preserve a claim of error for appeal." Rule 103(a).

Questions that use words such as "could," "might," or "possible" commonly call for speculation. Questions that ask about out-of-court statements or conversations must clear the hearsay hurdle.

Following recognition, the next task is to formulate a valid objection. Does the question truly call for speculation, or is it an acceptable lay opinion? Is the out-of-court statement inadmissible hearsay, or does it fall within one of the many exceptions? Even if there is a potentially applicable exception, is it possible to present a counterargument in favor of excluding the evidence? This is the sort of analysis that can fill pages in an appellate opinion or an evidence casebook, but trial counsel must undertake it within the five or ten seconds during which a viable objection can be made.

Finally, counsel must evaluate the tactical situation in order to determine whether the objection is worth making. It is well worth noting that not every valid objection needs to be made. There is little point to objecting if opposing counsel will be able to rectify the problem simply by rephrasing the question or if the information is not ultimately harmful to your case.

The decision to object must be made in reference to your theory of the case. Concerning every potential objection, always ask: Will the exclusion of the evidence contribute to my theory of the case? Unless the exclusion of the evidence actually advances your theory, there is probably no need to raise an objection.

The principal contribution that an objection can make to your theory of the case is to prevent the admission of truly damaging evidence. Hence the maxim, "Do not object to anything that doesn't hurt you." You can refine the decision even further by asking these two additional questions: Even if the information is harmful, can it be accommodated by other means? Even if the objection is sustained, will the information eventually be admitted after another question or through another witness?

Given the scope of modern pretrial discovery, there is no reason to postpone the objection decision until the very moment when the answer is falling from the witness's lips. The general content, if not the precise words, of most important testimony is known to all counsel before the witness ever takes the stand. Most documents and tangible exhibits must be tendered to opposing counsel in advance of trial.

Objection strategy should therefore be planned in the same manner as is direct or cross examination. For each opposition witness, counsel's preparation should include consideration of all possible objections to every reasonably anticipated area of testimony. The potential objections should be weighed against the standards discussed in the above sections, and counsel should come to at least a tentative conclusion as to whether an objection is worth making. The same process should be applied to every expected exhibit and document. It is also necessary to consider the likely content of the opposition's cross examination of your own witnesses and to determine the value of any possible objections.

The best of planning, of course, will not free counsel from the need to make split-second decisions. The evidence will rarely come in exactly as was expected, and the context of the trial may require last-minute adjustments to strategy and approach. Nonetheless, a good deal of the evidentiary background work can and should be done prior to trial.

C. Making and Meeting Objections

The format for making and meeting objections differs somewhat from state to state and even from courtroom to courtroom, so you will need to tailor your approach to objections to local practice. If in doubt about the requirements in a particular jurisdiction, one should always inquire. What follows here is a generalized description of the majority approach.

1. Making an Objection

The standard method of raising an objection is to stand and state the grounds for the objection:

"Objection, Your Honor, relevance."

"Objection, counsel is leading the witness."

"Your Honor, we object on the ground of hearsay."

"Objection, no foundation."

In a jury trial it may also be advisable to add a descriptive tag line so that the jury will understand the basis of the objection:

"Objection, hearsay, Your Honor. The witness cannot testify to what somebody else said."

"We object to the leading questions; counsel is testifying instead of the witness."

In any event, it is necessary to give the precise basis for the objection in order to preserve the issue for appeal. In most jurisdictions, simply stating "objection" is understood only to raise the ground of relevance. If such a "general objection" is made and overruled, all other possible grounds are waived for appeal. [5]

---

5. Note, however, that a "general objection" that is sustained may be affirmed on appeal if there is any valid basis for the objection.

a. Speaking objections

A speaking objection goes beyond the simple state-the-grounds formula described above. Some attorneys find it necessary or fulfilling to launch into an extended discourse on the bases for their objections before allowing the judge to rule or opposing counsel to speak:

> "Objection, Your Honor, that question calls for hearsay. The witness's personal notes constitute an out-of-court statement, even though the witness is present on the stand. They do not qualify either as business records or as past recollection recorded, and in any event there has been no foundation."

While there is no absolute rule against speaking objections, most judges do not like them. Since the judge is often ready to rule as soon as the initial objection is made, speaking objections are seen as time-wasting and laborious. Judges generally consider it their prerogative to request argument and may resent it when counsel fails to wait for the invitation.

b. Repeated objections

It is often necessary to raise the same objection to a number of questions in a row. Perhaps your initial objection was sustained, but your opponent is persistent in attempting to introduce the inadmissible evidence through other means. Perhaps your initial objection was overruled, and you feel bound to protect your record for appeal as opposing counsel asks a series of questions in elaboration. In any event, an awkward feeling inevitably arises when it is necessary to object repeatedly, on the same ground, to question after question.

The least obtrusive way to raise a repeated objection is to say "same objection" at the end of each of opposing counsel's questions. The judge can then repeat her ruling and the trial can proceed in a relatively uninterrupted fashion. If your objections are being sustained, the judge will no doubt tire of reiterating her ruling and will eventually instruct opposing counsel to move on to another line of questioning.

If your "same objections" are being consistently overruled, the judge is likely to tire of them even sooner. At some point she will probably inform you that "I have ruled on that issue, counsel. There is no need for you to continue to object." Now you will risk the judge's ire if you continue to object, but you also risk waiving an issue on appeal if some future question expands on the theme in a way that was not quite covered by your earlier objections.

The solution to this conundrum, which will often be suggested by the trial judge, is the "standing objection." The theory of the standing objection is that a single objection will be considered to "stand" or apply to an entire line of questioning, without the need for repeated interruptions. The problem with standing objections is that it may be difficult in the future to determine exactly which questions and answers were covered. Although the meaning of the standing objection may be apparent to everyone present in the courtroom, the cold transcript presented to the appellate court may seem to tell an entirely different story. It is for this reason that standing objections are to be avoided if possible.

c. Timing

Having determined what to say when initiating an objection, one must consider when to say it. The general rule is that an objection must be made as soon as it is apparent that it is called for. On the other hand, an objection may be premature if it interrupts an incomplete question or if it anticipates testimony that may or may not be given. To be timely, an objection must come neither too early nor too late.

Most objections to questions should be held until the examiner has had the opportunity to complete the question. Not only is it rude to interrupt, but the final version may turn out not to be objectionable. On a more pragmatic level, many judges will refuse to rule on an objection until the question has been completed. An interrupting objection, then, merely ensures that the question will be stated twice, thereby emphasizing its objectionable information or implications.

There are times, however, when it is necessary to interrupt the questioner. Some questions are objectionable not because of what they will elicit, but because of what they assert. A question may contain a damaging suggestion or proposition which, once heard by the jury, cannot be wholly remedied by objection. Such questions must be interrupted in order to cut off the interrogator's inadmissible statement. For example, a cross examiner may be about to question a witness about an inadmissible criminal conviction. Imagine this scenario:

QUESTION: Isn't it true that you were convicted of the crime of selling heroin?

OBJECTION: Objection, Your Honor, that was a juvenile offense. It is inadmissible under Rule 609(d).

THE COURT: Sustained.

Although the objection was sustained,[6] the jury has already heard the inadmissible, though nonetheless damning, truth about the witness. It would obviously have been far more effective to cut off the question earlier:

QUESTION: Isn't it true that you were con—

OBJECTION: Objection, Your Honor. Counsel is seeking information that is prohibited under Rule 609(d).

THE COURT: Sustained.[7]

Even if it does not interrupt a question, an objection may be premature if the examination has not yet reached the point where the inadmissibility of the answer has become certain. An objection must be made immediately before the inadmissible answer, not in anticipation of it. It is not uncommon for a diligent and eager lawyer to object one question too soon, as in the following example:

QUESTION: Did you have a conversation with Ms. Loughlin?

OBJECTION: Objection, Your Honor, hearsay.

THE COURT: Overruled. At this point the only question is whether a conversation occurred. The witness may answer.

ANSWER: Yes, I had a conversation with Ms. Loughlin.

QUESTION: Did Ms. Loughlin tell you anything about the investigation report?

OBJECTION: Hearsay, Your Honor.

THE COURT: Still too soon, counsel. Proceed.

ANSWER: Yes, she did.

QUESTION: What did Ms. Loughlin tell you about the investigation report?

OBJECTION: Objection on the ground of hearsay.

THE COURT: Sustained.

---

6.   In reality, it is most likely that this information would have been the subject of a pretrial motion in limine. For the purposes of this illustration, assume that for some reason no pretial motions were made.

7.   If the judge does anything other than immediately sustain the objection, the objecting lawyer will want to approach the bench for argument.

The first two objections were overruled because under the hearsay rule only the content of the out-of-court statement is inadmissible. The fact of the conversation is admissible evidence.

Timing the objections to questions is relatively easy. Often, however, a witness will respond to a seemingly proper question with a wholly inadmissible response. The timing in these situations is trickier since the answer was not foreshadowed by the question. The general rule is that an objection must be made as soon as the inadmissible nature of the answer becomes apparent. This necessarily means interrupting the witness.

d. Motion to strike

Unfortunately, it is not always possible to recognize and respond to inadmissible testimony before it happens. Counsel may be momentarily distracted or may suffer from rusty reflexes. And some witnesses, either innocently or by design, just have a way of slipping improper testimony into the record. When this happens, counsel's only recourse is the motion to strike:

QUESTION: Are you the comptroller of the defendant corporation?

ANSWER: The only thing I knew about skimming funds came through the rumor mill.

OBJECTION: Objection, hearsay. We move to strike that answer.

THE COURT: Sustained. The answer will be stricken from the record.[8]

In a jury trial it is also important that the judge instruct the jury to disregard the inadmissible answer:

QUESTION: Will Your Honor please instruct the jury to disregard that last answer?

THE COURT: Yes, certainly. Ladies and gentlemen, you are to disregard the answer that the witness just gave. Proceed.

---

8.   Note that the "stricken" testimony will not actually be deleted from the transcript. For the purpose of review on appeal, it is necessary that all of the witness's testimony, as well as all of the rulings of the court and the arguments of counsel, appear on the transcript. Thus, the testimony is stricken only in the legal sense, not literally.

While this sort of curative instruction is hardly a satisfying remedy, it is the best that can be done under the circumstances. In many jurisdictions the request for a curative instruction is a necessary predicate to raising the issue on appeal.

e. Witness voir dire

The basis for an objection may not always be apparent from the question or even the answer. Counsel may have access to information that is not yet in the record but which negates the admissibility of some part of a witness's testimony. This information can be brought to the judge's attention through witness voir dire. The term voir dire is derived from "law French," which was once in use in English courts; it means "speak the truth."

In the context of witness examination, voir dire refers to a limited cross examination for the purpose of determining the admissibility of evidence. The voir dire examination interrupts the direct and gives the opposing lawyer a chance to bring out additional facts that bear directly on the admissibility of some part of the balance of the testimony. Counsel who wishes to conduct voir dire must ask permission of the judge:

QUESTION: Whose signature is on that document?

ANSWER: It appears to be the defendant's.

OBJECTION: Your Honor, we object to that testimony and ask leave to conduct a limited voir dire of the witness.

THE COURT: You may proceed with voir dire of the witness.

OBJECTION: You did not see the document being signed, did you?

ANSWER: No.

OBJECTION: You have never seen the defendant sign his name, have you?

ANSWER: No.

OBJECTION: You have never received any signed correspondence from the defendant, have you?

ANSWER: No.

OBJECTION: Your Honor, it is obvious that the witness cannot identify the signature from her own personal knowledge. We renew our objection to the testimony and move to strike the previous answer.

Voir dire examination is most commonly utilized with regard to the qualifications of an expert witness or the foundation for a document or exhibit, but it can be used in other situations as well. Note that following voir dire the offering attorney is entitled to conduct additional examination aimed at reestablishing the admissibility of the evidence.

2. Responding to Objections

Many judges like to rule on objections as soon as they hear them, without even a response from opposing counsel. Believing that they know the law and have been attentive to the proceedings, judges often consider it a waste of time to entertain argument. In truth, a majority of evidentiary objections present no great problems in jurisprudence. A judge can sustain or overrule a good many objections without recourse to counsel's views.

It is common, therefore, for opposing counsel to make no response to an objection unless invited to do so by the judge. The judge might also signal the desire for a response nonverbally, perhaps by looking at counsel or by nodding in counsel's direction. It is important to be on the alert for such gestures, since failure to respond might be interpreted by the judge as waiver.

a. Requesting argument

Many objections will not be readily susceptible of summary disposition because they raise subtle or complex legal issues. Aspects of an objection may escape the judge or may require consideration of additional information that is not apparent from the record. In these circumstances counsel cannot rely on an invitation to argue from the judge and will need to inform the court, as politely as possible, that argument is necessary. It is preferable to do this before the judge has ruled, if that can be accomplished without interrupting. An effective signal is to stand while the objection is being made, in order to alert the judge that argument is desired.

Despite counsel's best efforts, the judge may rule on a disputed objection without input from the opposing side. If the point is important, counsel cannot be shy about letting the judge know that there is another side to the objection:

QUESTION: What did the police officer say to you?

OBJECTION: Objection, hearsay.

THE COURT: Sustained.

QUESTION: Your Honor, we would like to be heard on that.

THE COURT: Very well, what do you have to say?

QUESTION: The statement falls under the "present sense impression" exception.

THE COURT: I see. Overruled. The witness may answer.

b. Limited admissibility

Evidence may be inadmissible for some purposes yet admissible for others. When responding to objections it is extremely important to advise the judge of the precise purpose for which the evidence is offered.

For example, evidence that a dangerous condition has been repaired is generally inadmissible to prove negligence.[9] Counsel cannot argue to the jury, "Of course the owner of the car took inadequate care of the automobile; he had his brakes repaired just two days after the accident." On the other hand, evidence of the repair is admissible to prove ownership of the automobile. Counsel can argue, "The defendant denies that he was responsible for the upkeep of the car, but he was the one who ordered and paid for the repair of the brakes just two days after the accident."

With this dichotomy in mind, consider the possible objections and responses in the cross examination of the defendant:

COUNSEL: Didn't you have your brakes repaired just two days after the accident?

OBJECTION: Objection, Your Honor, this testimony violates Rule 407.

THE COURT: What do you have to say, counsel?

COUNSEL: We are offering it only to prove ownership and control, Your Honor.

THE COURT: The evidence will be received, but only for that limited purpose. Ladies and gentlemen of the jury, you are to consider this evidence only for the purpose of showing ownership and control

---

9.   See Rule 407, Federal Rules of Evidence.

of the automobile. You must not consider it as proof of any negligence on the part of the defendant.

If the court does not immediately give a limiting instruction, one should be requested by the attorney whose objection was overruled.

c. Conditional offers

The admissibility of certain testimony, particularly with regard to relevance, may not always be immediately clear. This is a frequent occurrence on cross examination since counsel may be utilizing the technique of indirection[10] or otherwise attempting to avoid being too obvious about the direction of the cross. Nor is such subtlety unknown on direct examination. In either case, the ultimate admissibility of the evidence might depend upon other testimony to be developed through later witnesses.

In these circumstances counsel may respond to an objection by making a "conditional offer." This is done either by promising to "tie it up later" or, preferably, by explaining to the court the nature of the evidence that is expected to follow. For example:

COUNSEL: Isn't it true that you had an important meeting scheduled for the morning of the accident?

OBJECTION: Objection. The witness's business schedule is not relevant.

THE COURT: What is the relevance of that inquiry, counsel?

COUNSEL: We intend to introduce evidence that the defendant had a meeting scheduled with a prospective client, that he was already late for the meeting at the time of the accident, and that he stood to lose a great deal of money if he didn't arrive on time. The question is therefore directly relevant to show that he was speeding and inattentive.[11]

THE COURT: Based on that representation I will allow the testimony, subject to a motion to strike if you don't tie it up.

---

10. See Chapter 4, Section V B(3), *supra* at p. 94.

11. Depending upon the sensitivity of the information, it would be appropriate to request that the argument on such an objection be conducted outside the presence of the witness.

A conditional offer is always subject to the actual production of the later evidence. The testimony can, and should, be stricken if counsel's representations are not fulfilled.[12]

d. Anticipating objections

Being specific is a challenge. When you are interrupted in mid-examination by a maddening objection, the precise, and hopefully devastating, reply may not spring spontaneously to mind. It is therefore essential to plan for likely objections as part of the overall preparation for trial.

Planning for relevance objections should be nearly automatic since it is really part and parcel of developing your theory of the case. Recall that every question you ask, indeed every item of evidence you put forward, should be calculated to advance your theory of the case. By definition, then, you will have considered the probative value of each question before the trial ever starts. To respond to a relevance objection, you will really need to do nothing more than explain to the judge why you offered the evidence in the first place. In other words, "The testimony is relevant, Your Honor, because it contributes 'X' to my theory of the case."

Other objections may not be as easy to anticipate. At a minimum, however, trial preparation should include an evaluation of the admissibility of every tangible object, document, or other exhibit that you intend to offer into evidence or use for demonstrative purposes. It is similarly necessary to do an "admissibility check" on all testimony involving conversations, telephone calls, meetings, and other out-of-court statements. Finally, potential objections should be considered for all opinions, conclusions, calculations, and characterizations you expect to elicit. Why is the evidence relevant? What is the necessary foundation for its authenticity? Does the witness have sufficient personal knowledge? Is there a hearsay problem? Might it be privileged?

e. Judicious nonresponses

It is not necessary to fight to the death over every objection. Counsel can frequently avoid an objection by rephrasing the offending question, either before or after the judge rules.

Since the precise language of a question is seldom of vital importance, it should be possible to circumnavigate virtually any objection as to form. Leading questions, compound questions, and

---

12. See Rule 104(b), Federal Rules of Evidence.

vague questions can all be cured. Even if your original question was perfectly fine, you may be able to move the trial along, and earn the gratitude of judge and jury, by posing the same inquiry in different words.

Other objections that can be undercut through rephrasing include personal knowledge, foundation, and even relevance. For example:

QUESTION: Did the plaintiff follow his doctor's advice?

OBJECTION: Objection. Lack of personal knowledge.

QUESTION: Let me put it this way. Did the plaintiff say anything to you about his doctor's advice?

ANSWER: Yes.

QUESTION: What did he say?

ANSWER: He said that he would rather risk the consequences than stay in bed all day.

Note that in this scenario the examination was made stronger by rephrasing the question in response to the objection.

Making and meeting objections involves a certain amount of gamesmanship. No lawyer likes to be seen as an evidentiary naif or pushover. From time to time it may be tactically important to stand behind a question, if only to establish your mastery of the rules. Another alternative is to rephrase a question without saying so. In the above example the attorney neither withdrew the question nor overtly rephrased it, but rather said, "Let me put it this way." Problem solved.

D. Arguing Objections

1. Where

As an initial matter, lawyers usually argue objections from wherever they happen to be standing or sitting when the issue first arises. Even in a jury trial most objections are resolved without anyone moving from their location. The language of objecting is arcane, and in most circumstances it does no harm to have the discussion in the presence of the jury.

Occasionally, however, it is important that the jury not hear the content of the argument. It may be necessary to recite the expected testimony so the judge can rule on the objection, or to refer to other evidence that has not yet been admitted. In these circumstances either side may request that the argument take place out of the presence of the jury.

The most common way of insulating the jury from the attorneys' argument is for counsel to approach the bench and hold, in whispered tones, a sidebar conference. Alternatively, the jury can be excused from the courtroom while counsel argue. This latter approach is used fairly infrequently, and only in the case of extended arguments, since it is cumbersome and time-consuming to shuffle the jury in and out of the courtroom.

A sidebar can be called by the court or requested by either the party making or the party responding to the objection. Typically, the lawyer whose case is most likely to be harmed by disclosures in the course of the argument requests the sidebar. Ethical counsel, however, will volunteer the need for a sidebar whenever she realizes that her own argument may prejudice the other side. The opposition's failure to ask for argument outside the jury's presence should not be taken as license to make statements containing potentially inadmissible evidence. Unfortunately, this practice is all too common. It has no place in a trial conducted by professionals.

2. How

Arguments on objections should be conducted as a conversation between counsel and the court. The general scenario is for objecting counsel to argue first, followed by the attorney who offered the evidence, and concluding with a reply from the objector. In practice, however, the format is often much less formal, with the judge asking questions and counsel responding.

If there is one signal rule in arguing objections, it is that counsel should not argue with, or even address, each other. It is the judge who will make the ruling and the judge who must be convinced. It is ineffective, distracting, and even insulting to the court when counsel turn to each other to argue their objections.

No matter how foolish, trite, or easily disposed of the other side's position seems, avoid speaking directly to opposing counsel. All of your arguments should be made to the court. If, in the course of an argument, you are ever tempted to turn to opposing counsel, remember that she is being paid to disagree with you. There should be nothing in the world that you can say to make her alter her position. Her job is to take the other side of the issue. The judge, by contrast, is employed to keep an open mind. The judge can be persuaded, but only if you take the trouble to address the court directly.

Your evidentiary arguments will be most convincing if they are delivered with a tone of firm conviction. When you argue an objection, you are asking the judge to do something—either to admit or to exclude evidence. The wrong decision can lead to reversal, a matter of at least passing professional concern to the judge. Your argument, then, should give the judge a reason for ruling in your favor. Emotive histrionics will be counterproductive. The sort of diffidence or lassitude often displayed by attorneys when arguing to the bench is also unlikely to succeed. A judge, despite the robe, is human. If you do not believe in your argument, why should she?

E.   Once the Judge Has Ruled

The judge's ruling on an objection is not necessarily the end of that particular discourse. Counsel must remain alert to protect and develop the record. Both the proponent of the evidence (offering lawyer) and the opponent (objecting lawyer) may have more yet to do.

1. Objection Overruled

a. Proponent's job

The proponent's job when an objection is overruled is to ensure that the evidence actually makes its way into the record. In other words, the proponent must make sure that the witness answers the question that the judge has just ruled to be permissible. The following is an all-too-frequent scenario:

QUESTION: After the accident, what did the crossing guard say to you?

OBJECTION: Objection, Your Honor, the question calls for hearsay.

QUESTION: Your Honor, it has already been established that the crossing guard observed the accident immediately before making the declaration, so it qualifies as either an excited utterance or a present sense impression.

THE COURT: Yes, I think there is a hearsay exception there. Overruled.

QUESTION: What is the next thing that you did?

ANSWER: I went to a telephone and dialed 911.

Despite the court's ruling, the witness was never given an opportunity to answer the original question. The proponent, apparently flushed with victory, just went on to another subject.

Following an overruled objection, the proponent's safest course is to repeat the question, and to be sure to get a clear answer from the witness.

b. Opponent's job

The opponent's job following an overruled objection is to stay alert to the possibility of excluding all or some of the offending evidence.

In the first instance the opponent of the evidence should not withdraw an objection. Many lawyers, perhaps out of embarrassment or obsequiousness, seem to think that they can gain points with the trial judge by withdrawing an objection once it has been overruled. In fact, the opposite is probably true. Having already taken the court's time by making and arguing an objection, one can only convey indecision or lack of seriousness by withdrawing it immediately thereafter. Even more to the point, withdrawing an objection has the effect of waiving the issue for appeal.

In any event, once an objection has been overruled, the objecting lawyer must continue to scrutinize the subsequent testimony. Perhaps the witness will not testify in the manner that was promised by the proponent of the evidence in her argument to the court. For example:

QUESTION: After the accident, what did the crossing guard say to you?

OBJECTION: Objection, Your Honor, the question calls for hearsay.

QUESTION: Your Honor, it qualifies as either an excited utterance or a present sense impression.

THE COURT: Yes, I think there is a hearsay exception there. Overruled.

ANSWER: She said that she didn't really see what happened, but that it looked as though...

OBJECTION: Your Honor, I renew my objection. If the witness didn't really see the accident, then she can't have a present sense impression.

THE COURT: Yes. The objection will be sustained on those grounds.

Alternatively, other grounds for objection may become clear in the course of the testimony, or perhaps the witness will begin volunteering evidence that is inadmissible for some additional reason. In the above scenario counsel could also have objected on the ground that the declarant's statement ("it looked as though...") was speculative.

2. Objection Sustained

a. Proponent's job

A sustained objection means that the proponent of the evidence has been denied the opportunity to place the testimony or exhibit into the record. This ruling leaves the proponent with two options.

i. Offer of proof

If the testimony (or exhibit) is sufficiently important, the proponent's first task is to protect the record by making an offer of proof. When a witness is not allowed to testify, the record is silent as to the content of the evidence. An appellate court reviewing the record, however, must know the content of the omitted material in order to determine whether the judge's ruling was reversible error. The offer of proof is the means by which counsel can place into the record a description of the excluded testimony[13] so that the right to an effective appeal may be preserved.[14] An offer of proof also gives the trial court an opportunity to reconsider its ruling on the basis of a more complete description of the excluded evidence.

There are three generally accepted ways to present an offer of proof. The first method is to excuse the jury and proceed with the examination of the witness. This approach has the obvious benefit of accuracy since the witness's actual testimony will be preserved. It is also time-consuming and somewhat awkward, and for those reasons it is only employed in exceptional circumstances.

The most frequently utilized method of presenting an offer of proof is for counsel to summarize the excluded testimony. Although certainly time-efficient, the summarization method has its drawbacks. One problem is that it is very easy to leave out crucial information. A further problem is that enterprising and less than scrupulous lawyers have been known to pad their summaries with

---

13. When a proffered exhibit, as opposed to testimony, is not admitted, it usually remians part of the record as an exhibit "for identification" as opposed to an exhibit "in evidence." Thus, exhibits can generally be reviewed by an appellate court without the need for an offer of proof.

14. Rule 103(a)(2), Federal Rules of Evidence. Note that an offer of proof need not be renewed following a "definitive" ruling by the court.

"testimony" far more favorable than the witness ever would have produced.

The third approach to offers of proof is the submission to the court of witness statements, reports, or deposition transcripts. This method can have the benefit of both thoroughness and brevity. It is used relatively infrequently, however, due at least in part to the difficulty of assembling the right written materials at exactly the right time.

ii. Keep trying

The proponent's second task in the face of a sustained objection is to keep trying to have the evidence admitted. When a judge sustains an objection, the ruling usually applies only to the specific question (or answer) and grounds that were then before the court. Unless the judge says so explicitly, the ruling does not extend to the ultimate admissibility of the underlying evidence. In other words, a sustained objection says only that "the evidence cannot be admitted based on the testimony and arguments heard so far." It does not say that "the evidence cannot ever be admitted no matter what you do." Counsel generally has the option to offer the evidence through other means.

These "other means" may consist of nothing more than rephrasing a question. Any objection as to form—leading, compound, vague, argumentative—can be cured by altering the language of the inquiry. Leading questions on direct examination can easily be restated:

QUESTION: You had the green light when the defendant's car hit yours, didn't you?

OBJECTION: Objection, leading.

THE COURT: Sustained.

QUESTION: What color was your light when the defendant's car hit yours?

ANSWER: It was green.

Objections are frequently sustained not because of the form of the question but because of some missing predicate in the testimony. Objections to foundation can be cured by eliciting additional foundation. Objections to a witness's lack of personal knowledge can be remedied with further questions showing the basis of the witness's information. Relevance objections can be overcome through continued questioning aimed at demonstrating the probative value of the original question.

The same approach can work for hearsay objections. Additional facts can often be established that will qualify a statement for an exception to the hearsay rule. Moreover, out-of-court statements may sometimes be recast in the form of conduct or observations. In the following example a police officer has just testified on direct examination that she received a radio dispatch that a crime had been committed:

QUESTION: What was the content of the radio bulletin from the dispatcher?

OBJECTION: Objection, hearsay.

THE COURT: Sustained.

QUESTION: What did you do immediately after receiving the alert?

ANSWER: I drove to the corner of Grand Avenue and State Street.

QUESTION: What did you do there?

ANSWER: I began looking for a suspect wearing glasses and a white lab jacket.

The effect of the sustained hearsay objection was avoided by continuing the examination on the admissible subject of the witness's actions, as opposed to the inadmissible subject of the dispatcher's out-of-court statement.

It is not always possible to overcome a sustained objection. Some testimony will be flatly inadmissible no matter how many approaches counsel attempts. On the other hand, there are often numerous routes to admissibility, and a sustained objection usually closes off only one. Keep trying.

b. Opponent's job

When an objection is sustained, the opponent of the evidence has been successful. This should bring satisfaction to the objector, and in some cases even rejoicing, but it is never a reason to rest on your laurels. The very next question may ask for the identical evidence, in which case an additional objection must be made. A sustained objection will be a temporary victory indeed if the proponent of the evidence succeeds in having it admitted later in the witness's testimony. This is not uncommon. Successful objections can come undone as soon as the objector relaxes vigilance:

QUESTION:	Who told you to begin your financial investigation?
ANSWER:	I received an anonymous note charging that—
OBJECTION:	Objection, hearsay.
THE COURT:	Sustained.
QUESTION:	What caused you to begin investigating?
ANSWER:	There was a charge that money had been skimmed from one of the trust accounts.
QUESTION:	How did you learn of the charge?
ANSWER:	I received a note.

The opponent of the evidence in this case let down her guard. When the first hearsay objection was successful, she allowed her attention to lapse. She therefore failed to notice that the identical testimony was being introduced as the "cause" of the investigation. The information, of course, is no less hearsay (and no less anonymous) the second time around. A second objection should have been made.

The cardinal rule when your objection is sustained is don't fall asleep.

3. Limiting Instructions

If the evidence is admitted for a limited purpose, the opponent's job is to ask for a limiting instruction that explains the nature of the court's ruling. Most judges give such an instruction as a matter of course. Counsel may occasionally want to forego the limiting instruction, on the theory that it will only call attention to the harmful evidence.

THE BASICS

Summary of Objection Rules

- Consider objections carefully
- Direct all arguments to the judge
- Request sidebars (if allowed)
- Raise objections appropriately
    Stand up
    Object and state your grounds
    Pause for the judge to consider the objection
    If appropriate, respond to the court
    Request voir dire of the witness when necessary
- Time objections appropriately
- Respond to objections appropriately
    Wait for the judge's cue to respond
    If appropriate, request to be heard
    Respond specifically and inform the court of limited admissibility or
    a conditional offer
    Cure the objection whenever possible
- Follow up the judge's ruling

  Objection Overruled
  Proponent's job: ensure that the question is answered and evidence is heard
  Opponent's job: stay alert for new grounds to exclude the evidence

  Objection Sustained
  Proponent's job: keep trying to have the evidence admitted
  Opponent's job: stay alert to different attempts to offer the same evidence

III. ETHICS AND OBJECTIONS

Ethical issues frequently arise in the context of making and meeting objections. Because the objecting process is one of the most confrontational aspects of the trial, it often tests counsel's reserves of good will, civility, restraint, and sense of fair play. The three most common problems are discussed below.

A. Asking Objectionable Questions

As we have discussed above, assessing the likely admissibility of evidence is an essential component of trial preparation. There is no question that counsel may offer any evidence that she believes is either clearly or probably admissible. What about evidence that is probably inadmissible? Is it ethical to offer such testimony in the hope that either opposing counsel will fail to object or that the judge will make an erroneous ruling?

It is ethical to offer any evidence over which there is a reasonable evidentiary dispute. Our adversary system calls upon each attorney to make out the best case possible, and relies upon the judge to rule on disputed issues of law. Valuable evidence should not be preemptively excluded on the basis of counsel's assessment, so long as there is a reasonable basis in the law for its admission.

This principle does not, however, relieve counsel of all responsibility to cull inadmissible evidence from the case. A corollary to counsel's right to offer evidence for which there is a reasonable basis is the obligation to refrain from offering evidence for which there is no reasonable basis. As stated in the Model Rules of Professional Conduct, a lawyer shall not

> [I]n trial, allude to any matter that the lawyer does not reasonably believe is relevant or that will not be supported by admissible evidence...[15]

In other words, it is unethical to offer evidence knowing that there is no reasonable basis for its admission. Even though opposing counsel might neglect to object, and even though the court might err in its ruling, the adversary system does not extend so far as to allow the intentional use of improper evidence. Indeed, one of the justifications for the adversary system is precisely that counsel can be relied upon to perform this minimum level of self-policing.

An appropriate rule, therefore, is to consider it improper to offer evidence that cannot be supported by an articulable theory of admissibility. Counsel should be able to complete, with specific and recognizable legal arguments, the sentence that begins, "This evidence is admissible because..." If the only conclusion for the sentence is "Because it helps my case," then there is not a reasonable basis for the offer.

Finally, it is unethical to attempt to use the information contained in questions as a substitute for testimony that cannot be obtained. Some lawyers apparently believe that the idea of zealous advocacy allows them to slip information before a jury by asserting it in a question, knowing full well that the witness will not be allowed to answer. The usual scenario is something as follows:

LAWYER: Isn't it true that you were once fired from a job for being drunk?

OBJECTION: Objection, relevance.

LAWYER: I withdraw the question. (*Sotto voce*: Who cares about the ruling? I never expected to get it in,

---

15. Rule 3.4(e), Model Rules of Professional Conduct.

but now the jury knows that the witness is a drunk.)

This conduct, even if the information is true, is absolutely unethical. Testimony is to come from witnesses, with admissibility ruled upon by the court. It subverts the very purpose of an adversary trial when lawyers abuse their right to question witnesses in order to slip inadmissible evidence before the jury.

B. Making Questionable Objections

The same general analysis applies to the use of objections as it does to the offer of evidence. Counsel need not be positive that an objection will be sustained but must only believe that there is a reasonable basis for making it. Again, under the adversary system it is up to the judge to decide whether to admit the evidence.

The license to make questionable objections is available only if counsel is truly interested in excluding the subject evidence. That is, an attorney may make any reasonable or plausible objection, but only so long as the purpose of the objection is to obtain a ruling on the evidence. As we will see in the following section, objections may also be employed for a variety of ulterior purposes, most of which are unethical.

C. Making "Tactical" Objections

Many lawyers, and more than a few trial advocacy texts, tout the use of so-called "tactical" objections. Since an objection is the only means by which one lawyer can interrupt the examination of another, it is suggested that objections should occasionally be made to "break up" the flow of a successful examination. An objection can throw the opposing lawyer off stride, or give the witness a rest, or distract the jury from the content of the testimony. This advice is usually tempered with the admonition that there must always be some evidentiary basis for the objection, but the real message is that an objection may be used for any purpose whatsoever so long as you can make it with a straight face.

This view is unfortunate. It amounts to nothing more than the unprincipled use of objections for a wholly improper purpose. No judge would allow a lawyer to object on the ground that the opposition's examination is going too well. The fact that disruption can be accomplished *sub silentio* does not justify it. The same is true of other "tactical" uses of objections. It is unethical to use a speaking objection to communicate with the jury or to suggest testimony to a witness.

The tactical use of objections is widespread and seldom punished. The use of "colorable" objections to accomplish impermissible goals can insulate a lawyer from discipline, but it does not make the practice right.[16] The "true exclusion" standard being urged here may well be unenforceable by judges; it is virtually impossible to evaluate a lawyer's thought process to determine the underlying reason for any particular objection. The standard is, however, attainable by any lawyer who is committed to practice in good faith.

IV. A SHORT LIST OF COMMON OBJECTIONS

A complete discussion of evidentiary objections is beyond the scope of this book. The following list of some frequently made objections (and responses) is intended only as a reference or guide, not as a substitute for a thorough knowledge of evidence and procedure.

This section provides a brief description of the grounds for each objection followed by an equally brief statement of some possible responses. Where appropriate, citations are made to the Federal Rules of Evidence (FRE).

A. Objections to the Form of the Question (or Answer)

1. Leading Question

A leading question suggests or contains its own answer. Leading questions are objectionable on direct examination. They are permitted on cross examination. *See* FRE 611.

Responses. The question is preliminary, foundational, directing the witness's attention, or refreshing the witness's recollection. The witness is very old, very young, infirm, adverse, or hostile. Leading questions can most often be rephrased in nonleading form.

2. Compound Question

A compound question contains two separate inquiries that are not necessarily susceptible of a single answer. For example, "Wasn't the fire engine driving in the left lane and flashing its lights?"

Responses. Dual inquiries are permissible if the question seeks to establish a relationship between two facts or events. For example, "Didn't he move forward and then reach into his pocket?" Other

---

16. Racial or religious discrimination can also be accomplished, at least on a small scae, through undectectable means. One can often find an arguable excuse for bad actions. In this context it is easily recognizable that hiding one's motivation does not justify the result.

than to establish a relationship, compound questions are objectionable and should be rephrased.

3. Vague Question

A question is vague if it is incomprehensible, or incomplete, or if any answer will necessarily be ambiguous. For example, the question, "When do you leave your house in the morning?" is vague since it does not specify the day of the week to which it refers.

Responses. A question is not vague if the judge understands it. Many judges will ask the witness whether he or she understands the question. Unless the precise wording is important, it is often easiest to rephrase a "vague" question.

4. Argumentative Question

An argumentative question asks the witness to accept the examiner's summary, inference, or conclusion rather than to agree with the existence (or nonexistence) of a fact. Questions can be made more or less argumentative depending upon the tone of voice of the examiner.

Responses. Treat the objection as a relevance issue and explain its probative value to the court: "Your Honor, it goes to prove…" (It will not be persuasive to say, "Your Honor, I am not arguing." It might be persuasive to explain the nonargumentative point that you are trying to make.) Alternatively, make no response, but wait to see if the judge thinks that the question is argumentative. If so, rephrase the question.

5. Narratives

Witnesses are required to testify in the form of question and answer. This requirement ensures that opposing counsel will have the opportunity to frame objections to questions before the answer is given. A narrative answer is one which proceeds at some length in the absence of questions. An answer that is more than a few sentences long can usually be classified as a narrative. A narrative question is one that calls for a narrative answer, such as, "Tell us everything that you did on July 14." Objections can be made both to narrative questions and to narrative answers.

Responses. The best response is usually to ask another question that will break up the narrative. Note that expert witnesses are often allowed to testify in narrative fashion since technical explanations cannot be given easily in question-and-answer format. Even then, however, it is usually more persuasive to interject questions to break up big answers.

6. Asked and Answered

An attorney is not entitled to repeat questions and answers. Once an inquiry has been "asked and answered," further repetition is objectionable. Variations on a theme, however, are permissible, so long as the identical information is not endlessly repeated. The asked and answered rule does not preclude inquiring on cross examination into subjects that were covered fully on direct. Nor does it prevent asking identical questions of different witnesses. (Judges do, however, have the inherent power to exclude cumulative testimony. See FRE 611(a).)

Responses. If the question has not been asked and answered, counsel can point out to the judge the manner in which it differs from the earlier testimony. Otherwise, it is best to rephrase the question so as to vary the exact information sought.

7. Assuming Facts Not in Evidence

A question, usually on cross examination, is objectionable if it includes as a predicate a statement of fact that has not been proven. The reason for this objection is that the question is unfair; it cannot be answered without conceding the unproven assumption. Consider, for example, the following question: "You left your home so late that you only had fifteen minutes to get to your office?" If the time of the witness's departure was not previously established, this question assumes a fact not in evidence. The witness cannot answer yes to the main question (fifteen minutes to get to the office) without implicitly conceding the unproven predicate.

Responses. A question assumes facts not in evidence only when it utilizes an introductory predicate as the basis for another inquiry. Simple, one-part cross examination questions do not need to be based upon facts that are already in evidence. For example, it would be proper to ask a witness, "Didn't you leave home late that morning?" whether or not there had already been evidence as to the time of the witness's departure. As a consequence of misunderstanding this distinction, "facts not in evidence" objections are often erroneously made to perfectly good cross examination questions. If the objection is well-taken, most questions can easily be divided in two.

8. Nonresponsive Answers

It was once hornbook law that only the attorney who asked the question could object to a nonresponsive answer. The theory for this limitation was that opposing counsel had no valid objection so long as the content of the answer complied with the rules of evidence. The more modern view is that opposing counsel can object if all, or some part, of an answer is unresponsive to the question, since counsel is entitled to insist that the examination proceed in question-and-answer format. Jurisdictions that adhere to the traditional view may still recognize an objection that the witness is "volunteering" or that there is "no question pending."

Responses. Ask another question.

B. Substantive Objections

1. Hearsay

The Federal Rules of Evidence define hearsay as "[a] statement, other than one made by the declarant while testifying at the trial or hearing, offered in evidence to prove the truth of the matter asserted."[17] Thus, any out-of-court statement, including the witness's own previous statement, is potentially hearsay. Whenever a witness testifies, or is asked to testify, about what she or someone else said in the past, the statement should be subjected to hearsay analysis. Statements are not hearsay if they are offered for a purpose other than to "prove the truth of the matter asserted." For example, consider the statement, "I warned him that his brakes needed work." This statement would be hearsay if offered to prove that the brakes were indeed defective. On the other hand, it would not be hearsay if offered to prove that the driver had notice of the condition of the brakes and was therefore negligent in not having them repaired. There are also numerous exceptions to the hearsay rule.

Responses. Out-of-court statements are admissible if they are not hearsay or if they fall within one of the exceptions to the hearsay rule.

In addition to statements that are not offered for their truth, the Federal Rules of Evidence define two other types of statements as nonhearsay. The witness's own previous statement is not hearsay if (A) it was given under oath and it is inconsistent with the current testimony; or (B) it is consistent with the current testimony and it is offered to rebut a charge of recent fabrication; or (C) it is a statement of past identification. In addition, an admission of a party opponent is defined as nonhearsay, if offered against that party.[18]

Some of the more frequently encountered exceptions to the hearsay rule are as follows:

Present Sense Impression. A statement describing an event made while the declarant is observing it. For example, "Look, there goes the President." Rule 803(1).

---

17. Rule 801(c), Federal Rules of Evidence.
18. Rule 801(d)(2), Federal Rules of Evidence.

Excited Utterance. A statement relating to a startling event made while under the stress of excitement caused by the event. For example, "A piece of plaster fell from the roof, and it just missed me." Rule 803(2).

State of Mind. A statement of the declarant's mental state or condition. For example, "He said that he was so mad he couldn't see straight." Rule 803(3).

Past Recollection Recorded. A memorandum or record of a matter about which the witness once had knowledge but which she has since forgotten. The record must have been made by the witness when the events were fresh in the witness's mind and must be shown to have been accurate when made. Rule 803(5).

Business Records. The business records exception applies to the records of any regularly conducted activity. To qualify as an exception to the hearsay rule, the record must have been made at or near the time of the transaction by a person with knowledge or transmitted from a person with knowledge. It must have been made and kept in the ordinary course of business. The foundation for a business record must be laid by the custodian of the record or by some other qualified witness. Rule 803(6).

Reputation as to Character. Evidence of a person's reputation for truth and veracity is an exception to the hearsay rule. Note that there are restrictions other than hearsay on the admissibility of character evidence. Rule 803(21).

Prior Testimony. Testimony given at a different proceeding, or in deposition, qualifies for this exception if (1) the testimony was given under oath; (2) the adverse party had an opportunity to cross examine; and (3) the witness is currently unavailable. Rule 804(b)(1).

Dying Declaration. A statement by a dying person as to the cause or circumstances of what he or she believed to be impending death. Admissible only in homicide prosecutions or civil cases. Rule 804(b)(2).

Statement against Interest. A statement so contrary to the declarant's pecuniary, proprietary, or penal interest that no reasonable person would have made it unless it were true. The declarant must be unavailable, and certain other limitations apply in criminal cases. Rule 804(b)(3).

Catchall Exception. Other hearsay statements may be admitted if they contain sufficient circumstantial guarantees of trustworthiness. The declarant must be unavailable, and advance notice must be given to the adverse party. Rule 807.

2. Irrelevant

Evidence is irrelevant if it does not make any fact of consequence to the case more or less probable. Evidence can be irrelevant if it proves nothing or if it tends to prove something that does not matter. Rules 401, 402.

Responses. Explain the relevance of the testimony.

3. Unfair Prejudice

Relevant evidence may be excluded if its probative value is substantially outweighed by the danger of unfair prejudice. Note that evidence cannot be excluded merely because it is prejudicial; by definition, all relevant evidence must be prejudicial to some party. Rather, the objection only obtains if the testimony has little probative value and it is unfairly prejudicial. The classic example is a lurid and explicit photograph of an injured crime victim offered to prove some fact of slight relevance, such as the clothing that the victim was wearing. The availability of other means to establish the same facts will also be considered by the court. Rule 403.

Responses. Most judges are hesitant to exclude evidence on this basis. A measured explanation of the probative value of the testimony is the best response.

4. Improper Character Evidence, Generally

Character evidence is generally not admissible to prove that a person acted in conformity with his or her character. For example, a defendant's past burglaries cannot be offered as proof of a current charge of burglary. A driver's past accidents cannot be offered as proof of current negligence. Rule 404(a).

Responses. A criminal defendant may offer proof of good character, which the prosecution may then rebut. Rule 404(a)(1).

Past crimes and bad acts may be offered to prove motive, opportunity, intent, preparation, plan, knowledge, identity, or absence of mistake. Rule 404(b).

5. Improper Character Evidence, Conviction of Crime

As noted above, the commission, and even the conviction, of past crimes is not admissible to prove current guilt.

The credibility of a witness who takes the stand and testifies, however, may be impeached on the basis of a prior criminal conviction, but only if the following requirements are satisfied: The crime must have been either (1) a felony, or (2) one which involved dishonesty or false statement, regardless of punishment. With certain exceptions, the evidence is not admissible unless it occurred within the last ten years. Juvenile adjudications are generally not admissible. Rule 609.

Note that the impeachment is generally limited to the fact of conviction, the name of the crime, and the sentence received. The details and events that comprised the crime are generally inadmissible.

Responses. If the crime was not a felony, the conviction may still be admissible if it involved dishonesty. If the conviction is more than ten years old, it may still be admissible if the court determines that its probative value, supported by specific facts and circumstances, substantially outweighs its prejudicial effect. Rule 609.

6. Improper Character Evidence, Untruthfulness

As noted above, the past bad acts of a person may not be offered as proof that he or she committed similar acts. Specific instances of conduct are admissible for the limited purpose of attacking or supporting credibility. A witness may therefore be cross examined concerning past bad acts only if they reflect upon truthfulness or untruthfulness. Note, however, that such bad acts (other than conviction of a crime) may not be proved by extrinsic evidence. The cross examiner is stuck with the witness's answer. Rule 608(b).

Responses. Explain the manner in which the witness's past bad acts are probative of untruthfulness.

7. Improper Character Evidence, Reputation

Reputation evidence is admissible only with regard to an individual's character for truthfulness or untruthfulness. Moreover, evidence of a truthful character is admissible only after the character of the witness has been attacked. Rule 608(a).

Responses. Explain the manner in which the reputation evidence is probative of truthfulness or untruthfulness.

8. Lack of Personal Knowledge

Witnesses (other than experts) must testify from personal knowledge, which is generally defined as sensory perception. A witness's lack of personal knowledge may be obvious from the questioning, may be inherent in the testimony, or may be developed by questioning on voir dire. Rule 602.

Responses. Ask further questions that establish the witness's personal knowledge.

9. Improper Lay Opinion

Lay witnesses (nonexperts) are generally precluded from testifying as to opinions, conclusions, or inferences. FRE 701.

Responses. Lay witnesses may testify to opinions or inferences if they are rationally based upon the perception of the witness. Common lay opinions include estimates of speed, distance, value, height, time, duration, and temperature. Lay witnesses are also commonly allowed to testify as to the mood, sanity, demeanor, sobriety, or tone of voice of another person.

THE BASICS

Admissibility Checklist ☑	
❑ Is this evidence irrelevant?	Does this information fail to make at least one fact of consequence to the case more or less probable? *If so, it is irrelevant.*
❑ Is this evidence unfairly prejudicial?	Does the unfairly prejudicial nature of this evidence outweigh its probative value? Is there also something about the evidence that is inflammatory or unfair? *If so, it may be unduly prejudicial.*
❑ Is this information beyond the witness's personal knowledge?	Is the testimony about something the witness saw, heard, smelled, touched, or tasted? *If not, the witness is probably speculating.*
❑ Is this an opinion only an expert could reach?	Is this an opinion that requires special training, education, or knowledge? *If so, the witness is giving an improper lay opinion.*
❑ Is this inadmissible hearsay?	Is this an assertion that is being used to prove its own truth? If so, does a hearsay exception apply? *If not, the statement is inadmissible hearsay.*
❑ Is this improper character evidence?	Can this prior bad act be used to prove motive, opportunity, intent, preparation, plan, knowledge, or identity? Does this information go to a witness's reputation for truthfulness? Is this a felony that occurred within the past ten years or is it a crime that goes to the witness's truthfulness? *Unless the answer to at least one of the above questions is "yes," the information is improper character evidence.*

10. Speculation or Conjecture

Witnesses may not be asked to speculate or guess. Such questions are often phrased as hypothetical in a form such as, "What would have happened if..."

Responses. Witnesses are permitted to make reasonable estimates rationally based upon perception.

11. Authenticity

Exhibits must be authenticated before they may be admitted. Authenticity refers to adequate proof that the exhibit actually is what it seems or purports to be. Virtually all documents and tangible objects must be authenticated. Since exhibits are authenticated by laying a foundation, objections may be raised on the ground of either authenticity or foundation. This subject is discussed in greater detail in Chapter Nine.

Responses. Ask additional questions that establish authenticity.

12. Lack of Foundation

Nearly all evidence, other than a witness's direct observation of events, requires some sort of predicate foundation for admissibility. An objection to lack of foundation requires the judge to make a preliminary ruling as to the admissibility of the evidence. Rule 104. The evidentiary foundations vary widely. For example, the foundation for the business records exception to the hearsay rule includes evidence that the records were made and kept in the ordinary course of business. The foundation for the introduction of certain scientific evidence requires the establishment of a chain of custody. The following list includes some, though by no means all, of the sorts of evidence that require special foundations for admissibility: voice identifications, telephone conversations, writings, business records, the existence of a privilege, dying declarations, photographs, scientific tests, expert and lay opinions, and many more. This subject is discussed in greater detail in Chapter Nine.

Responses. Ask additional questions that lay the necessary foundation.

13. Best Evidence

The "best evidence" or "original document" rule refers to the common law requirement that copies or secondary evidence of writings could not be admitted into evidence unless the absence of the original could be explained. Under modern practice, most jurisdictions have significantly expanded upon the circumstances in which duplicates and other secondary evidence may be admitted.

Under the Federal Rules of Evidence, "duplicates" are usually admissible to the same extent as originals. Duplicates include carbons, photocopies, photographs, duplicate printouts, or any other copies that are made by "techniques which accurately reproduce the original." Rules 1001–1003.

Other secondary evidence, such as oral testimony as to the contents of a document, is admissible only if the original has been lost or destroyed, is unavailable through judicial process, or if it is in the exclusive possession of the opposing party. Rule 1004.

Responses. Ask additional questions demonstrating either that the item offered is a duplicate or that the original is unavailable.

14. Privilege

Numerous privileges may operate to exclude otherwise admissible evidence. Among the most common are attorney-client, physician-patient, marital, clergy, psychotherapist-patient, and a number of others that exist either by statute or at common law. Each privilege has its own foundation and its own set of exceptions. Rule 501 did not change the common law privileges, but note that state statutory privileges may not obtain in federal actions.

Responses. Virtually all privileges are subject to some exceptions, which vary from jurisdiction to jurisdiction.

15. Liability Insurance

Evidence that a person carried liability insurance is not admissible on the issue of negligence. Rule 411. This exclusion is necessary because it is generally assumed that juries will be promiscuous in awarding judgments that they know will ultimately be paid by insurance companies. The improper mention of liability insurance may be considered so prejudicial as to warrant a mistrial.

Responses. Evidence of liability insurance may be admissible on some issue other than negligence, such as proof of agency, ownership, control, or bias or prejudice of a witness. Rule 411.

16. Subsequent Remedial Measures

Evidence of subsequent repair or other remedial measures is not admissible to prove negligence or other culpable conduct. Rule 405. The primary rationale for this rule is that parties should not be discouraged from remedying dangerous conditions and should not have to choose between undertaking repairs and creating proof of their own liability.

Responses. Subsequent remedial measures may be offered to prove ownership, control, or feasibility of precautionary measures, if controverted. Evidence of subsequent repair may also be admissible in strict liability cases, as opposed to negligence cases.

17. Settlement Offers

Offers of compromise or settlement are not admissible to prove or disprove liability. Statements made during settlement negotiations are also inadmissible. Rule 408.

Responses. Statements made during settlement discussions may be admissible to prove bias or prejudice of a witness or to negate a contention of undue delay.

— CHAPTER NINE —
Foundations and Exhibits

I. EVIDENTIARY FOUNDATIONS

A. The Requirement of Foundation

Before any evidence can be considered at trial there must be some basis for believing it to be relevant and admissible. This basis is called the foundation for the evidence. Depending upon the nature of the evidence, the foundation may be painfully complex or strikingly simple. The question of foundation is directed to the judge, who must make a preliminary determination as to whether the particular evidence will be received.[1]

B. Components of Foundation

There are three universal aspects to virtually all evidentiary foundations. To be received, evidence must be shown to be (1) relevant, (2) authentic, and (3) admissible under the applicable laws of evidence. While the discrete elements of foundation will differ according to the nature of the evidence and the purpose for which it is offered, these three considerations must always apply.

1. Relevance

Relevance defines the relationship between the proffered evidence and some fact that is at issue in the case. Evidence will not be admitted simply because it is interesting or imaginative. Rather, it must be shown to be probative in the sense that it makes some disputed fact either more or less likely. The relevance of most evidence is generally made apparent from the context of the case, but occasionally it must be demonstrated by the establishment of foundational facts.

---

1. See Rule 104, Federal Rules of Evidence.

2. Authenticity

The concept of authenticity refers to the requirement of proof that the evidence actually is what the proponent claims it to be.[2] In other words, evidence is not to be admitted until there has been a threshold showing that it is "the real thing." The judge decides whether an item of evidence has been sufficiently authenticated, and the criteria vary according to the nature of the evidence involved. In many jurisdictions the strict rules of evidence do not apply to the court's preliminary determination of admissibility.[3]

We generally think of authentication as it applies to tangible evidence such as documents, physical objects, or photographs. Is that really the contract that the parties executed? Is this actually the machine part that caused the injury? Does the photograph fairly and accurately depict the scene of the accident? Before any exhibit can be received, a foundation must be established that adequately supports the proponent's claim of authenticity. Note that the court's initial ruling on authenticity is preliminary. It bears only on admissibility and is not binding as a factual determination. Opposing counsel may continue to controvert the genuineness of the exhibit, and the trier of fact (either judge or jury) remains free ultimately to reject the exhibit.

The requirement of authenticity is not, however, limited to tangible objects. It also applies to certain testimonial evidence. For example, a witness generally may not testify to a telephone conversation without first establishing her basis for recognizing the voice of the person on the other end of the line.[4] That is, the identity of the other speaker must be authenticated.

3. Specific Admissibility

While evidence will generally be received if it is relevant and authentic, the law of evidence contains a host of specific provisions that govern the admissibility of various sorts of proof. In many cases evidence can be admitted only following the establishment of foundational facts. Most exceptions to the hearsay rule, for example,

---

2.   See Rule 901(a), Federal Rules of Evidence, which provides: "The requirement of authentication or identification as a condition precedent to admissibility is satisfied by evidence sufficient to support a finding that the matter in question is what its proponent claims."

3.   See *e.g.*, Rule 104(a), Federal Rules of Evidence: "Preliminary questions concerning the...admissibility of evidence shall be determined by the court.... In making its determination it is not bound by the rules of evidence except those with respect to privileges."

4.   Alternative means for authenticating telephone conversations are discussed in Section II B(2), *infra* at p. 250.

require such a preliminary showing. Similarly, a foundation must be laid for the admission of evidence of habit or routine practice[5] or for the admission of evidence of subsequent remedial measures.[6] It is impossible to generalize about such prerequisites except to say that the advocate must be aware of the rule of evidence under which each item of evidence is proffered. As is discussed in detail below, a foundation can then be tailored to meet the rule's requirements.

THE BASICS

The Components of Foundation	
• Relevance	Testimony and exhibits must be shown to make some fact at issue in the case either more or less likely.
• Authenticity	Testimony and exhibits must be shown to be what the proponent claims them to be.
• Specific Admissibility	Testimony and facts must be shown to be admissible under the specifically applicable rules of evidence.

C. Establishing Foundations

1. Using a Single Witness

The most common approach to the establishment of a foundation is simply to call a witness who can provide the necessary facts, and then to offer the evidence after that testimony has been elicited. Consider this example from the direct examination of the plaintiff in our fire engine case:[7]

QUESTION: Do you recognize the object that I am showing you, which has been marked as Plaintiff's Exhibit 12?

ANSWER: Yes, it is the neck brace that I got from my doctor.

QUESTION: When did you get it from your doctor?

---

5. See Rule 406, Federal Rules of Evidence.
6. See Rule 407, Federal Rules of Evidence.
7. This example is slightly truncated. A fuller discussion of the steps for offering real evidence is found in Section III (B)(1), *infra* at p. 269.

ANSWER: When I was discharged from the hospital fol-
              lowing the accident.

QUESTION: What is it made of?

ANSWER: Stiff plastic.

QUESTION: Do you still wear it?

ANSWER: Yes, I have to wear it at least eight hours a
              day.

Counsel may now offer the neck brace into evidence. Its relevance to the issue of damages is apparent from the context of the
case, its authenticity as the actual neck brace has been established
by the witness, and there are no special evidentiary considerations
that govern the admission of this real evidence.

2. Using Multiple Witnesses

Some foundations cannot be laid by a single witness. In such
cases counsel must establish separate parts of the foundation from
each of several witnesses before offering the evidence. In a purse-
snatching case, for example, it may be necessary to call two witnesses in order to lay the foundation for the admission of the stolen
purse. First, the arresting officer:

QUESTION: Officer, do you recognize Prosecution Exhibit 1?

ANSWER: Yes. It is a lady's purse that was in the posses-
              sion of the defendant when I arrested him.

The officer has laid some of the foundation, but not all of it. The
defendant's possession of a purse is not relevant until it is shown to
have been stolen. It is therefore necessary to call the crime victim:

QUESTION: Ma'am, do you recognize Prosecution Exhibit 1?

ANSWER: Yes. It is my pocketbook.

QUESTION: Before today, when was the last time that you
              saw it?

ANSWER: The last time I saw it was when it was ripped
              off of my shoulder by a purse snatcher.

Now the purse is admissible. The victim provided the missing
aspect of relevance, and she also authenticated the purse as the object that was stolen.

Note that it is possible to combine both direct and cross examinations to lay a single foundation. Thus, defense counsel can begin to lay a foundation during the cross examination of a plaintiff's witness and can conclude the foundation during the defendant's case in chief. Assume, for example, that the defendant wants to introduce a letter from the plaintiff. To be admissible it must be shown both that the plaintiff wrote the letter and that the defendant received it. Defense counsel can begin the foundation during the plaintiff's case by having the plaintiff authenticate his own signature on cross examination. The foundation can later be completed by having the defendant testify during her own case that the letter was actually received.

3. Conditional Admissibility

It is not always possible to complete a foundation during the testimony of a single witness. However, a witness who is responsible for part of the foundation will in many cases have other important information concerning the exhibit. In the absence of a special rule, this witness could not testify about the exhibit until a second witness had been called to complete the foundation. Only then could the first witness return to the stand to complete his testimony about the exhibit.

Fortunately, such an awkward and inefficient procedure is generally not necessary. The rule of conditional admissibility allows the temporary or conditional admission of the evidence based upon counsel's representation that the foundation will be completed through the testimony of a subsequent witness.[8]

In the above purse-snatching case the prosecution might want to elicit further testimony about the purse from the arresting officer:

PROSECUTOR: Officer, do you recognize Prosecution Exhibit 1?

ANSWER: Yes. It is a lady's purse that the defendant was concealing under his jacket when I arrested him.

PROSECUTOR: Officer, please show us how the defendant was concealing the purse when you arrested him.

---

8.   Rule 104(b) of the Federal Rules of Evidence provides: "When the relevancy of evidence depends upon the fulfillment of a condition of fact, the court shall admit it ... subject to ... the introduction of evidence sufficient to support a finding of the fulfillment of the condition."

DEFENSE:	Objection. There is no foundation for this demonstration.
PROSECUTOR:	Your Honor, we will complete the foundation when we call the victim, who will testify that Exhibit 1 is the same purse that was stolen from her.
COURT:	On the basis of counsel's representation, the objection is overruled.

The further testimony of the officer has been conditionally allowed, subject to the perfection of the foundation. In the event that the victim does not identify the purse, all of the conditionally accepted testimony will be subject to a motion to strike.

4. Using Adverse Witnesses

Potentially complex foundations can often be simplified through the use of adverse examination. In a case where executed contracts have been exchanged through the mail, for example, it may be extremely difficult for one party to authenticate the other party's signature. This problem can be completely alleviated, however, simply by calling the opposing party as an adverse witness:

QUESTION:	Are you the defendant in this case?
ANSWER:	I am.
QUESTION:	Is this your signature at the bottom of Plaintiff's Exhibit 1?
ANSWER:	Yes, it is.

The signature has now been authenticated.

5. Cross Examination

Foundation requirements apply equally during cross and direct examinations. Testimonial foundations must be laid on cross examination for personal knowledge, voice identification, hearsay exceptions, and in every other circumstance where a foundation would be necessary on direct examination. In addition, there are special foundations for certain cross examination techniques such as impeachment by past omission or prior inconsistent statement.

It is also often necessary to use cross examination to lay the foundation for the admission of exhibits. Defense counsel in particular can avoid the need to call adverse witnesses by attempting to establish foundations for her own exhibits while cross examining a plaintiff's witness.

In some jurisdictions, however, exhibits cannot actually be offered other than in counsel's case in chief. In such jurisdictions you may proceed to elicit the appropriate foundational testimony during cross examination, but you must delay actually offering the exhibits until the other side has rested. Following this rule, a plaintiff's attorney who develops the foundation for exhibits while cross examining defense witnesses must wait until the defense has rested, and may then offer the exhibits on rebuttal.

The "case-in-chief" rule is very difficult to justify analytically. Counsel can develop affirmative testimonial evidence on cross examination, and there is no good reason to treat real or documentary evidence any differently. Moreover, delaying the offer of an exhibit until after cross examination also delays any objections to the exhibit. This may prove awkward in situations where an objection is sustained for some technical reason and the witness is no longer on the stand to cure the defect.

It is far preferable to be able to offer exhibits on cross examination. Nonetheless, the case-in-chief rule must be followed where it exists.

II. FOUNDATIONS FOR TESTIMONIAL EVIDENCE

A. Personal Knowledge

Witnesses are expected to testify from personal knowledge.[9] The most common sort of personal knowledge is direct sensory perception: information gained through sight, hearing, touch, taste, and smell. Witnesses may also have personal knowledge of more subjective information such as their own intentions or emotions or the reputation of another person.

Whatever the content of the witness's testimony, it is necessary to lay a foundation showing that the witness is testifying either from personal knowledge or on the basis of an acceptable substitute, as in the case of expert testimony.[10]

---

9. See Rule 602, Federal Rules of Evidence: "A witness may not testify to a matter unless evidence is introduced sufficient to support a finding that he has a personal knowledge of the matter. Evidence to prove personal knowledge may, but need not, consist of the witness's own testimony."

10. Expert witnesses are not required to testify from personal knowledge. The foundation for expert testimony is discussed in Chapter 7, Section II, *supra* at p. 166.

In the case of sensory perception, the basic foundation is simply that the witness was in a position to observe or otherwise experience the relevant facts:

QUESTION: Where were you on the afternoon of March 17?

ANSWER: I was at the corner of State and Madison.

QUESTION: What were you doing?

ANSWER: I was watching the St. Patrick's Day parade.

QUESTION: Please tell us what you saw.

In ordinary circumstances it is not necessary to establish more than the witness's general basis for testifying. Witnesses are assumed to have all of their senses in order, so, for example, counsel is not required to show that the witness's eyesight is unimpaired.

In some situations, however, additional foundation may be called for to establish fully the basis of the witness's testimony.

QUESTION: What happened when you were standing in the workshop?

ANSWER: I heard a high-pitched, mechanical, whining sound in the next room.

QUESTION: Could you tell what it was?

ANSWER: Yes.

QUESTION: How could you tell?

ANSWER: I have worked in the workshop before, and I heard that sound when I saw the machines operating.

QUESTION: What was the sound?

The foundation in this scenario was actually slightly overdone. In simple cases, most witnesses will be allowed to provide the basis of the perception either before or after testifying to the facts. Thus, in the machine shop example most judges would allow the witness first to identify the noise and then to explain why she could recognize it.

B. Special Foundations for Certain Testimonial Evidence

While most testimony requires a showing of personal knowledge, certain testimony calls for the establishment of additional foundational facts.

1. Conversations

Witnesses are often called upon to testify to conversations between two or more parties. In order to authenticate the conversation, and thereby allow opposing counsel to conduct a meaningful cross examination, testimony concerning a conversation generally must be supported by a foundation establishing the date, time, and place of the conversation, as well as the persons present at the time. For example:

QUESTION: Did you complain to anyone about the quality of the printing job?

ANSWER: Yes, I spoke to the store manager, Alex Rose.

QUESTION: When did you speak to the manager?

ANSWER: On April 18, the same day that I refused to accept the product.

QUESTION: About what time was that?

ANSWER: I believe that it was just before noon, but it may have been somewhat later.

QUESTION: Where were you when you spoke?

ANSWER: We were at the service counter.

QUESTION: Was anybody else present?

ANSWER: There was a clerk nearby, but she wasn't involved in the conversation.

QUESTION: Please tell us what was said during that conversation.

This foundation demonstrates the authenticity of the conversation. The witness's ability to relate the time, date, place, and participants provides sufficient evidence that the conversation happened as she says it did. It is not necessary to lay the foundation with minute precision. In the above scenario the witness would not be required to provide the clerk's name or the exact time of the conversation. The foundation is sufficient so long as it fulfills its purpose of providing opposing counsel with reasonably sufficient information with which to challenge or contest the witness's testimony.

Note, however, that the authentication of the conversation does not resolve any hearsay or other evidentiary problems that may be raised by its content. Those issues must be addressed separately, often necessitating the development of additional foundation.

2. Telephone Conversations and Voice Identification

The foundation for a telephone conversation includes the additional element of voice identification or of a reasonable circumstantial substitute.

a. Voice recognition

Voice identification can be based on personal familiarity that either precedes or postdates the telephone conversation in question.[11] For example:

QUESTION: Did you complain to anyone about the quality of the printing job?

ANSWER: Yes, I telephoned the store manager, Alex Rose, as soon as I opened the first package.

QUESTION: How do you know that you were speaking to Mr. Rose?

ANSWER: I recognized his voice. I have been going to that print shop for years, and I have spoken to Alex many times in person.

The witness could also base voice identification on a subsequent contact with the store manager:

QUESTION: Did you complain to anyone about the quality of the printing job?

ANSWER: Yes, I telephoned the store manager, Alex Rose, as soon as I opened the first package.

QUESTION: Had you ever met Mr. Rose?

ANSWER: Not at that time.

---

11. See Rule 901(b)(5), Federal Rules of Evidence.

QUESTION: How do you know that you were speaking to Alex Rose on the phone?

ANSWER: I spoke to him in person the next day, and I recognized his voice as the same person from the phone call.

There is no strict time limit for voice identification based on subsequent contact, although a lengthy time lapse will obviously detract from the weight to be given to a contested identification.

b. Circumstantial evidence; listed numbers

In the absence of a basis for voice identification, circumstantial evidence can be used as the foundation for a telephone conversation. A telephone call placed by the witness can be authenticated by showing that the call was made to a listed number.[12] Again:

QUESTION: Did you complain to anyone about the quality of the printing job?

ANSWER: Yes, I telephoned the store as soon as I opened the first package.

QUESTION: How did you obtain the number?

ANSWER: I looked it up in the telephone book.

QUESTION: Did you dial the number that was listed in the book?

ANSWER: Yes.

QUESTION: What did you say when the telephone was answered?

ANSWER: I said that I wanted to complain about the quality of the printing job that I had just picked up.

Under the Federal Rules of Evidence, the above foundation is sufficient in the case of a business, so long as the conversation related to "business reasonably transacted over the telephone."[13] There is a presumption that the person who answers a business telephone is authorized to speak for the business.

---

12. See Rule 901(b)(6), Federal Rules of Evidence, which uses the phrase "the number assigned at the time by the telephone company to a particular person or business."

13. *Id.* at 901(b)(6)(B).

In the case of an individual, however, the foundation must also include "circumstances, including self-identification, [that] show the person answering to be the one called."[14]

c. Other circumstantial evidence

Numerous other circumstances can be used to authenticate telephone conversations. Subsequent verifying events can form the foundation for telephone calls either placed or received by the witness. In the following example, the witness both placed and received a telephone call:

QUESTION: Did you ever speak to Mr. Hill after the incident?

ANSWER: Yes, I looked his number up in the telephone book, and I called his home.

QUESTION: Did you speak to Mr. Hill?

ANSWER: No, a woman answered the telephone.

QUESTION: What did you do?

ANSWER: I left my name and number, and I asked for Mr. Hill to call me back.

QUESTION: Did you ever receive a return call?

ANSWER: Yes, I received a call the next day.

QUESTION: What did the party say?

ANSWER: He said, "This is Arthur Hill. I am returning your call from yesterday."

Note that the placement of a call to an individual's listed number is not alone sufficient to lay the foundation for a conversation. Additional verifying facts must be established. In this example both the first and second conversations are verified by the following circumstances of the return call: (1) Hill's self-identification; (2) the stated response to the initial message; and (3) the listing of Hill's number in the telephone directory.

Circumstantial evidence authenticating telephone calls received by a witness must include specific information that tends to identify the caller. Calls placed by the witness are commonly authenticated circumstantially on the basis of the number dialed.

---

14. *Id.* at 901(b)(6)(A).

Such evidence can include reference to listings other than in the telephone directory, perhaps on company stationery or advertising material.

3. Prior Identification

Under the Federal Rules of Evidence, a witness may testify to his or her previous out-of-court identification of an individual.[15] While such evidence is most commonly offered in criminal cases to bolster the in-court identification made at trial,[16] it also has its uses in civil matters. The foundation for this testimony is that the out-of-court identification was made by the witness after perceiving the person identified:

QUESTION:	Were you able to see the person who stole your car?
ANSWER:	Yes. He was driving away in it just as I got home from work. I saw him from the shoulders up.
QUESTION:	How far away were you when you first saw him?
ANSWER:	I was about thirty feet away.
QUESTION:	Did you ever see him again?
ANSWER:	Yes, I picked him out of a lineup.
QUESTION:	Where and when was that?
ANSWER:	About four days later at the police station.
QUESTION:	Please describe the circumstances of the lineup.
ANSWER:	There were five men standing in a row. They were all about the same height and they were

---

15. Rule 801(d)(1)(C), Federal Rules of Evidence. Note that the statement of prior identification are excluded from the definition of hearsay and therefore are admissible to "prove the truth of the matter asserted."

16. In-court identifications may be less than compelling since the physical arrangement of the courtroom will often serve to point the witness in the direction of the party to be identified. In criminal cases, for example, the defendant will usually be seated at counsel table next to the defense lawyer. Out-of-court identifications, on the other hand, are more likely to test the witness's initial observation. Proof that the witness picked the defendant out a lineup, for example, will significantly bolster the subsequent in-court identification.

all wearing blue jeans and flannel shirts. I identified the man who was second from the left.

QUESTION: Was that the same man whom you identified here in court today?

ANSWER: Yes.

4. Habit and Routine

Testimonial evidence of habit or routine practice may be admitted as circumstantial evidence that a person or organization acted in a similar fashion on a particular occasion.[17] The subject matter of such testimony can range from an individual's clothing preferences to a business's routine for mailing letters. In each case, the evidence of a regular custom or practice is offered to prove that the individual or business acted in the same way at a time relevant to the issues at trial.

To lay the foundation for evidence of habit or routine practice, it is necessary to call a witness with personal knowledge of the regular conduct of the person or organization involved. Furthermore, counsel must establish that the asserted conduct was, in fact, of a consistently repeated nature. This can be accomplished through proof of either extended observation or the existence of a formal policy or procedure.

a. Individual habit

The most common foundation for an individual's habit is through evidence of a pattern of conduct repeated over a substantial period of time. The alleged habit must be clearly differentiated from independent or distinct activities.

In the following example, assume that the defendant is charged with stabbing a man to death. Pleading self-defense, the defendant claims that it was the victim who attacked him with a knife, which he took away and used to defend himself. Habit evidence will be offered by the prosecution to show that the defendant always carried a knife:

QUESTION: How long have you known the defendant, Jason Rosenberg?

ANSWER: About five years.

---

17. Rule 406, Federal Rules of Evidence.

QUESTION: In what context do you know him?

ANSWER: We are neighbors. He lives next door to me.

QUESTION: During the last five years, how often have you seen the defendant?

ANSWER: On average, I would say that I have seen him at least twice a week.

QUESTION: On those occasions, did you ever see Jason Rosenberg carry a knife?

ANSWER: Yes. He always carried a hunting knife strapped to his belt.

QUESTION: How often did you see the defendant with a hunting knife?

ANSWER: Whenever he went out of the house, he always had that knife on his belt.

QUESTION: Did you ever see him go out of the house without a knife on his belt?

ANSWER: Only once.

QUESTION: What was that occasion?

ANSWER: He was going to a wedding in a tuxedo.

The evidence of the defendant's constant habit over an extended period of time is admissible to prove that he was carrying a knife on the date in question.

b. Business practice

The routine practice of a business or organization may be established either through direct observation or through evidence of an existing policy or practice. In the following example, assume that a dispute exists over whether an employee's references were checked before she was hired by a large corporation. Although the employee's file was marked "OK," no one can specifically remember making the reference checks. The company must therefore rely on proof of their business practice. First, through direct experience:

QUESTION: What is your position at the Judson Corporation?

ANSWER: I work in personnel. I am in charge of checking references.

QUESTION: How long have you held that position?

ANSWER: Six years.

QUESTION: How do you go about checking references?

ANSWER: Once a potential employee has been approved by the department head, the next step is to check references. The file comes to me, and I personally telephone every listed reference.

QUESTION: What happens after you telephone the references?

ANSWER: If all of the references are positive, I mark the file "OK" and send it on to the personnel manager. If they are negative, I mark it "failed" before I send it on.

QUESTION: Have you ever marked a file "OK" when you haven't telephoned the references?

ANSWER: No. Not in my entire six years at the Judson Company.

QUESTION: Was that the practice that you followed during April of last year?

ANSWER: Absolutely.

QUESTION: Did anyone else handle reference checks during that period?

ANSWER: No. I was the only one.

The witness's testimony of her own business routine is proof that she adhered to that custom during the time period in question.

Now assume that there were a number of employees who did reference checks during the relevant time period and that several of them have left the company. Furthermore, the "OK" notation on the file was made by a rubber stamp:

QUESTION: What is your position at the Judson Corporation?

ANSWER: I work in personnel. I am in charge of checking references.

QUESTION: How long have you held that position?

ANSWER: Six years.

QUESTION: Do other employees also check references?

ANSWER: Yes. Over the years there have been four or five of us who have made the actual telephone calls.

QUESTION: Does the Judson Company have a written policy regarding reference checks?

ANSWER: Yes. Once a potential employee has been approved by the department head, the next step is to check references. The file comes to our department and someone personally telephones every listed reference. If all of the references are positive, the file is stamped "OK" and sent on to the personnel manager. If they are negative, it is stamped "failed" before it is sent on.

QUESTION: Was that policy provided in writing to every employee in your department?

ANSWER: Yes.

QUESTION: Does the written policy of the Judson Company permit a file to be stamped "OK" if the references have not been telephoned?

ANSWER: Definitely not.

QUESTION: Was that policy in effect during April of last year?

ANSWER: Yes it was.

Even without personal observation, the witness's knowledge of the company's business policy[18] provides a sufficient foundation for the introduction of the routine practice.

18. Since the witness testified to the content of a written policy, further foundation might be necessary to comply with the "best evidence" or "original writing" rule. See Section V B, *infra* at p. 297.

5. Character and Reputation

Evidence of a person's character generally is not admissible to prove that "action in conformity therewith on a particular occasion."[19] For example, counsel may not offer proof of a person's dislike of children as evidence that he committed a kidnapping. There are, however, a number of exceptions that allow the admission of character evidence for a variety of purposes.[20] Each exception requires the establishment of its own foundation.

a. Other crimes or past misconduct

Following the general rule, evidence of past crimes or other wrongful conduct is not admissible to prove the occurrence of a specific event. Three previous burglaries cannot be offered to show that a defendant is a burglar, nor can three previous automobile accidents be used to prove that a tort plaintiff was guilty of contributory negligence. Past misconduct, including uncharged crimes, may, however, be admitted for other purposes "such as proof of motive, opportunity, intent, preparation, plan, knowledge, identity, or absence of mistake or accident."[21]

The foundation for such evidence must include the specifics of the past act as well as the circumstances that make it usable for a permissible purpose in the case at trial. Assume that the defendant in the following example is an employer who is being prosecuted for intentionally failing to pay last year's employee-withholding taxes to the government. The defendant admits the conduct but claims that it was an unintentional oversight. The prosecution has called a tax examiner to the stand:

QUESTION: What is your occupation?

ANSWER: I am an auditor for the Internal Revenue Service.

QUESTION: Have you audited the records of the defendant's business?

ANSWER: Yes, I audited the records for the last seven years.

QUESTION: Exactly what records did you review?

---

19. Rule 404(a), Federal Rules of Evidence.

20. The uses of character evidence for impeachment are discussed in Chapter 5, Section IV, *supra* at p. 148.

21. Rule 404(b), Federal Rules of Evidence.

ANSWER:	I looked at all of the payroll records, including the time sheets and check stubs for every employee.
QUESTION:	Were you able to determine anything with regard to withholding taxes?
ANSWER:	Yes. In each of the last seven years the amount of money withheld from employees' paychecks was more than the amount paid over to the government.
QUESTION:	What was the difference last year?
ANSWER:	Last year the defendant withheld $55,000 more from employees than was paid to the government for their withholding taxes.
QUESTION:	And in the preceding six years?
ANSWER:	The amounts for the previous six years were $40,000; $32,000; $51,000; $39,000; $46,000; and $42,000.
QUESTION:	Did the defendant submit withholding tax returns in each of the last seven years?
ANSWER:	Yes. They were submitted and signed by the defendant in each of the last seven years, but they never accurately reflected the amount of money deducted from employees' paychecks.

The defendant has not been charged with failing to pay withholding taxes other than in the most recent year. The government may not offer the other tax records to show that the defendant was an habitual tax cheat. Nonetheless, evidence of the past misconduct is admissible to show either intent or absence of mistake in filing last year's return.

b. Reputation for untruthfulness

Once a witness has testified it is permissible for the opposing party to offer evidence of the witness's reputation in the community for untruthfulness. This is typically done by calling another witness to the stand who has knowledge of the first witness's reputation in the community. This evidence can be offered only to reflect on the credibility of the first witness's testimony.

The foundation for such reputation evidence includes identification of the relevant community, the basis of the witness's
knowledge, and the nature of the first witness's reputation during
a relevant time period. Note that the "community" involved may be
residential, professional, social, or the like. Assume that the plaintiff
has already testified in our fire engine case. The defendant has now
called a witness to testify regarding the plaintiff's reputation for
untruthfulness:

QUESTION:	Do you know the plaintiff?
ANSWER:	Yes, I have known her for four years.
QUESTION:	In what context do you know her?
ANSWER:	We belong to the same hiking club. It's called the Campside Walkers.
QUESTION:	Are you familiar with the plaintiff's reputation for truth and veracity among the Campside Walkers?
ANSWER:	Yes. Her reputation is very bad. She is regarded within the club as an untruthful person.
QUESTION:	Was that her reputation as of last Tuesday when she testified?
ANSWER:	Yes it was.

In many jurisdictions a witness may also testify as to her opinion of a previous witness's untruthfulness.[22] The foundation is similar to that for reputation testimony:

QUESTION:	Do you know the plaintiff?
ANSWER:	Yes, I have known her for four years.
QUESTION:	In what context do you know her?
ANSWER:	We belong to the same hiking club, the Campside Walkers.
QUESTION:	How often have you spoken to the plaintiff during those four years?
ANSWER:	Well, the club meets once a month and both of us usually attend the meetings. In addition, we

---

22. Rule 405(a), Federal Rules of Evidence.

have gone on many long hikes together, and on at least three occasions we went on weekend camping trips.

QUESTION: Based on your contacts with the plaintiff, do you have an opinion concerning her truthfulness?

ANSWER: Yes, I do. My opinion is that she is not a truthful person.

Once a witness has given reputation or opinion evidence concerning another's untruthfulness, the cross examiner may then inquire as to "relevant specific instances of conduct."[23] Additionally, once the character of a witness has been attacked, the proponent of the witness may proceed to offer evidence of the witness's good reputation for truthfulness.

c. Character traits of criminal defendant or crime victim

Notwithstanding the general rule, a criminal defendant may always offer evidence of a pertinent character trait such as honesty, truthfulness, or peacefulness. This evidence may come in the form of reputation or opinion. Courts have also been known to allow evidence of specific incidents of good conduct, often under the rubric of "foundation" for the witness's opinion or reputation testimony. Once the accused has offered evidence of good character, the prosecution may offer the same sorts of evidence in rebuttal.[24] It is up to the defendant to initiate the admissibility of character evidence; the prosecution may not launch a preemptive attack.

In the same vein, a criminal defendant may offer evidence of a relevant character trait of the crime victim, which may then be rebutted in similar fashion by the prosecution.[25] Finally, even in the absence of initial evidence from the defense, the prosecution may use reputation, opinion, or specific conduct evidence of the "peaceful"

---

23. *Id.*

24. Rule 404(a)(1), Federal Rules of Evidence.

25. Note that Rule 412, Federal Rules of Evidence, places severe restrictions on the admissibility of evidence concerning the past conduct or reputation of victims of rape or sexual assault. Specifically, "evidence offered to prove any alledged victim's sexual predisposition is not admissible" A similar provision applies to direct evidence of the victim's past conduct. Virtually every state has adopted some version of this important and beneficial rule.

character traits of a homicide victim in order to prove that the victim was not the "first aggressor."[26]

Foundations for Testimonial Evidence	
• Personal Knowledge:	Testimony by all witnesses (except expert witnesses) must be shown to be based on personal knowledge.
• Conversations:	Testimony about conversations must include when and where the conversation took place, a listing of the parties present, and (in case of telephone conversations) how the other person's voice was identified or authenticated.
• Habit and Routine:	Testimony about another's habit or routine practice must be shown to be based on personal knowledge of a consistently repeated activity.
• Character and Reputation:	Testimony about another's character or reputation must be shown to be used for an admissible purpose, and must include the specifics of how that information was learned and why it is reliable.
• Hearsay:	Testimony of an out-of-court statement that is used to prove the truth of the matter asserted must be shown to be nonhearsay or to fit into an exception to the hearsay rule.

C.   Foundations for Hearsay Statements

The rule against hearsay excludes evidence of out-of-court statements if offered to prove the truth of the matter asserted.[27] Numerous exceptions to the hearsay rule allow for the admissibility of out-of-court statements, provided that the necessary foundation is established. The foundations for those exceptions that apply primarily to testimonial evidence are discussed below. Foundations for hearsay exceptions that typically apply to documentary evidence are discussed in a later section.[28] The following sections are intended only as an outline of the foundations for the various hearsay excep-

---

26. Rule 404(a)(2), Federal Rules of Evidence.
27. Rule 801(c), Federal Rules of Evidence.
28. See Section V C, *infra* at p. 299.

tions, not as a complete treatment of the complexities or rationale for the hearsay rule itself.

1. Party Admissions

Out-of-court statements made by the opposing party are generally admissible to prove the truth of the matter asserted. Party admissions constituted a hearsay exception at common law and are excluded from the definition of hearsay under the Federal Rules of Evidence.[29] Notwithstanding the approach of the Federal Rules, most lawyers continue to find it convenient to refer to the "exception" for admissions by a party-opponent.

In brief, the previous statements of the opposing party are admissible if: (1) the witness can authenticate the statement, (2) the statement was made by the party against whom it is offered, and (3) the statement is adverse to the opposing party's claim or defense.[30] In the following example the witness is a police officer who investigated an automobile accident. The direct examination is being conducted by plaintiff's counsel:

QUESTION: Officer, did you speak to anyone after you arrived at the scene of the accident?

ANSWER: I spoke to both drivers, Mr. Weiss and Ms. Gable.

QUESTION: Was that the same Mr. Weiss who is the defendant in this case?

ANSWER: Yes.

QUESTION: Who was present when you spoke with Mr. Weiss?

ANSWER: Only the two of us.

QUESTION: When did that conversation take place?

ANSWER: At approximately 10:00 a.m. on December 19.

QUESTION: Where did it take place?

ANSWER: At the intersection of Ridge and Central.

---

29. Rule 801(d)(2), Federal Rules of Evidence.

30. Party admissions may be received in written as well as testimonial form. The foundation for a written party admission—such as a letter, memorandum, or report—is the same as that for an oral one. Where the admission is contained in a document, however, all of the other general requisites for the admissibility of an exhibit must be present.

QUESTION: Did Mr. Weiss say anything about the cause of the accident?

ANSWER: Yes. He said that he never saw the other automobile until just before the impact.

The defendant's out-of-court statement is admissible. The witness heard the statement and can identify it as having been made by the party against whom it is being offered. The content of the statement itself demonstrates its adverse nature. The party admission doctrine applies only to statements offered against the party-declarant. The plaintiff in the above example could not elicit her own favorable statements to the investigating police officer.[31]

The party admission exception also applies to statements made by certain agents or employees of a party. In these situations the exception is available when (1) a party has adopted the statement or manifested a belief in its truth, (2) a party has authorized the declarant to make a statement concerning the subject, or (3) the statement was made by a party's agent or servant, during the existence of the relationship, concerning a matter within the scope of agency or employment.[32] In the following example, assume that the plaintiff is the Quickset Printing Company, which has sued the defendant for nonpayment on a large duplicating order. The defendant is testifying on direct examination:

QUESTION: Did you speak to anyone at Quickset after you received the order?

ANSWER: Yes. I went back to the shop and I spoke to the manager.

QUESTION: How do you know that you were speaking to the manager?

ANSWER: I have been doing business with Quickset for years, and I have spoken to the manager many times.

QUESTION: What did you say to the manager?

ANSWER: I said that the order was defective and that I would not pay for it.

---

31. The plaintiff's statements to the officer might, however, be admissible on some other theory such as "excited utterance" or state of mind. See Sections II C(3) and (4), *infra* at pp. 266–267.

32. Rule 801(d)(2)(B–D), Federal Rules of Evidence.

QUESTION: Did the manager respond?

ANSWER: Yes. He said that he didn't expect anyone to pay for defective work and that he would speak to the owner of the company.

Agency and scope having been established, the manager's out-of-court statement is admissible. Note that the testimony also contained a reference to the defendant's own out-of-court statement concerning the defective nature of the order. While the defendant could not offer her own statement as a party admission, it is admissible to provide the context for the manager's response.

2. Present Sense Impression

The present sense impression exception allows the admission of out-of-court statements "describing or explaining an event or condition made while the declarant was perceiving the event or condition, or immediately thereafter."[33] The foundation for the exception, then, is that (1) the declarant perceived an event; (2) the declarant described the event; and (3) the description was given while the event occurred or immediately afterward. A witness may testify to her own previous statement of a present sense impression, as in this example taken from the fire engine case:

QUESTION: Where were you at about 8:20 a.m. last March 17?

ANSWER: I was at the corner of Sheridan and Touhy, walking west on Touhy.

QUESTION: Were you with anyone?

ANSWER: Yes, I was with my two children, who are four and six years old. My neighbor was also with us.

QUESTION: Was your attention drawn to a vehicle at that time?

ANSWER: I saw a fire engine headed west on Touhy Avenue.

QUESTION: Was the fire engine using its warning signals?

ANSWER: It was flashing its lights and sounding its siren.

---

33. Rule 803(1), Federal Rules of Evidence.

QUESTION: Did you say anything about the fire engine to anyone?

ANSWER: Yes. I told my children to listen to the siren and to look for the fire truck. I think that my exact words were something like, "Listen kids, whenever you hear a siren like that it means that you have to look out for a fire engine."

QUESTION: When did you say that to your children?

ANSWER: Right as the fire truck was passing.

A witness also can often testify to a present sense impression statement made by another. It is generally necessary for the statement to have been made in the witness's presence in order to satisfy the foundational requirement of personal knowledge.[34]

3. Excited Utterance

The excited utterance exception is quite similar to the present sense impression rule, allowing for the admission of hearsay when the statement relates "to a startling event or condition made while the declarant was under the stress of excitement caused by the event or condition."[35]

The foundation for an excited utterance is that (1) the declarant perceived a startling event or experienced a stressful condition; (2) the declarant made a statement concerning the event or

---

34. It is possible, however, to "stack" hearsay exceptions so as to allow testimony concerning secondhand statements. Imagine, for instance, the following chain of events in the fire truck case: A passenger in the defendant's car heard the siren and described it to the defendant, saying, "Listen, I think I hear a fire truck siren." The defendant later mentioned the passenger's remark to the investigating police officer. The officer would be allowed to testify as follows:

Question: Did the defendant say anything to you about a siren?

Answer: Yes. The defendant said that his passenger told him something like, "Listen, I think I hear a fire truck siren."

The passenger's statement is a present sense impression, and the defendant's recounting of it is a party admission. Each out-of-court statement falls under an independant exception to the hearsay rule. Assuming that the proper foundations are laid, the police officer's testimony is therefore admissible. *See* Rule 805, Federal Rules of Evidence.

The further intricacies of the treatment of "hearsay within hearsay" are beyond the scope of this chapter and will not be discussed in any greater detail.

35. Rule 803(2), Federal Rules of Evidence.

condition; and (3) the statement was made while the declarant was under the stress of the event or condition.

As with present sense impressions, a witness may testify to her own excited utterance or to that of another.

4. State of Mind

"State of mind" provides one of the broadest exceptions to the hearsay rule, as it allows the admission of statements concerning the declarant's "then existing state of mind, emotion, sensation, or physical condition (such as intent, plan, motive, design, mental feeling, pain, and bodily health)."[36]

The foundation for this exception is that the statement actually be probative of the declarant's mental, emotional, or physical condition. This can best be demonstrated by the content of the statement itself. Apart from the content of the statement, there is no special foundation for the state of mind exception. However, the witness still must establish the authenticity of the statement by testifying as to (1) when the statement was made, (2) where it was made, (3) who was present, and (4) what was said. Note also that the statement must have been made during the existence of the mental, emotional, or physical condition that it describes.

5. Statement Made for Medical Treatment

The foundation for this exception is that the declarant made a statement for the purpose of obtaining medical care or diagnosis. The statement may be made to a physician, medical worker, or other person, so long as its purpose was to obtain or facilitate treatment. The statement may include medical history or past symptoms, but it must relate to a present bodily condition.[37]

6. Dying Declaration

The hearsay exception for dying declarations requires the following foundation: (1) The declarant made a statement while believing that his or her death was imminent, (2) concerning what he or she believed to be the cause of death.[38] At common law it was also required that the declarant actually had died, but under the Federal Rules it is sufficient that the declarant be unavailable as a witness.[39]

---

36. Rule 803(3), Federal Rules of Evidence.
37 Rule 803(4), Federal Rules of Evidence.
38. Rule 804(b)(2), Federal Rules of Evidence.
39. Rule 804(b), Federal Rules of Evidence.

The declarant's belief that death was imminent can be established by surrounding circumstances, such as the nature of an illness or injury, or by the declarant's own words. The content of the statement will generally be sufficient to show that it related to the declarant's belief as to the cause of death.

Under the Federal Rules, dying declarations are admissible only in civil cases or homicide prosecutions. The exception is not available in criminal cases other than homicides.

THE BASICS

Is This Inadmissible Hearsay?

Is it an out-of-court statement offered to prove the truth of the matter asserted?

- Does it assert some fact?
- Are you using the statement to prove the truth of that fact?

If the answer to both of these questions is "yes," go on to the section below.

Is it an admission by a party opponent?

- In criminal cases: did the defendant or a conspirator of thedefendant make the statement and is it being used against thedefendant right now?
- In civil cases: did the plaintiff or defendant or any of their agents make the statement and it is being offered against that party now?

If the answer to the applicable question is "yes," the statement is not hearsay. If the answer is "no," go on to the section below to determine whether an exception to the hearsay rule applies.

Is there an exception that applies?

- Is the statement a present sense impression?
- Is the statement an excited utterance?
- Is the statement being used to illustrate the declarant's state of mind or the effect of the statement on the person who heard it?
- Is the statement itself a business record or is it included within one?
- Is the statement a dying declaration?

If the answer to any of these questions is "yes," the statement is admissible. If the answer to each question is "no," check the less common hearsay exceptions to see if one applies. If none apply, the statement is inadmissible.

III. EXHIBITS

A.   The Role of Exhibits

Exhibits are the tangible objects, documents, photographs, video and audiotapes, and other items that are offered for the jury's consideration. Exhibits are the only form, apart from the testimony of witnesses, in which evidence can be received. Spoken testimony typically presents the jury with a recitation of the witness's memories and perceptions. As effective as testimony might be, it remains a secondhand account that is, at best, once removed from the jury's own experiences. Exhibits, on the other hand, allow the jurors to utilize their own senses and perceptions. It is one thing to hear somebody describe, for example, the texture of a piece of cloth; it is far more striking actually to run your hand over the material itself. Your direct experience will be infinitely more informative than listening to another person's description. Having touched the cloth, you will remember it better, you will appreciate more of its nuances or details, and you will be much less likely to change your mind about it in the future.

Life is full of experiences that cannot truly be described, and exhibits bring reality into the courtroom in a way that spoken testimony will never approach. Imagine the melody of the last popular song that you heard on the radio. No matter how simple the tune, even the most gifted critic cannot recapture it in words. The use of an audiotape, however, can re-create the experience almost exactly. The same is true of visual exhibits. Think of a scene as commonplace as the street immediately outside the room in which you are sitting. It would take hours to describe everything that you could see there, and even then you would be unable to capture all of the colors, distances, spatial relationships, angles, and other particulars. A photograph can depict these details, and numerous others, all at once.

At trial, exhibits enhance or supplement the testimony of the witnesses. Exhibits can make information clearer, more concrete, more understandable, and more reliable. The sections immediately following will discuss the general procedures for the introduction of exhibits.

B. Types of Exhibits

While the categories tend to overlap and the lines cannot be drawn with precision, it is often helpful to think of exhibits as falling into these three categories: (1) real or tangible evidence, (2) demonstrative evidence, and (3) documentary evidence.

1. Real Evidence

The term "real evidence" generally refers to tangible objects that played an actual role in the events at issue in the trial.

The proceeds or instrumentalities of the crime are often introduced in criminal cases. Typical examples might include the "marked money" recovered in a suspect's possession, the bullet casing found at the scene of the crime, an item of clothing that the defendant was wearing when arrested, or a quantity of narcotics seized by the police.

Real evidence is also used in all categories of civil cases. In personal injury cases it is common for plaintiff's counsel to introduce objects that allegedly caused or contributed to the injury. Such real evidence might include a frayed wire that led to a steering failure or a rusty canister that failed to contain a corrosive liquid. Similarly, defense counsel in a tort case would be expected to introduce the actual safety devices that were available to, but ignored by, the plaintiff. Real evidence in a commercial dispute might include samples of allegedly nonconforming goods.

Photographs, while obviously different from tangible objects, are so close to reality that they are also often treated as real evidence.

Documents such as contracts, memoranda, letters, and other primary writings can also be considered real evidence, although the special rules that apply to out-of-court writings generally make it more convenient to treat "documentary evidence" as a separate category.

2. Demonstrative Evidence

The term "demonstrative evidence" refers to exhibits that did not play an actual role in the events underlying the case but that are used to illustrate or clarify a witness's testimony. Demonstrative evidence can take the form of models, graphs, diagrams, charts, drawings, or any other objects that can explain or illustrate issues in the case.

A familiar form of demonstrative evidence is the simple intersection diagram on which a witness can indicate the locations of the automobiles involved in an accident. The intersection itself, not the diagram, would constitute real evidence of the configuration of the streets. The diagram, however, may be used to demonstrate the relative positions of the cars, traffic signals, and witnesses. It is easy to see why demonstrative evidence can be superior to real evidence— the intersection cannot be transported into the courtroom. And even if the jury were to be taken to the scene of the accident, it would still be extremely difficult for the lawyers to push real automobiles around at the instruction of the witnesses.

More complex displays may range from an anatomical model to an elaborate "day in the life" videotape depicting the daily routine of a disabled accident victim. An anatomical model of a human shoulder can be used to show the effects of surgery on an individual's ability to move or work. "Day in the life" videotapes have been used with great impact to demonstrate the limitations and obstacles faced by accident victims and the extraordinary effort and expense that is necessary to cope with severe injuries.

The production of demonstrative evidence is a creative task. It allows counsel, in effect, to dream about ways of presenting a case and then to fashion those dreams into a persuasive reality. The attorney must constantly ask, "How can I make this testimony more concrete?" Or, "How can I help the jury visualize this point?" Or, "Is there a way to accentuate the relationship between these two ideas?" The answer will often be found in the development of demonstrative exhibits.

3. Documentary Evidence

"Documentary evidence" is the term used to refer to virtually all writings, including letters, contracts, leases, memoranda, reports, ledgers, printouts, and business records. Written documents, almost by definition, contain out-of-court statements, and they are typically offered because their contents are relevant to the case. Thus, most documents face hearsay hurdles in a way that real and demonstrative exhibits do not. Tangible objects are admitted into evidence because of what they are; documentary exhibits are admitted because of what they say.

Documentary evidence has the power to document past events. Barring fraud or forgery, contemporaneous writings often provide the best proof possible. Perhaps more than any other form of evidence, however, documents have the potential to overwhelm the trier of fact. Only the most determined judge or juror will have the patience to wade through a foot-tall stack of reports in order to extract some evidentiary gem. Thus, your presentation of documents must be judicious. Truly important exhibits can be emphasized effectively only if trivial or repetitive ones are omitted. The final section of this chapter deals in greater depth with the persuasive use of documentary evidence and other exhibits.

C. Offering Exhibits at Trial

Whether they consist of real, demonstrative, or documentary evidence, there is one basic protocol for offering exhibits at trial.

Although the details vary somewhat from jurisdiction to jurisdiction, the following steps form a nearly universal procedure.[40]

1. Mark the Exhibit for Identification

Every exhibit should be marked for identification before it is offered into evidence or even referred to in the course of a trial. Marking the exhibit identifies it for the record so that it will be uniquely recognizable to anyone who later reads a transcript of the proceedings. References to "this letter" or "the first broken fastener" may be understood in the courtroom, but they will be meaningless to an appellate court. "Defendant's exhibit three," on the other hand, can mean only one thing, assuming that the exhibit was appropriately marked and identified.

Exhibits are generally marked sequentially and further identified according to the designation of the party who has first offered them. Thus, the exhibits in a two-party trial will be called plaintiff's exhibit one, plaintiff's exhibit two, defendant's exhibit one, defendant's exhibit two, and so forth. In multiple-party trials it is necessary to identify an exhibit by the name, and not merely the designation, of the party who offers it. Accordingly, you will see references to plaintiff Bennett exhibit one or Weber exhibit two. In some jurisdictions plaintiffs are expected to use sequential numbers for their exhibits, while defendants are requested to use letters. Hence, plaintiff's exhibit one and defendant's exhibit A. The details of the particular marking system are unimportant so long as it produces a clear and understandable indication of which exhibit is which.

The "mark" itself usually takes the form of a sticker placed directly on the object or document. Stickers are available in a variety of forms. Many attorneys use color-coded sets that already contain the words plaintiff or defendant, with a space left blank for the number assigned to each exhibit.

The term "marked for identification" means that the exhibit has been marked and can be referred to in court but has not yet been admitted into evidence. Exhibits that have been marked for identification may be shown to witnesses and may be the subject of limited examinations for the purpose of establishing a foundation, but they usually may not be shown to the jury.

---

40. Subsequent sections of this chapter will discuss the foundations for various sorts of exhibits. Most sections will include examples of these foundations. For the sake of brevity, these examples will be limited to the evidentiary foundations and will not include the technical protocol for offering the exhibits. Readers should assume that in each example the sponsoring attorney would go on to follow the general procedure for offering exhibits as is outlined below.

2. Identify the Exhibit for Opposing Counsel

Exhibits should be identified for opposing counsel before they are shown to the witness. This may be done by referring to the exhibit number or by indicating its designation in the pretrial order if one has been prepared. In some jurisdictions you may be expected actually to hand or display the exhibit to opposing counsel before proceeding.

In any event, these common courtesies allow opposing counsel to confirm that the exhibit is the same one that was produced during discovery or that was discussed and marked at the pretrial conference. Opposing counsel is also afforded an opportunity to make an early objection to the use of the exhibit.

3. Examine the Witness on the Foundation for the Exhibit

Having identified the exhibit, you may now proceed to lay the foundation for its admission.

a. Show the exhibit to the witness

The first step is to show the exhibit to the witness. This is typically done by handing it to the witness.[41] If the exhibit is something as large as a life-sized model or an enlarged photograph, you may point to it and direct the witness's attention. In either case you should announce for the record what you are doing, using a shorthand description of the exhibit as well as its identification number:

COUNSEL: Ms. Harris, I am handing you defendant's exhibit eleven, which is a letter dated July 26.

Your initial description of the exhibit must be scrupulously neutral. While you are allowed to ask a leading question on preliminary matters, you are not allowed to begin arguing your case under the pretext of laying a foundation. Thus, you cannot say:

COUNSEL: Ms. Harris, I am handing you defendant's exhibit eleven, which is the letter in which the plaintiff agreed to provide repair service at no additional cost.

The date of the letter, and perhaps the name of its author, would be sufficient. If the very description of the exhibit is in issue, you may briefly describe what it "purports" to be.

---

41. In some jurisdictions it is necessary to obtain the court's permission before you approach the witness. In other courtrooms you may simply walk up to the witness, so long as you do it politely.

b. Identify the exhibit

The next step is to have the witness identify the exhibit. The witness should state the basis for her familiarity with the exhibit and then describe it in some detail:

QUESTION: Have you ever seen Plaintiff's Exhibit 7 before?

ANSWER: Yes, I have seen it many times.

QUESTION: What is Plaintiff's Exhibit 7?

ANSWER: It is a piece of the stationery that I received when my order was delivered from Quickset Printing.

QUESTION: How is it that you recognize it?

ANSWER: I remember how it looked when I took it out of the box.

Numerous variations are possible once the witness has examined the exhibit: "Are you familiar with the exhibit? Do you recognize the exhibit? Are you able to identify the exhibit?" While it is technically necessary to establish initially that the witness has a basis for giving a description, it is often possible to elicit the description first: "What is it? How do you know?"

c. Complete the foundation for the exhibit

In some situations, particularly those involving real evidence, the identification of the exhibit will provide a sufficient foundation for admission. In other circumstances the foundation will be much more elaborate, perhaps calling for chain of custody or the establishment of a hearsay exception. These and other foundations for the introduction of real, demonstrative, and documentary evidence are discussed at length in subsequent sections of this chapter.

THE BASICS

Offering an Exhibit at Trial	
STEP	**EXAMPLE**
Mark the exhibit for identification	• Prosecution Exhibit 10
Identify the exhibit for opposing counsel	• (To counsel) I'm going to show the witness what has been marked Prosecution Exhibit 10.
Show the exhibit to the witness	• (To judge) Your Honor, may I approach the witness? • (To witness) Detective Evin, I'm handing you what has been marked as Prosecution Exhibit 10.
Ask the witness to identify the exhibit	• (To witness) Please tell the jury what that is. • How do you know that is the knife found at the defendant's home? • Why do you put your initials on items recovered from crime scenes? • On what day was this knife found?
Complete the foundation	• Please tell the jury exactly what you did with the knife after you found it.
Offer the exhibit	• Your Honor, we offer Prosecution Exhibit 10 in evidence. • Your Honor, we move the admission of Prosecution Exhibit 10.

4. Offer the Exhibit into Evidence

Once the foundation has been completed, the exhibit can be offered into evidence. Jurisdictions vary as to the formality with which this must be done. In the simplest version:

COUNSEL: Your Honor, we offer Plaintiff's Exhibit 3.

Some courts, however, expect a more highly mannered presentation:

COUNSEL: Your Honor, we move that the identifying mark be stricken and that Plaintiff's Exhibit 3 be received as Plaintiff's Exhibit 3 in evidence.

In any case, the exhibit must be shown to the judge, who will then ask opposing counsel if there are any objections to its admission.[42] At this point it is sufficient to recall that objecting counsel is entitled to request a limited cross examination of the witness (voir dire), which will be restricted to the subject of the admissibility of the exhibit.

5. Publish and Use the Exhibit

Once an exhibit has been received, it can be "published" to the jury and also used as a basis for further testimony.

a. Publication

The term "publication" refers to the communication of the exhibit to the jury. Exhibits may be published in a variety of ways. Large objects and oversize graphics are usually turned toward the jury. Smaller objects typically are handed to the jurors and passed among them. Documents can be enlarged and displayed, projected on a screen or monitor, passed among the jurors, or read aloud. The choice of publication method is customarily left to counsel, although the court may deny leave to use overly dramatic, prejudicial, or dangerous means.[43]

While the right of publication follows inherently from the admission of the document, the court still exercises discretion over the timing and manner of publication. Consequently, it is necessary to obtain the judge's permission to communicate an exhibit to the jury:

COUNSEL: Your Honor, may I show Defendant's Exhibit 6 to the jury?

Or,

COUNSEL: May I have leave to publish Plaintiff's Exhibit 3 by passing it among the jurors?

Or,

COUNSEL: Your Honor, may the witness read Prosecution Exhibit 9 to the jury?

There is no requirement that the entire exhibit be published. In the case of a lengthy document or voluminous record, it is appropriate to ask a witness to read only the portions that you deem most important. The entire exhibit, however, must be made available to

---

42. The process for arguing objections is discussed in Chapter 8.

43. Section VI, *infra* at p. 307, discusses the persuasive use of exhibits, including effective methods of publication to the jury.

the jury for inspection, as well as to opposing counsel for use on cross examination.

b. Using the exhibit

Once an exhibit has been admitted in evidence, it can be used to illustrate or amplify a witness's testimony. In addition to publishing it to the jury, a witness can give further testimony that interprets or otherwise explains the significance of the exhibit.

Tangible objects can be used in demonstrations. A witness can show how a gun was aimed or how a tool was used. Maps, diagrams, and photographs can be used to illustrate the movement of persons and vehicles, the locations of incidents, or the relationship and distances between stationary objects. It is permissible to have a witness mark directly on the exhibit or to use velcro "stick-ons" to elaborate on her testimony. These techniques will be discussed further in the section below on demonstrative evidence.

Additionally, once an exhibit is in evidence, a witness can testify about its contents:

QUESTION: Do the words in Defendant's Exhibit 9 have a particular meaning in your profession?

QUESTION: Why was the color of the stationery, Plaintiff's Exhibit 1, so important to you?

QUESTION: What did you do once you received Plaintiff's Exhibit 12?

QUESTION: What was your reaction when you saw Lynn Stromski holding Defendant's Exhibit 4?

The right to testify about an exhibit is constrained by the applicable rules of evidence. Contrary to a frequently heard objection, however, an exhibit is not required to "speak for itself."

Finally, be aware that once an exhibit has been admitted it may be used, subject to the rules of evidence, in the examination of any witness, not only the witness who introduced it.

IV. FOUNDATIONS FOR REAL AND DEMONSTRATIVE EVIDENCE

A. Real Evidence/Tangible Objects

Real evidence must be shown to be relevant and authentic. Did the object actually play a role in the facts of the case? Does it tend to prove (or disprove) some issue in contention? Is the object in court really the one that we are talking about? If these conditions are met, the evidence will usually be admitted.[44]

The relevance of real evidence is typically established by the context of the case and often requires no additional attention when it comes to laying the foundation. Authenticity, on the other hand, must always be carefully established, as it is the fact of authenticity that qualifies the exhibit as *real* evidence.

In many cases the authenticity of real evidence can be shown by a witness's recognition of the exhibit. Other cases require a more detailed and complex foundation, usually referred to as chain of custody.

1. Recognition of the Exhibit

The authenticity of real evidence can be established through the testimony of a witness who is able to recognize the item in question. Many objects can be identified by virtue of their unique features. Others may have been given some identifying mark in anticipation of litigation. In either case, the witness must testify (1) that she was familiar with the object at the time of the underlying events, and (2) that she is able to recognize the exhibit in court as that very same object.

In the following example, the plaintiff in a property damage case will be asked to lay the foundation for an item of personal property:

QUESTION: Do you recognize Plaintiff's Exhibit 1?

ANSWER: Yes, it is an oil painting that was left to me by my grandmother.

QUESTION: How is it that you can recognize it?

ANSWER: Until the fire, it hung over our mantle and I used to look at it almost every day.

QUESTION: Was it in your house at the time of the fire?

ANSWER: Yes it was. It was one of the first things that I tried to salvage after we were allowed back into the house.

---

44. Rule 403, Federal Rules of Evidence, provides an exception: "Although relevant, evidence may be exluced if its probative value is substantially outweighed by the danger of unfair prejudice, confusion of the issues, or misleading the jury, or by considerations of undue delay, waste of time, or needless presentation of cummulative evidence."

This provision is often applied to real evidence.

QUESTION: Is Plaintiff's Exhibit 1 the same oil painting that you removed from your house after the fire?

ANSWER: Yes.

QUESTION: Is Plaintiff's Exhibit 1 in the same condition as it was when you removed it from your house after the fire?

ANSWER: Yes, it is.

While an oil painting is likely to be unique and easily recognizable, other exhibits are more fungible. Police officers and others who are familiar with litigation often solve this problem by placing identifying marks on tangible objects. In the following example a police officer will lay the foundation for a child's safety seat that was found at the scene of an automobile accident:

QUESTION: Officer, did you recover any personal property at the scene of the accident?

ANSWER: Yes, I removed a child's safety seat from the back seat of the plaintiff's automobile.

QUESTION: What did you do with the car seat after you removed it?

ANSWER: I wrote my initials on the back of the seat, along with the date of the accident.

QUESTION: Showing you Defendant's Exhibit 6, is this the same child's safety seat that you removed from the back of the plaintiff's automobile on the date of the accident?

ANSWER: Yes, it is.

QUESTION: How do you know?

ANSWER: Because it has my initials and the date written on the back, in my own handwriting.

QUESTION: Is Defendant's Exhibit 6 in the same condition as it was when you retrieved it from the plaintiff's automobile?

ANSWER: Yes, it is.

The above foundation is sufficient for the admission of the car seat, so long as the exhibit is being offered only to prove the presence of the child seat in the plaintiff's automobile. The question on condition is technically superfluous unless the condition of the car seat is in issue. Nonetheless, judges are accustomed to hearing the "same condition" question, so it is usually a good idea to include it in the foundation for any tangible object.

An exhibit may still be admissible even if its physical condition has changed between the incident and the time of the trial. Under those circumstances the foundation must include an explanation of any changes:

QUESTION: Have there been any changes to the car seat since the time that you retrieved it from the plaintiff's automobile?

ANSWER: Yes. It is now much dirtier, and some of the plastic has been chipped or scratched.

QUESTION: Other than those changes, is Defendant's Exhibit 6 in the same condition as it was when you removed if from the plaintiff's car?

ANSWER: Yes.

In both the oil painting and the car seat examples it was unnecessary for the witness to account for the whereabouts of the exhibit between the incident and the trial. This is because the witnesses were able to supply all of the information necessary to authenticate the exhibits. In other circumstances, however, a foundation will need to include a chain of custody.

2. Chain of Custody

A chain of custody establishes the location, handling, and care of an object between the time of its recovery and the time of trial. A chain of custody must be shown whenever (1) the exhibit is not uniquely recognizable and has not been marked, or (2) when the exhibit's physical properties are in issue.

a. The need for a chain of custody

Many objects are not inherently identifiable. A case might involve a defective piece of industrial machinery, a damaged automobile part, a contaminated food product, or a misapplied hospital dressing. In none of these situations is a witness likely to recognize the relevant object with any certainty. While it is possible that some of these items might have been marked for later use in litigation, most people (other than police officers and trial lawyers) do not go around scratching their initials on objects to ensure their admissibility. Furthermore, some exhibits cannot be marked at all. For example, vegetation samples, tissue samples, liquids, and narcotics all have physical properties that defy marking.

A chain of custody is also necessary when the exhibit has been subjected to testing or analysis or when other aspects of its condition or composition are at issue in the case. An object that has been tested is likely to have passed through many hands on its way to the courtroom. Because the test results can be invalidated by mishandling, tampering, or alteration of the exhibit, it is necessary to account for its possession and care at least between the time that it was recovered and the time that it was analyzed. The same holds true for an item that is used to display some physical property in the courtroom; a chain must be established to show possession of the exhibit from the time of the underlying incident until its production in court.

b. Establishing a chain of custody

A chain of custody must, at a minimum, be sufficient to show that the object in the courtroom is the same one that was involved in the events being considered at trial. This can usually be accomplished by tracing the possession of the item as it passed from hand to hand. In some situations it is also necessary to show that the object was stored during the intervening period in a manner that was secure from tampering or inadvertent change. In either case it may be necessary to call more than one witness in order to complete the chain.

In the following example an automobile mechanic was injured when a tire exploded as it was being mounted. The tire manufacturer has been sued, and the defective tire will be offered solely to show that it was manufactured by the defendant. The first witness is the garage manager:

QUESTION: Where were you when the plaintiff was injured?

ANSWER: I was standing about thirty feet away when I heard the noise of a loud explosion.

QUESTION: What did you do?

ANSWER: I ran over to where the plaintiff was lying on the ground. He was covered with blood, and there was a ragged tire lying right next to him.

QUESTION: Were there any other tires nearby?

ANSWER: No, that was the only one.

QUESTION: Did you do anything with the tire?

ANSWER: Yes. I picked it up and put it in my office.

QUESTION: Were there any other tires in your office at the time?

ANSWER: No.

QUESTION: Did you ever do anything else with the tire that you found next to the plaintiff?

ANSWER: Yes. About a week later a company superintendent came to investigate the injury. He asked to take the tire, and I gave it to him.

QUESTION: Had the tire been in your office the entire time between the injury to the plaintiff and the time that you gave it to the company superintendent?

ANSWER: Yes.

QUESTION: Were there any other tires in your office during that time?

ANSWER: No.

The garage manager has completed the first part of the chain. Note that the tire has not yet been produced in court. The next witness is the company superintendent:

QUESTION: Did you obtain a tire in the course of your investigation of this injury?

ANSWER: Yes. I went to speak to the garage manager about two weeks after the incident, and he gave me a tire that he had kept in his office.

QUESTION: What did you do with that tire?

ANSWER: I brought it back to company headquarters and placed it in my office.

QUESTION: From that day until today, were there any other tires in your office?

ANSWER: No.

QUESTION: Did the tire that you got from the garage man-
             ager ever leave your office?

ANSWER: Yes, I brought it with me to court today.

QUESTION: Showing you Plaintiff's Exhibit 1, is this the
             tire that you obtained from the garage man-
             ager and that you brought with you to court
             today?

ANSWER: Yes, it is.

The chain of custody is now sufficient to establish the identity of the tire. Even though the company superintendent did not
witness the accident or initially recover the tire, there is enough
evidence to show the continuity of possession. Since in this example
the tire is being offered only to prove who manufactured it, physical
properties are not in issue. It is therefore unnecessary to show that
the tire was kept under lock and key during the intervening period.
While it is remotely conceivable that someone could have sneaked
into either office and affixed a fraudulent logo to the tire, it is usually unnecessary for a chain of custody to exclude all such unlikely
possibilities.[45]

If the tire had been given to an engineering consultant for
stress analysis, a more elaborate foundation would be required. It
would be necessary to show that measures were taken to safeguard
the condition of the tire from the time it was recovered at least
until it reached the laboratory for testing. With most exhibits this
is accomplished by placing the item in a sealed container, usually
marked with a date and a person's initials or some other distinc-
tive notation. If the exhibit is removed for testing, the container is
typically resealed and re-marked once the test has been completed.
Organizations that frequently collect evidence, such as police departments and hospitals, generally have developed routine chain of
custody procedures for isolating and preserving potential exhibits.

---

45. If there were evidence of such tampering, however, a more elaborate chain
would be required.

Foundation for Physical Evidence and Tangible Objects

Recognition

- Can the witness simply identify the object by virtue of its unique appearance or other features?

Identifying marks

- Was the object marked or tagged for the purpose of later identification?

Chain of Custody

- Is the object fungible, or other wise incapable of specific identification?

- Is the condition of the evidence an issue in the case?

- Was the evidence subjected to testing or analysis?

- Is there a legitimate possibility that the evidence has been tampered with or altered?

- Can the object be accounted for, from the date of recovery to the date of trial?

- If the object was tested, were the procedures sufficient to ensure that there was no mishandling or misidentification?

- If tampering, alteration, or deterioration are in issue, was the evidence kept in a secure location and condition?

B. Photography and Other Recording Devices

Photographs and other recordings bridge the gap between real and demonstrative evidence. While a visual or audio recording of any sort is, strictly speaking, an illustration of a past event, its capacity to portray a scene with accuracy is so great that many courts treat photographs and other recordings as tantamount to real evidence.

1. Still Photographs

The basic foundation for the admission of a still photograph is that it "fairly and accurately" portrays the scene shown. In all but a few situations it is not necessary to call the photographer to the stand. It is generally possible to introduce a photograph through the testimony of any witness who is familiar with the scene as it appeared at a relevant time. In the following example the witness is the owner of a home that was destroyed by fire. A photograph of the house will be offered as evidence of damages.

QUESTION: Were you the owner of the house located at 208 Oak Street?

ANSWER: Yes.

QUESTION: How long did you live there?

ANSWER: About eight years, until the fire.

QUESTION: So, of course, you are familiar with the appearance of your home before the fire.

ANSWER: Yes, certainly.

QUESTION: Does Plaintiff's Exhibit 11 fairly and accurately show your home at 208 Oak Street as it appeared on the day before the fire?

ANSWER: Yes, it does.

Because the witness is familiar with the appearance of the house, it is not necessary to call the photographer or to inquire into the circumstances in which the photo was taken. Nor is it necessary to show that the photo was taken on the day before the fire, so long as the picture "fairly and accurately" depicts the house as it appeared on the relevant day.

If there had been any alterations in the appearance of the house, the photo could still be admitted once the changes had been explained. The admissibility of the photo will depend upon the significance of the changes.

QUESTION: Were there any changes in the appearance of your house between the time of Exhibit 11 and the time of the fire?

ANSWER: Yes. The house had been painted, so the color was blue instead of white.

Because the value of the destroyed property will not be affected by the color of the paint, this foundation is sufficient. It is certainly possible, however, for the admission of a photograph to be refused because of discrepancies between the scene at the time it was taken as opposed to the scene at the time of the relevant events.

In some circumstances it may be necessary to call the photographer to the stand, as in cases where the photograph was taken using special or unusual techniques. Additionally, while most photographs are offered to show how something looked at a particular time, some photographs are offered to prove that something occurred at a certain time. It is usually necessary to produce the testimony of the photographer if the date or occasion of the occurrence in the photograph is in issue.

One last word about magic words. It has become a virtual reflex for lawyers to introduce photographs by asking whether they "fairly and accurately" depict the scene portrayed. Many judges have come to rely on the phrase "fairly and accurately depict" as a required part of the foundation for a photograph. It is not. Any language should be acceptable, so long as it authenticates the photograph as a reliable representation of a relevant scene. Nonetheless, it may be advisable to use the magic words. Judges often expect them and opposing counsel will be less likely to object.

2. Motion Pictures and Videotapes

As with photographs, a motion picture or videotape may be authenticated by any witness who is familiar with the scene or scenes portrayed. It is necessary to call the operator of the camera only if special features were employed or if the date of the filming is in issue.

A more difficult problem arises in the case of remote taping, when no person actually observed the events as they were recorded. In these circumstances the foundation must include additional information on operating procedures as well as the condition of the equipment.

3. Audiotapes and Sound Recordings

The foundation for an audiotape recording depends upon the purpose for which it is offered. A tape recording that is submitted merely as a voice exemplar, for example, may be authenticated by any witness who is able to recognize the voices of the various speakers. The same holds true for recorded music, as might be offered in a copyright dispute. The foundation can be laid by any witness who is familiar with the material recorded.

Audiotapes are perhaps most commonly offered to prove the content of a conversation. Such tapes have often been made surreptitiously, as in the case of police wiretaps.[46] As might be expected, the foundation for these tapes may be quite involved. The simplest case is presented when the tape was made by a participant to the conversation, or where the conversation was overheard by a person who may be called as a witness:

> QUESTION: Did you have a conversation with Rafael Amit on September 21?
>
> ANSWER: Yes, I did.

---

46. Note that the legality of surreptitious audiotaping differs from jurisdiction to jurisdiction. In some states it is illegal to tape a conversation without the consent of every person involved. In other states "one-party" consent is sufficient. Law enforcement taping and wiretaps, of course, must comply with search and seizure law.

QUESTION:	Was that conversation recorded?
ANSWER:	Yes. I recorded it myself.
QUESTION:	Is Prosecution Exhibit 8 the recording that you made of that conversation?
ANSWER:	Yes.
QUESTION:	How do you know?
ANSWER:	Because I have listened to it several times.
QUESTION:	Does Prosecution Exhibit 8 contain an accurate recording of the conversation that you had with Rafael Amit on September 21?
ANSWER:	Yes, it does.

While this foundation is generally adequate,[47] many lawyers prefer to elicit more extensive testimony concerning the reliability of the equipment used in the recording and the safekeeping (chain of custody) of the tape between the time of the recording and the time of trial. Such a foundation may be necessary if the authenticity of the tape is in issue, or if no witness is available to testify to the content of the conversation as it occurred.

4. Medical Imaging

Radiological images such as X-rays, computerized axial tomography (CT scans), and magnetic resonance imaging (MRIs) are comparable to photographs of the body's internal composition. While it is a scientifically reliable fact that X-rays generally produce a "fair and accurate" representation of the bone structure, there is no person who can provide eyewitness testimony comparing an X-ray and a live patient's actual skeleton. Fortunately, courts have long been willing to take judicial notice of the validity of X-rays, and the same now holds true for CT scans, PET scans, and MRIs.

Consequently, the foundation for the admission of these technologies has been streamlined since the time when it was considered necessary to prove the scientific basis for the process, the competency of the technician, and the good working condition of the particular machine.

It is now generally considered sufficient for a physician or other qualified person to testify that an X-ray, CT scan, or MRI is a fair

---

47. Note that the authentication of a tape recording does not obviate the need for the recorded conversation to be brought within an exception to the hearsay rule.

representation of the internal structure of a given patient's body. The identifying marks on the film (which allow the physician to recognize which X-ray belongs to which patient) are usually considered to be business records of the hospital or clinic.[48]

C. Demonstrative Evidence

Demonstrative evidence is used to illustrate, clarify, or explain other testimony or real evidence. When such an exhibit is sufficiently accurate or probative, it may be admitted into evidence and even given to the jury when they retire to deliberate. A closely related type of exhibit is the "illustrative aid," which may be used to assist a witness in explaining testimony but cannot be given to the jury as evidence.

The line between "evidence" and "aid" cannot be clearly drawn, but it is possible to imagine a continuum based on accuracy. Scale exhibits, such as models, maps, and diagrams, are extremely accurate and are usually considered demonstrative evidence; rough freehand drawings may be useful devices, but their lack of precision makes them more likely to be limited to use as visual aids.

1. Admissible Demonstrative Evidence

a. Maps, charts, and diagrams

The foundation for a map, chart, blueprint, or other diagram is essentially the same as that for a photograph. The witness must be familiar with the scene, location, or structure as it appeared at a relevant time and must testify that the exhibit constitutes a fair representation.

Additional foundation is necessary if the exhibit is drawn to scale. If the witness prepared the exhibit herself, she may testify to the manner in which she prepared it and the steps she took to ensure its accuracy. Following this approach it may be necessary to call two witnesses: one who prepared the exhibit and another who can testify regarding the facts or events in issue. Note that in many cases witness testimony will not be necessary to establish scale since the notation on official maps, plats, and surveys may be self-authenticating,[49] and the court may take judicial notice of the accuracy of commercially produced maps and charts.[50]

---

48. Rule 901(b)(9) allows authentication of "a process or system" via evidence "describing a process or system used to produce a result and showing that the process or system produces an accurate result." Regarding the foundation for the business records exception to the hearsay rule, see Section V C(1), *infra* at p. 300.

49. See Rule 902(5), Federal Rules of Evidence.

50. See Rule 201(b), Federal Rules of Evidence.

b. Models and reproductions

The foundation for a model or reproduction is similar to that for a photograph. The witness must be familiar with the real location or object and must testify to the model's accuracy. Issues regarding scale are identical to those concerning maps and diagrams.

Litigation often calls for the use of generic, as opposed to specific, models. A medical expert in a personal injury case might want to use an anatomical model to illustrate her testimony. A scale representation of a human shoulder joint will not be an exact model of the plaintiff's own shoulder joint. Nonetheless, it should be possible sufficiently to authenticate such a model. To do so the witness must testify that the model will be useful in explaining her testimony:

QUESTION: Doctor, what is Plaintiff's Exhibit 12?

ANSWER: It is a scale model of a human shoulder joint.

QUESTION: Would the use of Plaintiff's Exhibit 12 assist you in explaining the injury to the plaintiff's shoulder?

ANSWER: Yes. All human shoulder joints are basically the same.

A final type of model is the "similar" object. If the actual object is unavailable, a similar object may be used to illustrate a witness's testimony. A defective product, for example, might be destroyed in the same accident that causes an injury. A defect could be "modeled," however, by using an identical product produced by the same company.

2. Illustrative Aids

Exhibits that are insufficiently accurate to be allowed into evidence may often still be used for illustrative purposes. The foundation includes a witness's testimony that the exhibit will assist in explaining her testimony, as well as a general explanation or description of the inaccuracy. In the following example the witness has produced a freehand drawing of an intersection:

QUESTION: What is Defendant's Exhibit 5?

ANSWER: It is a drawing of the intersection of Forest and Main.

QUESTION: Did you make that drawing yourself?

ANSWER: Yes, I did.

QUESTION:	Does Defendant's Exhibit 5 generally show the configuration of the streets at Forest and Main as they appeared on the date of the accident?
ANSWER:	Yes, it shows the location of the streets and the locations of the traffic signs.
QUESTION:	Is Defendant's Exhibit 5 drawn to scale?
ANSWER:	It is the best I could do, but it is not drawn to scale.
QUESTION:	Would Defendant's Exhibit 5 still help you to explain your testimony about the accident?
ANSWER:	Yes, it would.

The above foundation is sufficient to allow the witness to use the diagram in the course of her testimony. The eventual admissibility of the diagram, however, will depend upon the court's assessment of its accuracy. Freehand drawings are often inadmissible because they tend to distort distances, spatial relationships, angles, sight lines, and similar information. For that reason, as well as the notorious unreliability of witness-produced drawings, it is generally preferable to use professionally prepared diagrams.

V. FOUNDATIONS FOR DOCUMENTS

In addition to the usual issues of relevance and authenticity, the foundation for a document usually includes two other elements. Because documents invariably contain out-of-court statements, they must be brought within an exception or exclusion to the hearsay rule. Additionally, the proffer must comply with the "best evidence" or "original writing" rule.

A. Authentication

The authentication of documents typically requires proof of authorship or origin and may also call for proof of transmission or receipt. The existence of a lease, for example, may not be probative unless it can be shown to bear the signatures of the contending parties. Similarly, the existence of a product recall letter is likely to be meaningless unless it was transmitted to the affected consumers. Thus, unlike tangible objects, the foundation for documentary evidence may include more than simple recognition.

On the other hand, it is unusual for the physical condition or safekeeping of a document to be in issue. Chain of custody, therefore, is seldom a component of the foundation for documentary evidence, although it may be required if the paper has been subjected to testing or if the writing appears to have been altered or amended.

1. Handwriting and Signature

The signature or other handwriting on a document can be authenticated through a variety of means. A witness may recognize a signature based on past observation or may authenticate it on the basis of circumstantial evidence. Other possibilities include expert testimony and in-court comparison by the trier of fact.

A witness may always authenticate her own handwriting or signature. A witness may also authenticate the handwriting of another if sufficient familiarity can be shown:

QUESTION: Please examine Defendant's Exhibit 2 and tell me if you recognize the signature at the bottom of the page.

ANSWER: Yes, I do recognize the signature.

QUESTION: Whose signature is it?

ANSWER: It is Ruth Arroyo's.

QUESTION: How are you able to recognize it?

ANSWER: I have seen Ruth sign her name many times, and I recognize the handwriting as hers.

It is not necessary, however, for the witness actually to have seen the person sign her name. Circumstantial evidence can also support the required degree of familiarity:

QUESTION: How is it that you are able to recognize Ruth Arroyo's signature?

ANSWER: We have corresponded over the years, and it is the same signature that I have seen on her letters.

QUESTION: How do you know that those letters came from Ms. Arroyo?

ANSWER: Because she would usually answer questions that I had written to her in my letters.

Note that extended correspondence is not a requisite. A non-expert witness can identify a signature on the basis of a single past event or sample so long as familiarity was not acquired for the purpose of litigation.[51]

An expert witness can authenticate a signature on the basis of comparison to a single identified specimen,[52] and the trier of fact, either court or jury, can make its own comparison on the basis of an authenticated exemplar.[53] In the case of comparison to be made by an expert or the trier of fact, the known specimen must still be authenticated. This can be accomplished through the testimony of a witness, as above, by stipulation, or by having the alleged signer write out an exemplar in open court.

2. Circumstantial Evidence of Authorship or Origin

Many documents are printed or typewritten and do not contain signatures or other handwriting. Unless such a document is somehow uniquely marked, it will need to be authenticated via circumstantial evidence. Such evidence can be in the form of a letterhead, seal, or stamp, or it can be provided by the context of the case:

QUESTION: Do you recognize Defendant's Exhibit 6?

ANSWER: Yes, it is a price list that I received from Quickset Printing.

QUESTION: How do you know that Defendant's Exhibit 6 came from Quickset Printing?

ANSWER: Well, it is on stationery that says Quickset Printing at the top of the page.

QUESTION: Is there any other reason that you know that Defendant's Exhibit 6 came from Quickset Printing?

ANSWER: Yes. I called the telephone number listed for Quickset in the directory, and I asked the person who answered the phone to send me a price list. This price list arrived in the mail two days later.

The above foundation is more than sufficient to authenticate the document. Note that, notwithstanding the admission of the document, the opposing party remains free to controvert its origin or

---

51. Rule 901(b)(2), Federal Rules of Evidence.
52. Regarding the qualification of an expert witness, see Chapter Seven.
53. Rule 901(b)(3), Federal Rules of Evidence.

authorship. Authentication is a threshold question, and it is not dispositive of the ultimate issue.

3. Mailing or Delivery

The admissibility of a document will often depend upon its receipt by, or at least transmission to, another party. This is an authenticity issue since the document is made admissible only by its status as one that was actually or constructively received. In other words, proof of mailing authenticates the document as truly having been sent to the other party.

Mailing can be proven either directly or through evidence of a routine business practice.[54] Direct proof of mailing can be given in a single sentence: "I placed the document in an envelope, with the correct address, and I deposited it in the United States mail with sufficient postage." The following is an example[55] of the "business practice" approach to proof of mailing:

QUESTION: Does your organization have a routine practice for the handling of outgoing mail?

ANSWER: Yes, we do.

QUESTION: Please tell us, step by step, what that practice is.

ANSWER: The secretary prepares an envelope as soon as a letter is typed, taking the address from the address block on the letter itself.

QUESTION: What is the next step?

ANSWER: Then the letter and the envelope are given back to the person who wrote it. That person proofreads the letter and signs it if there are no corrections.

QUESTION: What happens next?

ANSWER: The letter is given back to the secretary, who makes any necessary corrections. If there are no corrections, or once any corrections have

---

54. See Section II (B)(4), *supra* at p. 254, for a discussion of the foundation for habit and routine practice evidence.

55. In a real trial the witness would probably be permitted to explain the entire mailing procedure in a single, narrative answer. This example uses multiple questions and answers in order to underscore the individual elements of the foundation, as well as to avoid giving the impression that narratives are generally allowed.

been made and approved, the secretary seals
the letter in the envelope and places it in the
out box.

QUESTION: What is the next step?

ANSWER: The letters in the out box are picked up twice
each day by someone from the mail room. The
letters are taken to the mail room where they
are weighed and run through the postage me-
ter. The metered mail is taken to the local post
office twice each day, once at about noon and
once at 5:00 p.m.

QUESTION: Was that procedure in place on December 19?

ANSWER: Yes, it was.

The postal service was once the only common means of trans-
ferring documents. Today there are numerous others, including
messengers and overnight express services. The basic foundation
for proof of transmission is the same no matter which mode of communication is utilized. A witness may provide direct proof of transmission or may testify as to the organization's practice for handling
outgoing documents.

4. Faxes and E-Mails

Various forms of electronic transmission have become increasingly common, and in some areas virtually dominate communications. The foundations for telefaxes and e-mails vary somewhat from
standard letters and telephone calls, but rely upon the same basic
principles. In both cases, the technologies have become sufficiently
well known that courts will take judicial notice of their reliability,
making it unnecessary (except in unusual circumstances) to introduce evidence that the "process or system…produces an accurate
result."[56]

For faxed documents, then, it is sufficient to provide either direct evidence ("I put it in the fax machine and entered the listed
number") or to offer proof of an organization's practice for outgoing
documents (I filled out a fax sheet and handed it to my secretary").
In addition, most fax machines now provide documentation for all
transmissions, which may be offered as business records.[57]

Incoming faxes present a slightly different problem, since the
sender's identity will usually need to be authenticated. If the sender's

---

56. Rule 901(b)(9), Federal Rules of Evidence.
57. See section C 1, below.

fax number appears on the document (as is required by a federal statute), that will usually provide sufficient authentication—so long as the number itself can be linked to the sender through a directory or other means. In the alternative, a fax may be authenticated circumstantially, as with any other document.

The authentication of e-mails is somewhat trickier. For outgoing correspondence, it must be shown that the e-mail was actually sent to the intended recipient. Thus, the e-mail address must be linked to the recipient, either through a directory or some other means. Many businesses and other organizations publish such directories, but in other situations the validity of the address may have to be established circumstantially, as in this example in a simple contract case:

QUESTION: How did you transmit your acceptance of the offer?

ANSWER: I sent an e-mail to Louis Robbins.

QUESTION: What e-mail address did you use?

ANSWER: It was louis-dot-robbins-at-jacksonville-dot-net.

QUESTION: How do you knowthat was the correct address?

ANSWER: Louis and I had corresponded by e-mail for several months, and all of his replies came from that address.

Traditionally, the "mailbox rule" provided a rebuttable presumption that properly mailed letters were in fact received. That presumption may have to be relaxed a bit in the case of e-mails, however, since some transmissions "bounce" and others may be mistakenly deleted as unwanted "spam." The only certain way to prove receipt of an e-mail, therefore, may be to call the recipient as a witness or to subpoena her computer (or to achieve the same result through a request to admit facts.)

Incoming e-mails will have to be authenticated the same way, either by establishing reliable knowledge of the sender's e-mail address or through other circumstantial evidence. In the case of both outgoing and incoming messages, the proponent's printout of the e-mail will usually have to qualify as an exception to the hearsay rule, perhaps as a business record (outgoing) or party admission (incoming).

In an extreme case, it might be necessary to prove in detail that a particular e-mail was actually transmitted from one computer to another. Though complex, this can be done by establishing the routing chain, as the e-mail (or rather, the electronic impulses) passed through various servers en route from sender to recipient. Fortunately, the documentation at each stage will usually qualify as a business record, and authentication may be made by certification, thus making it unnecessary to call a series of witnesses.[58]

5. Website Postings

Website postings have become increasingly important in commercial and consumer litigation. Information that was once found in catalogs and brochures, or on price lists and other printed documents, is now disseminated even more broadly over the Internet. Proof of a website's content may therefore be relevant in contract, warantee, consumer fraud, and even tort cases.

It is a fairly simple matter for a proponent to prove the content of its own website, as the necessary documentation will generally qualify as a business record. It will usually be sufficient, therefore, for a witness to testify that a certain page was posted on the date in question. As with faxes and e-mails, most courts will accept the reliability of the technology and not require proof of the process by which the postings actually appear at a given web address.

Extra steps are required when the propoent offers evidence from someone else's website. In that case, it must be shown that the site is actually operated at a certain URL (universal resource locator) by a particular person, organization, or entity. Such proof may be readily available, if the site has an easily identifiable inscription or logo. Otherwise, an admission or circumstantial evidence may be necessary. Consider the following example:

Question:	Where did you find the pricing information that you relied on?
Answer:	It was posted on the website for Quickset Printing, which was www-dot-quicksetprinting-dot-com.
Question:	How do you know that was Quickset's website?
Answer:	It had their logo, street address, and telephone number.

---

58. Rule 902(11), Federal Rules of Evidence.

Question: Anything else?

Answer: Yes. I have frequently order products through that website. My payments were always accepted and the products always arrived.

Because websites are not static, it will often be necessary to establish the date of the posting as well, either through documentation (a printout of the page in question) or specific testimony.

B. The Original Writing ("Best Evidence") Rule

The so-called "best evidence" rule was once a formidable obstacle to the admission of documentary evidence. In its harshest form the rule excluded all but the original copy of any writing unless certain conditions could be met. Today, the rule has been softened considerably and now allows for the easy admissibility of most copies.[59] The rule constitutes an authenticity requirement, but its terms are sufficiently unique so as to call for separate treatment.[60]

The essence of the "original writing" rule is that the content of a document can be proved only by producing the original, or an acceptable duplicate, unless the original is lost, destroyed, or unavailable. Because under most circumstances a duplicate is admissible on the same terms as the original, the rule now operates primarily to exclude testimonial summaries or paraphrases of a document. Note also that the original writing rule applies only to proof of a document's content, not its signing, acknowledgment, or delivery.

A duplicate may be substituted for the original in most situations. The Federal Rules of Evidence define the term "duplicate" quite broadly so as to include essentially all accurate reproductions,

---

59. Rule 1002, Federal Rules of Evidence, states the basic original writing requirement: "To prove the content of a writing, recording, or photograph, the original writing, recording, or photograph is required, except as otherwise provided in these rules or by Act of Congress."

Rule 1003, however, goes on to allow the admissibility of most duplicates: "A duplicate is admissible to the same extent as an original unless (1) a genuine question is raised as to the authenticity of the original or (2) in the circumstances it would be unfiar to admit hte duplicate in lieu of the original."

60. As everyone knows, the "best evidence" rule has nothing to do with whether a document is the best evidence of any particular proposition, which is why most commentators now choose to refer to it as the "original writing" or "original document" rule. Judges and lawyers, perhaps becuase they thrive on confusion, have persisted in using the "best evidence" terminology.

including carbons, photocopies, telefaxes, and computer-generated duplicates.[61]

Duplicates are not admissible, however, where "a genuine question is raised as to the authenticity of the original."[62] Thus, for example, a photocopy of a contract cannot be offered if one of the parties can support a claim that her signature was forged on the original.

In any event, there are exceptions to the original writing rule. The original is not required if it (1) has been lost or destroyed, (2) is unobtainable, or (3) is in the possession of an opponent who has refused to produce it.[63] Invocation of an exception requires the establishment of a foundation.

In the following example the witness claims to have received a threatening letter from the defendant:

QUESTION: Did you receive a letter from the defendant?

ANSWER: Yes, I did.

QUESTION: How do you know that it was from the defendant?

ANSWER: I recognized his handwriting, which I have seen many times.

QUESTION: Do you still have the letter?

ANSWER: No, I do not.

QUESTION: What happened to it?

ANSWER: I lost it when I moved to a new apartment.

QUESTION: What did the letter say?

---

61. See Rule 1001(4), Federal Rules of Evidence, which provides as follows: " A 'duplicate' is a counterpart produced by the same impression as the original, or from the same matrix, or by means of photography, including enlargements and miniatures, or by mechanical or electronic re-recording, or by chemical reproduction, or by other equivalent techniques which accurately reproduce the original."
62. Rule 1003(1), Federal Rules of Evidence.
63. Rule 1004, Federal Rules of Evidence.

The witness, having explained the loss of the original, may now testify as to the letter's content.[64] Similar foundations are necessary for the other exceptions to the rule.[65]

Foundation for Documents	
Authentication	• Can you establish authorship and origin? • If necessary, can you show that the document was received, reviewed, or transmitted? • Can the signatures, if any, be sufficiently authenticated?
Original Writing	• Does the "Best Evidence Rule" apply? • Does the document qualify as a duplicate? • Has the original been lost, or is it otherwise unobtainable?
Hearsay	• Is the document offered for a non-hearsay purpose, such as notice or acceptance? • Does the document qualify for a hearsay exception, such as business records, recorded recollection, public records, prior testimony, or another? • Was the document written, signed, or adopted by an opposing party, thus qualifying as a party admission?

C. Foundations for Hearsay Exceptions

The offer of a document inevitably sets the hearsay bell ringing in opposing counsel's mind. While writings may be admissible for nonhearsay purposes, such as proof of notice or acceptance, they are frequently submitted precisely to prove that their contents are true. Various exceptions are available to allow the use of such documents, each requiring its own foundation. The more common exceptions are discussed in the following sections.

---

64. Note that compliance with the original writing rule goes only to authenticity. A document may still be excluded if it is otherwise hearsay. In this example, however, the letter, having been written by the defendant, qualifies as a party admission.

65. The most involved foundation is necessary when the original is asserted to be in the possession of a party opponent. The Federal Rule allows secondary evidence if "[a]t a time when an original was under the control of the party against whom offered, that party was put on notice, by the pleadings or otherwise, that the contents would be a subject of proof at the hearing, and he does not produce the original at the hearing ..." Rule 1004(3), Federal Rules of Evidence.

1. Business Records

Business records can include ledgers, accounts, calendar entries, memoranda, notices, reports, statements, and similar writings. All of these documents constitute hearsay if they are offered to prove that their contents are true. Thus, the entries in a loan company's account book would be hearsay if submitted as proof that a certain loan was not repaid in time.

Fortunately for the world of commerce, the "business records" exception to the hearsay rule allows for the admission of most such records, so long as they can be shown to meet certain requirements. Under the Federal Rules the records of any regularly conducted activity are admissible if they (1) were made at or near the time of a transaction or event; (2) were made by, or based on information transmitted from, a person with knowledge; (3) were kept in the course of a regularly conducted business activity; and (4) were made as a part of the regular practice of that business activity.[66]

It is not uncommon to use the approximate words of the rule in order to lay a foundation for the exception:

QUESTION:	Are you employed by the Quickset Printing Company?
ANSWER:	Yes, I am the accountant and bookkeeper.
QUESTION:	Do you recognize Plaintiff's Exhibit 3?
ANSWER:	Yes I do. It is our ledger book.
QUESTION:	What is the function of your ledger book?
ANSWER:	We use it to record all of our credit sales and all of the payments that we receive.
QUESTION:	Are the entries in Plaintiff's Exhibit 3 made at or near the time of the sales or payments?
ANSWER:	Yes.
QUESTION:	Are the entries made by or transmitted from a person with knowledge of the sales and payments?
ANSWER:	Yes.
QUESTION:	Are those entries made as a part of the regular business practice of Quickset Printing?

---

66. Rule 803(6), Federal Rules of Evidence.

ANSWER: Yes.

QUESTION: Is the ledger book, Plaintiff's Exhibit 3, kept in the regular course of business?

ANSWER: Yes, it is.

The foundation for the exception is now complete. Note that the witness does not need to be the keeper or custodian of the records, but may be any "person with knowledge."[67] The term "business" is defined broadly to include any "business, institution, association, profession, occupation, and calling of every kind, whether or not conducted for profit."[68] Furthermore, the absence of an entry is also admissible on the basis of the same foundation so long as it is the type of matter of which a record was regularly kept.[69]

The basic foundation for the business records exception can be expanded upon as circumstances dictate. In dealing with records that are more complex, intricate, questionable, or exotic than ledger books, it is often desirable to have the witness spend more time explaining their use and reliability. It is worth keeping in mind, however, that judges are accustomed to hearing the foundation's magic words and that objections are less likely to be made or sustained when you use them too.

2. Computer Records and Printouts

Computer-generated printouts have become a common form of business record. In the early days of computing it was considered necessary to prove that computer data entry and retrieval systems were reliable means for storing information, but this is no longer the case.

The Federal Rules specifically recognize "data compilations" as an acceptable form of business record. Thus, the foundation for a computer printout is basically the same as that for any other business record:

QUESTION: Are you employed by the Quickset Printing Company?

ANSWER: Yes, I am the accountant and data manager.

QUESTION: Do you recognize Plaintiff's Exhibit 3?

---

67. *Id.*
68. *Id.*
69. Rule 803(7), Federal Rules of Evidence.

ANSWER: Yes, I do. It is a printout of our accounts receivable.

QUESTION: How was Plaintiff's Exhibit 3 generated?

ANSWER: We use a computer program to record all of our credit sales and all of the payments that we receive. We can then print out the information whenever we need it.

QUESTION: Are the entries made on your computer system at or near the time of the sales or payments?

ANSWER: Yes.

QUESTION: Are the computer entries made by or transmitted from a person with knowledge of the sales and payments?

ANSWER: Yes.

QUESTION: Are those entries made as a part of the regular business practice of Quickset Printing?

ANSWER: Yes.

QUESTION: Are your computer records kept in the regular course of business?

ANSWER: Yes, they are.

Note that only the computer entries, and not the printout, need to have been made "at or near the time of the transactions."

3. Summaries

Many business records or other sets of data are so lengthy and ponderous that they cannot be conveniently produced in court. Even if they could be produced, they may be so extensive and technical as to be impenetrable. In these circumstances it is permissible to substitute a "chart, summary, or calculation" that fairly presents the relevant information in a usable or understandable form.[70]

The foundation for such a summary includes these elements: (1) the original documents are so voluminous that they cannot be conveniently examined in court; (2) the witness has examined the original data; (3) the witness is qualified to produce a summary of

---

70. Rule 1006, Federal Rules of Evidence.

the information; and (4) the exhibit is a fair and accurate summary of the underlying information. The witness in the following example is an economist who has been called to testify regarding a company's net worth:

QUESTION: What is your occupation?

ANSWER: I am an economist.

QUESTION: Have you examined certain records of the Quickset Printing Company?

ANSWER: Yes.

QUESTION: Please describe all of the documents that you examined.

ANSWER: I looked at all of the books and records of the company, including their pay records, tax records, fringe benefit records, insurance records, accounts payable, accounts receivable, inventories, mortgages, and appraisals of their real property.

QUESTION: Why did you examine those records?

ANSWER: It was necessary to look at all of that information in order to arrive at a figure for their net worth.

QUESTION: Can you describe the volume of the materials that you examined?

ANSWER: All in all, I would say that they would fill three or four large binders.

QUESTION: Do you recognize Plaintiff's Exhibit 19?

ANSWER: Yes, it is a summary that I prepared of the Quickset records.

QUESTION: What does Plaintiff's Exhibit 19 contain?

ANSWER: It shows their outstanding assets and liabilities, which then gives us their net worth.

QUESTION: Is Plaintiff's Exhibit 19 a fair and accurate summary of the corporate records of Quickset Printing?

ANSWER: Yes.

It is also necessary for the original records to be made available for examination by the other parties. This aspect of the foundation can be established through testimony or by stipulation.

4. Recorded Recollection

A witness's written notes or other recorded recollection may be admitted in evidence only if the witness, at the time of trial, "has insufficient recollection to enable the witness to testify fully and accurately."[71] The foundation for this exception to the hearsay rule comprises these elements: (1) the witness once had personal knowledge of the relevant facts or events; (2) the witness cannot currently recall the events fully and accurately; (3) the witness previously made an accurate memorandum or record of the facts; (4) at a time when the events were fresh in his or her memory.

The witness in the following example has sued an insurance company for failure to pay a property damage claim:

QUESTION: Is it possible for you to name all of the items that were destroyed in the fire at your home?

ANSWER: No, we lost everything. I am sure that I would not be able to name every item, or even most of them.

QUESTION: Before the fire, had you ever made a list of your belongings?

ANSWER: Yes, I inventoried all of the more valuable or significant items, and I put the list in my safe deposit box.

QUESTION: How did you make that list?

ANSWER: It was easy. I went from room to room and wrote down each thing as I saw it.

QUESTION: Was the list accurate when you made it?

ANSWER: Yes, it was.

QUESTION: Showing you Plaintiff's Exhibit 1, is this the list of belongings that you made?

ANSWER: It is.

---

71. Rule 803(5), Federal Rules of Evidence.

QUESTION: After reviewing the list, would it be possible for you to remember all of the items on it?

ANSWER: No, there are too many.

The foundation for the witness's recorded recollection is now complete. Note that the witness testified that she could not recall all of the items even after reviewing the list. This testimony fulfills the requirement that the witness be unable to testify "fully and accurately." If the witness could recall all of the items, then her recollection would be "refreshed," and this particular hearsay exception would not be available. The witness would, of course, be able to testify as to her renewed recollection.[72]

Under the Federal Rules a document containing a recorded recollection may only be read into evidence; the record itself cannot be received as an exhibit unless offered by the adverse party.[73] Some state jurisdictions simply allow the admission of the document.

5. Public Records

There are a number of hearsay exceptions that allow for the admissibility of public records, statistics, and reports. Such records are generally admissible if they were made by a public office or agency and they set forth (1) the activities of the office or agency; or (2) matters observed pursuant to a duty imposed by law; or (3) in limited circumstances, certain investigative findings; or (4) officially required records of vital statistics.[74]

Because most government records are "self-authenticating," it is not usually necessary to call a witness to testify to their authenticity.[75] While it is technically necessary to call a witness to establish the "governmental duty" elements of the foundation, most courts will take judicial notice of the fact that agencies are required by law to record their activities and observations, particularly where the obligation is imposed by a statute or regulation.

Note that the Federal Rule places two limits on the use of this hearsay exception in criminal cases. First, "matters observed by police officers and other law enforcement personnel" do not qualify for the exception, even if contained in a report made pursuant to a duty imposed by law. Second, investigative findings are admissible in criminal cases only if offered against the government.

---

72. The techniques for refreshing recollection are discussed in Chapter 3, Section II E, *supra* at p. 34.

73. Rule 803(5), Federal Rules of Evidence.

74. See Rule 803(8) and 803(9), Federal Rules of Evidence.

75. Rule 902, Federal Rules of Evidence.

6. Absence of Public Record or Entry

Public records may also be used to show the nonoccurrence of events. The foundation for this evidence is (1) that such events, occurrences, or matters were regularly recorded in some form; (2) by a public office or agency; and (3) that a diligent search has failed to disclose a record of a particular fact or event. This evidence may be offered by certification from the appropriate official, in which case no witness needs to be called. The evidence may also be offered via testimony:

QUESTION: Do you hold a public position in this state?

ANSWER: Yes, I am the chief clerk at the Liquor Control Commission.

QUESTION: Does your agency keep records of the liquor licenses issued in this state?

ANSWER: Yes, we keep a record of every license as it is issued, as well as the payment of each annual licensing fee.

QUESTION: Are those records regularly made and preserved as part of the public business of your agency?

ANSWER: They are.

QUESTION: Have you conducted a diligent search to determine whether this state has ever issued a liquor license to an organization called the Park City Club?

ANSWER: Yes, I have.

QUESTION: What was the result of that search?

ANSWER: No such license has ever been issued.

7. Previous Testimony

The transcript of a person's previous testimony may be admitted into evidence if (1) the declarant is currently "unavailable" to testify; (2) the testimony was given under oath in court or at a deposition; (3) the party against whom the testimony is being offered had a fair opportunity to examine the witness when the testimony was originally given.[76] Note that this exception allows the admission of the earlier statement as a substitute for current testimony. Unlike the use of prior testimony for impeachment, there is no requirement that the previous testimony be inconsistent with the declarant's current position.

Under the Federal Rule a witness can be deemed "unavailable" for a variety of reasons, including: (1) the valid assertion of a privilege; (2) persistent refusal to testify; (3) inability to attend the hearing due to illness; (4) death; (5) failure of memory; or (6) absence from the hearing notwithstanding the efforts of the proponent of the testimony to procure attendance.

The elements of the foundation for this exception will frequently be established through judicial notice. The court, for example, will usually take notice of the fact that a party had an opportunity to cross examine the declarant at the earlier hearing or deposition. It may occasionally be necessary to produce proof of unavailability, as in the case of a witness who failed to respond to a subpoena.

8. Party Admissions

The party admission exception applies to documents as well as to oral statements. A party admission can be contained in a letter, report, memorandum, journal, progress chart, or virtually any other form of writing. Once the exhibit has been authenticated the only remaining foundation is that it was made or adopted by a party against whom it is being offered or by an agent, servant, or employee of such a party.

VI. PERSUASIVE USE OF EXHIBITS

The previous sections dealt with the technical aspects of offering exhibits. The admission of an exhibit, however, is only part of counsel's task. It is equally important to ensure that exhibits are presented and used as persuasively as possible. The following sections cover traditional courtroom exhibits, such as physical objects, photographs, and drawings. Computer-generated visuals will be discussed in Chapter Ten.

A. Magic Words

When offering exhibits, counsel must always reckon with the potency of magic words. Many foundations—including those for photographs, business records, and the authenticity of conversations—have become routine to the point that convenient phrases are now

---

76. Rule 804(b)(1), Federal Rules of Evidence.

frequently confused with legal requirements. No matter what some judges may think, though, it is not necessary to introduce every photograph by asking whether it "fairly and accurately depicts" the scene involved. As far as the law of evidence is concerned, it would be just as acceptable to ask whether the photograph "shows everything in the scene just as it appeared on the date in question." Hundreds of other variations would serve just as well.

Nonetheless, there is not much advantage to be gained by arguing with judges or opposing lawyers who are determined to hear the magic words. In the end it is just easier to say "fairly and accurately depict" than it is to convince the court that your more thoughtful and elegant version of the foundation is legally sufficient.

Magic words get results and must therefore be part of every attorney's repertoire. For the benefit of a jury you will often want to lay a foundation in more readily understandable language, but this should not prevent you from falling back on the expected jargon, either in response to an objection or as an extra "fail-safe" line of questions at the end of your preferred foundation.

B. Developing Exhibits

The most valuable exhibits in any case seldom step forward and present themselves. Rather, they must be sought after, searched out, and discovered. Often they must be developed and created. Even those exhibits that are simply handed to counsel by the client can be presented in an enhanced form.

All exhibits fall essentially into two categories: those that predate the litigation and those created by the attorneys. The pre-litigation, or integral, exhibits must be taken as they are found, but counsel has wide latitude in shaping and developing other exhibits for use at trial. Some of the more common sorts of lawyer-generated exhibits are discussed below. The creation of these, and similar, exhibits should be considered in virtually every case.

1. Deposition Transcripts

Although not commonly thought of as exhibits, deposition transcripts are indeed physical objects that did not exist before the litigation. They come into being only as a consequence of arrangement and questioning by counsel. The words on the printed page can under some circumstances be shown to, as well as read to, the jury. An enlargement of a key section of an adverse witness's testimony can make an extremely effective exhibit when used on cross examination.

2. Photographs and Videotapes

As we noted in the foundation section, it is extremely easy to have photographs admitted in evidence. They only need to portray accurately a relevant scene in order to be received. With this in mind you will almost always want to photograph important objects or locations that bear on your theory of the case.

Although it is not necessary to call the photographer in order to authenticate a photograph, it is often a good idea to employ a professional photographer to take any desired photographs. Amateurs, even working with good equipment, can make errors in focus, lighting, or composition. A professional will understand how to capture the desired scene while avoiding extraneous or misleading information.

It is now possible to use videotapes in much the same way that still photography has been used for years. Instead of photographing the scene of an accident, for example, counsel should consider videotaping not only the scene, but also the viewpoints of the parties as they approached the scene. A still photograph can capture only a limited amount of information about a physical space, while a videotape can more accurately convey information concerning perspective, spatial relationships, and even speed.

3. Models

Models can be simple or elaborate, but they are almost always useful in explaining a series of events. Depending upon the size of the case and the available litigation budget, models can range from to-scale duplicates of entire buildings to commercially available reproductions of human organs or joints.

4. Diagrams and Maps

Diagrams are perhaps the simplest and most ubiquitous form of lawyer-generated exhibit. Virtually no automobile accident case would be complete without an intersection drawing, and many other cases use street grids, floor plans, or other diagrams on which to place the occurrence of physical events. One of the advantages of a diagram is that it can be marked to indicate the locations of signs, objects, or witnesses, as well as the movement of persons and things.

5. Explanatory Graphs and Charts

Photographs, models, and diagrams all represent physical objects and occurrences. Graphs and charts, on the other hand, help explain concepts and ideas. A simple "time line," for example, can clarify the sequence in which crucial events occurred. Similarly, a pie chart can help a witness explain loss of income or allocation of damages. It is entirely permissible for a witness to illustrate her testimony in addition to describing it in words. Counsel can help the witness communicate by assisting in the development of graphs and charts.

C.   Presenting Exhibits

The presentation of an exhibit can be as important as its composition or foundation. No matter how well thought out, no matter how solidly admissible, an exhibit will not accomplish its purpose if it is not understood and accepted by the trier of fact. As with any aspect of witness examination, there are certain principles that can generally be applied to the presentation of exhibits at trial:

1. Advance Preparation

The best exhibits are usually those prepared in advance of trial. This principle applies to both selection and design.

While some cases involve only two or three exhibits, many cases will see the production of dozens, if not hundreds, of documents. A careful trial plan will determine precisely which of these exhibits are the most significant and will treat them in such a way as to emphasize their importance. As with direct examination, clutter is the enemy of coherent document presentation. It will not do to wait for the witnesses' testimony before you decide which exhibits to highlight. First, your decision about the value of the exhibits should drive the preparation of your witness examinations, not the other way around. Second, the documents that you intend to rely upon most should be enlarged, or otherwise prepared for an impressive presentation.

In addition to selecting key integral documents for enhanced presentation, effective trial preparation also involves the design of lawyer-generated exhibits. Particularly when it comes to diagrams and graphs, an ounce of professional preparation is usually worth several pounds of courtroom drawing. The lawyer must decide whether a witness's testimony can be improved through the use of a chart, graph, or diagram. If so, the desired exhibit should be developed in advance of trial.

While it is permissible for witnesses to draw on blackboards or poster boards while testifying, this approach usually should be avoided. Freehand drawing is unreliable under the best circumstances, and witnesses are notoriously prone to make embarrassing mistakes when called upon to draw in a courtroom.

Essential features of an exhibit such as scale, perspective, and proportion can only be assured when entrusted to a professional illustrator. If professional assistance is not an alternative, then counsel must take care to create the best diagram possible.

2. Size

Exhibits must be seen to be appreciated. When creating an exhibit, create a big one. When using integral exhibits, such as preexisting documents, make enlargements.

There is no reason for a lawyer-produced exhibit to be visually inaccessible. Charts, graphs, and diagrams should be made on oversize pieces of stiff poster board. Thin tagboard is unacceptable since even a masterpiece will be useless if it cannot be made to stand up. It is also necessary to ensure that a display easel will be available in the courtroom.

Ordinary documents can be enlarged. While it is neither necessary nor desirable to enlarge every document, the crucial few should be enlarged to poster size and mounted for display. The most important exhibits to enlarge are those that support your theory of the case. In a case involving extended correspondence over the terms of a contract, for example, counsel may want to enlarge only the two letters showing the final offer and acceptance. Alternatively, trial strategy might dictate enlarging letters that contain certain terms or conditions. In any event, the enhanced presentation of a limited number of exhibits can underscore their importance and drive home your trial theory.

Photographs, whether preexisting or taken at counsel's direction, should also be enlarged. Even an 8" x 10" photograph cannot easily be seen from the usual distance between the jury box and the witness stand. If the film quality permits, crucial photographs should be further enlarged to poster size or reproduced as 35mm slides.

Electronic displays and visuals are discussed in the following chapter.

3. Copies

Counsel should enter the courtroom with enough copies of every exhibit. At a minimum this should include an original, additional copies for the witness and the judge, and copies for each opposing attorney if they have not already been produced. Distributing copies at the appropriate time in the examination will prevent delays and can forestall objections. There is little more awkward and distracting than a lawyer leaning over a witness's shoulder while they attempt to share an exhibit.

When enlargements are impractical or unavailable, counsel should also make enough copies of the exhibits, whether documents or photographs, to distribute to the jurors. With the court's permission the copies can be given to the jurors as the witness testifies to the foundation. Alternatively, counsel might wish to delay passing out the copies until the exhibit has been admitted, or even until the end of the examination, so as to avoid having the jurors' attention distracted during the witness's testimony.

It is increasingly common for documents to be admitted at the pretrial conference. When this occurs it is possible to assemble all of the documents into a bound or loose-leaf "exhibit book," copies of which can be provided to the court, to each juror, and to witnesses as necessary.

— CHAPTER TEN —
Electronic Visuals

by Edward R. Stein

I. GENERAL CONSIDERATIONS

A. Introduction

Electronic visuals have become readily available to trial lawyers. Hardware and software are affordable and reliable. A number of federal districts and many county court systems have equipped one or more of their courtrooms with presentational devices that permit trial lawyers to bring a computer into the courtroom and to plug and play.

Nonetheless, electronic visuals have yet to become a mainstay of courtroom graphic presentation. This is not because electronic visuals are ineffective—just ask any lawyer who has used them. It is more likely the result of the generally conservative nature of lawyers and judges and their reluctance to embrace something new. After all, it was not so many years ago that trial lawyers were hesitant to use flip charts in front of juries.

B. The Advantages of Electronic Visuals

1. Familiarity

Most experienced trial lawyers understand that electronic visuals can be extremely effective in educating and persuading a jury (or a judge). We have all become accustomed to clear, concise, attractive graphic displays on television news, weather reports, and even sportscasts. We are used to receiving our visual information from a screen (whether a television, computer, or projection screen). Why would any trial lawyer not want to provide jurors with the same graphic quality and medium that they experience in most other aspects of their lives? The only way to duplicate that experience is to bring electronics into the courtroom.

2. Ease

When prepared appropriately, electronic graphics are extremely easy to use. Some lawyers like to do it all themselves with their own hands on the computer. They understand that even lawyers can master the technological challenge, for example, of typing a number and hitting the Enter key. That is all one has to do to put a Power-Point® slide on the screen. It is even easier to ask a legal assistant to bring up slide number 12 or, with a well-prepared index, Exhibit 12.

It is far easier to store, retrieve, and project digital visuals than it is to use an overhead projector with transparencies (where there is at least a 50 percent chance that they will first be projected upside down or inside out), or 3N x 5N blowups (try arranging twenty of them for convenient handling). Similarly, for many lawyers, it is far easier to display an electronic list than to painstakingly write it on a flip chart, interrupting the flow of whatever else is happening and chancing the exigencies of handwriting and spelling.

3. Speed

Projecting an image is usually the product of one or two keystrokes or mouse clicks. The total time is typically less than two seconds. That should be contrasted with finding and positioning transparencies or blowups, circulating an exhibit among jurors, or writing something on a flip chart. If there is anything all judges are likely to agree on in the twenty-first century, it is the need to, "Move things along, counsel." Electronic visuals give us the ability to comply.

4. The Ability to Build a Visual

Perhaps the most important advantage of electronic displays is the ability to build a visual, piece by piece, in front of the jury. Electronic building is the easiest way to insure that the jury is looking at what we are talking about, when we are talking about it. If, for example, there are five items on a list, the jury will stay focused on item 3 only if items 4 and 5 are not yet displayed. Once they are displayed, human nature will pretty much compel the jury to read them, leaving the lawyer as the only person in the courtroom still focused on item 3.

5. Cost

Although cost was once a disadvantage to the use of electronic visuals, things have changed dramatically. At least by comparison to professionally prepared graphic boards, electronic visuals are a bargain.

Sophisticated electronic displays can be created with presentational software that most lawyers already have on their computers. All the visuals can be brought to court in a moderately priced laptop, something else most lawyers already have. The only substantial cost is for a projection device (see below). The cost of those devices has been reduced dramatically in recent years, and excellent projectors now cost $2,000 or less. The cost, of course, can be amortized over several cases and several years. Moreover, if the courtroom already has a projection device, as an increasing number do, that cost disappears.

6. Strategic Benefit

Where you have technology working for you and your opponent does not, there is often a significant psychological edge. Lawyers who are unfamiliar with courtroom technology are frequently flummoxed by their opponents' use of it and resort to ill-prepared objections or attempts at ridicule. Neither is very effective.

So long as technology is used appropriately, most jurors will not wonder why a lawyer is using it, only why her opponent is not. In interviews with both mock and real jurors, the response to electronic visuals is overwhelmingly positive.

C. Disadvantages

1. Judges and Courtrooms

Like anything new, technology prompts some judges to respond, "Not in my courtroom." This can sometimes be overcome with patient explanation and a demonstration of how technology will help the jury. Moreover, almost all judges are likely to be persuaded by a showing that technology will help speed the trial along. For judges who still resist technology, the best strategy is to raise the issue well in advance of trial, providing an example of something simple and straightforward, such as an enlarged picture or document. In other words, start with something that resembles a non-electronic visual. Once the judge accepts a simple electronic visual, she may be more receptive to things like labeled diagrams, document callouts, and eventually argument slides.

Technology can be a problem in many older courtrooms in terms of lighting, power outlets, sight lines, and space. If the court staff is cooperative, however, and if one addresses these issues well in advance of trial, the problems can usually be solved.

2. Disclosure to One's Opponent

When they learn that their opponent plans to use electronic visuals, many lawyers ask to see them in advance so they can raise objections. Although judges rarely, if ever, require lawyers to tell their adversaries what they plan to say to a jury or ask a witness, some judges require lawyers to disclose what they plan to display electronically. This is especially likely in opening statement.

If what one intends to display is simply an enlarged exhibit, no harm should result from disclosure. If, however, disclosure would prematurely reveal a line of cross examination or a line of closing argument, damage could result. Where there is a concern, in camera disclosure to the judge alone should ameliorate the problem.

3. The Comfort Factor

It takes time and experience to become comfortable with technology in the courtroom. Many lawyers believe that in trial there is enough to worry about without adding the exigencies of something novel. This is a problem that can be solved only with familiarity and practice. Of course, if such problems were insurmountable, we would all still be getting around by horse and buggy. The easiest way to become comfortable with technology in the courtroom is simply to use it.

4. The Glitch Factor

We have not yet reached the stage where hardware and software are 100 percent glitch-free. Computers (especially with Windows operating systems) occasionally freeze, projector bulbs burn out, and one piece of hardware or software may not easily integrate with another.

Careful preparation and practice can reduce the likelihood of a courtroom glitch, but not eliminate it entirely. Therefore, electronic visuals require backup: backup technical personnel and hardware if the case justifies the expense, or a backup system (e.g. transparencies with an overhead projector or thumbnail hard copies with a document camera such as an Elmo). Of course, the flip chart is an ever-reliable, if limited, backup.

D. The Technology

1. Software

The least expensive and most widely accessible software appropriate for courtroom use is general presentational software.

By far the most popular of these programs is PowerPoint, part of Microsoft's Office suite. PowerPoint is extremely stable and easy to learn for anyone familiar with other Microsoft products. Perhaps even more importantly, NITA has published two excellent books on PowerPoint for litigators.

PowerPoint is limited, however, in that it cannot easily accommodate cases involving hundreds or thousands of documents, any one of which may have to be displayed at a moment's notice. For those cases, software that combines document management and presentation works best. TrialDirector® and Sanction® are widely used. Those programs also enable the user to highlight documents and create document callouts on the go. That, alas, is something PowerPoint cannot yet do. Highlighting and callouts in PowerPoint must be created in advance.

2. Hardware

Virtually any current mainstream laptop computer can easily accommodate the demands of electronic courtroom visuals. That does not include, however, the five-year-old laptop that has been gathering dust in the corner of your office. In order to reliably run today's software and drive today's display devices, the computer should be manufactured by a reliable source (e.g., Dell, Gateway, HP (Compaq), IBM, Sony) and should be no more than two or three years old.

The choice of display devices is threefold:

A data projector with a screen;

A large-screen digital television or computer monitor, or

Several smaller digital television or computer monitors.

The least expensive option is the projector and screen. High quality, high intensity (1,000 or more lumens) projectors are usually less expensive than large-screen digital television sets or computer monitors. Moreover, the projectors generally provide an image that is large enough so that it can be seen by jury, judge, and the attorneys. It is difficult to find a single television set or monitor that can be seen by everyone without a lot of repositioning or squinting.

Some lawyers use regular (non-digital) large screen television sets with an S-video cable from the computer. This is the most economical system, but can result in degradation of image size or quality.

II. APPLICATIONS OF ELECTRONIC VISUALS

A. Lists

Trial lawyers frequently organize information into lists because they are easy for a jury to understand and remember. The use of any list, whether in argument or witness examination, may benefit from the use of an accompanying visual. With presentational software, lists are quite easy to create and can be displayed item by item.

An effective list can be something as simple as the names and roles of witnesses or the elements of a legal concept. Here is an example of the latter:

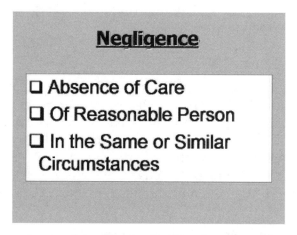

Lists can be used to illustrate the elements of an expert witness's testimony. For example, where a neurologist is testifying about the findings necessary to connect epilepsy to a trauma, this slide can be displayed:

For Trauma to Cause Epilepsy:

- Skull Fracture
- Loss of consciousness
- Clinical evidence of brain injury beyond loss of consciousness
- Blood in cerebral-spinal fluid

Lists can be more creative and complex, especially in closing argument. One might start with a list of the opponent's four claims and, after rebutting each, have it electronically disappear. Or one could create an electronic checklist (the checks appearing one by one as the testimony is summarized) to illustrate whether the facts favor the plaintiff's or defendant's position on an issue. For example:

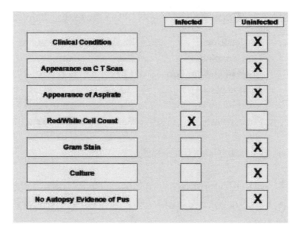

One of the most helpful lists, where chronology is important, is a time line in which the entries appear one at a time. Here is an example of plaintiff's opening statement time line where plaintiff claimed that the defendant-doctors committed malpractice by failing to timely diagnose her cervical cancer:

Contrasting lists can also be quite effective. Here, for example, in another malpractice case, is a list of the expected results of plaintiff's surgery contrasted with what actually occurred:

Outcome of Lisa Ford's Surgery	
Expected	**Actual**
• Tiny incisions	• Major multiple incisions
• Little scarring	• Extensive scarring
• Short hospitalization	• 171 days in hospitals
• Limited pain	• Severe pain – months
• Short recovery time	• Six additional surgeries
• Full recovery	• Permanent disfigurement

The type and effectiveness of electronic lists should be limited only by the facts of a given case and the imagination of the lawyer handling the case.

B. Documents

It is the rare case that does not involve important documentary evidence. The documents may come in myriad forms including correspondence, contracts, reports, medical records, and financial records. The difficulty in using documents as effective exhibits is that they are typically 8½" by 11", far too small to be seen at a distance. Even when enlarged to poster size, they cannot easily be read by a jury unless the enlargement is placed almost in the jury box, a practice frowned upon by many judges. If the enlargement is big enough for the jury to read at an appropriate distance, it is likely too big to be easily handled in the courtroom, at least without a team of movers.

Another problem using documents (especially if they are collected into exhibit books for each of the jurors) is that it is difficult to keep jurors focused on a single line or section. Thus, a lawyer may be questioning a witness about paragraph 2 of a contract while jurors are trying to read and interpret paragraph 4.

These problems can be addressed electronically with document callouts created with presentational software such as PowerPoint. A document callout typically consists of three components:

- The full relevant page(s) of the document with its exhibit number;
- The key section highlighted; and
- The key section enlarged.

The components appear on the screen one by one, and look like this when complete:

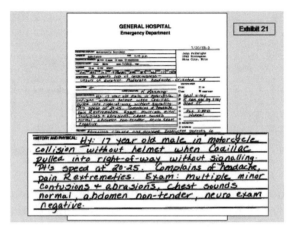

A variation on this theme is a re-keyed callout where the highlighted portion, instead of being enlarged is retyped. The advantage of the re-keyed callout is that it can accommodate a larger area of focus, a part of which can itself be highlighted. It looks like this:

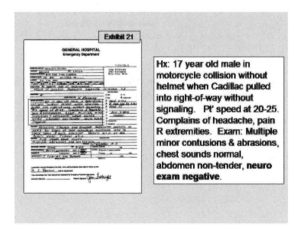

Where a handwritten document presents the additional challenge of legibility, the callout and re-keyed callout can be combined as follows:

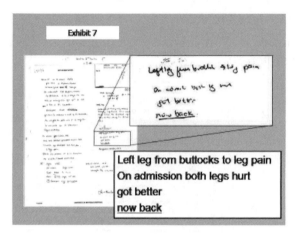

Often the significance of a multipage document is found by combining several provisions. Here is an example that combines two clauses of an insurance agreement:

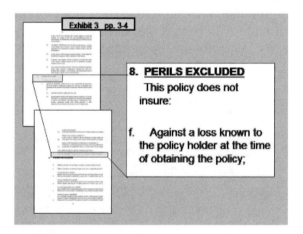

C. Photographs

Photographs can be enlarged electronically just as they can by traditional photographic techniques. But electronic enlargements are much less expensive and can be labeled for emphasis. Here is an example:

Electronically displayed photos also allow a lawyer to show the jury a wide view, then focus on and enlarge a small part of the photograph. This is usually accomplished with a series of three slides, the first showing the full photo, the second a cropped version, and the third an enlargement of the cropped version. This can all be done quickly and easily within PowerPoint and looks like this:

D. Graphs and Charts

Financial data are typically presented outside a courtroom in spreadsheets created by software such as Excel®. The problem with using spread sheets in the courtroom is that they can be too detailed, and their individual entries too small to serve as effective visuals. It is usually far more effective to display data as a graph which can be created in PowerPoint as it can in Excel. With PowerPoint, the added advantage is that the graph's segments can be displayed one after the other, giving the jury time to comprehend each.

Here are three types of graphs created within PowerPoint:

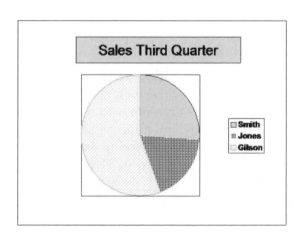

E. Radiology Images

Increasingly, hospitals and radiology facilities are storing images (X-rays, CT scans, MRIs) digitally. It is usually inexpensive to obtain copies of the digital files and easy to create electronic visuals with them. One cannot only electronically display a digital image, but label it and pair it with another image for contrast. Here, for example, is a slide contrasting a normal spine to the plaintiff's spine with its two extruding intervertebral disks:

One can also combine several images taken over time to show gradual change:

F. Text

Displaying text can be very important to provide jurors with a clearer understanding than they can obtain merely by hearing something. Jury instructions are a prime example. Here is a complex

instruction with the principal components highlighted to help insure juror comprehension:

> If an injury suffered by plaintiff is a
> combined product of both a preexisting injury
> and the effects of defendant's negligence, it
> is your duty to determine the damages
> caused by defendant's conduct alone. You
> must separate the damages caused by
> defendant's conduct from the condition
> which was preexisting if it is possible to to
> so. However, **if** after careful consideration,
> **you are unable to separate the damages**
> caused by defendant's conduct from those
> which were preexisting, **the entire amount of
> plaintiff's damages must be assessed
> against the defendant.**

G. Video

Videotape can be economically digitized, and video is now commonly recorded directly in digital format. From either source, it is
easy to create vignettes that can be shown through PowerPoint or
more sophisticated trial presentation software.

Video vignettes can include portions of video statements and
depositions, and even trial testimony in those courtrooms where the
record is created on videotape. Digital vignettes allow a lawyer to
quickly access particular segments without the annoying delay of
having to fast-forward and rewind (often several times) through a
videocassette to find the right place on the tape. This is especially
helpful in showing a series of vignettes, for example, to underscore
how someone's story has changed over time.

III. STRATEGIC CONSIDERATIONS

A. Introduction

Once you have mastered the ability to create and display electronic visuals, you must still decide when, with whom, and how to
use them. Like any other aspect of trial practice, there is no substitute for careful preparation.

B. Opening Statement

1. Judges' Attitudes

With those judges who are reluctant in general to allow electronic visuals, the reluctance is especially strong with respect to
opening statement. Many judges are concerned that the opening not

include argument, or at least what they consider argument. Still others believe that lawyers are entitled to speak to jurors in opening, but not to show them anything. Still others may permit lawyers to show exhibits to the jury in opening statement, but enforce a blanket rule prohibiting PowerPoint. These judicial attitudes, coupled with some lawyers' propensity to object to anything novel, mean that one should gingerly approach the use of electronic visuals in opening statement.

Even skeptical judges, however, may allow electronic visuals to display an enlarged diagram, photo, or document that has been preadmitted. Thus, where a judge's attitude toward technology is not clearly positive, the best course might be to use only the simplest visuals (and to obtain judicial permission in advance). Certainly one should not prepare an opening statement with critical use of electronic visuals unless there is a substantial degree of certainty that the judge will permit them.

2. Timing

Even with the growing number of judges who are quite comfortable with computer graphics, you should be careful not to rely too heavily on them in the opening statement. The opening is a time of adjustment for the jury. They adjust to their place in the courtroom, to each other, to the judge, to the lawyers, and to the facts of the case. All that takes some time and, on the lawyer's part, some patience. Early in the opening is probably too early for visuals; better to give the jury time to settle in and get to know you.

When the jury is ready—and it may take only a few minutes—it is usually best to start slowly and to limit the graphics to simple lists and exhibit enlargements. Even in the absence of judicial reluctance, the opening statement is too early for argumentative visuals. We know jurors start most trials believing that the lawyer's job is to manipulate them. Displaying visuals that do more than preview facts can easily feed into that preconception.

C. Witness Examination

1. Exhibits

Whether on direct or cross examination, electronic enlargements of exhibits can be extremely effective. They can be displayed almost instantly, eliminating the rhythm-breaking delay occasioned by searching through hard copy enlargements. The size and clarity of electronic exhibit enlargements make explanations simpler on direct examination and elusiveness far more obvious on cross examination.

Judges are more likely to accept exhibit highlighting and call-outs in witness examination than in opening statement. Nonetheless, some lawyers may object because a highlighted exhibit, or one with a callout, is not a precise copy of the actual exhibit. The response should be that it is permissible to ask the witness to read or focus on a certain part of the exhibit, and that highlighting or call-outs allow the jury to do the same. Moreover, the objecting lawyer is free to highlight or call out any other part of the exhibit he desires (if only he knew how to do so).

2. Testimonial Aids

In direct examination, providing visuals that highlight a witness's testimony can be very helpful in keeping both the witness and the jury on track. These visuals can include lists, definitions, or just a written iteration of something important the witness said. The potential problem in using electronic visuals for these testimonial aids is that they can look too prepared. The jury may wonder whether the testimony is coming from the witness or from the computer that has been programmed by the lawyer.

At least in part, this problem can be ameliorated when the witness explains to the jury that the testimony is hers, not the lawyer's:

QUESTION: In preparing for the trial, have you told me what your testimony would be?

ANSWER: Yes.

QUESTION: And have I shared with you several Power-Point slides that accurately reflect your testimony:

ANSWER: Yes.

QUESTION: Will it be helpful for you if the jury can see those slides as you testify?

ANSWER: Yes, it will.

True, this exchange is a bit leading and self-serving, but at least it gives the witness ownership of her testimony and signals the jury that something important might be coming.

Testimonial aids are especially important for expert witnesses whose testimony may be long, technical, and obtuse. One purpose of a visual may be to simplify and summarize the thrust of a lengthy direct examination. This is especially valuable for subjects like economics with which the jury may have no background and little interest.

Lawyers who have presented economists on direct examination understand that the jurors' eyes often glaze over within the first five minutes. Within five more minutes, the examining lawyer's eyes may glaze over. At times, even the witness's eyes start to lose their focus. Little can be done to make economic testimony exciting, but a simple PowerPoint slide, with its elements appearing one at a time, can summarize the witness' formula and the numbers he plugs into his formula. Here, for example, is a slide summarizing the testimony of plaintiff's economist in an employment case in which the plaintiff claims damages because she was wrongfully denied a law firm partnership and had to switch to law teaching (a less lucrative career):

Lost Income – Discrimination	
Earnings as a partner	$8,588,104
minus:	
Earnings as a teacher	-$2,254,730
equals:	
Total lost income	**$6,333,374**

A more dramatic way to emphasize an expert's opinion is to give it substance in a computer animation. Over the last decade, animations have become much more sophisticated and at least relatively more economical. They can depict with astonishing realism how a collision occurred, how a product failed, how an infection consumed a vital organ, or even how an intruder appeared to a householder just before the householder shot and killed him.

There is not yet a substantial body of law regarding the use of computer simulations. What law there is, clearly conditions their use on the discretion of the trial judge. Of course, there must be an appropriate foundation, and the judge ought to instruct the jury that the animation is not to be taken as a recreation of the event but only an illustration of a witness's testimony. So long as a qualified expert witness testifies that the animation accurately reflects her opinions, and so long as her opinions themselves are admissible, a reasonable judge will allow the animation to be shown to the jury. Although there is no universally accepted foundation, here is an example of the components that many judges look for:

QUESTION: Has the animation been created under your supervision?

ANSWER: Yes.

QUESTION: Is it substantially similar to the event as you believe the event occurred?

ANSWER: Yes.

QUESTION: Will it be helpful to you in explaining your opinions to the jury?

ANSWER: Yes, it will.

QUESTION: Were the data inputted into the computer to create an animation reasonably complete and accurate?

ANSWER: Yes.

QUESTION: Was the program used to create the animation generally accepted within your field in creating animations of this type?

ANSWER: Yes.

QUESTION: Was the computer used to create the animation working properly?

ANSWER: Yes, it was.

Even where the witness's opinions pass Daubert muster, and where the proponent has laid a proper foundation, a judge may still prohibit the use of an animation because of its possible unfair prejudice. Courts have expressed concerns that animation may cause jurors to confuse art with reality, and that an animation's dramatic power may be difficult to limit with an instruction. Moreover, where there is a substantial discrepancy in resources between the parties, a judge might find unfair prejudice if only one party can afford to present something as compelling as a realistic computer simulation.

D. Impeachment

Impeachment can be made much more dramatic where the witness and jury are presented with a visual of the witness's prior inconsistent statement. The visual can be written questions and answers from a deposition, a vignette of the relevant portion of a videotaped deposition, or both.

Software is available that can synchronize a visually recorded deposition to page and line numbers of the stenographic transcript. Where such software is used at the deposition, visual impeachment (whether by word, vignette, or both) requires little advance preparation for trial. Where such software was not used initially, preparation is more complex. Because a cross examining attorney rarely knows when a witness will change his testimony, the lawyer must have visual impeaching material available for all important points. For example, the cross examining lawyer will want to have PowerPoint slides which include digitized vignettes of all portions of a witness' deposition that might have to be used for impeachment. Only in that manner will visual impeachment be accessible easily, quickly, and smoothly.

Bar coding systems are available that allow a lawyer to affix bar coded labels to her trial notes or deposition transcript. When impeachment becomes appropriate, she need only aim a bar code reader at the label to signal the computer to send the appropriate slide to the projection device. In less than a second, the jury can see the transcript, or see and hear the prior statement coming from the witness' mouth. Where only the transcript is used, a PowerPoint slide can be created that displays the questions and answers one at a time.

The impeachment should take no longer than it does without a visual. Assuming the jury already knows the important aspects of deposition testimony (e.g., under oath, closer in time to the event, signed transcript), the impeachment can be as simple as this:

QUESTION: Did you say on direct exam that the light was red?

ANSWER: Yes.

QUESTION: But the fact is that the light was actually green, isn't that so?

ANSWER: No.

QUESTION: Why don't you look at page 32, lines 4–8 of your deposition while we watch a videotape of your testimony? [If only the transcript is displayed, the impeaching lawyer should read aloud each question and answer as it appears.]

The impact upon a witness of impeachment with a video vignette can be striking. In a recent civil case, plaintiff's counsel twice impeached the defendant's expert by displaying vignettes of his inconsistent deposition testimony on a large screen. When the witness changed his testimony a third time, this occurred:

QUESTION: You're saying that a reasonable physician can rely on a single negative Pap smear to rule out cervical cancer?

ANSWER: Yes.

QUESTION: That's not how you testified at deposition, is it?

ANSWER: I suppose you're going to show the tape again.

E.   Closing Argument

Closing argument is a fertile opportunity for visual persuasion. You can marshal the facts that support a conclusion in a simple list, or you can use something more graphically imaginative like this:

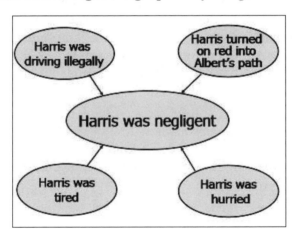

You can also combine the facts with the key elements of the judge's instructions. Here is an example from a gender discrimination case:

Elements	Proof
1. Female and an employee	1. Both are admitted
2. Unwelcome sexual advances	2. "Come fly with me to the Bahamas."
3. Her refusal led to job detriment	3. "You'll regret this, I promise you."

Graphics can give substance to what otherwise might be an amorphous concept. For example, plaintiffs' lawyers often try to underscore the relatively light burden of proof required by a preponderance of evidence. Here is what the burden could look like in a two-slide visual that creates the appearance of a tipping standard:

Preponderance of the Evidence

Preponderance of the Evidence

Similarly, the concept of comparative negligence may also be depicted. Here, for example, is the plaintiff's closing argument visual in a case where a teenage driver was killed in an accident with a RiteTruck semitruck, and where plaintiff's attorney attempted to minimize the decedent's comparative negligence:

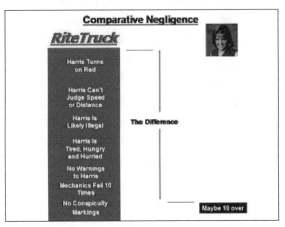

Exhibits can be electronically displayed in closing arguments, just as they can in opening statement or witness examination, but in closing they can be labeled and highlighted in argumentative fashion. Thus an overhead photograph can include more than simple identifying labels:

Moreover, exhibits can be combined in closing argument visuals. Here, for example, is a PowerPoint slide comparing the radiologic image of the plaintiff's spine with an excerpt from his medical records:

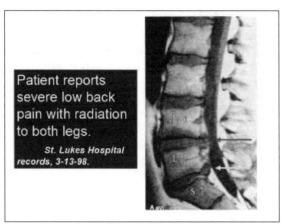

In personal injury cases, the plaintiff often introduces photographs that depict the extent of his damage (e.g., before and after photos, injury photos, photos of the decedent). In closing argument, such photographs can be displayed one after the other until they form a collage of substantial emotional impact. If there is an audio recording of particularly pointed testimony, that can be added as well. No, violins are not permitted.

IV. TECHNIQUE

A. Less Is More

Electronic visuals can be very seductive—for some lawyers, too seductive. True, we can use them effectively in virtually any part of the trial. But that does not mean they will retain their effectiveness if we use them in all parts of the trial or if we use too many of them.

Electronic visuals are tools along with all the other tools that help persuade jurors. They do not substitute for painstaking preparation, for clear direct examination, for controlled cross examination, or for logical and articulate opening statements and closing arguments. No matter how clever an electronic visual may be, it will never establish a lawyer's credibility. That occurs only when the jury has come to know the lawyer and understands that what she says is credible and dependable. Absent that, electronic visuals will be unpersuasive pixels.

In planning whether and when to use an electronic visual, a lawyer must understand that often the most effective focus for the jury is the lawyer-witness exchange or, in opening or closing, the lawyer alone. At those times a blank screen is the lawyer's friend. Lawyers should not jettison the time-honored crafts of trial practice for the quick fix of the electronic visual. But when an electronic visual is appropriate, a blend of solid trial technique with the impact of the visual can make an unbeatable combination.

At other times, a visual can be helpful, but not necessarily an electronic visual. For example, in closing argument in a contract action, it can be very effective to hold the contract in your hand when discussing the legal sanctity of a written agreement. Pointing at a screen cannot have the same effect.

B. Still Less Is More

When an electronic visual is appropriate, it has to be an effective visual. A document callout on a dark blue or gray background can help focus jury attention to the key phrase or passage. The same callout on a chartreuse background will call attention to itself and have the jury wondering what the lawyer's living room must look like.

Software like PowerPoint provides almost unlimited choices for colors, fonts, clip art, sounds, and graphic schemes. The great majority of them are inappropriate for the courtroom. Just imagine a slide with an Old English font, a green and pink color scheme, and the sound effects (whoosh, crash, screech) that PowerPoint makes available. The following slide might be great for a sales rally, but "screen clutter" is unlikely to work well in trial:

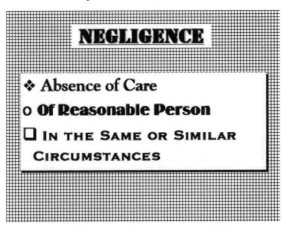

Slides should be compelling for their content, not their form. The form should be simple and straightforward: fonts like Tahoma and Arial; colors like black, gray, dark blue, and white. For emphasis, yellow highlighting (easily done only in the most recent versions of PowerPoint), red underlining, and red arrows are appropriate. But flashing, flying, spiraling arrows are not. And no sound effects.

Just as the form should be uncluttered, the content must be concise enough for the jury to easily and quickly understand it. Here are two examples of professionally prepared PowerPoint slides that simplify complex concepts (note how the designer enhanced the attorneys' rough sketches):

Here, on the other hand, is an ill-advised slide created by an eager young lawyer in an effort to diagram the underlying transaction in a legal malpractice case:

C. Combining the Actual Exhibit, the Electronic Visual, and the Record

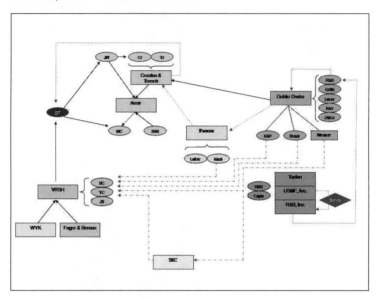

Where an electronic enlargement of an exhibit is used in witness examination, it can be very effective to start with the actual exhibit in the witness's hand and then move to the enlargement so that the jurors understand that they are seeing an accurate copy. It is also important that the record reflect what is being shown to the jury and (for those judges who want the record to contain hard copies of all electronic visuals) an identification of the visual. Once that is done, the examining lawyer can move to the highlighting and the callout on the visual. Here is an example of such an examination:

QUESTION: Please look at plaintiff's Exhibit 4, which is on the witness stand in front of you.

ANSWER: Okay.

QUESTION: What is it?

ANSWER: It is the contract I signed with Americraft Industries.

QUESTION: Your Honor, may I put it on the screen so everyone can see it?

The Court: Yes.

QUESTION: To legal assistant: Please bring up Plaintiff's Slide #18, Exhibit 4. Now please highlight Section 3 of Exhibit 4. And now please enlarge Section 3. Pause while jury reads it.

QUESTION: To the witness: Now let me ask you this ...

In this way the record clearly reflects what is displayed for the jury. The highlighting and callout are sourced to the original document, and the witness and opposing counsel have the document to make sure there is no electronic chicanery.

Once this has been done, it is usually a good idea for the examining lawyer to move to the screen, or to ask the witness to move to the screen, or both. This reduces the jury's points of focus from three (lawyer's lectern, witness box, screen) to one or two. This will make it easier for the jury to appreciate the testimony and the visual at the same time. Alas, some courtrooms provide small, individual monitors for each juror, located in or just in front of the jury box. In this arrangement, there is no convenient way to reduce the points of focus.

Finally, it is extremely important to remember to get the graphic off the screen when you are finished with it. Otherwise, the jury's attention may linger on the visual while you are trying to move on to another point. Getting the graphic off the screen can be accomplished as simply as turning to the legal assistant who is operating the computer and saying, "Thank you." That signals the legal assistant to put a black slide on the screen, giving the appearance that the electronics are turned off.

— CHAPTER ELEVEN —
Opening Statements

I.   THE ROLE OF THE OPENING STATEMENT

A.   The Opening Moment

Opening statement, the advocate's first opportunity to speak directly to the jury about the merits of the case, marks the beginning of the competition for the jury's imagination. This moment is crucial since the mental image that the jurors hold while hearing the evidence will directly influence the way they interpret it. The attorney who is successful in seizing the opening moment will have an advantage throughout the trial because the jury will tend to filter all of the evidence through a lens that she has created.

The importance of access to the jury's imagination cannot be underestimated. We are accustomed to receiving most of our information through the sense of sight, but at trial the jurors will obtain most of their information through the oral testimony of witnesses. They will hear descriptions and recountings of past events, but in almost all cases they will not actually see an enactment of the crucial occurrences. They will, however, envision the events as they believe them to have occurred. Each juror will summon her own mental images of the facts, objects, locations, and transactions that are described from the witness stand. The details and context of these images will, in turn, influence the juror's decision.

Consider, for example, the image that is brought to mind by the words "billiard parlor." Each person who hears that term is likely to think of a specific location that she once visited (or saw on television or in a movie) and to use it as a reference in calling up a mental picture of a similar locale. Billiard parlors, in most people's experience, are probably formal, reserved, well-lighted, reasonably open, and fairly respectable. Thus, events occurring in a billiard parlor will have a certain cast to them. Jurors with this scene in mind will tend to fit the events into that image, that is, to view them in a "billiard parlor" sort of way.

On the other hand, consider the image evoked by the words "pool hall." Now many people would probably envision a place that is smoky, dark, perhaps slightly threatening, and probably a little seedy. Things happen differently in pool halls than they do in billiard parlors. Visibility is better in a billiard parlor; things happen more furtively in a pool hall. A stranger might be questioned in a billiard parlor, but a confrontation is more likely in a pool hall. In other words, the initial mental image dictates, or at least suggests, a variety of assumptions about the nature, context, and likelihood of events.

These assumptions, of course, are not graven in stone. They can be altered, dispelled, or contradicted by the evidence. Still, the creation of an initial image can be a powerful tool. Recall how Professor Henry Hill in *The Music Man* convinced the citizens of River City to purchase the instruments for a boys' band. He described their "trouble with a capital T and that rhymes with P and that stands for pool." The townsfolk listening to Professor Hill envisioned their children sinking en masse into depravity and delinquency because of the mental picture evoked by "Pool." He would not have been a quarter so persuasive if he had preached that they had "trouble with a capital T and that rhymes with B and that stands for billiards." The image just isn't that compelling.

Your task in an opening statement is to engage the jury's imagination—to help them begin to imagine the case your way. As we shall see below, this forensic task is complicated by the legal function that the opening statement plays in the conduct of the trial.

B. Legal Function

Opening statements exist in order to assist the jury in understanding the evidence to be presented at trial. Of course, we hope that the evidence will be self-explanatory, but in even the best-organized cases evidence is often presented in a disjointed if not utterly discontinuous manner.

To reduce the possibility of jury confusion as a result of the manner in which evidence is introduced, the courts have developed the concept of the opening statement. At the very beginning of the trial jurors are presented with an overview of the case so that they will be better equipped to make sense of the evidence as it is actually presented. The institutional purpose of the opening statement, then, is to ease the jury's burden by making the trial more understandable; it is not intended to give the lawyers another crack at pleading the case.

Thus, we have the basis of the "nonargument" rule. The courts and commentators are virtually unanimous that opening statements may only be used to inform the jury of "what the evidence will show." Counsel may not argue the case during opening, but is restricted to offering a preview of the anticipated testimony, exhibits, and other evidence. This limitation results in a highly stylized set of rules for the presentation of opening statements, and it informs almost everything else that there is to be said on the subject.

C. Advocacy

As an advocate your governing principle in presenting an opening statement should be to use it as an opportunity to advance your theory of the case. This is not as easy, or as obvious, as it sounds. Many lawyers take the approach of simply listing the witnesses or describing the general tenor of the expected testimony and exhibits. In other words, they discuss only what the "evidence will be." This is a serious mistake, as it squanders the potential benefits of the opening moment.

A far more useful, and equally permissible, approach is to discuss what the "evidence will show" rather than merely what it will be. The distinction is not semantic. Telling the jury "what the evidence will be" is a neutral formulation geared toward providing a simple synopsis of the trial to come. Explaining "what the evidence will show," on the other hand, requires you to consider the relationship between the expected evidence and the conclusions and outcomes that you want the jury to reach. In our intersection case, for example, the projected evidence might be that a fire truck approached the intersection and that the defendant did not stop his car. From the plaintiff's perspective, however, the evidence hopefully will show that the defendant had ample opportunity to observe the fire truck, which was flashing its lights and sounding its siren, but that he was so distracted that he did not notice it.

Counsel need not feel limited to an antiseptic listing of the evidence to come. Rather, explain to the jury what propositions will be proven and exactly how they will be proven. So long as you avoid lapsing into argumentative form, you may explicate your theory of the case. While you may not urge the jury to reach certain conclusions, you may arrange your discussion of the facts so that the conclusions are inevitable. Many tools are available to accomplish this goal. In brief, a well-developed opening statement will take advantage of some or all of the following concepts:

Choice of facts. In every opening statement you must decide which facts to include and which to leave out. While you will obviously want to emphasize the facts that you find helpful, there is also considerable risk to telling an incomplete or illogical story.

Sequencing. The order of facts may be as important as the nature of the facts. Recall the question that resulted in the downfall of the Nixon administration: "What did the President know and when did he know it?"

Clarity of description. It is one thing to mention a fact, but it is better to describe it with sufficient detail and clarity as to engage the jury in your own mental portrait.

Common sense. Common sense is used both to judge and to predict outcomes. An opening statement cannot be successful if its story doesn't jibe with everyday experience. On the other hand, a jury's reflexive resort to common sense can be used to lead them to a desired conclusion. Consider an opening statement that begins this way: "The defendant woke up late; he had an important meeting to go to; the meeting was to be held far from his home; the defendant drove to the meeting." Without saying more, common sense suggests that the defendant was in a hurry.

Moral attraction. An opening statement can be made more attractive when it tells a story that people want to accept. The evidence can be described in a context of shared values or civic virtues so as to add moral force to your client's position. In the intersection case, for example, the plaintiff's evidence will be that she stopped for the fire truck. On the other hand, the evidence will show that the plaintiff knew that it was important not to get in the way of a fire engine, and so she stopped to let it pass.

In the final analysis the most successful opening statements are those that explain exactly how you intend to win your case.

II. THE LAW OF OPENING STATEMENTS

A. The Rule Against Argument

As we noted above, the rule against argument is inherent in the very concept of the opening statement.

1. Defining the Rule

The rule against argument is easier to state than to define. Moreover, application of the rule will vary from jurisdiction to jurisdiction, and even from courtroom to courtroom. No matter how the rule is articulated it is almost never hard and fast. Most judges recognize that "argument" is a relative concept and allow lawyers a reasonable amount of latitude.

As a general rule, opening statement ends and argument begins when counsel attempts to tell the jury how they should reach their decision. Difficulties arise when the advocate engages in interpretation or exhortation. You may not urge the jury to draw inferences from facts or to reach certain conclusions. You may not explain the importance of certain items of evidence or suggest how evidence should be weighed. It is improper to comment directly on the credibility of witnesses. Finally, an opening statement may not be used to appeal overtly to the jury's sense of mercy or justice.

For example, it would be proper to tell the following story to a jury during the opening statement in a personal injury case:

> Just before the accident the plaintiff was sitting in a tavern. In less than an hour and a half he consumed at least four shots of whiskey. He bought a round for the house and then he left. He left in his car. The accident occurred within the next twenty minutes.

It would be improper argument, however, to continue in this vein:

> The plaintiff was obviously drunk. No person could drink four whiskeys in that amount of time without feeling it. Only an alcoholic or a liar would even claim to have been sober under those circumstances.

The second paragraph violates the argument rule not only because it draws the conclusion that the plaintiff was drunk, but also because it tells the jury how to evaluate the plaintiff's anticipated testimony: "Only an alcoholic or a liar would claim to have been sober."

2. Guidelines

A number of guidelines or rules of thumb have been developed for determining when an opening statement has drifted into argument.

The witness test. One possible test is to question whether a witness will actually testify to the "facts" contained in the opening statement. If so, the opening is proper. If not, it has become argument. In the tavern example above, for instance, witnesses will be able to testify to the plaintiff's presence in the bar and his consumption of liquor; therefore, the initial paragraph is appropriate. No such witness, however, would be allowed to testify to the conclusion that the plaintiff is a liar or an alcoholic. Accordingly, the second paragraph is impermissible.

The verification test. An alternative measure is to determine whether the content of the opening statement can be verified, the theory being that facts are verifiable while argumentative conclusions are not. Note that this analysis can be more flexible than the witness test since the comment that the plaintiff was drunk is subject to verification. On the other hand, the "alcoholic or liar" comment continues to fail under this test as well.

The "link" test. A final approach is to consider whether the opening statement contains facts with independent evidentiary value or whether the attorney has had to provide a rhetorical link in the probative chain. Again we see that the first paragraph above is just fine; it consists entirely of classic evidence. The second paragraph, however, is pure rhetoric. It becomes probative only when counsel supplies the explanation, or link, that "no person could drink that amount of whiskey without showing it."

Each of these tests is more holistic than legalistic. There are no case holdings or rules of court that detail how a particular jurisdiction will apply the rule against argument. Even a seasoned trial judge may not be able to explain exactly why an objection was sustained to some portion of an opening statement. As a practical matter it may be best to keep in mind the principle that "argument" occurs when counsel seeks to tell the jury how they should go about reaching their decision.

3. Other Considerations

In addition to the words spoken and the evidence marshaled by counsel, a variety of other considerations may lead a judge to conclude that an opening statement has crossed the line into argument. Some of these are detailed below:

Tone of voice. Words that appear neutral on the printed page may become argumentative by virtue of the tone in which they are delivered. Sneering, sarcasm, volume, or vocal caricature can all transform an acceptable opening into an impermissible one.

Rhetorical questions. The use of rhetorical questions is inherently argumentative. Such questions can be used to suggest disbelief, as in, "What could she possibly have been thinking of?" Alternatively, they can be used as a statement of incontrovertible certainty, such as, "What other answer could there be?" In either case they strongly signal argument when used in an opening statement.

Repetition. Although an excellent persuasive device when used elsewhere in a trial, repetition can lead an opening statement into forbidden territory. In the tavern scenario above, for example, imagine that the first paragraph of the plaintiff's opening statement was embellished this way:

> Just before the accident the plaintiff was sitting in a tavern. In less than an hour and a half he consumed at least four shots of whiskey. Not two or three, but four. He bought a round for the house and then he left. He left in his car. That's right, he drove away from the tavern. He opened the car door, got behind the wheel, put the key in the ignition, started the engine, shifted into first gear, and proceeded to drive down the road. There will be two witnesses who will testify to plaintiff's consumption of alcohol. And three different witnesses will testify that they saw the plaintiff drive away from the bar in his own car.

Although each of the facts in this extended paragraph could stand as nonargumentative, some judges would no doubt consider the extreme repetition as going too far.

B. Comments on the Law

Closely related to the rule against argument is the general proscription against discussing law during opening statements. The rationale is the same. Opening statements are allowed for the purpose of organizing and previewing the evidence for the jury. Not until the end of the case will the court instruct the jurors on the law. The instructions presumably will be comprehensive and therefore will not require a preview. Indeed, it is usually impossible to predict all of the jury instructions until all of the evidence has been admitted. In any event, to the extent that the jury requires advance information about the law, this can come from the judge in the form of a preliminary instruction.

Nonetheless, it is virtually impossible for counsel to avoid some discussion of the law during any but the simplest opening statement. It is the law, after all, that determines the relevance and importance of the facts being previewed. Without some explanation of the legal issues, a jury will have no way to tell whether certain facts are significant or merely window dressing.

Most judges attempt to steer a middle course when it comes to discussion of the law during opening statements. It is almost always permissible to frame the legal issues for the jury. A sentence or two devoted to an explanation of the legal significance of the evidence will also usually be allowed. Once the discussion of the law becomes intricate, lengthy, or controversial, however, an objection will usually be sustained.[1]

C. Persuasion

While argument is prohibited during opening statements, persuasion is not. So long as counsel refrains from suggesting conclusions to be drawn from the facts it is permissible to arrange them in an order that maximizes their favorable impact. Furthermore, persuasive ordering of the facts by both counsel will typically assist the jury in understanding the case since they will then be able to see just how the parties' stories diverge.

The persuasive ordering of facts can be accomplished either through incremental development or through contrast. Incremental development involves the successive ordering of a series of discrete facts, each building upon the last, until the desired conclusion becomes obvious. Although the facts will be related, they need not be presented in chronological order. The following example demonstrates how the plaintiff might use incremental development in our fire engine case:

> The defendant awoke at 7:00 a.m. He had an important meeting scheduled with a potential new client for 8:30 that morning. The client had not yet decided whether to hire the defendant, but the account would have been worth a lot of money. The meeting was to be held downtown, which was sixteen miles from the defendant's home. The defendant showered, shaved, dressed, and ate a quick breakfast. He went to his car, which was parked about a block away. All of this took approximately fifty minutes. By the time the defendant got to his car it was 8:00 a.m. He had thirty minutes left before the new client was scheduled to arrive at his office.

Note that the example begins when the defendant woke up, skips ahead to the information about the scheduled meeting, and then goes back to describe the rest of the defendant's morning routine. Other facts, of course, could be added to show how seriously late the defendant was, and therefore how likely he was to drive carelessly or too fast. The point is that the individual events build upon each other to explain, without saying so, why the defendant would have been driving negligently.

---

1. It should go without saying that an incorrect statement of the law is objectionable, even if made only in passing or for the purpose of framing the issues for the jury.

Contrast is the juxtaposition of contradictory facts, most often used in an opening statement to demonstrate the implausibility of some aspect of the opposing case. The defendant in the fire engine case might use contrast this way:

> The plaintiff in this case is seeking damages for pain and suffering and lost income. She claims a permanent disability. You will see medical bills offered into evidence that start with the date of the accident and which continue right through to last December 10. You will also see a receipt for the purchase of a new backpack and camp stove, purchased by the plaintiff last August 17. She went to the doctor on August 15, she bought her backpack on August 17, and she went camping at Eagle River Falls on August 31. She returned to town on September 3. Her next visit to the doctor was not until October 19.

Without resort to argument, the simple contrast between the medical bills and the camping trip casts doubt on the plaintiff's allegation of permanent injury.

The line between persuasive ordering and argument is crossed when counsel attempts to inject judgments, conclusions, or other means of reaching a decision into the opening statement. It is fair game to present facts showing, say, that the plaintiff requires a large judgment to be fully compensated:

> Each morning when the plaintiff wakes up, he needs assistance in getting out of bed. He cannot walk to the bathroom himself. He cannot bathe or clean himself. He cannot fix his own breakfast. If he wants to read a newspaper or a book, someone must get it for him. Each day, for twenty-four hours, he must pay a nurse or housekeeper to do all of the things that other people are able to do for themselves.

It is not fair game, however, to continue in this vein: "The plaintiff could just as easily be your own neighbor or relative; he deserves your generosity."

III. STRUCTURE AND ELEMENTS

If a trial is a persuasive story, the opening statement is the attorney's first opportunity to tell the whole story without distraction or interruption. Not until final argument will counsel again be able to speak directly to the jury. All other communication will be filtered through the awkward, and often opaque, process of witness examination. If your theory is to be presented in its entirety, opening statement is the time to do it. Because of the conventions that control the content and form of the opening statement, it is particularly important to pay careful attention to its structure and elements.

A. Communicate Your Theory

The single most important rule concerning opening statements is to present a coherent theory of the case. You will, of course, have developed such a theory in your pretrial preparation since no case can be won without one. The challenge now is to communicate it clearly, succinctly, and persuasively.

Recall that a trial theory is the adaptation of a factual story to the legal issues in the case. Your theory must contain a simple, logical, provable account of facts which, when viewed in light of the controlling law, will lead to the conclusion that your client should win. In short, you will want to use the opening statement to explain to the jury why the verdict should be in your favor.

A successful theory will be built around a persuasive story. Ideally, such a story will be told about people who have reasons for the way they act; it will explain all of the known or undeniable facts; it will be told by credible witnesses; it will be supported by details; and it will accord with common sense. Thus, your opening statement should, at some point and in some manner, address all of these elements:

What happened? The crucial events in your story will be the ones that speak to the legal elements of your claim or defense. If you represent the plaintiff in a tort case, your opening statement should contain sufficient facts from which a conclusion can be drawn that the defendant was negligent. The defendant's opening, on the other hand, should emphasize facts pointing toward his own caution or the plaintiff's fault.

Why did it happen? It is not sufficient to list the facts. A story is most persuasive when it explains why events occurred as they did. It is particularly important to explain why individuals acted as they did, since a compelling reason for an action will tend to rule out or negate alternative possibilities. For example, you may explain that the defendant in a collision case was driving slowly and carefully just before the accident. This story will be more persuasive if it can be supported with a reason. Perhaps she was returning from an antique auction, carrying an expensive and fragile chandelier in her back seat. Obviously, then, she would be inclined to be more than normally cautious. Her reason for driving slowly not only supports her version of events, but it also makes less likely a claim by the plaintiff that she careened around a corner at high speed.

Which witnesses should be believed? Trials almost always revolve around conflicting testimony, with one set of witnesses supporting the plaintiff's theory and another supporting the defendant's. It is improper to argue the credibility of witnesses in your opening statement, but you may, and should, provide the jury with facts that bolster your own witnesses and detract from the opposition's. While too much background can easily clutter your opening statement and distract the jury, positive information—such as education, community ties, and family responsibility—should be provided to humanize your key witnesses. Bias, motive, prejudice, and interest in the outcome of the case are always relevant to a witness's believability. Explain the facts that demonstrate your own witnesses' lack of bias; include as well the facts that demonstrate the motive or interest of the opposition.

How can we be sure? As should be apparent from the examples above, the persuasiveness of an opening statement, indeed the persuasiveness of virtually any aspect of a trial, is often established through the use of details. Broad assertions can stake out territory and raise issues, but it is most often the details upon which the truth will be determined. An essential element of an opening statement, then, is the judicious use of details in support of the accuracy, dependability, or believability of your facts.

Does it all make sense? Finally, the theory you present in opening, or at any other point in the trial, must make sense when it is measured against the everyday experiences of the jurors. The provision of reasons, biases, or details, no matter how compelling they are to your way of thinking, will accomplish nothing if the jurors cannot place them into a context that they understand and accept. It is meaningless to suggest that a witness should be believed because she received an "A" on her contracts exam in law school. Although that detail may make her praiseworthy in some eyes, it is not a commonsense indicator of honesty.

B.   Communicate Your Theme

Your trial theme, as distinct from your theory, should be expressed in a single sentence that captures the moral force of your case. A theme communicates to the jury the reason that your client deserves to win. Thus, introducing a theme in opening is particularly effective as a persuasive matter since it can focus the jury's attention on a cognitive image that you will return to throughout the trial.

Nonetheless, using a theme in your opening statement presents some difficulty. Unlike a trial theory, a theme is intended to reflect upon or interpret the evidence rather than simply to describe or outline it. Overuse or constant repetition of your theme may bring you perilously close to argument. Most judges, however, will allow the statement of a theme at both the beginning and the end of an opening statement, especially when it is phrased in terms of fact as opposed to opinion or characterization.

C. Utilize Primacy

The principle of primacy posits that in all aspects of a trial a jury will remember best those things that they hear first. The opening statement therefore provides a double opportunity to utilize primacy. The first few minutes of your opening statement constitute the "beginning of the beginning" and therefore have the potential to be among the most memorable moments of the trial. Put them to good use.

It is essential not to waste your opening moments on trivia or platitudes. Get right to the point. State your theme. Explain the most important part of your theory. Lay the groundwork for a crucial direct or cross examination. Foreshadow your closing argument. Above all, do not spend your most precious minutes meandering through a civics-class exposition on the virtues of the American jury system.

In the fire engine case, the plaintiff might want to open something like this:

> This is a case about a defendant who was too busy to be careful. Because he failed to stop for a fire truck, he smashed his car right into the back of the plaintiff's automobile. The fire truck was flashing its lights and sounding its siren. All of the other drivers noticed the fire truck and stopped. Except the defendant. He had his mind on an important meeting, so he kept on driving until it was too late. Now the plaintiff will never take another step without feeling pain. Let me tell you exactly what happened.

The above opening is direct and to the point. It states theory and theme right at the outset and launches immediately into the facts that support the plaintiff's case. The three central points that the plaintiff will make are all mentioned: (1) The fire truck was clearly visible, (2) all of the other traffic stopped, and (3) the defendant was preoccupied and caused the accident.

Two principles can guide your selection of material for the beginning of the opening statement: impact and relationship.

Impact. Your opening statement should begin with the information that you hope will have the greatest impact on the jury. What facts most support a verdict in your favor? What issues will be most hotly contested? Which witness will you rely upon the most? Choose the point that you most hope the jury will take with them when they retire to deliberate.

Relationship. There will be many important evidentiary facts in most trials. Since you will want the jury to remember them all, it may be difficult to decide just which ones to begin with. This decision can be made easier if, in addition to impact, you consider the relationship of the information to some other aspect of the trial. Will the testimony of your key witness be attacked? Will you need to undermine or impeach the testimony of an opposition witness? Will your closing argument rely upon certain inferences or conclusions? You can use the first moments of your opening statement to begin developing the points to which you intend to return.

D. Utilize Issues

Your case can be only as persuasive as the theory behind it, and your theory can only be persuasive if it ties the evidence to the legal issues. Your opening statement, then, must address the legal issues in your case. Ultimately, the jury will not be asked to conclude whether a particular witness is a good person or whether events occurred in a certain order. Such decisions may be reached along the way, but they are only important to the extent that they affect the actual verdict in the case. Defense counsel may do a stunning job of convincing the jury that the plaintiff is foolish or forgetful, but she will lose her case unless she also persuades them that the defendant was not negligent.

It is imperative, therefore, that your opening statement explain to the jury why your facts are important to their decision. Although a statement of importance may seem to approach argument, recall that the opening statement's purpose is to assist the jury in understanding the evidence. A serial presentation of facts, no matter how beautifully organized or well delivered, cannot be understood clearly without some mention of the purpose for which the evidence will be offered. Accordingly, it would be unusual for a judge to disallow a reasonable explanation of the issues toward which the evidence is directed.

Assuming that the fire engine case is being tried in a comparative negligence jurisdiction, the defense may want to show that the plaintiff was partially at fault for the accident. The opening statement could simply list a set of facts that comprise the plaintiff's contribution to the accident, and hope that the jury draws the right conclusion: the plaintiff didn't pull over; the plaintiff's brake lights were not working; and, although she claims otherwise, the plaintiff may not have been wearing her glasses. It will be more persuasive, however, and truly more helpful to the jury, if the opening first explains the import of the evidence:

> One issue in this case is whether the plaintiff herself contributed to the accident. You see, even if the defendant was negligent in some way, the law still asks whether the plaintiff was partially at fault as well. And if she was at fault, then any damages would have to be reduced. The evidence will definitely show that the plaintiff was at fault. When she saw the fire truck she slammed on her brakes right in the middle of the road. She didn't pull over to the side. She didn't leave a clear lane for the car that was immediately behind her. That made it impossible for the following driver, my client, to avoid the accident. Furthermore, her brake lights weren't working on the day of the accident. She knew they weren't working, but she hadn't gotten around to getting them fixed. So when she slammed on her brakes, my client had no way of knowing that she was going to make a sudden stop instead of pulling over into the parking lane.

The statement of the law is an acceptable part of this opening statement because it is correct, neutral, and closely related to the facts that follow. It is helpful because it focuses attention on the import of the facts concerning the plaintiff's driving. The evidence is going to be offered not to show that the plaintiff was generally a poor driver, but rather to show exactly how she contributed to the accident in this case.

E. Utilize the Evidence, Don't Just Display It

There is a world of difference between utilizing evidence and merely displaying it. Displaying evidence is a vice most common to unprepared or disorganized lawyers, and it is frequently the result of insufficient attention to theory and analysis. While no diligent attorney would intentionally use the opening statement to list a series of facts in a purely random order, many lawyers are attracted to the allure of some seemingly natural organization. Utilization of the evidence, however, involves the purposeful ordering of the facts, as we have discussed above, in the manner most supportive of counsel's theory of the case.

1. Avoid Witness Summaries

The "witness-by-witness" approach, in particular, is to be avoided. It is a mystery why many lawyers think that they can help the jury understand the case by naming all of the witnesses and outlining the expected testimony of each. Recall that the very purpose of the opening statement, indeed its underlying justification, is to overcome the disjointed fashion in which the witnesses will produce evidence at trial. Witness-by-witness rendition of the facts is unlikely to produce a coherent story when the witnesses take the stand and testify for themselves. This method of organization becomes no more helpful simply because a lawyer has substituted a summary of the testimony for the actual direct and cross examinations.

2. Be Wary of Chronology

Chronology is an obvious, natural, and often useful organizing technique for opening statements. All events in the real world, after all, occur in chronological order. Moreover, we are all used to thinking of life in chronological terms. It is for this very reason, in fact, that opening statements have become part of the trial: to allow lawyers to take individual witness accounts and meld them into a single chronological narrative.

Still it is all too easy, and sometimes counterproductive, automatically to allow chronology to establish the organization of an opening statement. Simply because events occurred in a certain order is not a sufficient reason to present them that way to a jury. This is especially the case when your story involves simultaneous, or nearly simultaneous, events that took place in different locations.

a. The drawbacks of chronology

In the fire truck case, for instance, a strict chronology might begin with the time that the plaintiff left her home. The defendant probably left his home shortly thereafter, and the fire engine left the station last of all. None of this ordering should matter to either party's story, however, since the only important fact is their concurrent arrival at the fateful intersection. While it may not undermine either opening statement to detail the order in which the vehicles departed, it will certainly clutter the stories with useless, and perhaps confusing, details.

Chronology can also interfere with the logical exposition of your theory. The plaintiff's theory in the fire truck case is that she stopped for the fire engine, as required by law, but the defendant did not. The defendant was at fault because he was preoccupied and failed to keep a proper lookout. Perhaps he was speeding, and perhaps his brakes performed inadequately due to poor maintenance. The various elements of this theory both precede and follow the accident itself. For example, the defendant woke up late before the collision, but he grabbed his phone to cancel his meeting after the collision. Both of these facts directly support the theory that the defendant was in a hurry that morning. Even though they occurred at different times, they can have more impact if they are presented together.

Similarly, consider the importance of the defendant's failure to have his brakes repaired. If the opening statement were presented in strict chronology, that fact would be introduced to the jury before they had any way to measure its importance. Of course, no matter when the jury hears it, it sounds bad for the defendant to have ignored a warning about his brakes. But a chronological recitation will separate this fact from the moment of the accident, thus requiring the jury to reach back in their memories in order to recall its importance.

The brake story is most persuasive when it is added to the events of the accident, not when it precedes them. Presented first, the brake story, at best, will evoke curiosity: "I wonder why that will turn out to be important?" Presented after the account of the accident the brake story should result in understanding: "Oh, so that is why he didn't stop in time." As an advocate you should almost always prefer to have the jury understand your theory rather than wonder about it.

b. The uses of chronology

Despite the drawbacks mentioned above, the judicious use of chronology is an essential part of every opening statement.

Chronological development should always be used to explain independent events. Every trial can be understood as a series of sub-events, which fit together to comprise the entire story. The order of these sub-events is always open to manipulation by counsel. The sub-events themselves, however, have their own internal logic, which generally can be understood only when explained chronologically.

The fire engine case provides an excellent illustration of this principle. The plaintiff's case consists of at least the following four sub-events: (1) the collision itself; (2) the defendant's hurried morning; (3) the defendant's failure to repair his brakes; and (4) the fire department's policy of always sounding the siren on a vehicle that is responding to a call. These four elements—and of course there may be others—can be arranged in a variety of ways to make the case more persuasive. Once the overall structure has been determined, however, it will make most sense, as you reach each individual component, to detail it chronologically. Suppose that plaintiff's counsel has decided to organize her opening statement in the same order that the sub-events are given above. After going through the facts of the accident in the same sequence in which they occurred, she would proceed to develop the secondary components by relying upon the chronology of each one:

> Why didn't the defendant stop when all of the other traffic did? We know that he woke up late that morning and that he had an important meeting to attend downtown, which was scheduled to begin only an hour and a half later. By the time he washed and shaved and went to the garage where his car was parked, he had only about thirty minutes left to get to his meeting. It was sixteen miles from his home to his office. As he headed south on Sheridan Road, every delay made him that much later for his meeting.

> By the time he got to the corner of Sheridan and Touhy, he only had twelve minutes or so before his meeting was to start, yet he still had seven miles to go. We know that the fire truck was already at that corner, flashing its lights and sounding its siren. There is no evidence that the defendant intentionally ignored the fire truck, but he obviously didn't respond to it in time. Although at some point he hit his brakes, he still went crashing into the back of my client's car.

> Was there something wrong with the defendant's brakes? Could he have stopped in time if they had been working better? We know that just a week before the accident he had his car in for servicing. The mechanic advised him to have his brakes relined, but the defendant decided not to take the time to have the repair work done. He left the garage without having his brakes fixed.

> We also know that the fire truck gave the defendant plenty of warning. It was flashing its lights and sounding its siren. We know this because it has always been strict fire department policy to use these warning signals whenever an engine is responding to a call. And so it was that day. Engine Number 9 was responding to a call, so, as one of the firefighters will tell you herself, the lights and siren were being used with full force.

Note, by the way, the reference to the testimony of the firefighter in the paragraph about the fire truck's lights and siren. Even though the story is not being presented in a witness-by-witness fashion, it will often be helpful to refer to the source of certain evidence, particularly when you know that it will be disputed.

Although the sub-events as units are presented out of chronology, internally each one is detailed basically as it occurred. The result of this approach is that the jury will be able to understand the context of the entire story as well as the precise nature of the individual occurrences that comprise the story.

3. Use details persuasively

As we have seen, the utilization of evidence in an opening statement depends upon the persuasive arrangement of major propositions and supporting details. While the application of this approach will vary tremendously from case to case, the following few generalizations should prove helpful:

a. Big ideas, then details

As a general rule, an opening statement should be organized as a series of big ideas, each of which is immediately supported by persuasive details.

As we have discussed above, jurors will tend to resolve a case on the basis of certain turning points or crucial issues. Details can be marshaled to make your version of these turning points more persuasive. For example, one major issue in the fire truck case will be whether the engine was sounding its siren just before the accident. If the jury decides that there was a siren, it will be more likely to bring back a plaintiff's verdict; if there was no siren, then the defendant has a better chance. Thus, the use of the siren could be a turning point in the trial. The plaintiff's position on this issue can be made more likely through the addition of details: the fire truck was responding to a call; there is a departmental policy to use the siren whenever responding to a call; the driver of the truck was an experienced firefighter, well aware of the policy; other motorists stopped their cars.[2]

The details, however, have little meaning when offered on their own. They become important only in light of the turning point on which they are offered. The fact that the fire truck was responding to a call doesn't tell us anything about the way that the accident

---

2. In the absence of details, the "siren question" would simply be a matter of the plaintiff's word against the defendant's. Note, then, that one value of the details is that they add persuasive force to the plaintiff's theory without relying upon her own credibility. This, in turn, makes the plaintiff all the more credible, since her version of events is supported by objective facts.

happened, but it does tell us that the truck was almost certainly using its siren. In the same vein, the jury will have no reason to care about the experience level of the fire truck driver until it is first informed that the use of the siren is an issue in the case. It is for this reason that details are best used to follow up or support the initial explication of a bigger idea.

b. Weave in the witnesses

While the witness-by-witness approach is unlikely to result in an effective opening statement, this does not mean that individual witnesses should not be mentioned in the course of your opening. To the contrary, it is often quite important to inform the jury of the source of a specific fact or the precise nature of some anticipated testimony. The key is to weave the information about the witnesses into the narrative so that the witness references arise in the context of your theory of the case.

As we have been discussing, the use of the siren is likely to be a turning point in our fire truck case. The plaintiff says there was a siren, and the defendant says there was not. The plaintiff's opening statement can bolster her position by weaving in witness information when her narrative reaches the siren issue:

> Just as she reached the intersection, the plaintiff saw and heard an approaching fire truck. It was sounding its siren and flashing its lights. We know that the siren was operating because Lieutenant Sarah Sherman, the driver of the fire truck, will testify that she always sounds the siren when she is answering a call. That is fire department policy, and Lieutenant Sherman is a decorated firefighter who has been with the department for over ten years. Perhaps, for whatever reason, the defendant didn't hear the siren, but Lieutenant Sherman will testify that she is certain that she was doing her official duty—that is, using her audio and visual alarms—on the day when the accident occurred.

Used in this manner, the information about Lieutenant Sherman corroborates and strengthens the plaintiff's theory of the case. It neither stands alone as an isolated description of the witness, nor does it interfere with the flow of the narrative. Rather, it adds unapologetic support to the plaintiff's theory at the precise moment when support is likely to be most readily understood.

Opening Statement Preparation Checklist ☑	
❏ Did you refrain from arguing?	Are you interpreting the evidence or urging the fact-finder to draw inferences? Are you explaining the importance of evidence or suggesting the weight it should be given? Are you appealing overtly to the fact-finder's sense of mercy or justice? *If so, you are arguing and you should revise your opening statement.*
❏ Did you refrain from commenting on the law?	Are you going beyond straightforward explanations of the legal issues in the case? *If so, save the further discussion for closing argument.*
❏ Did you weave your theory and theme into your trial story?	Are you beginning with a clear statement of your theory and theme, and then giving the supporting facts in narrative form? *If not, rework your opening statement to make it more persuasive.*
❏ Did you order and contrast the facts of your case persuasively?	Did you use incremental development of the facts to support your theory and theme? Did you use contrast to point out the opposing party's factual weaknesses? *If not, rework your opening statement to make it more persuasive.*

IV. CONTENT

The range of triable subjects being virtually limitless, is it possible to define what goes into a good opening statement? Of course, every good opening statement, no matter what the case, contains enough information to help you win the trial, but not so much as to distract the jury or risk exploitation by the other side. The following considerations should be helpful in most trials.

A. True and Provable

Every fact that you include in your opening statement must be true and provable. We have already seen that the law limits opening statements to a preview of the evidence that will be presented once the trial begins. It is not enough, however, that some witness may be willing to make a certain statement. The ethics of our profession require that we never knowingly be involved in presenting false evidence. This stricture applies not only to offering testimony, but also to outlining the case during the opening statement.

As we discussed earlier, the concept of truth takes a very specific form in the context of the adversary system. Since the jury, or judge, is assigned the role of deciding the truth of facts, counsel is generally obligated only to present one competing version of events. An attorney does not need to subject potential witnesses to a polygraph examination or be convinced of a witness's truthfulness beyond a reasonable doubt. The attorney may not, however, present evidence known to be fraudulent. Stated conversely, while you needn't be persuaded to a moral certainty, you must have some reasonable basis for believing a fact to be true before you can offer it from the witness stand or use it during your opening statement. It does not matter how good it makes the story, it does not matter how well it fits your theory of the case, it does not matter how incontrovertible your position might be: no fact may be used in an opening statement unless it meets the "not knowingly false" test of validity.

Conversely, even assuredly true facts should not be used in an opening statement until they have been subjected to the test of provability. While there may occasionally be reasons to depart from this principle, you should, as a general rule, omit from your opening statement any fact that you are not certain you will be able to prove at trial.

An opening statement is in many ways a promise to the jury. By making a definitive statement about the future evidence, you have committed yourself to produce that evidence. If your witnesses turn out to be less conclusive than your opening statement, you may seem at best to have overstated your case. At worst, you may seem deliberately to have misled the jury. The same thing can happen when promised evidence fails to materialize, either because the court declines to admit it or because it turns out to be unavailable. Even if the jury doesn't immediately realize that there has been a gap between your opening and your proof, you can be certain that opposing counsel will point it out during final argument.

Your strongest evidence should generally be at the heart of your opening statement. The central evidence will be a combination of: (1) the facts most essential to your case, and (2) the facts least likely to be disputed.

In the fire truck case it is central to the plaintiff's position to prove that she did indeed stop for a fire engine. The opening statement, if it does nothing else, must firmly establish in the jury's mind the presence of the truck and its use of its warning signals. Even if these facts will be disputed, they must be developed in the opening statement because the plaintiff cannot win without them.

Additionally, the plaintiff's opening statement should make liberal use of undisputed evidence even if it is not absolutely necessary to the case. The plaintiff can win the fire truck case without proving that the defendant was in a hurry. On the other hand, many of the specifics of the defendant's rushed morning cannot be controverted, which obviously makes them all the more persuasive. Thus, the plaintiff should be sure to include facts such as the time and importance of the defendant's business meeting that morning, the distance from his home to his office, the route he had to drive, his parking arrangements, and his telephone call to the office immediately after the collision.

B. The Operative Facts

The most important part of any opening statement is its treatment of the operative facts. Facts win lawsuits. Everything else—organization, presentation, theme development—must be seen as an aid to communication of the facts of the case.

It goes without saying that there can be no recipe for presenting the facts of a case. Each trial is unique. Some call for delicate innuendo; others may benefit from a frontal assault. Some cases rest heavily on the credibility of witnesses, while others depend on the timing of events. Often, however, the operative facts of a case will include some or all of the following:

1. Action and Key Events

Many cases revolve around one or more actions or key events. Most cases involving personal injury, crimes, medical malpractice, or property damage, to name only a few, require the description of a series of physical occurrences. An earlier section discussed the importance of using chronology to detail a single discrete event, as well as its frequent misuse as a device to outline an entire case.[3] This section addresses other aspects of presenting an account of the key events.

Whether representing the plaintiff or the defendant, it is important to use the opening statement to begin to paint a picture of the events in a way that helps the jury visualize the case from your client's point of view. To do this effectively you must first have created your own mental image which will, of course, be consistent with the testimony to be given later by your own witnesses. The importance of preparation cannot be overemphasized. You must know precisely how, and in what terms, your witnesses will relate each incident. You must be familiar with all of the physical evidence, and you must, if possible, have visited the site of the events. Competent counsel should never risk the possibility of dissonance between the

---

3. See Section III E, *supra* at p. 354.

events portrayed in the opening statement and those that emerge from the witnesses' testimony.

In depicting events, nouns and verbs can be much more helpful than adjectives and adverbs. This may not be immediately obvious since we commonly think of modifiers as adding descriptive depth. Consider, however, which of the following accounts is more evocative of the crime. First, a short paragraph that makes maximum use of adverbs and adjectives:

> It was a heinous, horrible crime. The defendant's actions were inhuman and awful. He brutally grabbed at the victim's gold chain, fiercely yanking it away. He left an ugly, ugly bruise on the victim's neck. Unsatisfied with the proceeds of the armed robbery, the defendant then coldly and wantonly stabbed the victim twice, leaving his jacket lying in a bloody heap. It was indeed a cowardly act, taken against a defenseless victim.

Now consider a paragraph with virtually no modifiers at all:

> The defendant placed his knife against the victim's body. Without waiting, he grabbed the gold chain from the victim's neck and wrenched it until it snapped, leaving bruises on the victim's neck that didn't heal for over a week. Although he had already taken what he wanted, he twisted the knife into the victim's shoulder, turning it as he pushed, and watched as the blood welled to the surface. Then he stabbed the victim again, until the blood soaked the jacket all the way through.

The second paragraph is more vivid, not only because of its slightly greater length,[4] but primarily because it describes the deeds as they occurred. In contrast, the first paragraph actually short-circuits the action by substituting value-laden modifiers for an account of the events themselves.

Of course, it would be foolish, if not impossible, to attempt to deliver an opening statement free of modifiers. Adjectives and adverbs are useful precisely because they convey compact meanings. Often they are indispensable. It is impossible to describe a red rubber ball without using the word "red."

Counsel must bear in mind, however, that modifiers frequently stand for judgments rather than for descriptions. Words like heinous, brutal, and awful or lovely, wonderful, and grand may convey

---

4. It inevitably takes more words to write without adjectives and adverbs since one of the functions of a modifier is to compress concepts into a single word.

the lawyer's opinion about something, but they do not depict a vision of the events themselves.

2. The Physical Scene

The meaning and legal significance of events is often dependent upon their location. Actions that are lawful or innocuous in one locale may become the basis of liability if they occur somewhere else. It is negligent to drive an automobile on the wrong side of the road. It may be an unfair labor practice for management to approach potential union members in their homes. It may violate a zoning ordinance to operate a law practice in a residential neighborhood. Similarly, the physical details of a particular setting may affect issues such as probability, credibility, or visibility.

It is important, therefore, to use your opening statement to set the scene for major events. While virtually all commentators agree that the scene should be set apart from a description of the action itself, there is divided opinion as to the sequence in which a scene should be described. Many lawyers suggest putting all of the details in place before going on to portray the action. In this way, the jury will already be aware of the physical details as the events unfold. Alternatively, you may describe the action first, and then go back to fill in the specifics of the setting. The theory behind this approach is that the importance of the events should be obvious, but the importance of the details will require some context to become apparent. There is no reason to care about the location of a stop sign until we know that there was a collision in the middle of the intersection.

Setting a scene involves describing a potentially unlimited number of details. Your opening statement should dwell on those details that are significant to your case while avoiding those that are merely clutter. In the fire truck case, for example, it is important for the plaintiff to note that the pavement was dry, since that would affect the defendant's stopping distance. The height of the curb, however, would be extraneous under virtually any theory of the case.

3. Transactions and Agreements

Most business cases involve written and oral communications far more than they do physical occurrences. In many ways these non-physical events may be more difficult to describe during an opening statement since there is little or no activity to depict. Nonetheless, when a case turns on the interpretation of a document or the meaning of a series of telephone calls, counsel must search for a way to bring the transaction to life.

The surest way not to bring a business transaction to life is to parse it out in minute chronological detail. It is generally far better to begin at the end. Explain the gist of the agreement and then go back to fill in only those details that are necessary to support your interpretation. There is no need, for example, to recount every telephone conversation that went into the negotiation of a purchase order. It will usually be sufficient to delineate the terms of the order itself, supported by an account of one or two crucial conversations.

It is not enough, however, simply to recite the terms of an agreement and then to point out that it was either kept or broken. While such an approach may, in the driest sense, convey your theory, it will not add moral weight to your case. Recall that your trial theme is intended to provide the jury with a reason for wanting to rule in your favor. This can only be done if you are able to explain the "rightness" of your interpretation of the contract. Why were the particular terms so important? Why was your client's reliance on the other party justified? Why will the other party's interpretation lead to chaos and disaster for the entire republic?

4. Business Context

Business context can be crucial to an appreciation of many agreements and transactions. Words may have specialized meanings, or unspoken expectations may be understood by all of the parties. Detailing the business context of a contract or other transaction may be the equivalent of setting the scene for an automobile accident.

Business context can include information on industry practice, course of dealings, production standards, insurability, cost of credit, lines of authority, agency, normal business hours, grievance procedures, and a host of other factors that may form the backdrop for even the simplest transaction.

5. Relationship of the Parties

As much as any physical detail, the past relationship of the parties can speak volumes about the merits of a case. It will add a whole new dimension to a contracts case if it is revealed that there had been a history of misunderstanding between the buyer and the seller. Past animus can be used to show motive or malice. A tradition of reliability, on the other hand, can be used to establish the reasonableness of a party's actions.

6. Motives and Motivations

As we have consistently seen, stories are more persuasive when they are told about people who have reasons for the way they act. An opening statement, therefore, should always attempt to stress the motivations for the parties' actions. The activity that you describe will be far more plausible if, at the same time, you are also able to explain why the people involved acted as they did.

It must be stressed, however, that the opening statement is not the time to speculate about a person's secret motives. The opening statement must develop motive in the same way that it treats everything else—through the preview of evidentiary facts. The rule against argument applies with full force, and probably then some, to the discussion of motive.

Thus, motivation must be carefully established through the use of discrete, incremental facts. You cannot say that the plaintiff is greedy. You can point out five previous occasions on which the plaintiff sued for breach of contract, each one based upon an imperceptible flaw in the goods delivered.

7. Amount of Damages

There are two schools of thought regarding the treatment of damages during the plaintiff's opening statement. One approach is to make the discussion of damages a significant part of the opening, explaining the nature of the injury and the amount that is being sought. The theory here is to acclimate the jury to the fact that the plaintiff will be requesting substantial monetary compensation. Where the amount sought is extremely large, many lawyers believe that it will take some time for the jury to become used to thinking about such big numbers. Thus, they like the process to begin as soon as possible.

Other lawyers believe that damage amounts will have little meaning until the jury actually has heard the evidence. It will be difficult for them to think in terms of awards until they have at least begun to make up their minds about liability. This is thought to be particularly true about big numbers, as it may make the lawyer and client seem greedy to begin talking about large verdicts before any evidence has been introduced. Lawyers who hold this view generally discuss the facts that support damages but do not mention a specific figure. Note, however, that there is little reason not to state a precise figure for damages in, for example, a commercial case where the amount is liquidated.

Finally, a majority of defense counsel refrain from discussing damages during the opening statement. Even where the plaintiff's damage figure is inflated or unrealistic, many defense lawyers fear that they will appear to concede liability if they seem to quibble about the amount of damages right at the outset of the case. Some lawyers choose to make only a passing reference to the plaintiff's request, stating something to the effect that, "Even if the defendant was at fault, the evidence will show that the plaintiff's number is far more than would be necessary for fair compensation." Others do not even go this far. Of course, where the defendant has admitted or stipulated to liability, the case will be tried only on the question of damages. Since the amount of compensation is the only issue, the defendant obviously must address it during the opening statement.

C.   The Opposition Case

It is always difficult to decide how much attention to give to the opposition case. Plaintiff's counsel must determine whether to anticipate and respond to the expected defenses. Defendant's counsel has to consider whether and how much to react to the plaintiff's opening.

1. Plaintiff's Opening

Unlike final arguments, there is no rebuttal in opening statements. The plaintiff gets to address the jury only once and without the advantage of knowing what the defendant's opening will be. No matter what defense counsel says, plaintiff's attorney will not be able to respond directly until the end of the trial. This can be especially troublesome in cases where the defendant presents an affirmative defense. Since an affirmative defense, by definition, raises issues that go beyond the plaintiff's own case, the plaintiff faces a delicate problem in dealing with them during the opening statement. Should the plaintiff ignore the affirmative defense, thereby foregoing the opportunity to reply to it at the outset of the trial? Or should the plaintiff respond to the defense in advance, in essence forecasting the defendant's case?

One solution to this problem is to construct the discussion of the plaintiff's own case in such a way as to blunt any rejoinders that the defendant might raise. In a simple automobile accident case, for example, plaintiff's counsel can build up the plaintiff's level of care and skill while driving, without ever mentioning the defense of contributory negligence.

Unfortunately, not all defenses are equally amenable to this approach. Assume, for instance, that you represent the plaintiff in a sales transaction. Your client contracted to sell industrial machinery to the defendant. Your client contends that the goods were shipped, but no payment was received. There are at least three possible defenses: (1) the goods were never received due to some fault of the plaintiff; (2) they were received, but they were defective; or (3) payment was made.

To negate fully any of these claims, the plaintiff, at a minimum, must refer to the defense itself. Consider the defense of defective products. To be sure, a general statement that the goods conformed to the contract will be sufficient to stake out the plaintiff's position. But a truly persuasive story will require the plaintiff to confront and refute each of the shortcomings asserted by the defense. In the absence of this discussion in the plaintiff's opening, the jury will hear only about what was wrong with the shipment. It is conceivable that plaintiff's counsel might run through every single specification, explaining that the goods conformed across the board, but this itemization could go on forever without informing the jury of the precise issue in dispute. It would make far more sense for the plaintiff to focus her opening statement on exactly the defects claimed by the defendant.

In some cases, then, the plaintiff has little choice but to anticipate the defendant's opening statement. Here are some guidelines:

Your case first. Give primary attention to the strongest aspects of your own case. The opening statement is your opportunity to begin to capture the jury's imagination. Don't get them started imagining the things that might be wrong with your case. Accentuate the positive. To the extent possible, defenses should be treated as technicalities or annoyances.

Be certain. The process of discovery should allow you to know with some certainty exactly which defenses will be raised. There is no reason to survey all of the holes that the defendant might try to punch in your case. Concentrate on the principal defenses.

No apologies, no sneers. When it comes time to discuss the opposition's case, your tone should be firm, unapologetic, and straightforward. If you seem overly concerned or worried about a defense, it will suggest that there are indeed problems with your case. By the same token, you shouldn't sneer or be entirely dismissive; after all, you are the one who is introducing the issue. Moreover, you can't expect the jury to share your disdain for the defendant's position when they haven't even had a chance to hear it yet.

Minimize witness references. There is an inherent difficulty in predicting what the other side's witnesses are going to say. Opening statements are allowed, after all, to allow you to assist the jury by previewing your own evidence. Not having prepared or organized the other side's case, you would be hard put to explain how you can help the jury by guessing at what it might be.

In this vein, it has even been suggested that it is improper for counsel to preview testimony from opposition witnesses. The theory behind this position is that you may only use your opening statement to explain what you expect the evidence to show and that you cannot be certain what the opposition evidence will be. Given the reality of deposition practice and pretrial orders, however, it is obvious that in most cases you will have a good idea of just how the opposing witnesses will testify. Even if a witness ends up not being called, in most jurisdictions you will have the opportunity to call the witness yourself.

Nonetheless, it is a good idea to refer to the other side's case in summary only and to avoid direct quotations from their witnesses. There is something discordant about a lawyer predicting how opposing witnesses will testify. Additionally, there is a tremendous chance that, following such an opening, the other side's witnesses will testify differently, if only to spite you. Finally, recall that the purpose of anticipating the defendant's opening statement is to allow you to build up your own case, not to expound on the details of theirs.

There are situations where explicit quotations may be helpful. It can be devastating to read from a document that the defendant produced or to quote directly from the defendant's own deposition. The key to this approach is to be sure (1) that the quotations are accurate, (2) that they are meaningful standing alone and do not require extensive context, and (3) that you have an independent evidentiary basis for introducing them yourself.

Finally, it must be noted that the Fifth Amendment prohibits prosecutors from so much as suggesting that the defendant will testify. The Fifth Amendment does not, however, prevent the prosecutor from reading from a confession or prior statement of the defendant so long as the statement itself has not been ruled inadmissible.

2. Defendant's Opening

Many lawyers believe that thorough preparation includes planning every word of the opening statement in advance. This is true only to a point. While plaintiffs and prosecutors have the luxury of knowing exactly how they will open their cases, defense lawyers must be more flexible. It is a tremendous advantage to deliver the second opening statement, and defense counsel can only take advantage of this opportunity by being ready to respond to at least some aspects of the plaintiff's opening. No matter how well you have prepared your case, it is a mistake to be tied to a scripted opening statement. Responses or rejoinders to the plaintiff's opening can be fruitful in the following situations:

Denials. The civil plaintiff's opening statement, and even more so the criminal prosecutor's, is essentially an accusation. Its entire thrust is to tell a story that accuses the defendant of negligence, breach of contract, criminal acts, or some other negative conduct. After hearing such an extended charge against the defendant, the jury's first inclination will be to ask the question, "Well, is it true?" The defendant, then, absolutely must respond with a denial. Anything short of a denial is likely to be regarded as evasion, equivocation, or worse, an admission of fault.

While defense counsel can plan to deny the plaintiff's allegations, it can be a mistake to plan exactly how to deny them. Generic denials tend to sound exactly like generic denials; they lack force because they do not meet the opposing party head-on. It can be much more effective and persuasive to pick up on the plaintiff's opening and to deny their claims using some of the same language in which they were made.

Care must be taken not to echo the insinuations of the plaintiff's charge. There is no reason to repeat all of the nasty evidence that the plaintiff claims to be able to produce. On the other hand, it is necessary to recognize that the plaintiff has made specific charges and to explain specifically how they will be rebutted.

The following is a poor example of a denial in a defendant's opening statement because it is too general to carry any weight:

> The defendant denies any and all negligence on his part.
> He denies that he was anything less than a careful driver,
> and he denies that he caused the plaintiff any harm.

This is a worse example because it gives too much credence to the plaintiff's case:

> The plaintiff has claimed that my client was preoccupied
> with an important business meeting on the morning of
> the accident. It is their position that he was thinking
> about how to attract a lucrative new client instead of pay-
> ing attention to the road. This is all untrue. We will prove
> that the accident was the plaintiff's own fault.

This is a better example; it responds directly to the plaintiff's central claim, but it does so by building up the defendant's own case, not by reiterating the plaintiff's:

> Contrary to the plaintiff's claim, my client was anything
> but "too busy to be careful." We will prove that he was
> driving well within the legal speed limit and that he was

keeping a proper and careful lookout. He had plenty of time to get to his office that morning, but the plaintiff herself stopped her car in the middle of the street rather than pulling over to the right as the traffic laws require.

Controverted evidence. It is also important to respond directly to the plaintiff's version of significant controverted evidence. Simply telling your own independent story is not sufficient since that will not allow you to explain why the facts in support of your version are superior. It is also risky to expect the jury to keep the plaintiff's opening in mind and then to appreciate the implications of the contrary facts as you reveal them. Instead, you should make it apparent that you are contradicting the plaintiff's factual claims:

> Plaintiff's counsel claimed that my client neglected to have his brakes repaired. The facts are that he took his car in for a tune-up and the mechanic said only that he should have his brakes "looked at" within the next 10,000 miles. The evidence will show that the defendant took care of all scheduled maintenance completely according to the manufacturer's timetable and that he had no reason to think that his brakes were not functioning properly.

If defense counsel simply began talking about brakes the jury might take it as a concession that defendant's brakes were a problem. The defense case is therefore made much stronger by pointing out how the defendant's facts contradict the plaintiff's claim.

Omissions. The absence of evidence can be as telling as the evidence itself. Defense counsel should therefore be ready to respond not only to what was said in plaintiff's opening but also to what was not said. While it would be argumentative to accuse opposing counsel of concealing information, it is perfectly proper to point out evidentiary gaps in the plaintiff's opening statement. Assume, for example, that liability has been stipulated in the fire engine case and that it is being tried solely on the issue of damages:

> Plaintiff's counsel spoke at some length about the plaintiff's injuries. She did not, however, give you all of the facts about the plaintiff's current physical condition. The evidence will show, for example, that the plaintiff spent a weekend last summer camping at Eagle River Falls. She carried a backpack, she slept on the ground, and she hiked every day. Plaintiff's counsel did not tell you that the trip was planned for a long weekend, and she stayed the full time. It was not necessary for her to leave early. After the long weekend of roughing it, she simply went home. She didn't go to a hospital, or even to her family doctor. On the

other hand, there will be absolutely no evidence in this case that the plaintiff lost any income as a result of her injuries.

Opening Statement Content Checklist ☑	
❏ Did you include only provable facts?	Is each fact you mention in your opening statement likely to be brought out during trial? *If not, take out the unprovables.*
❏ Did you include all the necessary facts?	Does your story describe the physical scene, actions, and key events and any transactions and agreements? *If not, add the operative facts to your trial story.*
❏ Did you include a reference to the other side's case (or are you prepared to do so at trial)?	If you represent the plaintiff/prosecution, did you address the defense theory (if known) in your opening statement? *If not, consider whether you can do so. (Recognize the limitations imposed by the Fifth Amendment in criminal cases.)* If you represent the defense, are you prepared to deny the opposition's accusations and address the controverted evidence? Are you ready to address possible omissions in your adversary's opening statement? *If not, continue your preparation until you are comfortable enough to do so.*

D. Bad Facts and Disclaimers

Should your opening statement ever mention negative information that is likely to come out about one of your own witnesses? There is divided opinion on this issue. The traditional view is that you will appear to be hiding any bad facts that you do not mention and that you can defuse the impact of such facts by bringing them out yourself. Thus, most lawyers favor making at least a casual reference to such matters as felony convictions, admissible "bad acts," and other provable misconduct.

More recently, however, it has been suggested that jurors do not expect lawyers to say anything negative about their own witnesses and that by doing so you actually call greater attention to the damaging information. There will be time enough to respond to charges after they have actually been made; there is no need to lead the bandwagon yourself.

Whether to introduce damaging information about your own witnesses remains a matter of judgment, and no doubt the answer will differ with the context of the case. A prudent approach, however, is always to keep bad information, or even the suggestion of bad information, to an absolute minimum. You will want to exhibit the highest possible level of confidence and belief in your own witnesses. Thus, negative information should not be mentioned until you have laid out all of the positive facts about the witness. If you believe that you must defuse a ticking bomb, do it quickly and without fanfare.

Defense counsel, of course, does not need to wonder if any of her witnesses will be attacked during the plaintiff's opening statement. She has the advantage of going second. Thus, for defense counsel there will seldom, if ever, be a situation where it is necessary to raise damaging facts in order to head off the opposition. If the jury didn't get the bad news when the plaintiff opened, there should be scant reason to deliver it during the defendant's opening statement.[5]

E. Legal Issues

As was noted above, it is frequently important to use the opening statement to introduce the legal issues to the jury.[6] A statement of legal issues will put the significance of the facts into clear perspective. Explanations of the law should be brief and to the point. It is far better to weave them into the context of the story as opposed to "string-citing" all of the legal issues at once.

F. Introductions

At some point in the opening statement it will be necessary to introduce yourself, your client, and any cocounsel. Even if the judge has already introduced all of you, it is a common courtesy to do it again yourself. While there is a natural inclination to begin with introductions, they are not really important enough to warrant the use of your opening moment. It is usually better to start with a strong statement of your theory and theme and then proceed to the introductions at a natural breaking point.

---

5. It is possible, of course, that the plaintiff will introduce negative information into evidence notwithstanding the fact that it was not mentioned during the opneing statement. Defense counsel should nonetheless be wary of advance disclosure during her opening. First, the plaintiff may decide not to offer the damaging evidence, or if offered, it may not be admitted. Second, much unpleasant information can be developed only on cross examination, in which case there will be time enough to defuse it (if that is your choice) during the witness's direct. Finally, the bad facts might be introduced during plaintiff's case in chief, in which case cross examination will be immediately available to the defendant, and it is unlikely to appear that the defendant was trying to conceal the material.

6. See Section II B, *supra* at 347.

G. Request for Verdict

Your opening statement should almost always conclude with a request for, or explanation of, the verdict that you will seek at the end of the trial. This request should be made in general terms: "At the end of the case we will ask you to return a verdict that the defendant was not guilty of negligence." The opening statement is not the time for a lengthy discussion of verdict forms or special interrogatories.

H. Bromides and Platitudes

There are numerous opening statement bromides and platitudes that have become venerated traditions among some members of the bar. While certain of these clichés have fallen from general use in recent years, others have taken on a life of their own, being repeated by generation after generation even though they have little, if any, intrinsic meaning. A few of the conventions have their limited uses. Here follows a short list of topics, phrases, and slogans that are usually best omitted from your opening statements.

The civics lesson. Some lawyers begin their opening statements with a paean to the American jury system. This invocation is unlikely to help your case since it has absolutely no persuasive value one way or the other. It may convince the jury that you are a patriotic lawyer, but it is just as likely to convince them that you have very little to say on the merits. There is a time to thank the jury for their service and to indicate your respect for the job that they are doing, but it is not at the beginning of your opening statement. The civics lesson, by the way, should be distinguished from a discussion in criminal cases of the concept of proof beyond a reasonable doubt. Reasonable doubt, unlike a generalized discourse on the jury system, is virtually always an essential element of the defendant's case that must be addressed during opening statements.

The neutral simile. It is not uncommon for a lawyer to begin an opening statement with an extended simile that is intended to explain the function of the opening. An opening statement, the jury might be told, is like the picture on the cover of a jigsaw puzzle box. Or it might be like a road map, or like the directions for assembly of a compact disc player. None of these similes is really worthwhile. They communicate absolutely nothing about your case, but they are damaging in the sense that they waste your opening moment. If your opening statement is good, the simile will be unnecessary. If your opening statement is disorganized or vague, no simile or metaphor will save it.

"Not evidence." Perhaps the hoariest opening line in the history of opening statements is the caution to the jury that "What I am about to say to you is not evidence; the evidence will be presented in the form of witness testimony, documents, and exhibits." Although this introduction is now heard less and less, it was once considered de rigueur for opening statements. Because it still survives in some quarters, the reasons for abandoning this line bear repeating. Telling the jury that your opening statement is not evidence is the rough equivalent of telling them to ignore what you are about to say. No one has ever claimed that opening statements are evidence, so there is no reason to disclaim the idea. You want the jury to pay attention to your opening; you should therefore say nothing that will tend to diminish its importance. There is one situation in which there may be some value to reminding a jury that an opening statement is not evidence. In criminal cases the prosecution often presents a very comprehensive and compelling opening statement. Since the defense may not wish to commit themselves to putting on a case, they are often left with very little to say in response. Moreover, the defense will frequently rely most heavily on cross examination as opposed to the development of an affirmative case. In these circumstances it can be helpful to use the opening statement to explain that the prosecution opening, no matter how powerful it seemed, simply was not evidence. Note that in these circumstances the "not evidence" disclaimer is raised about the opposition opening, not your own.

"The evidence will show." Opening statements are limited to a description of "what the evidence will show." This rule has led some lawyers to conclude that every fact mentioned in the opening statement must be preceded with an introductory phrase such as, "We expect the evidence to show that the fire engine was flashing its lights," or "we intend to prove that the defendant had not repaired his brakes," or "there will be evidence that the defendant was already late for an important business meeting at the time of the collision." There is no harm at all in occasionally reminding the judge and jury that you are indeed forecasting evidence that is yet to come. It is hopelessly distracting, however, to use such a phrase as a preface to every item of evidence. It is entirely possible to deliver a complete opening statement without ever once saying, "the evidence will show...." At most, the line should be used at wide intervals simply as an acknowledgment that the opening is a preview.

V.   DELIVERY AND TECHNIQUE

It would be very easy to overemphasize the significance of presentational skills in delivering an opening statement. While the popular misconception may be that polished style can win trials, the truth is that well-developed facts almost always triumph over dramatics. Only once you have generated your theory of the case and organized your opening statement to present it most effectively should you turn your attention to delivery techniques. This does not mean that delivery is irrelevant, but only that the substance of the case must come first.

Recognizing the secondary importance of technique, here are some useful guidelines.

A. Do Not Read

Do not read your opening statement from a prepared text. Only the most skilled professional actors can deliver a scripted speech and still appear to be spontaneous and sincere. Everyone else will seem to be stilted or labored. Your goal during the opening should be to communicate directly to the jury, not to lecture to them from a manuscript. You will want to make eye contact, you will want to pick up on the jury's reactions, and you will want to respond to objections and rulings by the court. Defense counsel, moreover, will want to reply to challenges, weaknesses, and omissions in the plaintiff's opening statement. A written opening statement will prevent you from doing any of these things effectively.

Much the same can be said of attempting to memorize your opening statement. While exceptional memorization is better than reading, you will still run the risk of forgetting a line (or more), of losing your place, or of being thrown off track by an objection. Very experienced lawyers may be able to deliver opening statements from memory. Novices should be wary of trying.

The best approach is often to deliver the opening statement from an outline. It should be possible to list all of your major points, as well as the most important supporting details, on one or two sheets of paper. An outline will allow you to organize the material as well as ensure that you don't leave anything out, while avoiding all of the perils of reading or memorization. Although some lawyers believe that any use of notes is distracting to the jury, it is far more likely that jurors understand the need to use some notes whenever you are speaking at length. The key, of course, is for your notes to be unobtrusive—hence, the outline as opposed to the text.

B. Use Simple Language and Straightforward Presentation

The opening statement should be reasonably straightforward and direct. It is a time to allow your facts to speak for themselves and not a time for emotional pleas or impassioned argument. In any event, the court will not allow you to make elaborate use of metaphors, literary allusions, biblical quotations, or any of the other rhetorical devices that can be so helpful during final argument.

While you should never talk down to a jury, simple language is generally the best. There is no word so eloquent that it is worth risking the understanding of a single juror. Your opening statement can be perfectly sophisticated without relying upon language that you won't hear on the evening news. There is no reason to say that the defendant in the fire truck case "procrastinated" in having his brakes repaired; say instead that he "put off having his brakes fixed."[7] Most of all, do not use legalese. It isn't impressive even to lawyers, and it will tend to confuse, bore, and even aggravate the jury.

C. Use Movement for Emphasis and Transition

To the extent that it is allowed by the judge,[8] you can add considerable force to your opening statement simply by moving about in the courtroom. Movement can be used most effectively to make the transition from one topic to another or to emphasize a particular point.

Movement for transition. Whenever you want to highlight a change of subjects during your opening statement, take a step or two to one side or the other. If you are standing at the lectern, your movement could be as slight as a shift to its side. By using your body in this manner, you signal to the jury that one subject has ended and another is about to begin. This motion, in turn, will have the effect of reinitiating primacy. The jury's attention will refocus, and you will then have a new "opening moment" in which to take advantage of the jury's heightened concentration and retention.

Movement for emphasis. Deliberate body movement always concentrates the jury's attention. Movement toward the jury will concentrate it even more. Whenever you reach a particularly important point in your opening statement, you can emphasize it by taking a step or two in the jury's direction. As your movement becomes

---

7. Readers have not doubt observed that this book does not shy away from big words. Nor should it; our language is rich, and it is made richer by the use of interesting and precise words. But writing for an audience of lawyers and law students is one thing, and trying cases is another.

8. In some jurisdictions counsel is required always to remain at the lectern. In a few jurisdictions the attorneys must conduct the entire trial while seated at counsel table. Most judges, however, allow lawyers to move rather freely about the courtroom, especially during opening statements and closing arguments. If you are not familiar with a particular judge's practice, make a point of finding out before the trial begins.

faster and more purposeful, you will increasingly emphasize the point. Two caveats regarding the use of this technique should be fairly obvious: don't run and don't hover over the jury. The invasion of their space can be seen as overbearing or even threatening. Note also that your important point should not be made while you are walking since the jury might be paying more attention to your motion than to your words. Instead, use a transition sentence while you are moving toward the jury, then stop, pause a moment, and deliver your crucial point while standing perfectly still. The contrast will emphasize the issue even more.

Pacing. Pacing is bad. It distracts the jury. Far worse, it also deprives you of the ability to use movement for emphasis. If you are constantly walking back and forth in the courtroom, you cannot use a few well-chosen steps to underscore the significance of a critical detail. This can be especially crippling in an opening statement since the rule against argument otherwise severely limits your ability to accent issues for the jury.

Lectern. Most, although not all, courtrooms come equipped with a lectern. Many experienced attorneys move the lectern aside during opening statements so that nothing will stand between themselves and the jury. They either speak without using notes, or they use a few small index cards. This is an excellent approach if you are able to use it. Most lawyers, however, need more notes and are more comfortable using a lectern as home base. There is nothing wrong with speaking from a lectern, and you will not lose your case if you take a note pad with you when you deliver your opening statement. The key is to use the lectern without being chained to it. Feel free to move out to the side of the lectern, or even across the courtroom, returning to your staging ground when you have finished emphasizing a point or when you need to refer to your notes.

D. Visuals and Exhibits

Your opening statement need not be confined to your words alone. The use of visual aids and exhibits can enormously enhance the value of your presentation.

Exhibits. Since the purpose of the opening statement is to explain what the evidence will show, you are entitled to read from or display documents and other exhibits that you expect to be admitted into evidence. If the case involves a contract, quote from the central clause. If you plan to offer a key letter into evidence, have it enlarged and show it to the jury during your opening statement. Use a pointer so that the jury can read along with you as you recite the opposing party's damning admission. During your opening statement you may be able to show the jury photographs, models, maps, and charts, as well as other tangible exhibits such as weapons, machinery, or even prosthetics. There is some risk, of course, in displaying an exhibit that may not ultimately be admitted. Under modern practice, however, this problem can usually be alleviated by obtaining a pretrial ruling on admissibility.

Visual aids. In addition to displaying actual exhibits, you may also use visual aids during your opening statement. The general rule is that any visual aid must be likely to help the jury to understand the eventual trial evidence. Thus, lawyers have been allowed to show "time lines" to the jury or to draw freehand diagrams that will not later be offered. There are limitations, of course. The visual aids must fairly summarize the evidence, they cannot be misleading, and they cannot be argumentative. You could not, for example, produce a chart captioned "Three Reasons Not to Believe the Plaintiff." Visual aids should be shown to opposing counsel before your opening statement begins. It is advisable also to show visuals to the court and to obtain advance permission for their use.

Other evidence. Not all exhibits are visual. It is permissible to play tape recordings during opening statements—such as legally tapped telephone conversations or 911 emergency calls—if they will later be offered into evidence. It is conceivable that creative counsel might even make use of olfactory or tactile evidence, although this possibility seems remote.

THE BASICS

Opening Statement Organization

- Begin with your theory and theme
- Introduce yourself and your client (if applicable)
- Tell the full story (avoiding a rigid witness-by-witness or chronological approach)
- Highlight the legal issues
- Request a verdict

VI. ADDITIONAL CONSIDERATIONS

A. Motions and Objections

Objections are fairly unusual during opening statements. It may seem rude to interrupt when the other lawyer is speaking directly to the jury, and a general convention has developed that most attorneys will try to avoid objecting during opposing counsel's opening. There are times, however, when objections are called for and should be made.

1. Common Objections

The most common objection during an opening statement is to improper argument. Most judges will sustain this objection only when the argument is extended or over-the-top. An argumentative sentence or two will be unlikely to draw an objection, and even more unlikely to see one sustained. Drawn out argument, however, should be objected to. There is no convention that allows opposing counsel to transform the opening statement into a final argument. Be particularly alert to extended argument on the credibility of witnesses.

It is also objectionable to discuss or explain the law during opening statements. Again, some brief mention of the applicable law is permissible and, in fact, unavoidable. Lengthy discourse on the law, and especially misstatement of the law, should draw an objection.

It is both objectionable and unethical for counsel to express a personal opinion during the opening statement or to assert personal knowledge of the facts of the case.[9] The purpose of this rule is to prevent attorneys from offering "facts" that will not be in evidence, and also to prevent the trial from becoming a referendum on the believability of the lawyers. This rule is intended to prevent lawyers from saying things like, "Believe me, I know what happened, and I wouldn't lie to you." It is not intended to preclude the occasional use of phrases such as "I think" or "I'm sure." An objection on this ground is most likely to be sustained when opposing counsel discusses her own investigation of the case or makes reference to her own credibility.

While opening statements are required to preview only the evidence that will ultimately come before the jury, objections usually will not be sustained on the ground that counsel is discussing inadmissible evidence. A lawyer is entitled to take a chance that her evidence will be admitted, and most judges will not rule on evidentiary objections during the opening statements. If you truly believe that evidence should be excluded, then your proper course of action is to make a motion in limine before the trial, not to raise an objection during opposing counsel's opening statement. On the other hand, it is possible that the opposition might take you completely by sur-

---

9.   In fact, it is unethical for counsel to express a personal opinion or assert personal knowledge of the facts at any point during the trial. See Rule 3.4(e), Model Rules of Professional Conduct; DR 7-106(C)(3) & (4), Model Code of Professional Responsibility.

prise by trying to slip some outrageously inadmissible and prejudicial tidbit into their opening statement. If that is the case, by all
means object. It is unethical for an attorney to "allude to any matter
that the lawyer does not reasonably believe is relevant or that will
not be supported by admissible evidence."[10]

It is entirely objectionable to refer to evidence that has been
excluded via motion in limine or other pretrial ruling.

Finally, it is worth noting that there is no such objection as
"That is not what the evidence will be." Opposing counsel presents
her case and you present yours. You will naturally disagree as to
what the evidence will show. If counsel ultimately fails to live up to
the commitments given during her opening statement, then you can
pound that point home during your final argument. For the same
reason there is also no such objection as "Mischaracterizing the evidence." If a characterization amounts to argument, object to it. Otherwise, opposing counsel is free to put whatever spin she can on the
evidence.

2. Responding to Objections

An objection during your opening statement can be distracting. Lengthy argument, however, can be even more disruptive. Any
time that you spend speaking to the court is time that you are not
speaking to the jury. In all but exceptional circumstances, then, it is
usually best to wait for the judge to rule on an objection and then to
proceed.

If the objection is overruled, you may thank the court and pick
up where you left off. If the objection is sustained, you must adapt
your opening to the court's ruling. For example, if your theme has
been declared argumentative, you must figure out a way to recast or
truncate it so that you can continue to use it without objection.

Consider the "too busy to be careful" theme that we have pos-
ited for the fire truck case. Although it is unlikely, imagine that the
court has sustained an objection to the use of that phrase during
your opening statement. Don't ask for reconsideration or try to explain why you weren't being argumentative. A small adjustment to
your opening should be sufficient:

> The evidence will show that the defendant was extremely
> busy on the morning of the accident. The evidence will
> also show that the defendant was not careful. He was busy
> because he had an important meeting scheduled with a

---

10. Rule 3.4(e), Model Rules of Professional Conduct; See also DR 7-106(C)(1),
Model Code of Professional Responsibility.

new client. He was running late for the meeting, and he wanted to get there on time. We know that he wasn't careful because he kept on driving when all of the other traffic stopped for a fire truck. The truck was flashing its lights and sounding its siren, but the defendant didn't notice it until it was too late.

Finally, many judges are adept at avoiding rulings on objections during opening statements. The following scenario is not uncommon:

ATTORNEY: Objection, Your Honor. Counsel is engaging in improper argument.

COURT: Argument is not permitted during opening statements. Proceed.

The judge has neither sustained nor overruled the objection. What should you do? The best approach is usually to modify your opening statement slightly as an indication to the court that you understand the need to avoid argument. The judge, in effect, has cautioned you, and you should not take that as license to binge on argumentation.

3. Motions and Curative Instructions

Once an objection is sustained the opening statement is allowed to continue. Occasionally the offending portion of the opening statement is so damaging that the objecting lawyer must request a curative instruction from the court. This should be done primarily when opposing counsel has engaged in lengthy argument or has referred to evidence that has already been excluded.

Curative instructions are obtained by asking the court to "instruct the jury to disregard counsel's comments." Some judges then instruct the jury in rather perfunctory terms, while others actually make some effort to ensure that the jury will not consider the improper comments. In either case, the decision to request a curative instruction is a touchy one since the instruction itself might serve to emphasize exactly the point that you want the jury to disregard.

Nonetheless, in many jurisdictions you cannot appeal on the ground of improper comments during opening unless you first objected and then requested a curative instruction. Paradoxically, it is not uncommon for appellate courts then to hold that the instruction rectified any harm.

In extreme cases a motion for a mistrial can be made on the basis of improper comments during the opening statement. To warrant a mistrial, opposing counsel's improper statement must have been so prejudicial and damaging as to have destroyed irrevocably the possibility of a fair trial.

B. Bench Trials

A judge, unlike a jury, is obviously familiar with the manner in which evidence is produced at trial. Does a judge ever require help in understanding the evidence? Is there a place for opening statements in bench trials?

In all but very complex cases, judges often prefer to eliminate or severely truncate opening statements. It may be conceit, but judges tend to believe that they can follow the evidence without the benefit of a preview. Counsel, however, should be reluctant to give up opening statements. It is just as important and valuable to capture the judge's imagination as it is to begin creating a mental picture for a jury. Indeed, it may be more important to impress your image of the case upon the judge since the court eventually will render its verdict without the benefit of deliberations. Even in the absence of opening statements, a jury will be composed of at least six people, all of whom will enter the jury room with different predispositions and experiences. A judge will have only her own background to rely on, and the opening statement may be your best opportunity to begin to persuade the court to see the case your way.

Nonetheless, in most jurisdictions the court has the right to forgo opening statements in bench trials. The surest way to be certain that opening statements will be allowed is not to abuse the privilege when it is granted. Your opening statement to the court should be particularly short, well-focused, and to the point. Many of the conventions and techniques that are aimed at juries should be eliminated when trying a case to the bench.

Judges hate long opening statements. You must do everything you can to shorten your presentation. For example, while repetition is effective in making a point to a jury, it can be deadly when opening to the court. There is seldom a need to repeat points, or to drive them home through a series of incremental steps, when your audience is a single judge. Do not omit significant details, but do not build them up in the same way that you would before a jury.

Similarly, there is certainly never any reason to go through a list of witnesses for the court. This technique has limited value in a jury trial, but it has absolutely no function in a bench trial. The judge will be able to understand who the witnesses are as they appear.

On the other hand, chronology and the ordering of facts continue to be important in bench trials. A clear picture of the occurrences will always help the judge's understanding. This applies not only to the sequence of events, but also to relationships among the various facts. If certain facts cast doubt on the credibility of a witness, tell that to the court. If a certain document will bolster or contradict a witness's testimony, tell that to the court.

Perhaps the most important consideration in opening to the court is to stress the legal issues. You should have much greater latitude in discussing legal issues in a bench trial. Tell the court what the claims and defenses are. Explain exactly how the principal facts and supporting details relate to the legal issues in the case. The judge will eventually arrive at a verdict by applying the applicable law to the proven facts. Your opening statement can be most effective if it presages this process.

C. Timing

1. When to Open

The plaintiff always opens at the very beginning of the case. The defendant, at least as a technical matter, usually has the option of either opening immediately after the plaintiff or waiting until the plaintiff has rested and the defense case is about to begin.

The overwhelming consensus view is that the defense should never delay opening. The plaintiff's (or prosecutor's) opening will portray their case in its strongest possible form. The defense can undermine that portrayal, and also create some discontinuity between the plaintiff's opening and the beginning of their evidence, by presenting their opening statement immediately after the plaintiff's. Delaying the defense opening will give the impression that the plaintiff's claims have gone unrebutted. On the other hand, opening at the outset of the trial will allow the jury to consider the defense position even while listening to the plaintiff's evidence. It will also create a context for defense counsel's cross examinations.

There are only a few possible justifications for delaying the defense opening until after the plaintiff has rested. It is remotely conceivable that you might have some surprise up your sleeve that you don't want to reveal before the plaintiff has concluded its case. Alternatively, criminal defense counsel sometimes prefer to evaluate the strength of the prosecution witnesses before deciding whether to present a defense. In these situations there may be some theoretical benefit to delaying the opening statement, although the same advantage can often be obtained by structuring an initial opening to achieve the same goals.

2. Multiple Parties

In cases with more than one plaintiff or defendant, the court will generally determine the order of opening statements. The plaintiff with the most at stake will typically be allowed to open first, followed by the others in descending order of potential recovery. Similarly, the defendant with the greatest exposure will usually be afforded the first opening statement. Other factors may also be considered, and the parties are customarily free to stipulate to some other order.

In a case with multiple defendants, it may be possible for one to open immediately after the plaintiff and for another to reserve opening until the beginning of the defense case. This approach provides the best of both worlds, although it obviously requires a fair level of cooperation among defendants. The court has discretion to grant or deny such a request.

— CHAPTER TWELVE —
Final Argument

I.   THE ROLE AND FUNCTION OF THE FINAL ARGUMENT

A.   The Whole Story

Final argument is the advocate's only opportunity to tell the story of the case in its entirety, without interruption, free from most constraining formalities. Unlike witness examinations, the final argument is delivered in counsel's own words and without the need intermittently to cede the stage to the opposition; unlike the opening statement, it is not bound by strict rules governing proper and improper content. In other words, final argument is the moment for pure advocacy, when all of the lawyer's organizational, analytic, interpretive, and forensic skills are brought to bear on the task of persuading the trier of fact.

If counsel has been successful, the opening statement painted a picture that the jury began to accept and internalize. The witnesses, documents, and exhibits fit neatly into that picture, reinforcing the image that counsel created. At final argument the attorney can then nail down the image by pointing out the crucial details, weaving together with witnesses' accounts, and explaining the significant connections. All three aspects of the trial—opening, witness examinations, and closing—should combine to evoke a single conception of events.

In sum, the final argument must tell the whole story of the case, but it cannot tell just any story. The final argument has to complement the portrait begun during the opening statement, and, even more important, must reflect and encompass the evidence in the case. This goal can be best accomplished only when the case is presented according to a well-defined theory.

B. Use of Theory and Theme

1. Theory

If nothing else, the final argument must communicate the advocate's theory of the case. Some witnesses can be disregarded, some details can be omitted, some legal issues can be overlooked, but the theory of the case is absolutely essential. This means that you must tell the jury, or the court, why your client is entitled to a verdict. A simple recitation of facts is not sufficient. Rather, the argument should bring together information from the various witnesses and exhibits in a way that creates only one result.

To be successful, the theory presented in a final argument must be logical, believable, and legally sufficient.

a. Logical

A trial theory, and consequently a final argument, must be logical in the sense that the component facts lead to the desired conclusions. It is often helpful, therefore, to reason backward, starting with the end result and then providing supportive facts. In the fire engine case the plaintiff's goal is to prove negligence. The starting point for her theory, then, is to ask which facts most strongly contribute to the conclusion that the defendant was negligent. Those facts will form the basis of the theory.

Reasoning in this manner, plaintiff's counsel will probably conclude that her strongest "theory" facts are: (1) the nature of the collision itself; (2) the presence of the fire truck; and (3) the defendant's hurried morning. Note that each fact has a logical connection to the conclusion of negligence: the collision was a classic "rear-ender," which shows that the defendant either failed to keep a proper interval or was driving too fast just before the accident. The presence of the fire truck explains why the plaintiff stopped her car and also demonstrates that the defendant failed to keep a proper lookout. The defendant's hurried morning adds proof that he was inattentive to the road.

Logic, however, is only the starting point for the final argument.

b. Believable

The most logical theory in the world will not win a case if the jury doesn't believe it. For a theory to be sound it must be based on facts that are likely to be accepted. There is no way to guarantee that the jury will accept your final argument; the purpose of the trial, after all, is to allow the judge or jury to decide which theory is more believable. It is possible, however, to construct a rough hierarchy of reliability that will assist you in evaluating the value of evidence for the purpose of the final argument. As is detailed below, the most believable evidence commonly takes the form of admissions from the opposing party, followed by the undisputed evidence that you produced. Concerning disputed evidence, it is generally best to rely first upon the common-sense value of the evidence and finally upon the credibility of witnesses.

i. Admissions

For the purpose of final argument, the most "believable" information is often that which was produced by the other side. The opposing party obviously would not offer self-damaging testimony unless it were unavoidably true. Consequently, it is particularly effective to argue against a party using his or her own words and documents. The defendant in the fire engine case, for instance, makes an admission when he testifies that he was late for a meeting at the time of the accident. This fact passes every test of believability when used in the plaintiff's final argument:

> How do we know that the defendant was distracted that morning? He said so himself. Just remember his own words. He said, "I woke up late that morning, and I knew that I would have to hurry up to get to my meeting."

This type of argument can continue, taking advantage of points that were scored on cross examination precisely for this purpose:

> The defendant's own words also tell us how preoccupied he was. After all, it was the defendant who testified about the importance of new clients. I'm sure you remember how he answered when I asked him if new clients mean money. He said, "Yes, that's what we're in business for." And then I asked him whether this particular new client was a valuable one, and he said, "Every new client is valuable." So there he was, late for his meeting with a valuable new client, worrying about how much money he might stand to lose.

Note that for the purpose of believability analysis, admissions need not be direct concessions, nor do they need to come in the form of testimony from the actual party. Anything can be exploited as an admission so long as it was produced by the other side. A strong closing argument can therefore make use of the opposition's witness testimony, exhibits, charts or graphs, tangible objects, or even comments made by the opposing counsel during the opening statement.

ii. Undisputed facts

Undisputed facts consist of the testimony, exhibits, and other evidence that you have offered and which the other side has not controverted. The opposition's decision not to produce contrary evidence greatly enhances the value of such undisputed facts.

While not quite so powerful as admissions from the other side, undisputed facts can provide a sturdy cornerstone for case theory and final argument:

> It is undisputed that there was a fire truck at the corner of Touhy and Sheridan. It is undisputed that the engine was answering a call. It is undisputed that other drivers slowed down or pulled over for the fire truck. It is undisputed that Lieutenant Sarah Sherman was driving the fire truck. And it is undisputed that fire department policy requires the siren to be used whenever an engine company is responding to a call. The defendant may claim that there was no siren, but he hasn't even tried to deny these uncontroverted facts.

Thus, undisputed facts are helpful not only in their own right, but also because they can be marshaled to cast light on disputed evidence.

iii. Common sense and experience

Admissions and undisputed facts are valuable precisely because it is impossible for the other side to take issue with them. Every trial, however, involves a core of facts and issues that are in dispute. It will be the rare final argument that can avoid entirely the necessity of explaining why the jury should prefer one version of contested facts over the other.

When key events or occurrences are in dispute, an effective final argument will first make use of common sense. As between any two stories or accounts, a jury is likely to choose the one that most closely agrees with its own experience. In structuring an argument, then, it is essential to bear in mind the relationship between your theory of the case and the jury's sense of what will or will not ring true.

A common-sense argument can be extremely helpful, as when defense counsel argues damages in the fire truck case:

> The plaintiff claims that her life's activities have been severely limited. Now pain is a subjective thing, so no one can step inside the plaintiff's body to see whether she is exaggerating. But we can look at her actions, and we

can interpret them in the light of our own common sense. The plaintiff went camping last Labor Day at Eagle River Falls. She carried a backpack and slept on the ground for four straight nights. She could have gone home after a night or two, but she chose to stay for the entire trip. Is this the action of someone who is in constant pain? Is this the action of someone whose life's activities are severely limited? Can you imagine how the plaintiff might have thought about such a trip: "Well, things are difficult here at home; I guess I'll go sleep on the ground for a long weekend." I don't want to minimize the plaintiff's real injuries, but common sense certainly tells us that someone in as much pain as she claims just wouldn't go camping for four nights.

iv. Credibility

The final method of establishing believability is to rely upon the credibility of the witnesses. While credibility is important, in relative terms it is probably the weakest method of proving your version of disputed facts.

There are two problems with credibility arguments. First, they rest almost entirely on subjective impressions. While an advocate may regard one witness as enormously more credible than another, there is no way to be sure that the fact-finder perceived the testimony in the same way. Second, credibility arguments ask the jury to think ill of a person, to conclude that she has omitted something, exaggerated, or even lied. Most lawyers consider it to be particularly difficult to persuade a jury to draw such adverse conclusions about any but the most disreputable witnesses.

This is not to say that counsel should always avoid credibility arguments, but only that they should be supported through the use of admissions, undisputed evidence, or invocations of common sense. For example:

> In addition to everything else, we know that the defendant didn't bother to have his brakes fixed just a week before the accident. Nate Lipton, a mechanic who operates his own garage, testified that he told the defendant that it was time to have his brakes relined. The defendant claims that Nate only suggested that he take care of the brakes within the next 10,000 miles. Well, who are we going to believe? Nate Lipton certainly has no reason to embellish his testimony. Unlike the defendant, Nate has no stake in the outcome of this case. But there is another reason

to believe Nate Lipton. The defendant admits that Nate mentioned the worn brakes, and it is undisputed that Nate Lipton has twenty years of experience as a mechanic. Our common sense tells us that no competent mechanic would open a brake drum, look at worn brakes, and then tell a driver that he could wait 10,000 miles to have them fixed. Why would Nate Lipton risk his own liability by suggesting that a customer drive out of the garage with badly worn brakes?

This credibility argument works because it is founded on the defendant's own admission as well as on common sense. In other words, the argument provides the jury with a reason to prefer the mechanic's testimony over the defendant's.

THE BASICS	

Keys to Reliability	
Admissions	• Statements by the opposing party or the opposing party's witnesses • Documents produced by the opposing party
Undisputed facts	• Evidence that has not been controverted
Common sense	• Evidence or conclusions that can be supported by common sense, plausibility, or everyday experience
Credibility	• Evidence that can be supported by the superior credibility, or undisputed neutrality, of a witness

c. Legally sufficient

The final cornerstone of a solid theory is legal sufficiency. The logic and believability of a final argument must lead to the desired legal result. In other words, a final argument must address the law as well as the facts.

A trial theory may be defined as the application of proven facts to legal issues. In the fire truck case, for example, the central legal issue is whether the defendant was negligent. The following might serve as an abbreviated statement of the plaintiff's trial theory:

We have proven that the defendant was distracted and rushed on the morning of the accident. He was negligent because he failed to pay sufficient attention to the road.

A lengthier theory statement would include a definition of negligence:

> Under the law, a driver must always exercise due care and caution when operating a motor vehicle. We have proven that the defendant failed to meet that standard on the morning of the accident. A driver exercising due care wouldn't rush down the road just because he was late to a meeting. A driver exercising ordinary caution wouldn't allow himself to become so distracted that he would miss seeing and hearing a fire engine. At a bare minimum, the standard of due care and caution must call for a driver to keep his eye on the traffic around him, but the defendant didn't slow down, even though every other car on the road either pulled over or came to a stop.

In either case, the thrust of the argument is to explain not only that the defendant was wrong, but that the defendant was wrong in a way that should result in a legal consequence.

Lawyers commonly use jury instructions as a framework for discussing legal issues during final argument.[1]

2. Theme

A good trial theme provides an incentive for the entry of a verdict in your client's favor. In addition to being logical and believable, a trial theme invokes shared beliefs and common values. Just as a theory explains why the verdict is legally necessary, the theme explains why the verdict is morally desirable.

Your trial theme should be a constant presence throughout the final argument. Unlike opening statement and witness examinations, where a theme can only be used intermittently, the entire final argument can be organized so as to emphasize your theme. You can begin with a statement of the theme and constantly return to it in each segment of the argument.

In the fire engine case, for instance, plaintiff's counsel's first words on final argument could be, "This accident occurred because the defendant was too busy to be careful." Plaintiff's attorney might then proceed through the argument by discussing issues such as the defendant's morning preparations, the accident itself, defendant's post-accident conduct, defendant's shoddy brake-repair record, and finally plaintiff's damages. At each stage of the argument, plaintiff's attorney would find a way to advert to the theme. In some situations

---

1. The uses, and occasional misuses, of jury instructions ar discussed below in Section IV F, *infra*, at p. 431.

the usage would be obvious: "The defendant didn't bother to have his brakes repaired because he was just too busy." At other points in the argument the reference might be somewhat more subtle. Consider the question of the siren:

> The defendant claims that the fire engine was not sounding its siren. But the defendant's claim cannot be believed. Remember that the fire truck was being driven by Lieutenant Sarah Sherman. Lieutenant Sherman, as we heard, is a decorated firefighter and the first woman ever to be promoted to lieutenant in this city. Not only is she well-trained, but she now teaches courses at the fire academy. Lieutenant Sherman knows full well that fire trucks are required to sound their sirens whenever responding to a call. It is part of her job to comply with that regulation. For Lieutenant Sherman, being busy and being careful are the same thing. We know that she was careful because she was busy.

As effective as the recurrent use of a theme can be on final argument, take care not to overdo it. No matter how compelling it is the first time, any single-sentence statement can become trite or bothersome if it is repeated *ad nauseam*. For this reason it is often wise to utilize the spirit of the theme in place of the mantra itself. For example, plaintiff's counsel in the fire truck case might describe the plaintiff's own attentiveness to the road by saying something like the following:

> She was not in a hurry that morning. She was on her way to the Art Institute, but she had over an hour until it opened. She had no reason to speed and every reason to stop as soon as she saw and heard the fire truck. There was nothing on her mind to distract her from her careful driving.

This argument employs the trial theme but does not repeat it, thus taking advantage of its moral force while avoiding an annoying echo.

C.   What Makes It Argument

Recall the cardinal rule of opening statements that you may not argue. In final argument, on the other hand, you may, should, and must argue if you are serious about winning your case. The gloves are off, and the limitations are removed, but what precisely distinguishes argument from mere presentation of the facts? The following are some of the most useful elements of "argument."

1. Conclusions

The attorney in final argument is free to draw and urge conclusions based upon the evidence. A conclusion is a result, consequence, or repercussion that follows from the evidence in the case.

In our fire engine case, for example, the plaintiff will no doubt offer this evidence: the defendant woke up late on the morning of the accident; he had an important meeting to attend that morning; he did not have sufficient time to get to the meeting; he stood to lose a potential new client (and therefore a lot of money) if he arrived late.

From this evidence several conclusions *may* be drawn: The defendant was in a hurry. The defendant was preoccupied. The defendant was trying to plan for his meeting while driving because he wouldn't have time to plan for it after he arrived at the office. The defendant allowed his thoughts to drift to the point that he became careless and inattentive to the road.

All of the above conclusions would be permissible in argument even though there is unlikely to be direct proof of any of them. That is what makes them conclusions; they follow logically, although not necessarily, from admitted evidence. In other words, the conclusion might or might not be accurate. It is possible for a driver to be exceptionally careful, even though late for a meeting. It is the force of advocacy, advanced through argument, that can lead the trier of fact to draw one conclusion as opposed to another.

Thus, it is not sufficient for a final argument to draw, or even urge, conclusions. The argument must go on to explain why the desired conclusions are the correct ones.

2. Inferences

While a final argument can and should include broad conclusions, it may also include the sort of narrow conclusions commonly known as inferences. An inference is a deduction drawn from the existence of a known fact. In other words, the inferred fact need not be proven so long as it is a common-sense consequence of some established fact.

Turning again to the fire engine case, assume that the defendant testified that his parking garage was located two blocks from his office. From that known fact it could be inferred that it would take him at least five minutes to walk from the garage to his office. It could further be inferred that the defendant knew how long it would take him to reach his office. Such inferences, based upon a combination of proven fact and everyday experience, could be used to support the larger conclusion that the defendant was in a rush at the time of the accident.

An inference will be accepted only if it is well-grounded in common understanding. For that reason it is often necessary or desirable to explain the basis of all but the most obvious inferences. For example, everyone will be willing to infer a child's age from knowledge of her grade in school. There is no need to explain that third graders are typically eight or nine years old. Other inferences, however, may be more complicated.

Recall the evidence in the fire truck case that the engine was being driven by veteran firefighter Sarah Sherman. It can be inferred from this fact that the truck's siren was sounding just before the accident, but the inference will profit from some explanation:

> The fire truck was being driven by Lieutenant Sarah Sherman, a ten-year veteran of the force. The first woman ever to be promoted to that rank, Lieutenant Sherman did not get where she is today by being careless or by ignoring departmental rules. A fire truck is required to sound its alarm whenever it is responding to a call. This is a simple safety precaution that alerts other vehicles to clear the way. It just doesn't make sense to argue, as the defendant claims, that Lieutenant Sherman would have carelessly neglected to use her siren that day at the intersection of Sheridan and Touhy.

The proven facts include Lieutenant Sherman's background and the departmental rules. The inference is that she sounded her siren on the date in question. The explanation—that the siren is a necessary safety precaution—bolsters the inference.

3. Details and Circumstantial Evidence

Final argument is counsel's only opportunity to explain the relevance and consequences of circumstantial evidence. Much of the art of direct and cross examination consists of the accumulation of details that lead to a certain conclusion or result. The knowledge of the individual witnesses, not to mention trial strategy and luck, may result in the scattering of such details throughout the trial. It is during final argument that the attorney can reassemble the details so that they lead to the desired result.

In a burglary prosecution, for example, there may have been no eyewitnesses to give direct evidence against the defendant. A number of witnesses, however, might provide detailed circumstantial evidence. Perhaps one witness saw the defendant running from the scene of the crime, while another found a single shoe in the doorway of the burglarized house. Yet a third witness might have heard the defendant complaining about her need for a new radio. The crime victim could testify that an expensive radio was taken in the burglary. Finally, on cross examination the defendant could be asked to try on the shoe to show that it fits.

None of these circumstantial details constitutes direct evidence of the defendant's guilt, particularly when they are adduced individually through the testimony of four or five different witnesses. They can, however, be organized into a powerful narrative leading irresistibly to conviction. Moreover, the circumstantial evidence becomes even more persuasive when all of the connections are explained in argument:

> No one saw the defendant commit the burglary, but the surrounding details point in only one direction. She was seen running, not walking, from the crime scene just after the house was robbed. That alone does not make her guilty, but it does tell us that she had a reason to run away from that house. Now consider all of the other evidence. She wanted a new radio so badly that she complained about it to her friends, and the largest item taken in the burglary was a brand new radio. It seems as though the burglar left a shoe behind that was caught in the door, and that shoe just happens to fit perfectly on the defendant's foot. It all falls together: The house was robbed, the defendant ran; she wanted a radio, a radio was stolen; the burglar left a shoe behind, the shoe fits the defendant. Perhaps one of these facts could be a coincidence, but all together they add up to guilt.

Trial lawyers understand that circumstantial evidence is probative and reliable. In the popular mind, however, the term "circumstantial" is often equated with doubtful or equivocal. It is therefore desirable to use final argument to explain the value and credibility of circumstantial evidence. This is frequently done through the use of an analogy, some of which have virtually become all-purpose classics:

> While no one saw the defendant commit the burglary, the circumstantial evidence is overwhelming. As the court will instruct you, circumstantial evidence can be just as credible as eyewitness testimony. We can all recognize the value of circumstantial evidence based on our experiences in everyday life. For example, think of the last time that it snowed in the night. If you looked out on your front yard in the morning and saw footprints in the snow, then you

knew for sure that someone had walked across your lawn. Even if you didn't actually see anybody, the footprints were circumstantial—and absolutely reliable—evidence that someone had been there. In this case, even though no one saw the defendant, there is no doubt that she left her footprints for everyone to see.

Analogies have many other uses at trial, some of which are detailed in the next section.

4. Analogies, Allusions, and Stories

a. Analogies

An analogy can explain human conduct through reference to everyday human behavior. A witness's testimony can be strengthened or diminished by comparing her version of events to some widely understood experience or activity.

Suppose that the defendant in the fire engine case testified that he saw the fire truck but that he did not slow down because the siren was not sounding. Plaintiff's attorney will want to characterize this conduct as unreasonable. Counsel can, of course, simply say as much: The defendant should have slowed down, and it was unreasonable to keep driving once he saw the fire truck. From a purely legal perspective, that should be sufficient to establish negligence. It could be more persuasive, however, to use an analogy:

> The defendant admits that he saw the fire truck but says that there was no siren, and so he did not feel it necessary to stop. Even if you believe him that he didn't hear the siren, there is nothing reasonable about conduct like that. By continuing to drive at the same speed, he was playing Russian roulette with the safety of every other driver on the road. Simple attentiveness to safety tells us that we should slow down when we see an emergency vehicle. Just because he didn't hear the siren doesn't mean that it wasn't sounding. You wouldn't expect someone to pick up a gun and fire it at somebody, claiming, "Well, I didn't see any bullets." Of course not. A gun is dangerous, and simple prudence means that you should always treat it as though it is loaded. Well, cars can be dangerous too. As soon as he saw that fire truck, the defendant should have recognized the possibility that traffic would slow or stop. He should have recognized the possibility that it was answering a call, whether he heard the siren or not.

Continuing to drive, without at least slowing down, was the equivalent of pointing a loaded gun down the road.

The above excerpt takes conduct that everyone will recognize as unreasonable and explains why the defendant's conduct falls into the same category.

Analogies can support testimony as well as deride it, and they can be short as well as extended. Consider the following example from defense counsel's final argument:

Fire trucks use their sirens to tell traffic to stop. We have all seen fire engines on the street that weren't responding to calls. Without their sirens they are just part of traffic. If you look up into the sky and see an airplane flying by, you don't say, "I'd better take cover; it's going to crash."

While analogies can be very powerful, there is always the danger that they can be inverted and exploited by the other side. Thus, so long as the opposing counsel has yet to argue, care must be taken to ensure that any analogies are "airtight." For the same reason, plaintiff's counsel often reserves the use of analogies until rebuttal when the defendant will no longer be able to reply.[2]

b. Allusions

An allusion is a literary or similar reference that adds persuasive force to an argument. In earlier days, before the advent of mass culture, trial lawyers' allusions were most commonly drawn from Shakespeare or the Bible. Perhaps the most frequently used quotation from Shakespeare is the suggestion that a witness "doth protest too much."[3] Today references are just as likely to be taken from motion pictures, television, popular songs, fairy tales, or, alas, advertisements. Defense counsel in the fire engine case might disparage the plaintiff's injury claim with a reference to "The Princess and the Pea":

The plaintiff claims that her life's activities are severely limited. She says that sometimes she can't even sleep. But last Labor Day she went camping at Eagle River Falls where she slept on the ground for four nights. Now that her case is on trial she claims that she was in pain, but the truth is that she stayed at the campground for the whole weekend. We all know the story about the princess who could feel a pea even though it was underneath a

---

2. Regarding the uses of rebuttal argument, see Section II C, *infra* at p. 410.

3. "The lady doth protest too much, methinks." William Shakespeare, *Hamlet*, Act III, scene 2, line 242.

stack of mattresses. But our law doesn't allow recovery for that sort of super-sensitivity. And this plaintiff, who had no hesitation about sleeping on the ground, certainly can't complain about peas under the mattress today. You can't be a backpacker when you want to and then a princess when the time comes to try for damages.

Advertising slogans are commonly used during final argument. For all that they lack in elegance and literary merit, they have the advantage of familiarity and catchiness.

c. Stories

Stories, in the form of either hypotheticals or anecdotes, can be used effectively in final argument. It is permissible to illustrate an argument with a hypothetical story so long as the story is based on facts that are in evidence. Again, from the plaintiff's argument in the fire engine case:

Imagine what the defendant's morning was like. His alarm clock didn't go off. He woke up, looked at the clock, and began to panic. He was late, and if he missed the meeting with this new client, he would lose money and damage his position with his firm. He rushed into the bathroom to shower and shave. Maybe he cut himself, as happens so often when you hurry. Think of all the things that people do when they are rushed in the morning. No time to read the newspaper. No time to eat breakfast. No time to stop for gas, even if the tank is low. You can be sure that the defendant hurried to his car that morning. This was not the day for a leisurely drive. This was a day to push the speed limit and to run yellow lights.

This reconstruction of the defendant's morning is hypothetical in that the details are all suppositions. It is proper argument because the entire story is derived from the defendant's own testimony.

Another form of argumentative storytelling is the illustrative anecdote. An anecdote is a sort of litigator's fable or folk tale, again used to elaborate on a theme in the case. Attorneys frequently draw upon real or imagined family wisdom:

My grandfather was a modest man who cared very little for life's material rewards. Although he loved other people's celebrations, he never wanted anything for himself. Especially birthday presents. "Please don't give me anything," he would say, "because every day is my birthday." When I got a little older I asked my mother why Grandpa always said that. She told me that Grandpa once almost died from a heart attack, and after that he considered every day to be a brand new gift from God; in other words, a birthday. I always thought that Grandpa was the happiest man in the world because every day was his birthday.

I think that we would all like to view life the way that Grandpa did, but the plaintiff will never be able to. She wakes up every morning in pain. Every movement must be measured and gauged. One wrong move and she risks having to spend the day in bed, or even going to the hospital. She can't think of every day as her birthday because each day is hell.

My grandfather had a joy in life and peace of mind that was an inspiration to everyone who knew him. More than anything else, that is the possibility that the defendant has taken from the plaintiff. She will never know simple pleasures again.

The use of the story serves to humanize the plaintiff. It is always difficult to ask for money, but to compare the plaintiff with the kindly, unassuming grandfather demonstrates both the severity of her loss and the relatively modest nature of her claim.

5. Credibility and Motive

Counsel may also use the final argument to comment on, and compare, the motive and credibility of witnesses. Many, perhaps most, trials involve competing renditions of past events, which the trier of fact must resolve in order to reach a verdict. Final argument is the only time when the attorney may confront directly the character of the witnesses and explain why some should be believed and others discounted.

Perhaps a witness for the opposing party was impeached through the use of a prior inconsistent statement[4] or omission.[5] While the inconsistency will to one degree or another speak for itself, the final argument can underscore just exactly how it undermines the witness's credibility. The following example is taken from the defense argument in a robbery prosecution:

We all heard the victim claim that the robber was easily recognizable by his long hair and moustache. But just thirty minutes after the robbery he was interviewed by Officer Larry Pinsky. At that time the robber was still at large, and the victim had every reason to give Officer

---

4. See Chapter 5, Section II, *supra* at p. 124.
5. See Chapter 5, Section III, *supra* at p. 142.

Pinsky the best description he could. That description is right here in the police report. Officer Pinsky got height, weight, age, race, clothing—but not one word about long hair and a moustache. That's right, a short thirty minutes after the crime the victim didn't have a word to say about long hair or a moustache.

What happened? How did long hair and a moustache get added to the description? Unfortunately, the police made a suggestion. They drove the victim around the neighborhood, pointing out "possible suspects." And to his misfortune, my client was one of the people they pointed out. He had long hair and a moustache, so those facts were added to the description at that time. I am not saying that the victim is lying, but that second description is not reliable; it was suggested by the police. If the robber really did have long hair and a moustache, the victim would have told that to Officer Pinsky right off the bat.

Witness examinations can bring out impeaching facts, and the opening statement can use apposition to contrast the credibility of different witnesses. But only on closing argument can counsel make direct comparisons. Consider the question of the siren as plaintiff's counsel might argue it in the fire truck case:

The plaintiff told you that she stopped because she saw a fire truck, which was flashing its warning lights and sounding its siren. The defendant has to concede that the truck was there, but he claims that it was not using its warning signals. Well, was there a siren or wasn't there? Who should you believe?

The defendant's story just isn't credible. Everyone agrees that the fire truck entered the intersection on its way to answer a fire scene. You have even seen the transcript of the 911 call that the truck was responding to. A fire truck would have to be using its siren under those circumstances. Only the most negligent firefighter would speed toward an intersection without sounding the siren, but this truck was being driven by Lieutenant Sarah Sherman, one of the most decorated firefighters on the force. Which is more likely, that Lieutenant Sherman neglected such an elementary duty or that the defendant is wrong about the siren?

The plaintiff heard the siren and stopped her car. The other drivers must have heard it as well since all of the other traffic pulled over. Of course, it is possible that the defendant testified the way he did because he simply didn't hear the siren, but that is another story. Why didn't he hear the siren? Why didn't he stop his car? For the answers to those questions we have to look at the events of his day and why he was "too busy to be careful."

Finally, motive can be argued on the basis either of proven facts or of logical inferences. Counsel may tell the jury why a witness would exaggerate, waffle, conceal information, quibble, or lie. The suggested reasons need not be based on outright admissions so long as they follow rationally from the testimony in the case.

6. Demeanor

It is fair game in final argument to comment on a witness's demeanor. Demeanor arguments are frequently negative in nature since it is easier to characterize untrustworthy conduct. An argument that counsel's own witness "looked like he was telling the truth" may tend to seem insincere or overprotective. Negative comments, on the other hand, can be effective so long as they are adequately based on observable fact.

It is not uncommon, for instance, to remark upon a witness's refusal to give a simple answer or to make an obvious concession. Similarly, counsel might mention that a witness averted his eyes or fidgeted on the stand as though hiding something. Comparable points can be made about witnesses who sneer, lose their tempers, scowl, or become impatient.

One caveat: Demeanor argument is based strictly on perception, and there is little way to ensure that counsel's perception of the witness will be the same as the judge's or jury's. Conduct that the attorney sees as evidence of deception might be regarded by a juror as a reasonable response to unfair questioning. Be careful. Demeanor argument can be best used only when the witness's behavior has been blatant and unambiguous.

7. Refutation

Another distinguishing feature of argument is refutation of opposing positions. Opening statements and witness examinations may recite and elicit facts that are contrary to the opposition case, but final argument can refute it directly by pointing out errors, inconsistencies, implausibilities, and contradictions. Consider this extract from the plaintiff's final argument in the fire engine case:

> The defendant claims that he was not distracted on the morning of the accident, but that cannot be true. We know that he woke up late and that he had an important meeting

to attend with a potential new client. New clients mean money, so missing the meeting, or even being late, could have had a devastating impact on the defendant's job.

By the time he got ready for work and got to his car, he was already at least thirty minutes behind schedule. By the time he reached the corner of Sheridan and Touhy, he was still running over twenty minutes late—he still had to drive downtown, get to his garage, park his car, and proceed to his office, all in less than twenty minutes.

There is no plausible way for the defendant to deny that he was preoccupied and in a hurry. His mind must have been elsewhere; certainly it wasn't on his driving. Every driver saw and heard the fire truck, but not the defendant. Every driver stopped or pulled over, but not the defendant. Those were not the acts of a careful man.

One last fact shows just how absorbed the defendant was. Right after the accident he jumped out of his car and took out his cell phone. He called his office. That meeting was so important to him that he didn't even check to see if the other driver was hurt. That meeting was more important to him than a possible injury. No wonder it was more important to him than safe, careful driving.

8. Application of Law

Final argument provides the attorney an occasion to apply the law to the facts of the case. Discussion of law is extremely limited during the opening statement and all but forbidden during witness examinations, but it is a staple of the final argument. In most jurisdictions counsel may read from the jury instructions[6] and explain exactly how the relevant law dictates a verdict for her client.

9. Moral Appeal

Final argument allows counsel to elaborate on the moral theme of the case. Recall that a trial theme states, usually in a single sentence, a compelling moral basis for a verdict in your client's favor. The theme invokes shared values, civic virtues, or common motivations. The theme can be stated during the opening statement and alluded to in witness examinations, but it can be hammered home in the final argument. Again, consider the plaintiff's final argument in the fire truck case:

---

6.   See Section IV F, *infra* at p. 431.

The defendant was "too busy to be careful." We know that from his actions and their consequences. But what was he busy doing? He was rushing to a meeting for the sole purpose of increasing his income. He was worrying about money, not about safety. It is true that he was late, but that was no one's fault but his own. And once he was late he was so obsessed with getting to the meeting that he threw caution out the window. He was so "busy" that he didn't even care to see whether the plaintiff was injured. No, that business meeting was all that mattered. Well, everyone is at risk when drivers behave that way. No one is safe on the road when people care more about their meetings than they do about the way they are driving. You cannot allow someone to think that it is all right to be "too busy to be careful."

Admittedly, the moral dimension of an intersection accident is not overpowering. Cases involving crimes, frauds, civil rights violations, child custody, reckless conduct, and even breach of contract will provide more fertile ground for the assertion of a moral theme. Nonetheless, even the most mundane case can be approached from the perspective of rectitude by explaining how and why your client's position makes sense for reasons other than strict legality.

THE BASICS

What Makes It Argument
• Conclusions
• Inferences
• Tying up circumstantial evidence
• Connecting details
• Analogies, allusions, and stories
• Comparing motives and credibility
• Commenting on demeanor
• Applying the law
• Overt moral appeals
• Referring to jury instructions
• Asking for a specific verdict

II. FORMAT

In most jurisdictions the parties' final arguments are divided into three distinct segments, which are presented in the following order: the plaintiff's (or prosecutor's) argument in chief, the defendant's argument in chief, and plaintiff's rebuttal.[7] While general principles of argument apply to all three, each segment also has its own unique set of uses, applications, and special techniques.

A. Plaintiff's Argument in Chief

The plaintiff (or prosecutor) must use argument in chief to define the issues and lay out the entire theory of the case. The plaintiff's argument in chief will not be successful unless it provides the jury with compelling reasons to find for the plaintiff on every necessary issue.

Because of the nature of our litigation system, the plaintiff's or prosecutor's initial argument must be comprehensive. The plaintiff in a civil case must usually prevail by a preponderance of the evidence, and the prosecutor in a criminal case must present proof beyond a reasonable doubt. In either situation the burdened party must establish all of the elements of her cause of action. Thus, a civil plaintiff must establish all of the elements of the particular tort or contract action and a prosecutor must prove all of the elements of the charged crime. Failing to address an element can be fatal.

In contrast, and as will be discussed below in more detail, the defendant may often be considerably more selective during final argument. The defense can frequently prevail simply by disproving a single element of the plaintiff's case and therefore need not address issues as comprehensively as the plaintiff.

To counterbalance this advantage a plaintiff's attorneys will often use the final argument to issue a series of challenges to the defendant, thus drawing the defense into a discussion of issues that they might prefer to leave alone. A prime example of such a challenge commonly arises in tort litigation, as in this abbreviated example from the plaintiff's argument in the fire engine case:

> We have seen that the defendant had a duty to drive safely on the public roadway and that he breached that duty by failing to look where he was going. There is no doubt that he struck the plaintiff's car from behind and that the accident severely injured the plaintiff. We have discussed

---

7. In a few jurisdictions the plaintiff is not allowed to argue first; thus, there are only two components: defendant's argument and plaintiff's rebuttal. The terms used to describe the components of final argument also vary from jurisdiction to jurisdiction. What we have called plaintiff's argument in chief, for example, is often called plaintiff's "opening," notwithstanding the potential for confusion with the opening statement. Final argument itself is also frequently referred to as closing argument, summation, or, in the United Kingdom, final address.

her injuries at length, so you know just how crippling they have been.

The defendant, of course, is going to tell you that the accident wasn't his fault. But the one thing he cannot deny is how much harm he caused to the plaintiff. I invite the defendant's attorney to stand before you to discuss damages. If he thinks that the plaintiff wasn't hurt, let him come forward and say so.

The plaintiff can win only by establishing all of the elements of the specific tort; in negligence cases the classical elements are duty, breach of duty, cause in fact, proximate cause, and damages. The defendant, on the other hand, can win by disproving any single element. For that reason defendants in many cases prefer to emphasize the issues of breach of duty or proximate cause (where they think they can win) and to avoid discussing damages (where the only result might be sympathy for the plaintiff). Plaintiff's counsel in the above example sought to cut off that route by issuing a specific challenge to address damages.

B. Defendant's Argument in Chief

The defendant generally has substantially more latitude than the plaintiff in determining the content of the argument in chief. While the plaintiff must address every element, the defendant is usually free to "cherry pick," selecting only those elements or issues in which counsel has the most confidence. The defense theory, of course, must be comprehensive in the sense that it explains all of the relevant evidence, but its legal thrust may be significantly more pointed than the plaintiff's.[8]

The defining characteristic of the defendant's argument in chief is that it is sandwiched between the two plaintiff's arguments. Defense counsel must respond to the plaintiff's argument in chief but will not be able to respond to rebuttal.

1. Responding to the Plaintiff's Argument in Chief

It is essential that the defense reply directly to the plaintiff's argument in chief. After listening to the plaintiff's prolonged excoriation of the defendant, every reasonable jury will immediately want to know what the defendant has to say in return. This does not

---

8. A defendant is certainly not required to focus on a single element or issue. The plaintiff's case may be vulnerable in many areas, and the defendant may wish to address them all. Furthermore, concentration on one element can be risky, as that approach may concentrate too many eggs in a single basket.

mean that defense counsel should adopt the plaintiff's organization or respond point by point, but the defendant's argument cannot be entirely divorced from the structure that the plaintiff creates.

At a minimum, the defendant should deny the specific charges leveled in the plaintiff's argument. It is a natural human response to deny unfair or untrue accusations. The jury will expect as much from a wrongly blamed defendant. Unless there is a good reason for doing otherwise, the denial should come early in the defendant's argument.

In a more general vein, the defendant should usually devote some time to debunking the plaintiff's case. While the defense may well have an extremely strong affirmative case of its own, it is quite risky to allow the plaintiff's assertions to stand unrebutted. The precise handling of the various arguments will be discussed below in the section on organization.

Finally, the watchword for the defendant's argument in chief is flexibility. While the plaintiff may have the luxury of composing her entire final argument,[9] the defendant must always be alert to new issues and nuances raised once the arguments have begun. It simply will not do for defense counsel to deliver a set piece. The defendant's argument is most effective to the extent that it rebuts the plaintiff's case as presented at the end of the trial. A particularly effective device is the "reverse analogy." In the following example assume that plaintiff's counsel used her argument in chief to tell a story about her modest grandfather, who took such delight in life's simple pleasures.[10] The defense attorney can attempt to turn the story around:

> The plaintiff's lawyer spoke to us at some length about his grandfather, and it was a moving story about a straight-forward man who regarded every day as his birthday. But you have to wonder what Grandpa would have thought about the plaintiff's case, which is anything but straight-forward. Don't you think that Grandpa would say that anyone who goes camping for four days can't be in too much pain? And don't you think that Grandpa would say that anyone who sleeps on the ground and carries a backpack can't be too limited? And, most of all, don't you think that Grandpa would say that no one would wait two

---

9. The plaintiff, of course, will not make final preparations for the final argument until the very end of the trial. However well prepared you may be beforehand, it is still necessary to hear all of the evidence and to know which jury instructions will be given.

10. An example of the plaintiff's use of the "modest grandfather" story is found in Section I C(4)(c), *supra* at p. 400.

months to see her doctor if she were really experiencing medical difficulties?

The defendant's attorney had no way of anticipating the grandfather story but was nonetheless able to use it as an effective reverse analogy. This is not to say that defense counsel should defer preparation until the end of the plaintiff's argument, but rather that good preparation includes the ability to modify one's original plan in order to accommodate the plaintiff's remarks.

2. Anticipating Rebuttal

The greatest difficulty for defense counsel is knowing that she cannot speak again following the plaintiff's rebuttal. The plaintiff may comment on, criticize, or even ridicule defendant's argument, but the defendant may not respond. Defense counsel may have perfectly good answers for everything that the plaintiff says on rebuttal, but no matter. The usual rule is that the defense may argue only once.

Under these circumstances it is extremely important that counsel do whatever is possible to blunt the rebuttal in advance. One approach is to anticipate and reply specifically to the plaintiff's possible rebuttal arguments, as in this example from the defendant's argument in the fire engine case:

> This entire accident could have been avoided if the plaintiff had only pulled over instead of slamming on her brakes in the middle of the street. If she didn't cause the accident, she at least contributed to it. Now when plaintiff's counsel argues again, she may claim that there was no time to pull over. Don't believe it. There was really plenty of time to pull over. Let's look at the evidence...

This approach has its drawbacks, not the least of which is the necessity of suggesting that, in fact, the plaintiff may not have had enough time to pull her car to the side. In any event, it may be just as effective to make the argument without referring to rebuttal.

Most lawyers choose to anticipate rebuttal only in the general sense, making sure to explain the phenomenon of rebuttal to the jury:

> When I am done speaking, the plaintiff's attorney will have another opportunity to argue. That is called rebuttal. Following rebuttal, however, I will not be allowed to stand before you again. The rules of procedure allow me to speak to you only once. It is not that I don't want to speak again, or that I will have no responses to what plaintiff's

counsel says, but only that I will not have the opportunity to give you my responses.

I have only one request to make of you. When plaintiff's counsel returns to argue, please bear in mind that, whatever she says, I will not be able to answer. I think you know from the evidence that I will have answers to her rebuttal argument. So please keep what I have said in mind and provide those answers for me.

The timing of this aspect of the argument is important. Because it relates solely to the rebuttal, it obviously is preferable to make these remarks near the end of the defendant's argument in chief. On the other hand, placing them at the very end would deprive the argument of a strong finish. Thus, it is generally best to use the discussion of rebuttal as the penultimate point, saving the final moment for the most compelling substantive argument.

C.   Plaintiff's Rebuttal

The plaintiff or prosecutor, as the burdened party, is generally afforded the opportunity to present the last argument. Rebuttal, therefore, is a powerful tool. The plaintiff can reply to all of the defendant's arguments and contentions, but the defendant must stand mute in response. Everyone likes to have the last word, and the rules of procedure in most jurisdictions guarantee that right to the plaintiff.

Effective use of rebuttal can be elusive. While the plaintiff's argument in chief can be completely planned in advance, and the defendant's argument in chief can be mostly planned, rebuttal must be delivered almost extemporaneously. Preparation for rebuttal typically takes place while plaintiff's counsel listens to the defendant's argument in chief. Nonetheless, there are certain principles that can be applied to make rebuttal more forceful and compelling. The most important principle of rebuttal is to organize it according to the plaintiff's own theory of the case.

A common approach to rebuttal is simply to make notes of the defense arguments and then to reply to the most important of them in the order in which they were delivered. This technique is easy to use, and it has the virtue of minimizing the potential for overlooking arguments. Its vice, however, is that it organizes the rebuttal according to the defendant's agenda rather than the plaintiff's. It also tends to promote a boring delivery since a rebuttal that follows this approach is likely to fall into a repetitive cadence of short paragraphs, each one beginning, "The defendant also argued…"

A more effective technique involves matching the defendant's arguments to the major propositions in the plaintiff's own case. To do this, plaintiff's counsel needs only to prepare a truncated outline of the three or four most important, or hotly contested, issues in the case, leaving a blank half-page or so under each heading. In this manner, four major arguments can be spread over two sheets of paper and can be arranged in the order most advantageous to the plaintiff. Then, as defense counsel argues, plaintiff's attorney can write her notes under the appropriate heading. When it comes time to deliver rebuttal, plaintiff's counsel will have automatically organized her notes of the defendant's remarks according to the plaintiff's own structure. The rebuttal can then be delivered topically, without regard to the order of argument used by the defendant.

A second principle of rebuttal is to present the plaintiff's case in an affirmative light. Even when it is well-organized, rebuttal is weakened if it becomes nothing more than a series of retorts. As with all argument it is more effective to present the positive side of your own case, and this is particularly important when you represent the burdened party. Consequently, even in rebuttal, every position should be framed as a constructive statement of the plaintiff's own theory, with the refutation of the defense being used to explain further or elaborate on the plaintiff's case. Consider this short example from the rebuttal in the fire engine case:

> I would like to talk to you once again about damages. I'm sure that you remember the plaintiff's own testimony about her efforts to cope with her injuries. She has done everything possible to bring her life back to normal. She is a courageous woman who won't give up. That is why it is particularly unfair to see defense counsel trying to exploit the plaintiff's camping trip to Eagle River Falls. Of course she tried to go camping. What does the defendant want her to do, give up on life and just sit at home? Unfortunately, her efforts didn't work out. As she told you, the camping trip was pure hell. She suffered every day, and she had to stay on her back in the tent for hours at a time. Why didn't she come home early? Because she and her family had all come in the same car, and she didn't want to ruin the trip for everyone else. Sure she tried to enjoy camping. But that only proves how brave and determined she is, not that she wasn't injured.

Many lawyers attempt to save a single, devastating argument for rebuttal, on the assumption that it will be even more effective if it stands unanswered. There is, no doubt, a great deal of truth to this theory, as it deprives the defendant of all opportunity to respond.

One caveat, however, is necessary. Rebuttal is technically limited to issues that were addressed during the defense argument in chief. If, for whatever reason, defense counsel does not raise a particular issue, then it is possible that the court will sustain an objection to its coverage on rebuttal.

Thus, it is inherently risky for the plaintiff to "sandbag" by completely omitting a subject from the argument in chief. Suppose, for example, the plaintiff in the fire engine case decided to defer all discussion of damages until rebuttal, thereby precluding the defendant from replying to the plaintiff's specific arguments. The defendant, in turn, could decide not to address damages at all. Some courts, then, would refuse to allow the plaintiff to raise damages for the first time on rebuttal, and the plaintiff would be entirely precluded from presenting any argument on damages.[11]

The rule requiring rebuttal to be within the scope of the defendant's argument is enforced with varying degrees of strictness from court to court. It is generally safe to assume, however, that the rule will be applied more rigidly to topics (such as damages) than to lines of argument (such as elaboration on a theme). Consequently, it usually is not risky to withhold the use of an analogy or story until rebuttal, thereby preventing the defendant from "reversing" it.

D. Variations

It is always within the discretion of the court to alter the usual order of argument so as to reflect the actual burden of proof in the particular case. In cases involving counterclaims or affirmative defenses, the defendant may be allowed to present the first and last arguments or may be given a sur-rebuttal to follow the plaintiff's rebuttal. In multiparty cases the court will determine the order in which the various plaintiffs and defendants will proceed.

It is also the judge's prerogative to apportion the time for argument, although the court may not deny a party an effective opportunity to argue its case. Finally, some courts do not provide automatically for rebuttal, but rather require the plaintiff affirmatively to reserve time from the argument in chief.

---

11. Note that the rule is that rebuttal may be used only to respond to issues covered during the defendant's argument in chief. Thus, even if the plaintiff had addressed damages during her argument in chief, the omission of the issue from the defendant's argument in chief would still technically rule out damages as a subject for rebuttal. Unlike the "sandbagging" situation, however, the plaintiff in this supposition did not forego the opportunity to discuss damages at the outset.

III. STRUCTURE

The structure of the final argument must be developed for maximum persuasive weight. The central thrust of the final argument must always be to provide reasons—logical, moral, legal, emotional—for the entry of a verdict in your client's favor. Every aspect of the final argument should contribute in some way to the completion of the sentence, "We win because..." In the broadest sense, of course, the desired conclusion should simply follow from the facts and law of the case. Few cases, however, will go to trial unless the facts are capable of multiple interpretations. Effective argument therefore places a premium on arrangement and explanation.

The use of topical organization is the guiding principle in the structure of final arguments. The following section will discuss the various methods of employing topical organization as well as the drawbacks and advantages of alternative structures.

A.   Topical Organization

The importance of topical organization in final argument cannot be overemphasized. Seemingly natural methods of organization, such as chronology and witness listing, will not present the evidence in its most persuasive form. Topical organization, on the other hand, allows counsel to determine the best way to address the issues in the case. Topical organization can use, or combine, any of the following strategies.

1. Issues

One of the simplest and most effective forms of organization is to divide the case into a series of discrete factual or legal issues. Large issues, such as liability and damages, are obvious, but they are also so broad as to provide relatively little help in ordering an argument. It is more useful to think of issues as narrower propositions of fact or law.

In the fire engine case, for example, the plaintiff might organize the liability section of her argument according to these factual issues: (1) the defendant's hurried morning; (2) the siren; and (3) the events of the accident. The first section of the argument would emphasize the reasons for the defendant's inattention; the second segment would explain why all of the other traffic stopped for the fire truck (and why the jury should not believe the defendant's claim that there was no siren); and the third segment would finally describe the actual collision.

A fourth portion of the argument could be devoted to the legal issue of comparative fault. Plaintiff's counsel can thereby isolate and explain all of the factors that made the plaintiff's own actions reasonable and non-negligent.

Note that this format, as opposed to strict chronology, will allow plaintiff's counsel to plan the discussions of motivation and credibility in a coherent and logical fashion. All of the considerations pointing to the defendant's preoccupation can be addressed at once, including events that occurred both before (being late for the meeting) and after (rushing to call the office) the accident. Similarly, the entire "siren question" can be resolved, making it clear that the siren was sounding, before discussing the collision. Finally, counsel can address the question of comparative negligence without interrupting or detracting from the drama of the collision.

These strategies, of course, are open to question and reevaluation. Perhaps the use of the siren should be raised within the scope of the events, leaving the defendant's credibility to be addressed later. The point is that only the use of issue-based organization allows counsel to make such tactical decisions.

2. Elements

A second form of topical organization revolves around elements and claims. Every legal cause or defense is composed of various discrete elements. A claim of negligence, for instance, must be supported by proof of duty, breach of duty, cause in fact, proximate cause, and damages. A plaintiff can therefore develop her final argument by discussing the evidence as it supports each of the distinct elements of her cause of action. A defendant, who needs to challenge only a single element in order to win, can use the same form of organization but can truncate it by focusing only on those elements that are truly likely to be negated.

3. Jury Instructions

In most jurisdictions an "instructions conference" is held immediately prior to the final arguments.[12] Armed with advance knowledge of the instructions that the court will give to the jury, counsel can use them to organize all, or more likely part, of the final argument.

---

12. In most jurisdictions the final arguments are given before the court instructs the jury as to the law. In a few jurisdictions, however, final arguments follow the court's charge. In either situation the attorneys know what the instructions will be before they deliver their arguments.

Jury instructions must be used selectively as an organizing device. They are boring enough when read by the judge, and there is no reason to repeat them fully in their typically mind-numbing length as part of your argument to the jury. Rather, counsel should pick out several of the most important instructions and use those to develop the central points of the final argument. Thus, the plaintiff in the fire engine case might focus on the instructions dealing with due care and credibility, while the defendant might choose to utilize the instructions on comparative negligence and damages.

4. Turning Points

Modern cognition theory tells us that jurors are likely to regard the information in a case as a series of turning points or problems. Rather than resolving the truth or falsity of every distinct fact, they are far more likely to focus on a limited number of contested issues. Once a juror decides those issues, she will be inclined to fit the individual facts into a picture that fits in with that view of reality. Thus, an attorney can persuade a jury by identifying the key turning points in the trial and explaining them in a way that agrees with the jurors' life experience and sense of reality.

Assume that the defendant in the fire engine case has raised the defense of comparative negligence and has also challenged the plaintiff's claim of damages. Defense counsel's final argument could easily be organized around turning points such as the plaintiff's failure to pull over (as opposed to merely stopping in the middle of the road) or the plaintiff's weekend-long camping trip.

Note how the turning-point approach tends to work. Defense counsel can argue (although with more details and at greater length) to the following effect:

> Everyone knows that you are supposed to pull over to the right when you see or hear an emergency vehicle. If the plaintiff stopped but did not pull over, it must have been because she didn't have enough time to do so. That means that the fire engine's warning devices must have become noticeable only at the last moment, since the plaintiff herself would have pulled over if she had seen or heard the truck sooner. This must mean that the siren was silent, or at least inaudible, since the siren can be heard long before the fire truck can be seen.

By persuading the jury that the plaintiff stopped in the middle of the road, defense counsel can also make progress in persuading them of the defendant's position on the siren issue. A juror who believes that the plaintiff did not pull over will look to her own life's experience for a reason or explanation and will tend to embrace other facts that make sense in that context. An inaudible or nonoperating siren provides such contextual support for the juror's conclusion that the plaintiff did not pull over. Thus, once a juror accepts that the plaintiff did not hear a siren, she will be far more likely to credit the defendant's claim that he had insufficient warning to stop his car.

5. Alternative Structures

a. Chronological organization

Chronology is the most obvious alternative structure for a final argument. Since the events in a case manifestly occurred in a chronological order, it seems obvious to review them in the same progression during final argument.

While chronology certainly plays an important role in final argument, it may not be the best approach to overall structure. The difficulty with chronology is that events are unlikely to have occurred in the most persuasive possible sequence. Early events can frequently be illuminated by their subsequent consequences. In the preceding section, for example, we saw the forensic relationship in the defendant's argument between proof of the plaintiff's failure to pull over and the fire engine's use (or nonuse) of its siren. Told in chronological order, an argument would address the siren first; the use of warning signals obviously must have preceded the plaintiff's response. This structure, however, deprives the story of its persuasive weight since it is the failure to pull over that tends to prove the absence of a siren.

Consider, then, the following two snippets of defense argument. The first is in chronological order:

> As the fire truck approached the intersection, it flashed its lights but it did not use its siren. The plaintiff saw the fire truck and stopped for it, but she did not have time to pull over. That is why the accident occurred. She saw the fire truck only at the last moment.

Now, the same argument presented topically:

> The plaintiff stopped her car in the middle of the street. She didn't pull over. This can only mean that the fire truck was not using its siren. Everyone knows that you must pull over as soon as you become aware of an emergency vehicle, and a siren can be heard blocks away. The location of the plaintiff's car tells us that she saw that fire truck only at the last moment.

While both arguments make the same point, the discussion is clearly more persuasive once it is freed of the chronological strait-jacket. It then becomes possible to move both backward and forward in time, in order to place events in the most compelling order.

There can be no doubt, of course, that chronology is an essential tool in the structure of a final argument. There will come a time, or several times, in every argument when key occurrences will have to be time-ordered. Indeed, the precise sequence of events can often be the central issue in a case.

Chronology often fails, however, when it is used as the primary organizational device, as though the entire story of the case can be presented in a single order. Rather, it is best to think of the case as consisting of a series of discrete sub-stories. Each sub-story can be set out in chronological order while maintaining an overall format of topical organization.

b. Witness listing

Some lawyers persist in presenting final argument as a series of witness descriptions and accounts, essentially recapitulating the testimony of each person who took the stand. This approach is unlikely to succeed, as it diminishes the argument's logical coherence and force. Where topical organization focuses on the importance of issues and chronological organization focuses on the real-life sequence of events, witness listing depends on nothing more than the serendipity of which witness said what. It is a lazy, and usually ineffective, method of organization.

To be sure, it will often be necessary to compare witness accounts in the course of a final argument. You may wish to demonstrate the consistency of your own witnesses as opposed to the contradictions among the opposition's. You may want to dwell on the integrity and credibility of your witnesses. Or you might want to point out the bias and self-interest of opposing witnesses. All of this can be accomplished through topical organization.

B. Other Organizing Tools

1. Start Strong and End Strong

The principles of primacy and recency apply with full force to the final argument. In presenting a final argument, counsel has a limited window in which to attempt to shape the jury's imagination of the acts, events, and circumstances at issue in the case. Anything that bores the jury, or that distracts them from the task at hand, must be eliminated from the final argument. And it is certain that

prime time—the very beginning and the very end of the argument—
must be devoted to the most important considerations in the case.[13]

The strength of a starting point can be measured against a
number of standards such as theory value, thematic value, dramatic
impact, or undeniability. What is the central proposition of your client's theory? What aspect of the evidence best evokes your theme?
What is the most emotional or memorable factor in the case? What
is the opposing party's greatest concession?

In the fire engine case plaintiff's counsel might choose to begin
the final argument with a compelling restatement of her theory:

> The plaintiff was driving safely in the southbound lane of
> Sheridan Road. A fire truck approached the intersection
> from the west. It was flashing its lights and sounding its
> siren, so, as the law requires and as every high school
> student understands, she stopped her car. All of the oth-
> er traffic stopped as well, with one awful exception. The
> defendant kept his foot on the accelerator, never slowing
> down and never swerving, and he crashed his car right
> into the plaintiff's automobile.

Alternatively, plaintiff's counsel could start with her theme:

> This accident happened because the defendant was too
> busy to be careful. He was so preoccupied with his thoughts
> of a new client that he failed to notice what every other
> driver on the road saw and heard. He was so late and so
> rushed and so distracted that he paid no attention to the
> traffic all around him. He was in such a hurry to get to
> his office that the fire truck's emergency lights and sirens
> had no impact on him at all. He was so busy that getting
> to work became more important than ordinary caution.
> And make no mistake—ordinary caution would have been
> enough to avoid this accident completely.

Dramatic impact also works:

> In a single instant the defendant's carelessness changed
> the plaintiff's life forever. In one moment she went from
> being an ordinary, healthy, active individual to being a

---

13. Accordingly, it is a mistake to begin the final argument with a lengthy introduction on the virtues of the jury system. It is also usually unnecessary to reintroduce counsel and clients to the jury to to dwell on your gratitude for their faithful
attention to the evidence. It is sufficient to thank the jury in simple language and
then to proceed to the heart of the argument. Remember that the final argument is
a story. No best-seller begins with a paean to the publishing industry, and no motion picture ever starts by thanking the audience for attending.

person who cannot take a step, lift a child, or even prepare a meal without pain.

As does undeniability:

The one thing the defendant cannot deny is that he failed
to stop for a fire engine. There is no doubt that the fire
truck was there, there is no doubt that it was answering
a call, there is no doubt that the other cars stopped, and
there is no doubt that the defendant kept driving right
into the back of the plaintiff's automobile.

The most important point is that the opening salvo in the final
argument should be directed at making the jury want to decide the
case in your favor.

The last few minutes of the final argument should serve the
same function, either summarizing the theory, utilizing the theme,
driving home the strongest evidence, or painting the most compelling picture. Note that ending on a strong and memorable note is
particularly important to the defendant, who will not be able to argue again following the plaintiff's rebuttal.

2. Affirmative Case First

Most final arguments will consist of two distinct components:
developing the affirmative case and debunking the opposing party's
claims and/or defenses. As a general rule it is preferable to build up
your own case first and then proceed to debunk the opposition.

Plaintiffs in particular should resist the temptation to begin by
criticizing the defense case. No matter how weak or ridiculous the
defenses, it is usually best to begin with the strong points of your
own case. The plaintiff, after all, bears the burden of proof and cannot win without establishing all of the elements of an affirmative
case. Thus, there is less to be gained by refuting the defense if you
cannot prove your own case first. Moreover, a plaintiff who launches
immediately into an assault on the defendant's case may be seen as
confessing a lack of confidence in her own position. And if the jury
does not jump immediately to that conclusion, you can be sure that
defense counsel will argue that precise inference: "If plaintiff's case
is so strong, why did counsel begin by attacking the defense? They
must be worried."

The defendant has more latitude. Having just heard the plaintiff's or prosecutor's argument, a jury is unlikely to draw any adverse inference should defense counsel begin by refuting the plaintiff's case. Indeed, most juries will be waiting to hear the defendant's
denial. Therefore, the defendant should almost always begin with a

denial. After all, that is the natural response to an hour or so of the plaintiff's accusations.

Once a strong denial has been made, however, the defendant should, if possible, proceed to support it through the development of an affirmative case. That is, the defendant should usually explain why she is right before going on to explain why the plaintiff is wrong. Thus, the defendant's argument in the fire truck case might—in extremely skeletal form—proceed as follows:

> The defendant was not the cause of this accident. It was the plaintiff's fault. The defendant was driving safely and carefully, well within the speed limit. The fire engine was not sounding its siren, but as soon as he saw it, he hit his brakes and started to pull over. Unfortunately, the plaintiff chose to stop dead in the middle of the road instead of pulling to the side as the traffic laws require.

The real argument, of course, would be far longer, but the organization of the above paragraph holds true. Counsel began with a denial, demonstrated that the defendant's actions were reasonable, and went on to explain the plaintiff's own negligence.

The most frequent exception to the "affirmative case first" rule is found in criminal cases. Since a criminal defendant is not required to present an affirmative case, it is not uncommon for a defense argument to focus solely (or primarily) on the deficiencies in the prosecution's proof.

The plaintiff's (or prosecutor's) rebuttal, of course, is technically limited to refutation of the defense. Within this stricture, however, it is still advisable to frame the argument in as affirmative a light as possible.

Note finally that the "affirmative case first" rule does not mean "affirmative case only." A substantial part of most final arguments should be devoted to the weaknesses in the opposition case. But not the first part.

3. Cluster Circumstantial Evidence and Accumulate Details

Final argument is the time for gathering details. Although the particulars may have occurred at widely different times and have been testified to by several witnesses, they can and should be aggregated to make a single point in final argument. So, for example, the plaintiff in the fire engine case will want to collect all of the details, both direct and circumstantial, that support her proposition that the defendant was preoccupied with thoughts of his important meeting:

> We know that his mind was not on his driving. Look at the details. He was late for work. He had an important meeting scheduled for 8:30 a.m., and he was still sixteen miles from downtown. He had to park his car, leave the garage, walk over two blocks to his office, and get up to the fourteenth floor. And look at what would happen if he was late. The defendant himself testified that he was meeting with a potential new client and that he hoped to land a valuable account. New clients mean advancement and raises. Losing a new client means losing money. You can't land a new client if you don't make it to the meeting. That meeting must have been the only thing on the defendant's mind. It was so important to him that the first thing he did after the accident was run to a phone and call his office. He didn't call an ambulance, he didn't call the police, and he didn't even check to see if the other driver was injured. No, first and foremost he cared about that new client. Everything else—driving, traffic, safety—was unimportant compared to his need to get to that meeting.

Note that the details in the above passage could have come from as many as three different witnesses and that they do not strictly follow the chronology of the accident. The argument makes coordinated use of both direct (the phone call after the accident) and circumstantial (the distance from the garage to his office) evidence. The argument also utilizes both positive (a new client means money) and negative (he didn't call an ambulance) inferences. It is the clustering or accumulation of all of these points that gives the argument its persuasive weight.

4. Bury Your Concessions

In the course of almost every argument it will be necessary to concede certain of the opposition's claims or facts, if only to minimize or discount them. As a corollary to the "start and end strong" rule, such concessions should usually be "buried" in the middle of your argument.

Suppose, for example, that your client was impeached on cross examination with a prior inconsistent statement. At some point in your argument you may well want to concede the inconsistency but explain why it should be of no consequence to the outcome of the case. That is a fine strategy, but do not do it at either the beginning or the end of your argument. There are sure to be many facts that you want the jury to remember more vividly than your client's inconsistent statements, no matter how adeptly you are able to downplay their significance. In other words, bury the concessions.

5. Weave in Witness Credibility

We noted above that witness listing is an ineffective format for final argument. Witness credibility, on the other hand, is often a subject that must be addressed. The solution is to weave discussion of the witnesses, and their relative credibility, into the fabric of the story.

In most cases it will be sufficient to discuss witnesses only at the point that they become important to the theory of the case. So, for example, the credibility of the fire truck defendant should not form a separate section of the plaintiff's argument. There will be relatively little value to a freestanding attack on the defendant's credibility; it will seem like just that, an attack. On the other hand, the jury will be most receptive to a credibility argument at a moment when its significance is apparent:

> Let us turn to the question of the siren. There is no doubt that a fire engine's siren is a signal that traffic must stop. Ignoring a siren is definite negligence. The defendant claims that there was no siren, but he cannot be believed. He has too much at stake in this case, and he knows that the siren is a vital piece of evidence against him. And remember that Lieutenant Sarah Sherman testified that she always used her siren when answering a call. She has absolutely no stake in this case and no reason to tell you anything but the truth. So it comes down to this: either you believe the defendant or you believe Lieutenant Sherman.

While the defendant might be unsavory and Lieutenant Sherman upstanding, it makes no sense to discuss their character traits in the abstract. By weaving the witnesses into the story, however, counsel can make full use of their disparate believability.

6. Damages

A special problem is raised by the issue of damages in civil cases, and especially in personal injury cases.

Most authorities agree that plaintiff's counsel should argue liability before proceeding to damages. Particularly where the damages are great or inchoate, a jury will be more inclined to accept the plaintiff's argument once they have been convinced of liability. Stated otherwise, the desire to award damages flows naturally from a conclusion of liability. The converse, however, is not true. Proof of damages does not necessarily imply that the defendant was at fault.

For the same reason, defendants are often advised to address damages first, if at all. It is discordant to argue, "The defendant was not at fault, but even if he was, the damages were not so great as the plaintiff claims." The subsequent discussion of damages may be taken as a concession of liability.

Of course, many defense cases are based primarily, if not exclusively, on the issue of damages. In these cases it should be obvious that damages should form the first, last, and most important part of the argument.

THE BASICS

Final Argument Structure

- Use topical organization whenever possible
- Use chronological and witness-by-witness organization strategically
- Start strong and end strong
- Argue your affirmative case first
- Tie up cross examinations
- Embrace or displace the burden of proof
- Accumulate circumstantial evidence and bury your concessions
- Address witness credibility throughout
- Recognize "turning points" and address problems
- Use jury instructions

IV. CONTENT

The specific content of any final argument will obviously be determined by the facts and issues in the case. It is possible, however, to enumerate certain sorts of information that should be considered for inclusion in every final argument.

A. Tell a Persuasive Story

Virtually every final argument should contain all of the elements of a persuasive story. The argument should detail the evidentiary support for counsel's theory of the case and should consistently invoke the trial theme.

We have previously discussed five substantive elements[14] to a persuasive story: It explains all of the known facts. It is told about people who have reasons for their actions. It is told by credible witnesses. It is supported by details. And it accords with common sense. These elements should be present at some point in all final arguments.

1. Known Facts—What Happened

A persuasive story accounts for all of the known facts. It is not premised on incomplete information, and it does not glide over or ignore inconvenient occurrences. This is not to say that a final argument must mention every minor detail in the case, but rather that it should, in some fashion, accommodate all of the established facts.

The final argument must, of course, cover the central facts of counsel's case, taking care to provide support for all of the legally necessary elements. It must also take into consideration the evidence produced by the opposing party.

Assume that the fire engine case has been tried along the lines that we have discussed in previous sections. The plaintiff has used "too busy to be careful" as a trial theme, introducing evidence of the defendant's hurried morning. Since there was no dispute as to details such as the defendant's scheduled meeting and various travel times, these have become "known facts" in the sense that the jury is not likely to regard them with doubt or disbelief. Defense counsel might believe that these facts are inconsequential to the issue of liability; after all, people can be late for work and still drive carefully. Nonetheless, the defendant's final argument should account for these facts either by refuting them or by explaining their irrelevance.

2. Reasons—Why Did It Happen

Explain the reasons for the actions of the parties and other witnesses. It is not enough to state that an individual did something. Rather, counsel should go on to reveal why those activities were consistent with that individual's self-interest, announced intentions, past behavior, lifestyle, or other understandable motivations.

The articulation of reasons gives logical weight to the argument and can transform it from an attorney's assertion into an acceptable statement of fact.

---

14. The sixth, nonsubstantive, element to a persuasive story is organization.

3. Credible Witnesses—Who Should Be Believed

The credibility of witnesses should always be addressed on final argument. At a minimum this means that the credibility of counsel's own witnesses should be developed in the course of establishing an affirmative case. This can usually be done subtly and indirectly, simply by providing the background information that tends to render your witnesses believable.

In cases where credibility is seriously in issue, it will be necessary to take a more frontal approach.

4. Supportive Details—How Can We Be Sure

As we have seen throughout, persuasion often rests on the accumulation of supportive details. An essential aspect of final argument is the marshaling of details that give weight to counsel's argument.

The inclusion or exclusion of details is a tricky problem. While the right details at the right time can add an airtight quality to your case, the use of too many details (or their use in support of unimportant propositions) can drag a final argument into the depths of boredom and despair. There is no single key to making judgments in this area, but it is safe to look to the following guidelines:

- Use details when important facts are in dispute. Whenever there is a disagreement as to an occurrence or incident, details can be used effectively to support your client's version of events.

- Use details when motivations are in issue. The presence (or absence) of motive can frequently be established through recourse to constituent facts. Explain why a party would want to act in a certain way. Look at the details that show the benefits of the actions' consequences.

- Use details to support an interpretation of the evidence. The meaning of certain evidence is often contested even when the underlying facts are not in dispute. Regarding damages in the fire engine case, for example, both parties will agree to the fact that the plaintiff went camping at Eagle River Falls. But how should that fact be interpreted? Does it mean that she was not really injured in the accident? Or does it mean that she is a brave woman trying to make the best of a difficult situation? Constituent details—Did she stay in the tent? Did she organize daily hikes? Did she express reluctance about going in the first place?—may help provide the answer.

- Do not use details for unimportant reasons. The judge or jury will have a limited tolerance for details. Every time you use one detail you are diminishing the effectiveness of those that you will use later. It is therefore necessary to reserve your use of details for truly important situations. For example, you will not want to use details, even if they are available, to attack the credibility of a witness whose testimony was not damaging to your case.

- Do not use details to establish uncontested facts.

THE BASICS

Guidelines for the Use of Details	
Use details when important facts are in dispute.	When there is a disagreement as to an occurrence or incident, details can be used effectively to support your client's version of events.
Use details when motivations are in issue.	The presence (or absence) of motive can frequently be established by looking at specific facts. Explain why a witness would want to act in a certain way.
Use details to support an interpretation of the evidence.	The meaning of certain evidence is often contested even when the underlying facts are not in dispute.
Do not use details for unimportant reasons.	The judge or jury will have a limited tolerance for details; every time you use a detail you diminish the effectiveness of those that follow.
Do not use details to establish uncontested facts.	If a fact is uncontested, you need only state it.

5. Common Sense—Is It Plausible

Perhaps the ultimate test of every final argument is plausibility. Even if an argument accounts for the known facts, gives reasons for every action, is supported by credible witnesses, and might be replete with convincing details, it still will not be accepted if it does not make sense to the jury. Almost every other failing can be overcome or forgiven. You cannot, however, win with an implausible argument.

It is essential, therefore, that every closing argument address the subject of common sense. Explain why your theory is realistic, using examples and analogies from everyday life. Plaintiff's counsel in the fire truck case, for instance, will need to explain why the plaintiff, who claimed crippling injuries, went camping at Eagle River Falls. The argument, of course, is that she did not want to be defeated by her disabilities. This argument can be strengthened by drawing on the jury's own observations and experiences:

> It is easy to understand why someone would not want to give in to her injuries. We all know, or have seen, people who refuse to be housebound just because they are disabled. I read a story in the newspaper yesterday about a young boy who lost his right arm to cancer—but he still tried out for his high school baseball team. I'm sure that he went through a lot of pain and disappointment, but he never would have made the team if he hadn't tried. That is what the plaintiff did at Eagle River Falls. She tried to live a normal life.

"Common sense" arguments can also be used to belittle or even ridicule the opposition case. It is every lawyer's dream that the jury will retire to the deliberation room and immediately conclude that the opposition case just doesn't stack up.

B.   Tie Up Cross Examinations

Final argument is the time to tie up the issues that were intentionally left unaddressed during cross examination. Recall the questions that are forbidden to the prudent cross examiner: Never ask a witness to explain; never ask a witness to fill in a gap; never ask a witness to agree with a characterization or conclusion. These questions, and others like them, all risk losing control of the witness. There is a strong consensus that it is better to refrain from asking the ultimate question and to make the point instead during the final argument.

Thus, if your cross examinations were artful and effective, you should be able to spend some portion of the final argument drawing the previously unspoken conclusions.

Assume that you represent the prosecution in a burglary case involving an alibi defense. The defendant, on direct examination, recited his alibi but left an apparent gap during the crucial window when the burglary was most likely to have occurred. As a skilled trial lawyer, you knew not to go into those gaps on cross examination, for fear that the defendant would fill them in with additional information as to his whereabouts. Final argument, however, is another matter:

> We know that this burglary occurred some time during the evening of November 7. The defendant claims that he was at work that entire time. He even produced his

time card, showing that he punched in at 4:00 p.m. and punched out at midnight. Other witnesses testified that they saw him at work at various times that night. But no one testified that they were with him during his dinner break. We know that he must have taken a break, or at least that he is entitled to one. It is the law in this state that no employee can be required to work for eight hours without a meal break of at least thirty minutes. So we have a full half hour that is unaccounted for. We know that the defendant could have slipped away, and absolutely no one testified that they were with him.

Confronted with this gap on cross examination, a clever defendant might come up with numerous explanations as to why he didn't take a break or why he went alone. By the time of final argument, however, it is too late. The gap stands unfilled, ready to be exploited by the prosecution.[15]

The same approach can be used with regard to explanations and characterizations. You did not ask a witness why something happened; be sure to use the final argument to tell the jury why it happened. You did not ask a witness to agree with a conclusion or characterization; be sure to use the final argument to draw the conclusion yourself.

C.   Comment on Promises

Attorneys on both sides of a case will inevitably make various promises and commitments to the jury during the course of the trial. These promises may be overt, as is often the case during opening statements: "We will produce a series of documents and work records that prove that the defendant was nowhere near the scene of the crime." Or the commitments may be implicit in the theory of the case. When a plaintiff claims damages for personal injury, there is obviously an implied promise of certain proof.

---

15. Is it unethical to use the final argument to lie in wait for a witness? Is a prosecutor entitled to obtain a conviction by depriving the defendant of an opportunity to explain himself during cross examination? The answer lies in understanding the adversary system. The decision to refrain from asking a question on cross examination does not deprive the witness of all opportunity to explain. The witness was free to provide whatever information he wanted during the direct examination, and opposing counsel had at least one additional opportunity to cure any defects during redirect examination. The prosecutor, or any lawyer, can fairly assume that the decision to omit a fact from direct examination means that the fact does not exist. The decision not to inquire further during cross examination, then, at most deprives the witness of yet a third chance to elaborate. It is at least possible, if not likely, that the witness would use that chance to invent facts or obfuscate the truth.

Whatever the case, final argument is the time for counsel to comment on promises made, kept, or broken. Point out the ways in which you fulfilled your commitments. Perhaps more importantly, and certainly more dramatically, underscore the ways in which the opposition failed to live up to their own promises. Consider the explicit promise in the alibi example used above:

> I am sure you remember defense counsel's opening statement. She told you that she would produce documentary evidence—work records—that would prove that the defendant was nowhere near the scene of the crime. Well, the trial is now over and all of the evidence is in. We have not seen any documentary evidence; there were no work records.

The approach needs to be modified only slightly for use with implicit commitments:

> When a plaintiff comes before you claiming injury, she makes a commitment about the proof that she will offer. You have the right to expect that she will produce evidence of the nature of the injury, that you will hear from doctors about her medical condition, or at least that you will hear from friends and neighbors about the changes in the plaintiff's life. In this case, however, there was no such proof. Of course, the plaintiff testified. But beyond her words there was absolutely no disinterested evidence that she was truly injured in any way.

Of course, the most effective final arguments are often those in which counsel is able to state that "We kept our promises and they broke theirs."

D. Resolve Problems and Weaknesses

Final argument can be used to solve problems and confront weaknesses. No matter how well the evidentiary phase of the trial proceeded, you are sure to be left with a number of difficult or troublesome issues. Once identified, these issues can be addressed and resolved in the course of final argument.

A classic instance of such a weakness is the government's reliance on informers in drug prosecutions. Informers are assailable witnesses to begin with, and in drug cases they are often further sullied with histories of their own substance abuse. Recognizing the problems created by reliance on such witnesses, prosecutors have developed over the years an almost standardized, and extremely effective, final argument approach. In its barest form it goes something like this:

> It is true that a number of the prosecution witnesses were informers and former drug users. They aren't the most upstanding citizens in the world. It was not the prosecution, however, who chose them as witnesses. The defendants chose these people as witnesses when they set out to sell illegal and dangerous drugs. Who can serve as witnesses to drug deals? Not clergymen, not doctors, not solid citizens or civic leaders. No, drug deals take place in a shadowy world that is populated by petty criminals and addicts. Those were the people who were present for this transaction, and those were the witnesses whom we had to call to the stand.

There are several schools of thought as to the best timing for addressing weaknesses or problems. Some authorities believe that weaknesses should never be addressed unless the opposing side raises them first. Others believe that at least certain weaknesses should be dealt with "defensively," on the theory that the sting can be preempted by discussing the issue first.

The decision is not always simple. Plaintiffs' attorneys have the choice of dealing with weaknesses during either argument in chief or rebuttal. Thus, they can either initiate the discussion, or they can wait to see whether the defense brings up the issue during its argument in chief. Defendants, on the other hand, must be more wary. Even if the plaintiff (or prosecutor) omits a problem area from the argument in chief, it might still be exploited mercilessly on rebuttal.

Because the jury's deliberation does not depend solely upon the final arguments, there may ultimately be some weaknesses that must be addressed whether the opposition mentions them or not. Assume that the plaintiff's attorney in the fire engine case delivered the entire final argument without mentioning the plaintiff's camping trip and that the subject was also omitted from the defense argument. Should the plaintiff's counsel rejoice and refrain from mentioning the subject in her rebuttal argument? The jury, after all, heard the evidence, which was damaging to the plaintiff's case. There is no guarantee that they will not consider it, or even base their verdict upon it, once they retire to the jury room. Because the evidence was both harmful and easily counteracted, it is probably wisest for plaintiff's counsel to make sure that the topic is covered during final argument. Since counsel's ability to discuss the issue on rebuttal is limited by the scope of the defense argument, the best approach might well have been to address the issue during the plaintiff's argument in chief.

E.   Discuss Damages

The trial of a civil case can usually be divided into the conceptual areas of liability and damages. Although liability is the threshold issue, it is a mistake to underestimate the importance of damages. Unless the trial has been bifurcated, plaintiffs in particular should devote a significant portion of the final argument to the development of damages.

It may be helpful to think of damages as comprising a "second persuasive story" in the case. Once liability has been established, damages can be addressed using all of the persuasive story elements that we have discussed above. Counsel should account for the known facts that bear on damages, give the reasons for the actions of the people involved, address the credibility of the specific witnesses, delineate the crucial details, and explain why the requested damage award accords with common sense.

There are two significant aspects involved in most arguments for damages: method and amount. It is important to explain to the jury precisely how damages have been (or should be) calculated. It is also usually important to request a specific amount rather than leaving the award to the jury's guesswork.

Some defense attorneys prefer to avoid or minimize the issue of damages, reasoning that any discussion may be seen as an implicit admission of liability.[16] Many lawyers, however, choose not to "roll the dice" on liability, concluding that a reduced damage award is the next best thing to winning the case outright. When discussing damages, defense lawyers have a choice. You may simply rebut the plaintiff's damage claim, or you may present a competing estimate of your own. The decision will rest upon the circumstances of the particular case. Note, however, that the presentation of a competing damage estimate may run a greater risk of seeming to concede liability.

F.   Use Jury Instructions

Some part of every final argument should be devoted to the court's forthcoming jury instructions as well as to the elements of the claims and defenses in the case. Jury instructions can be extremely important in the way that the jurors decide the case, and it

---

16. Defense lawyers often seek bifurcated trials to avoid this problem.

is to counsel's advantage to invoke some of the instructions during argument.

Care must be taken, however, not to overuse or dwell on the instructions. The charge to the jury is universally regarded as one of the most boring parts of the trial, and there is not much value in simply giving the jurors a lengthy advance notice of the instructions to come. The instructions should be used strategically as further evidence of your client's right to prevail on key issues in the case. Thus, discussion of the instructions should not form a single, extended part of the final argument. Rather, they should be used throughout the argument, read or referred to at the points where they can accomplish the most good.

Assume, for example, that the plaintiff in the fire engine case called an expert economist to testify to the plaintiff's expected future losses. The defense, on the other hand, did not produce expert testimony for fear of crediting the plaintiff's claim to damages. Assume also that the court agreed to give the standard expert witness instruction to the jury: they may reject all, or any part, of the testimony of expert witnesses, and the credibility of experts should be judged in the same manner as the credibility of any other witness. As defense counsel approaches the issue of damages during her final argument, she will therefore want to make use of the expert witness instruction. The defendant's final argument, then, might go as follows:

> It is true that the plaintiff offered the testimony of Dr. Staffileno, an economist. But, as the court will instruct you, you may discount or reject any part of Dr. Staffileno's testimony. You do not need to accept what he said just because he is an expert, and the facts of this case show that the plaintiff was not really injured that severely. As the court's instructions will make clear, expert witnesses can make mistakes, or even be biased, just like any other witness.

Thus, counsel can use the instruction to place the court's imprimatur on her position discounting the value of the expert witness.

Jury instructions are particularly useful when it comes to discussing the elements of the various claims and defenses. It is imperative that the plaintiff persuade the jury that she has established all of the legal elements of her claim. Since the concept of "legal elements" can often be confusing, it is frequently quite helpful simply to run through the court's instruction on elements, explaining at the same time the manner in which each requirement has been satisfied.

In similar fashion, the defendant can use the court's instruction to focus on one or more elements to show that they have not been satisfied by the evidence.

G.   Use Verdict Forms

In addition to jury instructions, the court will also provide the jurors with a set of alternate verdict forms. One of these forms will be the paper that the jury actually fills out as its official verdict in the case.

Use the verdict forms in your final argument. Show the jury the form that you want them to use, and explain how you want them to fill it out. You may persuade the jury that you are entitled to win the case, but that will do you little good if, by mistake, they end up entering the wrong verdict.

H.   Introductions and Thanks

By the time of final argument it should be unnecessary to reintroduce yourself and your cocounsel to the jury. If, for some reason, you believe that renewed introductions are called for, make them short.

You should, at some point, thank the jury for their time and attention. They have truly fulfilled an important civic duty, sometimes at considerable personal cost or inconvenience, and their importance should be recognized. It is, on the other hand, all too easy to overdo the acknowledgments. Lengthy encomiums to the jury system will quickly become cloying. Even worse are declarations of abject gratitude where counsel feels compelled to confess that the trial has been a boring ordeal. A simple statement of thanks on behalf of yourself and your client is usually sufficient.

V.   DELIVERY AND TECHNIQUE

Final argument is generally regarded as the advocate's finest hour. It is the time when all of the skills—no, the arts—of persuasion are marshaled on behalf of the client's cause. While a polished delivery will not rescue a lost cause, a forceful presentation can certainly reinforce the merits of your case.

Most of the persuasive techniques that we have discussed previously, and especially those used in opening statements, also have their applications in final argument.

A. Do Not Read or Memorize

It is a mistake to write and read your final argument. As we noted in the chapter on opening statements,[17] only the most skilled actors can truly appear natural while reading from a script. Memorization is only slightly more likely to yield an unaffected presentation, and it carries the extreme additional risk that you will forget your place or leave out a crucial part of the argument.

In addition to the purely forensic drawbacks of reading and memorization, the advance scripting of a final argument deprives you of the ability to respond to opposing counsel or to last-minute rulings by the court.

The most effective final arguments are those that are delivered from an outline. The use of an outline allows you to plan your final argument, to deliver it with an air of spontaneity, and to adapt to the arguments of the opposition.

Do not be reticent to use notes during final argument. It is all well and good to speak without notes if you are able to do so, but it is far better to refer to a page or two on your pad than it is to omit a crucial argument. Even if you are capable of arguing without notes you should still use the outline method of preparation rather than writing out and memorizing a speech.

B. Movement

A certain amount of body and hand movement will enliven your final argument and increase the attentiveness of the jurors. Gestures can be used to emphasize important points or to accent differences between your case and the opposition's.

Body movement can also be used for emphasis or transition. Pausing and taking a step or two will alert the jury that you are about to change subjects. Moving toward the jury will underscore the importance of what you are about to say. Moving away from the jury will signal the conclusion of a line of argument. Note that body movement can only be used effectively if you avoid aimless pacing. Constant movement is not only distracting to the jury, but it also deprives you of the ability to use movements purposefully.

Some courts require counsel to stand planted at a lectern or even seated at a table, but most allow the attorney to move fairly freely about the courtroom. Many authorities suggest that the use of a lectern places an obstacle between counsel and the jury. While

---

17. See Chapter 11, Section V A, *supra* at p. 376.

this may be true, it is easily possible to overstate the importance of abandoning the lectern. Use it if you need it.

C.   Verbal Pacing

The speed, tone, inflection, and volume of your speech can be important persuasive tools. Changes in speed, tone, inflection, and volume can be used to signal transitions and to maintain the jury's attention. It is important, of course, to avoid speaking too quickly or too loudly.

The pacing of your speech can be used to convey perceptions of time, distance, and intensity. If you describe an event rapidly, it will seem to have taken place very quickly. If you describe it at a more leisurely pace, the time frame will expand. In similar fashion, rapid speech will tend to magnify intensity and reduce distance. Slower delivery will reduce intensity and increase distance.

D.   Emotion

There are different schools of thought regarding the use of emotion in final argument. Many lawyers believe that emotion has little place at any point during the trial, while others believe that emotion can communicate as effectively as logic or reason. There is a clear consensus, however, that false emotion will backfire. Insincerity has a way of showing through, and there is little that is less persuasive than an overtly insincere attorney.

The best approach to emotion is to save it for the times when you are discussing the moral dimension of your case. There is no reason to wax passionate over the date on which a contract was signed. It is understandable, however, to show outrage or resentment toward a party who intentionally breached a contract, knowing that it would cause great harm to another.

The absence of emotion may be taken as a lack of belief in the righteousness of your case. What reasonable person would be unmoved when discussing crippling injuries to a child or perjury by the opposing party? There will be points in many trials that virtually call out for an outward display of feeling, and a flat presentation may be regarded as an absence of conviction.

E.   Visuals

As with opening statements, visual aids can be extremely valuable during final argument. Counsel is generally free to use any exhibit that has been admitted in evidence and also to create visual displays solely for the purpose of final argument.

Any item that has been admitted in evidence may be utilized during final argument. Thus, documents may be read out loud, displayed, or enlarged. Counsel can highlight key passages in important documents or can array various documents side by side. This last technique is particularly useful to demonstrate relational concepts such as contradiction or continuity.[18]

Physical evidence other than documents may also be used during final argument. It is permissible to exhibit items such as weapons, models, photographs, samples, and anything else that has been admitted by the court. It is also permissible to use the evidence to conduct demonstrations and reenactments, so long as they are consistent with the testimony in the case. In criminal cases, for example, it is common for the prosecutor to show the jury precisely how a weapon was held and used.

Counsel has wide latitude to create visual aids specifically for use during final argument. The only restriction on the use of such materials is that they must be fairly derived from the actual evidence. Visual aids may be "argumentative." In fact, it may be best to think of them as argument in graphic or physical form.

Thus, it is perfectly legitimate for an attorney to use a blackboard or marking pen to write in large letters "THREE REASONS NOT TO BELIEVE THE PLAINTIFF," and then to fill in three columns of reasons for discounting the plaintiff's testimony. Since counsel could obviously tell the jury the reasons not to believe the plaintiff, she may also write them down. In other words, anything that could be spoken may also be illustrated.

More sophisticated visual aids can take the form of charts, graphs, overlays, and enlargements.

F.   Headlines

A headline announces where the argument is going next. Just as newspapers use headlines to pique the interest of readers, so can they be used to focus the attention of jurors during final argument.

A headline can take the form of a simple statement, a rhetorical question, or a short "enumeration." The defendant in the fire truck case, for example, might use a headline as brief as the following headline when turning from liability to damages:

Now let us look at the plaintiff's claim for damages.

Alternatively, defense counsel might choose to make the transition more argumentative:

---

18. See Chapter 10 concerning the use of electronic visuals in final argument.

> Having seen how weak the plaintiff's position is on liability, let's turn to her damages claim.

Or the headline can be used to emphasize the importance of the coming subject:

> As I told you during the opening statement, the real heart of this case is damages. I want to show you now just how inflated the plaintiff's claim really is.

Rhetorical questions can also be useful, as in this example from the plaintiff's argument in the fire engine case:

> What could lead a person to drive so carelessly?

Or, more elaborately:

> How could the defendant have missed seeing the fire engine, when every other car on the road saw it and stopped?

Finally, the technique of "enumeration" might be the most effective of all. Every teacher, and probably most students, will recognize this phenomenon. As soon as the lecturer announces that there are "three reasons" or "four rules" or "six characteristics," every person in the room picks up a pen and begins to take notes. It seems that little serves to concentrate the mind more than the onset of a numbered list. This approach can also be used in final argument:

> The defendant was negligent in three different ways.

Or,

> There are four basic flaws in the plaintiff's claim for damages.

Or,

> There were three different moments at which the defendant could have avoided this accident. Let me explain them to you.

The technique of enumeration is particularly effective when it is used in conjunction with a visual aid. Do not simply tell the jury that the defendant violated three "rules of the road." Write the numbered headlines down in bold letters or project them on a screen.

G. Simple, Active Language

The chapter on opening statements contains a substantial discussion of the persuasive use of simple, active language.[19] The same rules apply equally to final arguments, with the additional

---

19. See Chapter 11, Section V B, *supra* at p. 376.

proviso that simple, active language may be applied in argumentative form.

One further point should be made. There is a strong temptation during final argument to use judgmental or conclusory terms such as heinous, brutal, deceptive, unfair, virtuous, naive, and the like. Although usually not permitted during opening statements, such language is allowed on final argument. Nonetheless, counsel would do well to remember that conclusory adjectives and adverbs tend to be less persuasive than active nouns and verbs. It is one thing to assert that a crime was heinous, and quite another to describe its awful, vivid details.

VI. ETHICS AND OBJECTIONS

The rules of ethics, evidence, and procedure combine to place a number of very real, though definitely manageable, limits on what can be said during final argument.

A. Impermissible Argument

1. Statements of Personal Belief

It is improper and unethical for an attorney to "assert personal knowledge of facts in issue...or state a personal opinion as to the justness of a cause, the credibility of a witness, the culpability of a civil litigant or the guilt or innocence of an accused."[20]

The purpose of this rule is twofold. First, it prevents lawyers from putting their own credibility at issue in a case. The jury is required to decide a case on the basis of the law and evidence, not on their affinity for or faith in a particular lawyer. While every advocate strives to be trusted and believed, it subverts the jury system to make an overt, personal pitch.

Moreover, a statement of personal belief inevitably suggests that the lawyer has access to off-the-record information and therefore invites the jury to decide the case on the basis of nonrecord evidence. Consider the following:

> I have investigated this case thoroughly. I have spent hours with my client, and I have visited the scene of the accident. I could tell, just from talking with her, how seriously she has been injured. Believe me, I would not take up your time if my client were not telling the truth. I have

---

20. See Rule 3.4(e), Model Rules of Professional Conduct.

handled many other cases of this type, and I can honestly say that this is one of the strongest plaintiff's cases that I have ever seen.

Here, the lawyer has not merely asked for the jury's confidence. Counsel has impliedly asked the jury to enter a verdict on the basis of out-of-court interviews and previously tried cases.

The rule against statements of personal belief is an important one. It should not be demeaned by a too-literal interpretation. It is difficult to purge your speech entirely of terms such as "I think" or "I believe." While good lawyers will strive to avoid these terms, it is not unethical to fall occasionally into first person references. Similarly, it is unnecessary to preface every assertion with statements such as "the evidence has shown," "we have proven," or the like.

It is unethical to ask the jury to decide the case, or any issue in the case, on the basis of its trust in counsel. Thus, the following argument for the plaintiff in the fire truck case is permissible, though some of its language would better be avoided:

> The defendant must have been worried about how late he was for his meeting. We have heard from the defendant's own mouth that his parking garage is almost three blocks from his office. It would take an average person about ten minutes to park his car and walk that far. I think that he also had at least another half hour or so of driving to do. Put the times together and you will see that he was at least twenty minutes late. That was enough to distract him from his driving.

The personal statement in the above example is really nothing more than an inference from the evidence. Of course, things would be different if counsel used an exaggerated tone of voice or series of gestures to emphasize personal belief as opposed to a conclusion drawn from the trial evidence.

On the other hand, this argument is definitely improper:

> I know that it would take at least ten minutes to walk from the defendant's parking garage to his office. I work downtown, and I have walked that distance many times myself. Believe me, it is at least a ten-minute walk.

Here it is clear that counsel is asserting personal knowledge, not admitted evidence, as a basis for the desired conclusion.

2. Appeals to Prejudice or Bigotry

It is unethical to attempt to persuade a jury through appeals to racial, religious, ethnic, gender, or other forms of prejudice. It is a sad fact of life that some jurors can be swayed by their own biases, but lawyers cannot and should not seek to take advantage of this unfortunate phenomenon.

An appeal to prejudice asks the jury to disregard the evidence and to substitute an unreasonable stereotype or preconception. Thus, such arguments violate the rule against alluding to "any matter that the lawyer does not reasonably believe is relevant or that will not be supported by admissible evidence."[21]

The mention of race, gender, or ethnicity is not always improper. It would, for example, be permissible to refer to a party's race if it is relevant to identification by an eyewitness.

On the other hand, it is definitely unethical to make racial or similar appeals implicitly or through the use of code words. An argument based on bigotry cannot be saved through subtle language.

3. Misstating the Evidence

While it is permissible to draw inferences and conclusions, it is improper intentionally to misstate or mischaracterize evidence in the course of final argument. Accordingly, defense counsel in the fire truck case could portray the plaintiff's camping trip as follows:

> The plaintiff admits that she went camping at Eagle River Falls. She did all of the things that ordinary campers do. She carried a pack, she slept on the ground, she went hiking. In other words, she willingly undertook all of the strains, exertions, and activities of backpacking. No one made her take that trip; she did it for recreation. Of course, she told a different story here on the witness stand. The only possible conclusion is that she has exaggerated her claim for injuries.

To be sure, the above example is replete with characterizations, but they are fair characterizations. Even if no witness actually testified that the plaintiff went camping voluntarily, it is a reasonable inference that "no one made her take that trip."

The following argument, on the other hand, definitely appears to misstate the evidence:

> The plaintiff was an enthusiastic and carefree camper. She carried the heaviest pack in the family, and she insisted on chopping the wood and pitching the tent. She would have gone camping again the next weekend, but her family couldn't keep up with her.

---

21. See Rule 3.4(e), Model Rules of Professional Conduct.

These are, by and large, assertions of fact, not simply inferences. (While the statement that the plaintiff was an "enthusiastic" camper might be seen as an inference, the statements concerning the "heaviest pack" and the plaintiff's desire to go camping the next weekend are clearly presented as proven facts.) They may not be made in final argument unless they are supported by the record.

Although the rule against misstatements and mischaracterizations is plain enough, judges, for obvious reasons, are usually loath to invoke it. No one is capable of remembering all of the evidence that was admitted at trial, and the line between allowable inferences and forbidden mischaracterizations is difficult to draw. Opposing counsel are, after all, expected to disagree about the content and interpretation of evidence. Thus, judges often try to refrain from ruling on objections based upon the misstatement rule. Instead, the court's typical response to an objection is merely to remind the jury that they are the sole judges of the evidence and that they should rely upon their own memories rather than upon counsel's presentation.

Nonetheless, in truly egregious situations a judge can and will sustain an objection to argument that misstates the evidence. What is more, appellate courts have been known to reverse judgments in situations where the prevailing attorney's argument strayed too far beyond the record.

Two lessons should be drawn concerning the "misstatement" rule. First, evidence should not be misstated. The courts' general reluctance to resolve questions raised by the rule should not be taken as license to ignore the rule. Second, the "misstatement" rule should not be used as an excuse to make spurious objections, to interrupt opposing counsel's argument, or to quibble over the meaning of the evidence. Objections should be made, but only when opposing counsel has seriously and prejudicially departed from the record.

4. Misstating the Law

In most jurisdictions attorneys may use final argument to explain the relevant law, to discuss the jury instructions, and to apply the law to the facts of the case. Counsel may not, however, misstate the law or argue for legal interpretations that are contrary to the court's decisions and instructions.

Thus, defense counsel in a criminal case could not argue that the jury must acquit the defendant "if there is any doubt whatsoever, no matter how insignificant or far-fetched it might be." By the same token, the prosecutor could not argue that a reasonable doubt only exists if the jury "is persuaded that there is a good chance that the defendant is not guilty." In both of these examples the attorneys offered definitions of reasonable doubt that are not found in any jurisdiction.

Courts vary in the degree to which they allow lawyers to paraphrase or summarize the law. Attorneys in some jurisdictions are given relatively free rein to argue, while others permit counsel only to read the jury instructions.[22]

Counsel is never free, however, to ask a jury to ignore or disregard the law. Although the potential for jury nullification plays an important role in both our civil and criminal justice systems, it is not a device that can be actively invoked by counsel. You may hope that the jury will refuse to apply a harsh, unfair, or inequitable law, but you may not urge them to do so.

5. Misusing Evidence

When evidence has been admitted only for a limited or restricted use, it is improper to attempt to use it for any other purpose. Suppose, for example, that the ownership of an automobile is at issue in a case. The court has allowed evidence that the defendant maintained insurance on the vehicle, ruling that while the existence of liability insurance is generally inadmissible, it can be received to show agency, ownership, or control.[23] Thus, the following argument is permissible, in keeping with the limited admissibility of the evidence:

> We know that the defendant owned the automobile, because she paid for the insurance on it. You have seen the policy, signed in her own handwriting. No one would sign up and pay for insurance on a car that she did not own.

This argument, on the other hand, is improper:

> We have all seen the insurance policy. The defendant in this case carried over $100,000 in liability insurance— you can see it right there in black and white. She can afford to pay for the damages, and she should pay for the damages.

The Federal Rules of Evidence contain many examples of the limited admissibility doctrine. Rule 404 provides that character evidence may not be admitted to prove actions in conformity with a person's character but that it may be used to prove motive, opportunity, intent, or preparation. Subsequent remedial measures, under Rule 407, cannot be admitted as proof of negligence, but they may

---

22. In yet other jurisdictions counsel is not permitted to read the jury instructions, but may paraphrase them.

23. See Rule 411, Federal Rules of Evidence.

be offered to prove the feasibility of precautionary measures. Offers of settlement or compromise are generally inadmissible, but Rule 408 does not require their exclusion if offered to prove the bias or prejudice of a witness.

In each of these situations final argument should only employ the evidence for the purpose for which it was admitted. Finally, it should go without saying that counsel may not use, or attempt to use, evidence that was excluded by the court.

6. Appeals to the Jurors' Personal Interests

An appeal to the jurors' personal interests invites the jury to decide the case on a basis other than the law and evidence. So, for instance, it is improper for defense counsel to tell a jury that a large verdict will raise taxes or insurance rates. Similarly, plaintiff's counsel cannot argue that an inadequate verdict will result in increased welfare payments. Other predictions as to the potential consequences of a verdict may be equally objectionable. Thus, a prosecutor cannot argue that an acquittal will increase the crime rate or endanger the citizenry.

A specific form of this principle is the so-called "Golden Rule," which prohibits counsel from asking the jurors to envision themselves in the position of one of the litigants. The following is an excerpt from a classic forbidden argument:

> The plaintiff in this case lost his right arm in an industrial accident. You must now determine how much money is necessary to compensate him for his loss. Let me ask you this question: How much money would you want if it had been your right arm? If someone offered you $1,000,000 to have your arm crushed, would you take it? Would you accept $2,000,000?

Such arguments obviously appeal to the jury's sympathy. They also ask the jurors to decide the case on the basis of their own self-interest, as though they were the people actually affected by the outcome of the case.

For much the same reason, counsel cannot refer to the possibility of reversal on appeal, pardon, parole, or other potentially curative measures. Such arguments appeal to the jurors' self-interest by inviting them to avoid making the hard decisions themselves.

7. Appeals to Emotion, Sympathy, and Passion

While there is an emotional side to virtually every trial, counsel may not use final argument to ask the jury to decide the case on the basis of sympathy or passion. Impermissible appeals to passion are often found when counsel dwells upon some dramatic but barely relevant aspect of the case, such as the nature of a plaintiff's extreme injuries when only liability is at stake.

We have already discussed the unethical nature of inflammatory arguments based on racial, religious, ethnic, and gender prejudice.[24] Equally objectionable, although perhaps less offensive, are arguments that appeal to local chauvinism or stereotypical concepts of wealth, education, political affiliation, physical appearance, and the like.

8. Comments on Privilege

It is unethical for the prosecutor in a criminal case to comment on the defendant's invocation of the privilege against self-incrimination. The prosecutor can neither point out nor ask the jury to draw any adverse inference from the defendant's decision not to testify or present evidence.

Jurisdictions are divided as to the rule in civil cases. In some states it is permissible to ask the jury to draw an adverse inference from a party's invocation of a privilege. Here is an example of such an argument:

> I am sure that you remember the cross examination of the plaintiff. I asked him where he was going on the morning of the incident, and he said that he was on his way to see the doctor. But he refused to answer when I asked why he was going to the doctor. He invoked what is called the physician-patient privilege. Now, the plaintiff had the right to invoke that privilege, and the court ruled that he did not have to answer my question. But I ask you, why was the defendant afraid of telling us the reason that he needed to see a doctor? What was he hiding? What is the awful secret? If it had just been an ordinary visit—a sore throat or the flu—you can be sure that he would have told us. So there must have been something about the visit that hurt his case.

In other states, however, the above argument would not be allowed since it would be regarded as infringing on the party's right to assert the privilege in question. Whichever approach a jurisdiction

---

24. See Section VI A(2), *supra* at p. 439.

takes, the same rule will usually apply to all privileges: attorney-client, physician-patient, husband-wife, clergy-penitent, and others. It is conceivable, however, that a court would allow counsel to comment on the assertion of one privilege but forbid it concerning the invocation of another. Familiarity with local practice is therefore essential.

9. Exceeding the Scope of Rebuttal

The proper scope of rebuttal was discussed previously.[25] It is objectionable to attempt to argue new matters on rebuttal.

THE BASICS

Objectionable Argument

- Statement of personal belief
- Suggestion of off-the-record information
- Appeals to prejudice or bigotry
- Misstating evidence
- Referring to excluded evidence
- Misstating the law
- Appeals to jurors' personal interests
- Appeals to sympathy or passion
- Comments on assertion of privilege

B. The Protocol of Objections

1. Making Objections

Objections during final argument follow the same general pattern as objections during witness examinations. Counsel should stand (unless local practice differs) and state succinctly the ground for the objection. There is usually no need to present argument unless requested by the court.

Some attorneys believe that so-called speaking objections should be employed during final argument, to ensure that the jury understands why counsel is objecting. Following this approach, you would not simply say, "I object, Your Honor, counsel is misstating the evidence." Instead, the objection might go as follows:

> I object, Your Honor. There was absolutely no evidence to the effect that the plaintiff carried the heaviest pack on

---

25. See Section II C, *supra* at p. 410.

that camping trip. In fact, she testified that her children had to help her with her pack every day.

This is not good form, and it may draw a rebuke from the court. Speaking objections should not be used to score substantive points with the jury. A far better approach is simply to make the identical point during counsel's own argument. There is some justification for defense counsel to make extremely limited use of speaking objections during the plaintiff's rebuttal since the defense attorney will not have the opportunity to argue again.

In any event, most attorneys attempt to avoid objecting during opposing counsel's final argument. It is considered a common courtesy to allow opposing counsel to speak uninterrupted. Moreover, the overuse of objections may result in the interruption of one's own final argument. This does not mean, of course, that seriously improper arguments should be tolerated.

It is unethical to make spurious objections simply for the purpose of interfering with opposing counsel's argument.

2. Responding to Objections

The best response to an objection is often no response. An objection disrupts the flow of final argument, and an extended colloquy with the court will only prolong the interruption. A dignified silence will usually be sufficient to allow the court to rule and to impress the jury with the basic rudeness of the interruption.

Once the court rules, whether favorably, unfavorably, or inscrutably, counsel should simply proceed by adapting the argument to the court's ruling.

3. Cautionary Instructions

When an objection to final argument has been sustained, the judge will usually caution the jury to disregard the offending remarks. If the court does not give such an instruction on its own motion, objecting counsel should consider asking for one. The downside, of course, is that a cautionary instruction may only serve to emphasize the content of the objectionable argument. Nonetheless, some jurisdictions require that counsel request such an instruction in order to preserve the issue for appeal.[26]

---

26. Paradoxically, appellate courts often hold that a cautionary instruction has cured the negative impact of an improper argument.

In extreme cases, and especially where a cautionary instruction may only exacerbate the situation, a motion for a mistrial may be appropriate.

VII. BENCH TRIALS

Most of the techniques discussed above can be used in both bench and jury trials. Judges, however, are famously impatient with long final arguments. Counsel should therefore strive to keep final arguments as short as possible in bench trials. Most of the adaptations discussed in the chapter on opening statements apply equally to final arguments.[27] In brief, counsel should be particularly alert to legal issues and standards when arguing to the court. The judge is likely to have followed and understood the evidence but will still want to know how the law should be applied to the facts of the case. It is permissible to cite case law during final argument to the bench. Finally, be prepared for the court to ask questions.

---

27. See Chapter 11, Section VI B, *supra* at p. 383.

— CHAPTER THIRTEEN —
Jury Selection

I.   INTRODUCTION

Jury selection is one of the least uniform aspects of trial advocacy. The procedures used to select and qualify jurors differ widely from jurisdiction to jurisdiction. In some courts the attorneys are little more than observers, while in others they are given wide latitude to question the panel of potential jurors. The trend for many years, however, has been to restrict, if not eliminate, attorney participation. While this is most often done in the name of efficiency, it is also a response to perceived abuses. Many lawyers have seen jury selection as an opportunity to begin arguing the case, or even to introduce evidence surreptitiously. Others have engaged in all manner of obsequious behavior aimed at currying favor with the jurors. In consequence, the heyday of attorney-conducted jury selection now seems past. In some highly publicized trials the process may still occasionally consume weeks or months, but the reality is that jury selection has been de-emphasized in many parts of the country. It is likely that this will continue to be the case.

In truth, it was never really possible to "select" a jury. Even in the most lenient jurisdictions the best that counsel could generally accomplish was to de-select or disqualify a certain number of potential jurors. Today, the goals of jury selection can probably be summarized as: (1) eliminating jurors who are biased or disposed against your case; (2) gathering information about the eventual jurors in order to present your case effectively; and (3) beginning to introduce yourself, your client, and certain key concepts to the jury.

As restricted as jury selection may have become, however, it does remain the one aspect of the trial when counsel can interact with and obtain direct feedback from the jury. At all other moments in the trial one can only observe and infer the jurors' reactions. During jury selection, even when it is conducted solely by the court, it is possible to learn directly from the jurors themselves. If this precious opportunity is to be preserved, lawyers must use it wisely and fairly.

II. MECHANICS OF JURY SELECTION

A. Terminology

Jury selection is markedly different from other aspects of the trial and has developed a lexicon of its own.

The "venire" or venire panel is the group of citizens from which juries are to be chosen. The venire, also called the jury pool, is typically assembled from lists of registered voters, licensed drivers, or other adults. Jurisdictions vary widely as to an individual's term of service on the venire. Some courts utilize a "one day or one trial" system in which potential jurors are released after one day unless they are seated on a jury. The more traditional approach, still employed by many courts, is to require potential jurors to be available for a set period of time, ranging from a week to a month.

"Voir dire"[1] is the process of questioning venire members, by either the court or the attorneys (or both) in order to select those who will serve on a jury.

In the course of voir dire counsel may seek to disqualify potential jurors. This is done by making a "challenge." A "challenge for cause" is an objection to the venire member's qualifications to sit on the jury either because she does not meet certain statutory requirements or because she has revealed significant bias or prejudice in the course of questioning. A challenge for cause must be ruled upon by the court and may be objected to by opposing counsel. There is no limit on the number of potential jurors who may be challenged for cause.

"Peremptory challenges," sometimes known as strikes, may be exercised without cause. The parties are typically allowed to excuse a certain number of potential jurors without stating their reasons. Except in the case of apparent racial or other discriminatory motivation, peremptory challenges must be allowed. The number of peremptory challenges available to each party is determined by statute or court rule.

In most states there are statutory "exemptions" that allow individuals to decline jury service. Traditionally, many occupational groups were exempt, including lawyers, physicians, dentists, clergy,

---

1. Juror voir dire should not be confused with witness voir dire as described in Chapter 8, Section II C(1)(e), *supra* at p. 213.

and even embalmers. In many states most of these automatic exemptions have been eliminated. Note that an exemption does not disqualify a person from serving on a jury, but only allows her the privilege of opting out. Even in the absence of an exemption, venire members can request to be excused from service on the basis of hardship.

There are also minimal statutory "qualifications" for jury service. While these differ from state to state, they typically include the ability to understand English, as well as an age requirement. Convicted felons are also frequently disqualified from jury service.

B. Questioning Formats

The voir dire of potential jurors may be conducted by the judge, the attorneys, or both. As noted above, the right of counsel to participate in jury voir dire has been greatly limited in many jurisdictions. Nonetheless, some state systems still permit wide-ranging attorney voir dire. In a few jurisdictions the judge is not even present for the questioning of potential jurors unless one of the parties so requests.

In a large number of federal courts the current practice is for the judge to conduct the entire voir dire, allowing counsel only to submit written questions which the court may use or discard. This model saves time and avoids abuses, but it is subject to the criticism that a judge's questions will necessarily be fairly superficial. The judge, after all, cannot possibly know as much about a case as the attorneys and is unlikely to be attuned to all of the possibilities for uncovering subtle prejudices.

Finally, a growing number of courts have adopted a mixed approach in which the judge conducts the primary voir dire but the attorneys are allowed to ask supplemental questions. This format attempts to accommodate both the court's need for efficiency and counsel's interest in participating in the voir dire.

C. Timing and Order of Voir Dire

The timing and exercise of challenges are determined in large part by the format for questioning the venire members.

1. Preliminary Statements

In all three questioning formats it is typical for the judge to make a preliminary statement to the entire venire panel, describing the voir dire process, the nature of the case, and the issues involved, and perhaps introducing the parties and their attorneys. In systems where attorney questioning is permitted, the lawyers may also be allowed to make preliminary remarks, or at least to introduce themselves and their clients if the judge has not already done so.

2. Size of the Venire Panel

The number of venire members brought to the courtroom should exceed the total needed for the jury as well as the total number of peremptory challenges available to all of the parties. Assume, for example, that our fire engine case is to be tried by a jury of six, with two alternates, and that the local rules of court allow three peremptory challenges for each party. Thus, the minimum size for the venire would be fourteen. It is possible, however, that some venire members will be challenged for cause; others may request to be excused for reasons of hardship or personal convenience. Consequently, it is likely that the voir dire will begin with a panel of at least twenty or twenty-four. In controversial or highly publicized cases, the initial panel may need to be much larger.

3. Questions to the Entire Panel

Many courts begin the voir dire with a series of inquiries to the entire venire panel. These questions typically require only "yes" or "no" responses and seek to develop information relevant to the particular case. Some judges have a standard set of questions, but most will also accept suggestions from counsel.

Venire members are asked to raise their hands if the answer to any question is "yes." Are you related to any of the attorneys or parties?[2] Do you or members of your immediate family work in the aerospace industry? Have you ever been the victim of a crime? Have you ever been asked to co-sign for a loan? Venire members who raise their hands may be asked follow-up questions by the court. In jurisdictions where the attorneys participate, the follow-up questions may come during the lawyers' voir dire.

The court may also ask the entire panel whether anyone requests to be excused by reason of hardship or whether any of the potential jurors falls under a statutory exemption.

Jury questionnaires may also be used to direct questions to the entire venire panel. In a large number of jurisdictions every venire member is asked to fill out a card providing information such as address, occupation, age, marital status, and the like. In some courts

---

2.   The court, of course, will name the attorneys and parties, perhaps also asking them to stand at this point. In addition, the court may also ask whether any of the potential jurors are related to certain named witnesses.

the attorneys are also allowed to fashion a more detailed question-naire containing questions relating to the specific trial. Such questionnaires are subject to court approval and are most likely to be used in particularly complex cases.

4. Questions to Individual Jurors

The questioning of individual jurors, either by the court or by counsel, may follow several models.

The jurors may be questioned one by one with the exercise of challenges following immediately. In extremely sensitive or highly publicized cases such questioning may take place in the judge's chambers.

It is more common for the venire to be questioned in groups. Frequently, twelve prospective jurors are seated in the jury box for voir dire. Sometimes smaller groups of four or six are questioned at one time.

5. Exercising Challenges

The timing for the exercise of challenges is governed by the approach used for questioning the venire members. When jurors are questioned singly, as noted above, challenges (either peremptory or for cause) are usually expected to follow immediately.

A variety of challenge sequences can be used when potential jurors are questioned as a group.

One approach is to question the venire in groups of four. Once the questioning is finished, either by the court or by the attorneys, counsel is first asked whether there are any challenges for cause.[3] The plaintiff (or prosecutor) is usually asked to make her challenges first. Defense counsel may object to the challenge and may also ask to conduct additional voir dire aimed at demonstrating that the juror can be fair. The judge will rule, either excusing or retaining the juror. Then the procedure is reversed, with the defense challenging and the plaintiff being given the opportunity to object.

If a challenge for cause is allowed, the excused juror will be replaced by another member of the pool who will then be questioned in like fashion.

---

3. In some jurisdictions the plaintiff questions the jurors and must then present any challenge for cause, followed by the defendant's questions and challenges. In other jurisdictions both parties complete their questioning before either is given an opportunity to raise challenges.

Once all challenges for cause have been ruled upon, the attorneys will then have the opportunity to exercise peremptory challenges. Again, the plaintiff and defendant will alternate. Unlike challenges for cause, there are no objections to peremptory challenges other than on the basis of unlawful discrimination.[4] Excused jurors will be replaced from the pool, and the new jurors will then be questioned. This process continues until there are no further challenges and the applicable number of jurors has been seated.[5] The questioning will then begin again with another group of four. Variations on this approach are also used with groups of six or twelve.

Most lawyers prefer to make their challenges at a sidebar conference in order to avoid offending the remaining members of the panel. If the judge requires challenges to be announced in open court, this should be done as politely as possible. Peremptory challenges can be made quite obliquely: "Your Honor, we request that Mr. Roth be thanked for his time and excused from further service." Challenges for cause will require more explanation, but they should still be courteous.

Note that courts vary as to the finality of an attorney's statement that she does not wish to exercise a challenge. In some jurisdictions counsel must present a challenge at the earliest possible time; otherwise it is waived forever. In other courts it may be permissible to "re-invade" the panel, usually because opposing counsel subsequently exercised a challenge. Following this approach, if plaintiff's counsel "passes" a group of jurors, she may only challenge one later if defense counsel has challenged a member of the same group.

An alternative approach, widely used in federal courts, is the "strike" system. Under this method the entire venire panel is questioned before any challenges are heard. The attorneys and the judge then meet out of the presence of the venire. The court first hears challenges for cause. Once these are decided, the attorneys take turns stating their peremptory challenges. The first twelve (or six) unchallenged panel members will constitute the jury. The necessary number of alternates will be selected in the same fashion. In some jurisdictions the attorneys will simultaneously submit written strikes, rather than alternating.

---

4. Concerning the impermissible use of peremptory challenges, see Section V C, *infra* at p. 470.

5. Depending upon the jurisdiction, jurors who are not challenged are referred to as having been seated, accepted, or "passed."

6. Preserving Error

What happens when the court erroneously denies a challenge for cause? In most jurisdictions the denial of a challenge for cause cannot be the basis of an appeal unless the challenging party has exhausted its peremptory challenges.

III. PLANNING AND CONDUCTING VOIR DIRE

In systems where lawyer participation is permitted, voir dire must be planned as carefully as any other aspect of the trial. Your areas of inquiry must be designed to obtain the maximum amount of useful information without overstepping the boundaries set by the court.

Bear in mind that a successful voir dire will accomplish at least three goals. First, it will allow you to uncover grounds to challenge jurors for cause. Second, it will provide you with enough information to make wise use of your peremptory challenges.

Finally, a well-conducted voir dire will give you a basis for adapting your trial strategy so as best to appeal to the jurors in the case. For example, suppose that voir dire in the fire truck case disclosed that one of the jurors had worked her way through college as an electrical inspector. While this information is unlikely to cause either party to want to challenge her, it does suggest that she will probably be receptive to arguments based on precision or safety standards. Thus, the plaintiff might want to use an analogy in her final argument to the effect that the defendant "broke the rules" when he failed to have his brakes repaired.

A. Permissible Inquiries

It is almost always permissible to question potential jurors on their backgrounds, work histories, and life experiences. In this vein, it is common to ask jurors about their past involvement with the legal system; their membership in civic, political, social, religious, and other organizations; their hobbies, reading interests, and other pastimes; their families and education; their business experience; and other similar topics.

It is also permissible to inquire as to the jurors' knowledge of or relationship to the parties, lawyers, and witnesses involved in the case. It is fair to ask about family relationships, friendships, business arrangements, debtor-creditor relationships, professional acquaintances, employment, or investment relationships.

Many courts likewise allow counsel to ask jurors about their attitudes and possible preconceptions or prejudices concerning legal and factual issues in the case. Thus, assuming relevance to the case, jurors can be questioned about their attitudes toward issues such as capital punishment, welfare, seat belt laws, or medical treatment. It is expected, for example, that defense counsel in criminal cases will ask potential jurors whether they understand the concepts of the presumption of innocence and proof beyond a reasonable doubt. Most courts draw the line, however, when purported questions about jurors' attitudes spill over into indoctrination or argument.[6]

Finally, it is almost always proper to inquire into an individual's exposure to pretrial publicity.

B. Question Form

Most authorities suggest that voir dire questions be asked in very open, nonleading form. Suggestive questions circumscribe the potential juror's answer and are therefore unlikely to result in much usable information. Open questions, on the other hand, have the potential to open a window on the juror's outlook or point of view. Consider the following examples. First, a suggestive question:

COUNSEL: Do you get the local newspaper?

JUROR: Yes, I read it every morning.

Now an open question:

COUNSEL: What magazines or newspapers do you read?

JUROR: I get the morning paper, and I also subscribe to Motor Sport, Car and Driver, and Automotive News.

By the same token, narrow questions are unlikely to uncover much about a potential juror's true attitudes. Consider these scenarios:

COUNSEL: Are you prejudiced against people who receive public assistance?

JUROR: No, I'm not prejudiced against anybody.

As opposed to:

COUNSEL: What do you think about public assistance?

JUROR: I suppose that it's necessary, but an awful lot of people get it just because it's easier than working.

---

6.   See Section V B, *infra* at p. 469.

Another reason to avoid leading questions is that they are almost certain to make the venire members uncomfortable. No one likes to be cross examined. And no matter how gentle we think we are, leading questions will probably feel like cross examination to potential jurors.

C. Stereotypes and Generalizations

The early literature on jury selection was typified by its reliance on ethnic, class, and racial stereotypes. North Europeans were considered to be conservative and prosecution-oriented in criminal cases. Latins and Mediterraneans were thought to be emotional and therefore sympathetic to plaintiffs in personal injury cases.

Most of this thinking has long since been abandoned. Virtually all modern research indicates that there is far more diversity within ethnic groups than there is between groups and that ethnicity is a poor predictor of complex attitudes.

This is not to say, however, that characteristics such as race, class, or gender are entirely irrelevant to jury selection. Recall from the discussion of opening statements that every advocate seeks to have the jury create a mental image that is helpful to her case.[7] That task is made far easier when at least some of the jurors have had personal experiences similar to those that counsel wishes to evoke.

A fact of contemporary life is that group identity can often be used as a proxy for certain life experiences. One obvious example is discrimination. While most Americans will say that they object to discrimination, members of minorities are far more likely to have seen or felt it directly. Thus, a lawyer whose case depends upon proof of discrimination will no doubt want minorities on the jury. This is not because minorities are inherently generous or sympathetic, but rather because it is more likely that they will comprehend the proof.

The use of group identification as a proxy for experience is not limited to minority groups. Union members, for example, will be more likely to understand concepts such as going on strike or the importance of paying dues, should those issues be relevant to a trial. Older people may have more experience with certain types of medical treatment; parents can be expected to have more relevant knowledge in cases involving children.

Closely related is a concept that might be called "affinity selection." Much psychological research suggests that jurors will be more likely to credit the testimony of persons who are like themselves.

---

7. See Chapter 11, Section I A, *supra* at p. 341.

Following this theory, lawyers will want to seek to impanel jurors who most resemble their clients and principal witnesses. To the extent possible, counsel would also want to exclude jurors who might be the counterparts of the opposing party or significant adverse witnesses. Tactical advantages notwithstanding, it is improper to use peremptory challenges to exclude minorities from juries.[8]

D. Juror Profiles

Jury selection often calls for snap decision making, requiring counsel to exercise (or waive) peremptory challenges on short notice with far less than perfect information. In jurisdictions where the judge conducts all or most of the voir dire, counsel may be left with dozens of unanswered questions, yet will still have to decide whether to strike a particular juror. Even in courts that allow wide-scale lawyer questioning, the exercise of peremptory challenges will still call for large amounts of intuition, guesswork, and seat-of-the-pants reckoning.

Faced with a daunting task under even the best of circumstances, many lawyers develop "juror profiles" to aid their decision making. This process involves creating a list of attributes that you would want in your "perfect juror." To do this, one must consider both the facts and circumstances of the case and the characteristics of your client and principal witnesses. For example, the facts of our accident case suggest that the plaintiff's perfect juror might be someone whose work requires careful attention to rules, as well as someone who has experienced and overcome physical injuries. Recall also that one of plaintiff's key witnesses will be Lieutenant Sarah Sherman, who will testify to fire department procedures. The plaintiff will therefore want jurors who will identify with Lieutenant Sherman and who may resent an aggressive cross examination of her—perhaps relatives of firefighters or women who have succeeded in traditionally male occupations.

In addition to profiling the preferred juror it is also necessary to imagine a "nightmare juror," the one whom you absolutely must avoid. For our intersection plaintiff, the juror from hell would probably be young, male, self-reliant, a lover of fast cars, and a successful entrepreneur. Such a juror would be inclined to identify with the defendant and to be skeptical of the plaintiff's damage claims.

Both lists will go on and on. And, of course, no single juror will ever combine all of the desired traits and experiences. Most real people will possess both positive and negative characteristics,

---

8.   See Section V C, *infra* at p. 470.

sometimes abundant quantities of each. Thus, the profiles will always necessarily involve some degree of rank ordering. Should the plaintiff strike a young, male entrepreneur—who also happens to be the brother of a female firefighter?

Jury consultants (see below) often prepare extensive "scoring" systems that assign positive and negative point values to each listed characteristic. In that manner, the profiles become virtual equations: plug in the values, try to keep the high scorers, and strike the low ones. When well-devised through sophisticated survey instruments and demographic data, these systems may be quite accurate. Otherwise, they may amount to little more than intuition painted by numbers.

In the absence of a qualified and proficient consultant, then, lawyers may best use profiling as a sort of shorthand, keeping ready track of important information until the time comes to reach a decision. In doing so, it is important to keep in mind that every human being is a multifaceted individual. Even the best, most rigorous attitudinal survey can only tell you what a specific person is likely to think; no profile can tell you how an actual individual will actually react to actual evidence and argument. Thus, it is entirely possible that an entrepreneurial race car driver might turn out to be the plaintiff's best juror or that a feminist firefighter might end up being her worst.

In short, jury selection is ultimately an exercise in interpretation. A well-conceived profile can be a useful template, but not a substitute for judgment.

E.   Jury Consultants

It is now possible to retain a consultant to assist with jury selection. There is a broad range of available services. Some consultants are professional psychologists who will sit at counsel table during voir dire in order to assess the venire members' responses and body language. Others are social scientists who will conduct surveys to determine the ideal juror profile. Some will assemble "shadow juries" or focus groups for pretrial preparation so that various arguments can be tried out on demographically representative samples.

Whatever their specialty, jury consultants are usually expensive. As a consequence they are generally used only in big-budget cases.

IV. VOIR DIRE STRATEGIES

Whether voir dire will be restricted or extensive, its value can always be maximized through careful planning. The first step is to understand your own goals. The selection process can be used to educate yourself about the jury panel, to develop (or counteract) challenges for cause, to test the panel's reactions to aspects of the case, to obtain commitments to fair treatment, and to begin the process of developing rapport with the jury.

Each goal carries its own implications for the conduct of voir dire.

A. Gathering Information

The legal justification for voir dire is to allow counsel to obtain information about the venire panel so that a fair jury may ultimately be seated. In an age of cynicism many advocates will announce that they really want an unfair jury—one that is biased in their favor and against their opponents. Be that as it may, the process itself is truly more designed to eliminate bias than it is to perpetuate it. The calculation is simple. With relatively few peremptory challenges at your disposal, you cannot hope to determine which jurors will serve in your case. The best you can do is to choose several who will not sit.

Your first goal, therefore, should be to assure your client a fair trial by identifying those potential jurors who, for whatever reason, cannot be objective about your client's case.

1. Identifying Bias and Preconceptions

Most people want to be fair. Most people think they are fair. Nonetheless, each of us views new data in light of our prior life's experiences. The sum of those experiences may exert an enormous influence over how new facts will be understood or perceived.

For example, one issue in our intersection case is whether the fire truck was sounding its siren immediately prior to the accident. Since departmental regulations required the use of the siren, it would be difficult to convince, say, a military officer that the regulation was not followed on the date in question. Thus, a soldier with command responsibility would be a "biased" juror in the sense of coming to the case with a settled preconception about the likelihood of certain events. On the other hand, a different member of the venire panel might once have worked in an environment where "rules were made to be broken." Quite apart from any conscious favoritism, that juror would have an entirely different outlook on the question of the siren's use.

Discovering a juror's set of preconceptions is a subtle and difficult task requiring delicate probing of the person's lifestyle, relationships, education, and personal history. Most important, you have to know what you are looking for. What sort of information will help you decide whether to keep or strike an individual juror? The facts you need will almost always be case-specific, turning on considerations of evidence, inference, and personality. As always, a good way to start thinking is by considering your theory and theme.

In the fire engine case, one component of the plaintiff's theory is that the defendant was late for an important business meeting, and, because he was distracted, he failed to notice that traffic had stopped for a fire truck. The plaintiff, therefore, will want jurors who are receptive to this theory. She will look for jurors who are especially responsible, punctual, careful. She will want to excuse jurors who are casual, absent-minded, or more easygoing about their obligations. Of course, this information cannot be gathered directly. Imagine an interchange like this:

QUESTION: Are you a responsible person?

ANSWER: Why, no I am not.

Obviously that will never happen. People universally think of themselves as responsible, and those who do not are unlikely to admit it. To obtain reliable information counsel will have to consider the elements of responsibility and then look for indicators. Obvious questions would go into the potential juror's educational and work history. Additional inquiries (with some follow-up) might include:

QUESTION: Have you ever been in a position where you supervised other people? Tell me about it.

QUESTION: Have you ever been in a situation where you had to depend on someone else to get something done? To be on time? How did they handle it? How did you?

QUESTION: Deadlines make a lot of people nervous; how do you feel about them?

QUESTION: Do you wear a watch? Do you carry a pocket calendar?

Some of these questions are trivial, but a resourceful advocate will easily be able to come up with more and better keys to the potential juror's thoughts and attitudes.

2. Identifying Affinity

Many psychological studies have shown that jurors are more likely to believe witnesses whom they like or with whom they have something in common. While this affinity link can usually be overcome, it is obviously preferable to begin the trial with an advantage in this area. Some aspects of affinity are apparent, such as age or gender. Other aspects are readily available, such as occupation, marital status, education, or address. Still other possibilities require more in-depth probing.

Consider all of the characteristics of your client and major witnesses. Which of these will become known to the jury? Is your client a parent? A jogger? A gourmet cook? A self-made professional? Also consider your client's overt personality traits. Is he aloof and short-spoken? Shy? Humorous? Go through the same analysis for the opposing parties and their major witnesses. While you would not want to dismiss a juror simply because he and the opposing party share the same hobby, the information might be helpful in deciding borderline cases. If you are down to your last challenge, and you truly can't decide which of two jurors to strike, why take a chance on the one who belongs to the same alumni association as the other side's most important witness.

Finally, remember that affinities can be transferred. The defendant in the fire truck case would not want to see a firefighter on the jury. Nor would he want the spouse, parent, sibling, best friend, sweetheart, or next-door neighbor of a firefighter. Nor would he want someone whose life had been saved by a firefighter, or someone who, as a child, had spent every free afternoon hanging around the firehouse. The only way to find out about these relationships is to ask.

3. Planning for Trial

The final reason to gather information is not to eliminate potential jurors, but rather to educate yourself about the jurors who end up sitting in your case. You will want to gather as much information about them as possible: Who are they, what do they care about, what have they done in their lives, what are their families like, who are their friends, what important decisions have they made?

The answers to these questions, and dozens of others like them, can help you shape your arguments so that they will be as persuasive as possible. For example, if you have learned that one of your jurors is an MBA who plays racquetball, you will avoid making disparaging comments about Yuppies, no matter how great the temptation to tweak the opposing party.

THE BASICS

Voir Dire Strategies	
Gather information	• Is it possible to identify biases or preconceptions? • Do any members of the panel have "affinity links" with your client? With the opposing party?
Plan for trial	• Can you learn anything about the jury that will help you prepare your case? • Do any of the jurors have occupations, hobbies, or experiences that may make them receptive (or hostile) to certain arguments?

B. Challenges for Cause

You may also use voir dire to develop (or counteract) potential challenges for cause. Because a fair and impartial jury is an essential element of due process, each party is entitled to an unlimited number of challenges for cause.

1. Developing Challenges for Cause

In most jurisdictions, statutes or court rules set out the minimum qualifications for jurors. Most courts utilize screening systems so that individuals who fail to meet the basic requirements are excluded from venire panels. You may, however, nonetheless come across jurors who are disqualified by reason of age, residence, or inability to communicate in the required language. These jurors may be excused for cause.

Jurors may also be excluded on the ground of bias. In the context of jury selection, "bias" means something more than simple bent or inclination; rather, it refers to an inability to serve as an impartial juror. The standard is usually a high one.

Sometimes, of course, the need to disqualify a juror may be obvious. The juror may be closely related to one of the parties or may have had an important experience quite similar to the events at issue in the case. For example, many courts will automatically exclude crime victims from cases that involve comparable offenses. By the same token it may be possible to excuse jurors who belong to affected occupational groups—say, insurance adjusters from personal injury cases, or nurses from medical malpractice trials. Nor is it unusual for members of the venire panel to disqualify themselves, stating that some element of the case would make it impossible for them to be impartial.

Nonetheless, jurors need not be removed for cause merely because they have some similarity to one of the parties or because they have had a passing exposure to the facts of the case. Thus, a challenge for cause will often have to be developed through further questioning once a possible premise for disqualification has been discovered.

Looking again at the fire truck case, recall that one of the primary witnesses for the plaintiff will be the fire department's first-ever female lieutenant. The defendant, of course, wants to avoid jurors who will identify too closely with this witness. Imagine, then, this interchange between defense counsel and a prospective juror:

QUESTION: Do you have any close relatives who are fire-fighters?

ANSWER: Yes, my daughter is a firefighter in another state.

At this point a challenge for cause will almost certainly be denied. Although it may seem likely that the juror would be disposed to accept a firefighter's testimony, there is no reason to think that the juror would not be able to decide the case fairly on its facts. More questioning is needed before a court will excuse the juror (in the absence of a peremptory challenge).

QUESTION: Would you mind telling us how your daughter came to be a firefighter?

ANSWER: Well, it's something that she always dreamed of doing. There's still a lot of prejudice against women in those positions, but she set her mind to it and she succeeded.

QUESTION: Did she have to overcome any special obstacles?

ANSWER: She sure did, but she just decided that she would be twice as good as everybody else.

QUESTION: This case is going to involve testimony from the first female fire lieutenant in our community. Do you think that she may have had to overcome the same sort of obstacles as your daughter?

ANSWER: I would think so.

QUESTION: Because of your own experience with your daughter, do you think that you might have some special insight into the career of another woman firefighter?

ANSWER: Probably, now that you mention it.

QUESTION: Would it be fair to say that you might be especially sympathetic to the challenges facing women in today's fire departments?

ANSWER: That would be fair.

QUESTION: Now, thinking of your daughter and what she went through, is it possible that you might feel uncomfortable listening to testimony that a woman fire lieutenant failed to follow regulations?

ANSWER: I might. It would depend on the testimony.

QUESTION: Well, let me ask you this. What do you think someone else might think about your reaction to a woman firefighter's testimony?

ANSWER: I suppose they might think that I'd be on her side.

QUESTION: Given that, do you think it might be better for you to sit on a different trial, one that doesn't involve an issue so close to home?

ANSWER: I guess that I would be more comfortable on a different case.

At this point a challenge for cause would get a more sympathetic hearing from the court. Still, it is not a sure thing. The juror's comfort level, though important, is not the ultimate determinant of a challenge for cause. The question is whether the juror can be fair and impartial. Thus, plaintiff's counsel (or the court, depending upon the judge's own approach) might attempt to rehabilitate the potential juror.

QUESTION: I'm sure you understand that this case has nothing to do with your daughter.

ANSWER: Of course.

QUESTION: So would you do your best to listen to the testimony in this case and evaluate it fairly, without thinking about your daughter?

ANSWER: I certainly would.

QUESTION: Does that mean you could put aside your pride in your daughter's accomplishments and give these parties a fair trial based on the evidence in this case?

ANSWER: I'm sure that I could.

Following this questioning it will be up to the judge to decide whether to allow the challenge for cause. Some judges will deny all challenges unless the juror virtually admits an inability to be fair. Other courts are more lenient, excusing jurors whenever there is a reasonable basis for inferring bias.

2. Presenting Challenges for Cause

No matter how skillfully done, a challenge for cause always has the potential to embarrass or offend the potential juror. For this reason lawyers prefer to make such challenges at sidebar or in chambers. Not every judge is accommodating, however, so it is often necessary to present challenges in open court.

In these circumstances tact is essential. The manner in which you present the challenge may be taken as an affront by the subject juror or by others on the panel. Thus, you should not announce that

"We challenge Mr. Levitt, who is clearly too prejudiced to serve impartially in this matter."

Rather, try something kinder and gentler, such as

"We move that the court excuse Mr. Levitt for cause and release him to serve on a different jury."

The court, of course, might not immediately agree with your assessment of the juror. You may therefore find yourself having to be more explicit about why the person is too biased to serve on the jury. Moreover, your opponent might well be primed to argue loudly and extensively (and in the presence of the entire venire panel) that you are being unfair yourself in impugning the integrity of so fine, objective, and impartial a citizen as the upstanding Mr. Levitt. In this uncomfortable situation there are three important things to bear in mind.

First, it is never too late to ask for a sidebar. Though the court has required you to make your challenges in open court, the judge might nonetheless be willing to hear argument outside the presence of the panel.

Second, no purpose can be served by abandoning diplomacy in the presence of the venire panel. Do not argue that the potential juror is a bad or bigoted person. Argue instead that his expressed views and experiences will make it impossible for him to decide the case objectively. The distinction is not trivial; it is the difference between a personal attack and a fair request. (On the other hand, do not be so polite as to concede your point, and remember that your argument will also constitute your record on appeal.)

Finally, be aware that no matter how well justified, you still might lose the challenge for cause. For this reason many lawyers insist that you should never make a challenge for cause unless you have at least one remaining peremptory challenge available to remove the juror even if the judge will not do it for you.

C.   Testing Reactions

A further strategy is to utilize voir dire as a means of testing jurors' reactions to aspects of the case. The purpose here is not to begin your argument or indoctrinate the juror, but rather to get an initial read on whether your anticipated positions are likely to make sense to the jury.

For example, the key to the defense in the fire truck case might well be to attempt to minimize the plaintiff's damages. Defense counsel might therefore want to ask each juror a question such as, "Do you think that people ever exaggerate their injuries?" The answers are all likely to be equivocal, "Some people do, some don't; I would have to hear the evidence." But the jurors' manner of answering the question could well give counsel some insight into how they, collectively, might accept an argument that the plaintiff was not injured as badly as she claims.

Of course, anything you learn may also educate your opponent. Try to be subtle.

D.   Obtaining Commitment

It is often thought that certain parties, in certain circumstances, begin each trial with a natural persuasive advantage. Conversely, other parties begin with a handicap no matter what the articulated standard of proof. For example, criminal defendants, personal injury defendants (particularly in cases involving serious injuries), large corporations, and lawyers either suing or being sued by their clients all can typically expect to face an uphill battle. Consequently, many lawyers for such parties use voir dire as an opportunity to gain a commitment from each juror to be fair and to follow the law.

In criminal cases it is virtually standard practice for defense counsel to emphasize the presumption of innocence and to underscore the prosecution's burden of proof beyond a reasonable doubt. Many defense lawyers conclude by asking for every juror's pledge to honor and apply that standard.

In a similar vein, a lawyer in civil cases might ask jurors to "give a corporation the same fair treatment that you would give to an individual." In personal injury cases jurors will probably be asked if they understand that liability and damages are separate questions and that a severely injured plaintiff is not automatically entitled to damages. To the opposite effect, plaintiff's counsel in a medical malpractice case might ask jurors to agree not to give extra weight to a doctor's testimony.

E. Developing Rapport

Voir dire is your only opportunity to converse directly with the members of the jury panel. You can speak to them during your opening statement and final argument, but you cannot ask them questions and they cannot answer you. Moreover, first impressions tend to be lasting impressions. Thus, it is essential to regard voir dire as your best opportunity to begin to develop a positive relationship with the jury.

Often the best way to make a good impression is to avoid making a bad impression. Never talk down to the venire panel, never overwhelm them with lawyerisms, never appear frustrated, never argue with a potential juror, never insult or mock a potential juror, and always attempt to make eye contact.

Almost every study of juror perceptions concludes that jurors are most receptive to lawyers who are well-organized, knowledgeable about the facts of the case, confident, authoritative, and polite.

Of course, you will do everything in your power to avoid inconveniencing or embarrassing members of the venire panel. You will not ask deeply probing questions unless they are clearly related to some objective in your case. You will not exhaust the panel (or any member) by dwelling on minutiae or pointless details. If your questions are going to be unavoidably embarrassing, you will ask the court to conduct the voir dire in chambers. You will be unfailingly considerate, even to jurors whom you intend to excuse. Remember, the members of the venire panel may have spent hours or days together before they ever were introduced to you. Members of the panel may have become quite friendly, so that an affront to one might be taken personally by others.

V. ETHICS AND OBJECTIONABLE CONDUCT

As was noted above, the conduct of voir dire has been subjected to increasing supervision by the courts. Here follows a survey of behavior that has been held unethical or improper.

A. Contact with Venire

Direct or indirect contact with the venire panel is unethical.[9] This is true when the contact is made for the purpose of gathering information, and it is doubly true when it is done in order to influence their opinions.

B. Improper Questioning

Many courts consider it improper to use voir dire as a means of arguing the case or indoctrinating the jury. While such a "persuasive" approach was once widely advocated, it is now generally frowned upon by most judges.

It is particularly unethical and objectionable to use voir dire as a means of presenting inadmissible evidence. For example, it would be wrong for plaintiff's counsel in a personal injury case to proceed in this manner:

> COUNSEL: Could you be fair to the defendant even though he is a business broker who earns over $100,000 a year?

Or,

> COUNSEL: Would you be influenced by the fact that the defendant is heavily insured?

While each of these questions is ostensibly designed to ascertain the juror's ability to be fair, in reality they are intended to exert improper influence on the outcome of the case.

It is permissible to inquire as to jurors' understanding and acceptance of the law, but counsel cannot use voir dire to misstate the law or to suggest an incorrect standard. Defense counsel in a criminal case could not ask this question:

> COUNSEL: Do you understand that the defendant cannot be convicted if you hesitate, even for half a second, to believe that he committed the crime?

---

9. See Rule 3.5(b), Model Rules of Professional Conduct.

Similarly, the prosecutor could not make this inquiry concerning the burden of proof:

COUNSEL: Do you understand that hundreds of defendants are convicted in this courtroom every year, so the standard cannot be that hard to satisfy?

It is likewise improper to use voir dire to begin arguing factual inferences or legal conclusions or to mischaracterize evidence in the guise of a predicate for a question.

Thus, in our accident case it would be wrong for plaintiff's counsel to ask an argumentative question such as the following:

QUESTION: If the evidence shows that the defendant was late for an important business meeting, do you think that might mean he was more likely to be a little distracted or careless?

Similarly, the next question asks the venire to accept an inaccurate statement of evidence:

QUESTION: The evidence will show that the defendant tried to drive through an intersection ahead of a fire truck that was responding to an alarm. Do you think that such conduct is ever justified?

Some lawyers may be tempted to pry into venire members' personal lives by asking unnecessarily embarrassing questions. While a certain amount of intrusion is inherent in the voir dire process, this should not be taken as license to invade a juror's zone of privacy.

Appeals to prejudice are as unacceptable during voir dire as they are at any other stage of the trial.

C. Impermissible Use of Peremptory Challenges

Peremptory challenges cannot be used for the purpose of excluding racial minorities from jury service. This rule applies to both the prosecution[10] and the defense[11] in criminal cases and to all parties in civil cases.[12]

If it appears that peremptories are being used in a racially discriminatory manner, the court must hold a *Batson* hearing to

---

10. *Batson v. Kentucky*, 476 U.S. 79 (1986).
11. *Georgia v. McCollum*, 505 U.S. 42 (1992).
12. *Edmonson v. Leesville Concrete Co.*, 500 U.S. 614 (1991).

determine whether there is a legitimate, nonracial basis for the challenge.

The United States Supreme Court has extended the *Batson* rule to challenges based on gender,[13] so that a mini-hearing may be necessary if it appears that one party has attempted to use peremptory challenges to exclude either female or male jurors. Lower courts have also applied the *Batson* rule to cases of religious or ethnic discrimination.

D. Making Objections and Motions in Limine

Objections may be raised in the course of voir dire just as in any other phase of the trial. Should opposing counsel stray from permissible questioning, it is appropriate to alert the court:

> "Objection, Your Honor, these are not proper voir dire questions."

Or,

> "We object, counsel is arguing his case."

It may sometimes be necessary to be more specific:

> "Your Honor, the defense objects to the plaintiffs' incorrect statement of the burden of proof."

If opposing counsel is adept at voir dire, the questioning of jurors may seem very much like a personal conversation, with lawyer and juror engaged in a friendly chat. In those circumstances an objection, no matter how well founded, may be taken as a rude interruption. Thus, most attorneys try to keep voir dire objections to a minimum and to keep them brief and polite.

On the other hand, an unskilled or overbearing opponent may step across the line separating advocacy from respect or good taste. The jury system does not profit when attorneys offend, frustrate, or anger members of the panel, particularly when the questions have no apparent relationship to the issues in the case. While it might be tempting to watch such a lawyer alienate the venire, the better tactic is probably to rescue the potential juror with an objection:

> "Objection, Your Honor, to the irrelevant and unnecessarily personal nature of counsel's questioning."

It is also possible to direct a motion in limine to the voir dire process. In many cases, particularly in jurisdictions where wide-open questioning is the norm, the court may be disinclined to limit voir dire in advance. So, for example, it could be difficult to prevail on a

---

13. *J.E.B. v. Alabama*, 511 U.S. 127 (1994).

motion to prohibit "argumentative" questions or questions that seek to "indoctrinate the panel." While such questions are improper, most judges will probably want to hear the actual voir dire before ruling. Of course, if opposing counsel has a reputation for abusing voir dire, then the motion should be made, supported by compelling facts.

Motions in limine are most likely to be successful when aimed at specific lines of questioning or specific items of evidence. So, for example, a court very well might allow a motion to prohibit all references to a disputed scientific test, an excluded document, or certain inflammatory evidence of questionable admissibility. A court might also direct counsel to refrain from questioning the venire in areas with great potential for prejudice—such as race, sex, or mental illness—depending upon the relevance to actual issues in the case.

Index